Nothing Can Stop Us

The Definitive History of 514 Squadron RAF

Nothing Can Stop Us

The Definitive History of 514 Squadron RAF

Simon Hepworth and Andrew Porrelli

with Harry Dison

Bomber Command Books

from

First published in the United Kingdom 2015 by Mention the War Ltd.

Cover design: Topics - The Creative Partnership www.topicsdesign.co.uk
A CIP catalogue reference for this book is available from the British Library.

ISBN-13: 978-0-9933360-2-7

ISBN-10: 0993336027

Cover image: 'Coming Home'. 514 Squadron Lancaster NG142, A2-H is pictured returning from a raid in 1944. The aircraft, christened 'The Lancashire Lass', completed 59 operations and survived the war, despite having been hit by flak on at least three occasions.

The painting is by renowned railway and aviation artist Don Breckon. Use of the image is by kind permission of Don's widow Meg and by David Evans, who owns the original painting.

514 SQUADRON, R.A.F., WATERBEACH, 1944

Photo: WMHM

Dedication

In total, 437 members of 514 Squadron lost their lives in the service of their country.

This book is gratefully dedicated to their memory and to all those who served in 514 Squadron, Royal Air Force 1943 to 1945.

The Authors

Simon Hepworth (left, with veteran wireless operator Frank Bell) is a police officer and writer. 'Nothing Can Stop Us' is his second book about 514 Squadron. Simon's great uncle, Sgt. Peter Gosnold, was a flight engineer with the squadron, losing his life over Homberg on 21st November 1944. Simon is also the author of 'Late Shift', a paranormal crime novel and 'The Dark Part of the Sky', an anthology of Bomber Command ghost stories. He lives in Leeds with his partner, Mandy, and son, William (Photo: William Hepworth)

Andrew Porrelli (right, with veteran rear gunner Robert Chester-Master), is an automotive engineer and Bomber Command historian. He co-authored 'Striking Through Clouds - The War Diary of 514 Squadron RAF' with Simon Hepworth. Andrew lives in New South Wales with his wife Leeanne and sons Jayden and Aaron. Andrew's grandfather, Sgt John Porrelli, was a rear gunner with 514 Squadron and lost his life returning from Valenciennes on 16th June 1944.

Sgt Harry Dison (left) served as a flight engineer with 514 Squadron between August and December 1944. Born in Liverpool in 1924, Harry volunteered for the RAF as a short spell on convoy duty in the Merchant Navy. His tour of operations was flown with the crew of F/O Hugh Richford. In 1999 Harry started compiling the accounts of squadron veterans in 1999. These were published as 'Some of the Story of 514 Squadron' and are reproduced in this book to ensure that it is a comprehensive operational and personal record of 514 Squadron. Harry lives in retirement in Cheshire.

Nothing Can Stop Us

Table of Contents

Nothing Can Stop Us

What is Our Destination?

What is our destination?
Said Skipper with trepidation.
Hope it's not Berlin again,
Twice in a week is a bit of a pain.
Hope the flak isn't heavy,
And the fighters not too keen
I'm concentrating on where we are going,
Not worrying where we've been.

What is our destination today?
Ah, I see it's Berlin again.
I have a coach full of passengers,
All veterans but now in friendship's name.
This time they'll be glad to see us,
And we'll be welcome with open arms.
We'll be carrying our good wishes,
None of us bearing arms.

by Amy and Holly of Bishop's Cleeve Primary School
with W/O (Ret'd) Ken Staveley,
Bomb Aimer, 514 Squadron.

Ken Staveley with the author, Simon Hepworth, in February 2015. Ken flew in NG142 (cover image) operationally whilst serving with 514 Squadron (Mandy Morgan).

W/O Ken Staveley (2nd from right) and crew of F/L Ted Morrish, RAF Waterbeach 1945 (Ken Staveley).

A Personal Foreword

Warrant Officer Ken Staveley, Bomb Aimer, 514 Squadron RAF

Greetings to 514 Squadron Society members and all who still have a link to the unit. I had no idea such a body existed until a few weeks ago when my daughters discovered the Facebook page. I had taken my late wife to a couple of reunions; most enjoyable but by then the RAF Airfield Construction Branch was occupying Waterbeach. Recently I and some of my family had the pleasure of a visit from Simon Hepworth and his partner Mandy and, over a cuppa, we were confirming dates and names etc. in the 514 Squadron War Diary, a copy of which I had received. The time just flew by.

One offshoot of all this is that my relics of time there, a photo or two, maps and other oddments, previously regarded as 'bits of Dad's RAF service', have gone up in the world and my girls and their families are most enthusiastic. Like myself they are looking forward to Simon and Andrew's next book. And so, with all your hard work and research to build up the 514 Squadron Society, your book will be a surefire success! I'm so looking forward to the next reunion in June.

Meanwhile, all the best,

Ken Staveley, April 2015

Acknowledgements

I am very grateful to everyone who has helped bring together the wealth of information that makes up the history of 514 Squadron RAF.

- Andrew Porrelli spent months transcribing barely-legible copies of the Operational Record Book which formed the basis of our first volume of the squadron's history, *Striking Through Clouds.* The daily diary tells us what went on throughout the two-year life of the squadron, but without the lifeblood of the story which could only be provided by those who served.
- Sergeant Harry Dison, who completed a tour as a flight engineer with the squadron in 1944, compiled a collection of first-hand accounts from fellow veterans, which he published privately in 1999 as *Some of the Story of 514 Squadron.* Harry has very kindly reproduced a large number of these contributions in this history and they add immeasurably to the story.
- Roger Guernon has contributed significantly by painstakingly checking details for accuracy, especially the names and details of crew members. Roger has also spent countless hours completing the database of individual sorties from the ORB. For the first time, every known operational flight by a 514 Squadron aircraft is recorded with full details.
- Andy Jones, of Topics – The Creative Partnership (*http://www.topicsdesign.co.uk*), has produced an excellent cover for the book. The nephew of 514 Squadron navigator, F/O Alf Wallen, Andy also generously contributed the cover designs for *Striking Through Clouds* and the forthcoming *Beach Boys and Bombers* to help preserve the squadron's memory.
- Oliver Merrington, Curator of Waterbeach Military Heritage Museum (WMHM), and Alan Shipp, of the Museum Trustees, have allowed me to reproduce numerous photographs held by the Museum. Proceeds from the book will help support the Museum in its work in preserving the memory of RAF Waterbeach and its wartime work.

I am hugely indebted to the other veterans who shared their stories, directly or indirectly.

- Warrant Officer Ken Staveley, Bomb Aimer, through a number of telephone conversations and visits, has shared many memories with me along with photographs and charts.
- Warrant Officer Peter Lowen, Navigator, who, supported by his family, shared many memories and stories.
- Flight Sergeant Don Say, Bomb Aimer, and veteran of two tours, who gave me useful technical advice about his role as well as sharing his experiences.
- Flight Sergeant Frank Bell, Wireless Operator, also compiled his memoirs, *Waterbeach 514 Squadron* and kindly allowed me to include many of his accounts in the book.
- Warrant Officer Geoff Payne, Air Gunner, who supplied many memories and illustrations as well as writing the foreword to the book. Geoff has been in regular contact with the authors.
- Flight Lieutenant Alex 'Red' Campbell, pilot and evader, who wrote the foreword to *Striking Through Clouds* has again been of great assistance with details of his operations and the loss of his Lancaster over France.
- Flying Officer Lou Greenburgh features prominently in *Nothing Can Stop Us*, his story being worthy of a film in its own right. Ed Greenburgh, Lou's son, and his family graciously allowed me to include many details from his biography of his father, *DFC and Bar*.
- The three standard works of reference for Bomber Command history were, as ever, invaluable:
  The Bomber Command War Diaries, Martin Middlebrook and Chris Everitt (Midland Publications 2000).
  RAF Bomber Command Losses 1943, 1944 and 1945, Bill Chorley (Midland Counties Publications 1998).
  Nachtjagd War Diaries, Theo Boiten (Wing Leader Books, 2011).
- 3 Group specialist historian Steve Smith provided ORB details for RAF Waterbeach and RAF Foulsham, along with 514 Squadron's Loss Reports and Evasion Reports as well as individual aircraft disposals for all aircraft used by the squadron.

- The National Archives have once again provided much source material; the Operational Record Books (ORBs) for squadrons and stations along with the Bomber Command Night Raid Reports are a gold mine of information for researchers.
- The National Archives (TNA), Auckland War Memorial Museum (AWMM), Australian War Memorial (AWM) and the Australian National Archives (ANA) for permission to reproduce the material contained in their records.
- Colin Pateman, author of *Unshackled Spirit* (Fonthill Media 2013, ISBN 9781781551912), kindly provided details from the book of the exploits and experiences of Flying Officer John 'Toppy' Topham and his crew, including the incarceration of three of their number in Buchenwald.
- Grub Street Publishing made details available of various 514 Squadron crew members who wound up in Stalag Luft 7, from *The Long Road* by Oliver Clutton-Brock and Raymond Crompton (GSP 2013, ISBN 9781909166202).
- Floyd Williston, brother of F/ Sgt Albert Williston, kindly allowed me to reproduce details and photographs relating to the loss of his brother's aircraft, from his excellent book *Through Footless Halls of Air*, (GSPH 1966, ISBN 9781896182445).
- My partner Mandy for her patience and understanding as I have been so absorbed in researching and writing this book, and my son William for all his help. The next generation is genuinely interested in what the crews experienced, achieved and sacrificed.
- Everybody with an interest in 514 Squadron and its members for their photographs, information and, of course, their efforts in keeping the squadron's memory alive.

Finally, on the 70th anniversary of VE Day, I would like to offer heartfelt thanks to the air and ground crews of 514 Squadron, RAF. Without you there would have been no history.

Simon Hepworth
Leeds, England, May 8th 2015

Foreword

by Warrant Officer Geoff Payne, Air Gunner.

It is a privilege to have been asked to write a Foreword to this impressive document, relating to the exploits of 514 Squadron RAF. The comments are mine alone, derived from times whilst serving with Bomber Command and of the aftermath that followed the ending of the Second World War.
With much encouragement, these young men from Britain, the Commonwealth and allied countries, donned their Air Force Blue and went off to war, knowing full well that their chances of survival were very slim. The press and the public supported the efforts of Bomber Command as at that time, it was the only means of taking the war back to Germany. However, just a few months later, after the ending of hostilities, the recriminations began. A few left wing politicians and blinkered clergy, crept out of the woodwork and, began a vitriolic campaign against Arthur Harris. This campaign eventually permeated through to his airmen who, began to suffer the brunt of these accusations.

These proud young men went to war to preserve our democracy and freedom against two of the most evil regimes in the history of mankind, yet, there are still these vociferous groups of politicians, clergy and media who continue to abuse this privilege of freedom for their own political expediency and, personal agenda.
As the years pass, many prominent authors have painstakingly researched and assembled facts with aircrew stories relating to the air war that Bomber Command waged against the Third Reich. There are also the many relatives of these aircrew who, joined forces, to bring into the public domain, the exploits of these airmen. Ordinary people such as Simon Hepworth, a Yorkshireman and Andrew Porrelli, also a Yorkshireman though long-time resident of New South Wales, Australia, both of whom had lost relatives whilst serving with 514 Squadron. These dedicated people and others, spent many hours piecing together the history and achievements of these airmen and airwomen of RAF and of this fine Squadron, culminating in two excellent books "Striking Through Clouds" and "Nothing Can Stop Us".
Now that the magnificent Bomber Command Memorial in Green Park, London has finally been dedicated and, the Bomber Command Clasp awarded to the Aircrews who participated in that terrible conflict, it is hoped that the unfair, politically motivated controversy surrounding the role' of Bomber Command can now be laid to rest.

On a final note, let me recall Philip Nicholson's "Return"

We have come home, dropping gratefully through friendly skies,
And though in tired brains the engines thunder on and images of death remain in reddened eyes,
Though nostrils sniff the legacy of oil and sweat and legs must learn to cope with solid ground,
We have come home and are at least alive, to mourn our friends, indifferent now to sight or smell or sound,

Geoff Payne 2015

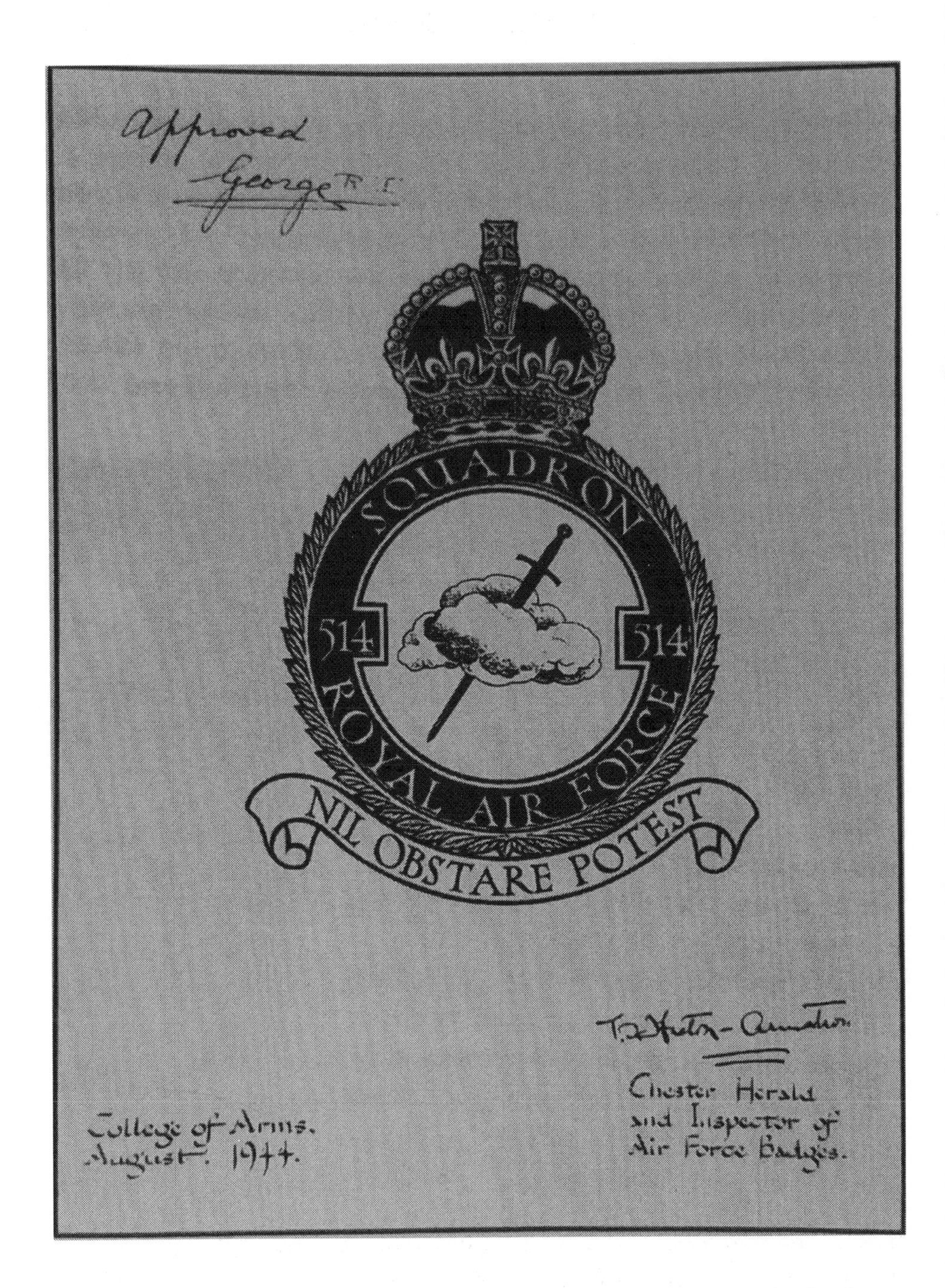

Approved by King George VI, the 514 Squadron crest was designed by F/O Harry Darby who was shot down on 30th / 31st March 1944, attacking Nuremburg, surviving as a POW (Harry Darby via Harry Dison)

Prologue: First Op

On 31st October 1944 we were told we were joining 514 Squadron at Waterbeach. We said our goodbyes to the other crews and were on our way. We liked the new camp immediately. It was a permanent RAF station with brick buildings, about five miles from Cambridge. The five of us who were NCOs were billeted in the Sergeants' Mess which was quite luxurious and comfortable compared with the old Nissen huts we had sometimes had to put up with. This was to be our home until we had done thirty operations. We had hope in our hearts and, like everyone else, we thought it wouldn't happen to us: The Chop! But we knew the odds were stacked against us, and that is why aircrew on operational squadrons got six days leave every six weeks. And, wonder of wonders, on top of our Sergeants' pay we also got aircrew danger pay in the princely sum of one shilling per day. We also received another perk, the customary meal of egg and bacon before every operation and the same post-operational meal on our return – if we returned.

On our second day we were interviewed by the CO of the station and also by the OC – 514 Squadron. We were given a pep talk and wished the best of luck and that was that. Now we had to get an operation under our belts so that we would be truly accepted into the squadron.

It was late in the evening of 3rd November 1944 when a battle order was pinned up on the notice board in the Sergeants' Mess. Our pilot's name was on it. So this was it: an early call was booked for 0515 hrs. This was obligatory; no one was allowed to be late for a briefing. Next morning at precisely 5.15 am we were awakened by hammering on the door and a shout of 'Wakey, wakey!' I was ready with fifteen minutes to spare so I took out of my pockets everything that would potentially identify me or give information away, putting it all in my locker. I was to learn that in future this was done in the briefing room. We were given a cloth bag to put everything in which was reclaimed if and when we returned. The only forms of identity allowed were the two official discs around our necks and I was allowed to take two or four pencils to write in the logs.

At 6am we went to the mess for breakfast. This was usually Corn Flakes or porridge, milk, tea, bread and the coveted bacon and eggs followed by toast, butter and jam. This was one of the luxuries operational air crew were afforded when going on an operation. It was also the same for the post operational meal except for cereal. If you arrived back in the early hours at 5 or 6am it wasn't unusual to see some plates untouched when leaving the table. Nerves were the usual explanation. I don't know exactly how you would describe it but it was a strange feeling one got, thoughts you tried to put to the back of your mind. It couldn't happen to you, it only happened to other crews. At the same time you knew damned well it could actually happen to you. It never put me off my food though; if I was going to get the chop I would do it on a full stomach.

514 Squadron's Wireless Operators in 1945. Circled is Sgt Leslie Holt, Wireless Operator with the crew of F/O LA Adams (Leslie Holt via WMHM).

After a final cup of tea and cigarette to steady the nerves it was time to walk down to our respective section headquarters for our own special briefing. As a wireless operator, mine was by the Signals Leader in the Signals building. This took about thirty minutes. We would be given the wireless information and frequencies, call signs for all 3 Group aircraft and the collective call sign for the whole force, along with the colours of the day for the Very cartridge gun. Also if it was a night raid and there was a

'Master of Ceremonies' (Master Bomber) there would be a special call sign for him and also for his deputy. There was always a Deputy Master Bomber in case the original was shot down which did happen now and again.
At 7.30 am everyone assembled in the main briefing room. The noise was terrific. The total number of crews varied depending whether or not it was to be a maximum effort with up to thirty crews, each at a separate table. We joined our own pilot and navigator who were poring over their charts. We sat there waiting and smoking until we were called to attention as the Station Commander and the C.O. of 514 Squadron plus the respective Flight Commanders and heads of sections walked in. The C.O. immediately put us at ease with "Gentlemen, you may smoke" and the main briefing commenced. There was a dais at the front of the room with a huge map of Europe on the wall but it was covered with a curtain to conceal the route and target. Now the C.O. pulled the curtain back to reveal all. Depending on the target and/or the length of red number of legs over Europe there would be howls and groans and various remarks. Distant and big city targets such as Berlin. Leipzig, Frankfurt and anything in the Ruhr would not be welcome. The Ruhr was heavily defended, not only by fighter aircraft but a few hundred anti-aircraft guns. It was a hotbed savagely defended right up to the end of the war.
Today the target was a town called Solingen in the Ruhr where synthetic oil was produced. First we were given the reason for our proposed visit and then each leg of the route was explained. The exact mileage of each leg, the compass bearing, wind velocity and strict speed to be maintained. We were allocated the height at which our squadron was to fly and which we had to stick to unless there were unforeseen circumstances which necessitated a change. There had to be valid reasons for doing so. All the flak area positions and fighter airfields en-route were marked; each leg of the route kept us as far as possible from these positions. We were told our bomb load was to be one 4,000lb Cookie; the blockbuster plus for this medium distant target ten 1,000lb high explosive bombs. This was our usual load. Sometimes it varied, the most likely alternative being a 4,0001b cookie plus ten or twelve cans of incendiary bombs. The further away the target, the smaller the bomb load and the more high octane petrol we carried to get us back again. A Lancaster could carry 2,150 gallons if required.

Next we would be given all the information about the total number of aircraft and types that would be operating on the raids and from which groups they would come. We were also told in which wave we would be, at what height we would fly and our time on target (T.O.T). Then at our own Squadron and Flight level we would be told with which other aircraft we would be flying and the letters on the side of those aircraft.

This training photo gives a good idea of the wide range of bomb sizes available, many different combinations of which could be carried by the Lancaster. 514 Squadron aircraft carried all sizes up to the 8,000lb 'blockbuster', though most loads tended to be a mixture of 4,000lb 'cookie', several 1,000lb or 2,000lb General Purpose (GP) and incendiaries (WMHM).

As our navigator had been specially trained on radar we were a G.H. leader and therefore three other aircraft would be looking to formate on us. We would be in charge of them. On the run in to the target they had to copy what we did. When our bomb doors opened they had to open theirs and when they observed us dropping our bombs they had to do likewise. We had to fly straight and level until they had all bombed. Once on the bombing run it was my job to get into the astrodome and watch these three Lancasters formating, and to tell the pilot once they had dropped their loads as well as to watch out for aircraft flying above us. They were never supposed to be, as there was supposed to be three minutes between first and second wave with different heights for each wave, say at 23,000ft for the leading one or two squadrons, reducing by 500 feet each time down to a minimum of 19,000 feet. Then the second wave commenced starting at the top height again. However over such a distance and time the

separation became non-existent and generally one or two squadrons at the end of the first wave, at an altitude of say 19,000 feet, would be overtaken by the first couple of squadrons of the second wave at their higher altitude. It was nothing unusual to be bombed from above by our own aircraft.
We would be informed of other raids taking place that day and the fighter escort we could expect either for the whole way or just part of the way. All this would be related by the C.O. of 514 Squadron and the Intelligence Officer. Next would come the Navigation Leader, then the Bombing Leader, then next the Signals Officer, the Gunnery Leader and finally, it would be the turn of the Met. man giving us all the weather expected going over and on our return plus the QFE (the local air pressure for our airfield). At that point we were given final instructions on the runway in use, the time we had to enter our aircraft, the time for starting our engines and checking everything, time to start taxiing to the runway in use. Permission for the first aircraft out to take off was finally given by the Flying Control Tower and also the control van at the end of the runway by giving the green light for take-off. At the end of the briefing the Station Commander would say a few words and wish everyone the best of luck.
As soon as the main briefing was over the room was filled with babble. It was like a saloon with the blue haze of cigarette smoke and everyone was talking at once. By that time it was about 8.45am and time to go to the nearby locker room to get into our flying kit, draw our parachute and Mae West. One of the crew drew the flying rations and each crew member had to draw and sign for his emergency escape kit at the intelligence office. This consisted of emergency rations such as chocolate, Horlicks tablets, sea water purifying tablets, hard biscuits, two or three small condensed maps of Europe for escape, and money in German, French, Belgian and Dutch currency. These escape packages were in a hard plastic see-through box to be handed in on return to base. Crews then had to test their oxygen masks on the portable testers in the crew room.
In the wireless operator's position in a Lancaster where I sat, the heating opening sent from the engines was directly opposite me and while other members of the crew, particularly the upper and rear gunners, were usually freezing, I was sometimes sweating. Those in the cockpit were usually just about warm. I usually flew in my ordinary battle dress uniform, a black wool sweater, thick black wool socks and my flying boots. I took two pairs of gloves in case I needed them; one pair chamois leather and one pair pure

silk. They had to be thin in order to write my wireless transmission log in pencil but I rarely had to wear any.
When everyone got themselves sorted out and into crews again we assembled outside the crew rooms waiting for the transport that would take us out to our aircraft at dispersal. Sometimes a dispersal would be at the other side of the airfield which was maybe up to a mile and half away. The drivers were always WAAFs; they were a good humoured lot, joking though they were aware of what we may be feeling. Three crews at a time were taken in the lorries and dropped off near their aircraft. We arrived at our dispersal with about 20 minutes to spare before the official time of getting in and starting up. Immediately the pilot went round the plane checking, making sure as far as was possible at this stage that everything was o.k. The rest of the crew entered and went to their positions depositing their parachutes and equipment. Personally I had to squeeze past the bottom of the mid-upper gun turret then over the main spar which served as my seat's back rest, stow my parachute in the container next to my seat and check my satchel. This contained pencils, W/T log, Q code book, Bomber Command code book and some sheaves of rice paper with other secret information on. These had to be chewed up and swallowed if we were forced down in enemy territory. I made sure everything was working, switching on the R1155 receiver and listening to the signals coming through my helmet head set. I then switched on the T1154 transmitter to make sure the valves were heating up and quickly pressed the Morse key, ensured the intercom was working and also checked the trailing aerial and earth connections including the HF fixed aerial leads from outside to the aerial board inside.
When all checks were completed we gathered outside chatting to the ground crew and have our last smoke before the off. As departure time drew near stomachs started to churn and adrenalin flowed. But there was an inner excitement too. I can't explain but ask any operational air crew and they would confirm the peculiar feeling one got. All we had trained for (23 months in my case) was now going into the boiling pot. Anyone who said he wasn't scared was either a liar or there was something lacking. I am trying to explain the feelings one had. It was a mixture of a love for flying, fear, pride to be fighting for your country and camaraderie with men in your crew. You lived for this day, that's all, because you knew the chances of your completing a tour was slim. We knew what we were

letting ourselves in for. There was no turning back, no L.M.F. (Lack of Moral Fibre: the official term for what was considered cowardice) for us.Time passed quickly now. Dead on 0930hrs we dumped our cigarettes and climbed into the aircraft. The entry door was at the rear of the aircraft just before the tail plane and rudders on the starboard side. There was a small steel ladder with about six rungs and this was drawn in and stowed by the last man in, usually one of the gunners. I put on my helmet with oxygen mask and microphone attached and waited for the pilot and the ground crew to start up the engines. My wireless equipment and electrical circuits were powered by large accumulator batteries charged constantly by an engine-driven generator in the starboard inner engine. Outside the ground staff would attach a trolley battery set to start up the engines so as not to drain the power from the aircraft's batteries. The pilot would signal to them which engine he was starting up then would press the button for that engine and the propellers would slowly start to turn and then with a staccato burst of noise would fire and burst into thunderous life. It was a sound vibrant with the emotion of power and when the four of them were running it was like sweet music to the ears. But it was loud! And I do mean loud. Once the motors were running I switched my equipment on making sure once again everything was o.k.

I wouldn't commence my w/t watch until we were airborne. I made sure the flare chute and the flares were secure as well as the Very pistol and cartridges with the correct colours of the day. Then I sat waiting, watching and listening to the usual paraphernalia that went on at this time. Each engine would be revved up to maximum to check it was running o.k. with no mag drop or oil pressure problems, overheating etc. After each engine was run on its own all four throttles would be opened up to clear each engine and what a din they made. If everything was to the skipper's satisfaction he gave the thumbs up to the ground crew, who would have previously disconnected the trolley accumulator before the engines were run up. They would then pull the chocks away ready for us to taxi out. The skipper would then check with each crew member to confirm that everyone and everything was o.k. and especially that for every position the oxygen supply was working and intercom was in order. At precisely 1000 hrs. we started to move out of our dispersal and the ground crew gave us the thumbs up and wished us good luck. Nearly all the aircraft round the field were moving around the perimeter track to the beginning of the runway in use. On the side of the runway was the controller's black and white checkered van. This was where the take-off control was done by the green light from the Aldis lamp and not by radio transmitter from the control tower. The take-off time of each Lancaster was recorded in a log in the control van with the letter of the aircraft and time then passed by landline telephone to the control tower where it was logged again. One Lancaster was lined up on the end of the runway waiting for the green light to be given to confirm it was clear to take off. There were two others in front of us. Butterflies were churning now. This was it. Take-off with full load of bombs and petrol was one of the most fateful moments. Anything could go wrong; there were so many potential causes or reason. That was why your heart was in your mouth and you sweated! The Lancaster on the runway started to move ever so slowly and began to pick up speed. It was travelling fast now and slowly its tail wheel came up then suddenly it was airborne. At last our turn came. We turned on the runway and the brakes squealed as we came to a halt all lined up, dead centre, ready for take-off. The skipper called us all up in turn on the intercom asking if we were ready and then on receiving the green light said "Right, here we go." Brakes full on he pushed the four throttle levers slowly, nearly to the fully open position and the engines roared! He released the brakes and slowly we began to move down the runway. There was always a few officers, airmen and women by the side of the control van to watch the take-offs and they would give us the thumbs up as we set off. In fact, we could see little groups of personnel scattered all over watching the take-off. The main road from Cambridge to Ely that ran along the whole length of the airfield was full of cars and sometimes a bus pulled up on hard standing, the people all watching.

I was sitting at my position looking out of the little rectangular window at my left hand side watching the huge Merlin engines and the two propellers which were just a blur. I was sweating with tension. Slowly we gathered speed and then we were roaring down the runway. The throttles were opened fully now and the roar of the engines increased. I could feel the extra surge in power. Now we were at the point of no return. We were committed to the take-off. Faster she went, the tail went up and we kept going, the end of the runway looming up with the ditch at the end of it and the road with the spectators watching. Then with a lurch suddenly we were airborne. What a lovely feeling. I started my wireless transmitter watch then noting the time we were airborne in the log, the E.D.G. (engine driven generator) readings, voltage and current of the accumulators. Looking at my watch I checked how long I had before tuning in for the 3 Group H.Q broadcast, wireless transmitter call sign 35/3 on 3190 kilocycles. These were sent on the hour and the half hour for three minutes. If they had no information for us they just sent call signs and identifying figures for late tuners. The number was included so logs could be checked that no broadcast was missed. This could be a chargeable offence. At quarter to and quarter past the hour broadcasts from H.Q. Bomber Command had to be picked up. There were nearly always winds that were transmitted and every navigator in the main force had to use them. This was usually a three minute transmission time. Now that we had gained height I could reel out the 300 foot trailing aerial weighted at the end with fifteen lead balls to prevent swinging beneath the aircraft. The steel wire aerial was on a winch near my left hand.

We started to climb to our orbit height, about 5,000 feet, and continued orbiting waiting for our followers. Sometimes we had two followers, other times three. We knew their aircraft code letters and they would know ours; each G.H. aircraft had two broad yellow stripes on its tail fins for identification purposes. These yellow stripes could be seen from quite a distance away so aircraft could spot a G.H. leader aircraft initially and converge to see if it was their leader. Within five minutes we had our three followers tagging along, all just aft of us, one on the port side, one on the starboard side, and one in the centre forming a kind of diamond. The one in the middle would fly a little lower or higher to avoid the wash of our propellers. Everywhere you looked now you could see little formations all over the sky and here and there a few loose Lancasters frantically dashing hither and thither looking for their leaders. Then at a certain time, 1030hrs on this occasion, it was time to set course for Germany, and Solingen. It was an amazing sight, all those Lancasters setting of for the Ruhr.

Immediately we set off on the actual first leg. Our squadron had to gain height up to 20,000 feet. As we had been circling over Cambridgeshire at about 5,000 feet it would take another half to three quarters of an hour to get up to our allocated height. Once we reached 10,000 feet it was time for our oxygen masks and microphones to be fastened on to the helmet. From now on we would be getting two or three puffs of pure

oxygen every minute until we reduced height again, usually as we approached the enemy coast homeward bound.
Now my job was routine, receiving the wireless transmission broadcasts from 3 Group and also Bomber Command. This would be every fifteen minutes for each. The winds from Bomber Command were passed immediately to the navigator. Everything was going smoothly but everyone was alert, expecting the unexpected. Hours of routine en-route to the target. The pilot flying the aircraft, the navigator still plotting his route and keeping track of just where we were or where we were supposed to be. The bomb aimer would be either helping the pilot or map reading to help the navigator with his pin points. The flight engineer would still be checking the engine gauges and temperatures as well as the fuel quantity left. Gunners would be searching the sky for enemy aircraft or anything unusual. No one could relax completely until we were back on Terra Firma.
Back to the route out. On the route to the target there would generally be 3 or 4 legs basically to try and fool the enemy fighters and the radar controllers as to which was the actual target destination. After bombing, it would be precisely the same legs home. If there was trouble in any form the quickest route in a straight line could be taken making sure hot spots were by-passed if possible. The noise of the four Merlin engines throbbing away was terrific and you did get used to it. The helmet cut down the din a little.
Sometimes you would see the target well under attack long before you were anywhere near it if the weather was clear, but if it was dense cloud bombing it would be by sky markers and you would never see the ground or target, although you knew it was there.
Flak would be coming up thick and fast just before the bombing run. I would get into the astrodome and observe our followers and any aircraft who might just be flying above us or somewhere near.
We were now on our bombing run and very vulnerable as we had to fly straight and level as well as getting on the correct heading. I was listening on the crew intercom hearing the dialogue between the pilot, navigator and bomb aimer and also watching our followers. I then heard "bomb doors open" and started to sweat knowing that any hit from flak now, either direct or just hot shrapnel on the blockbuster, would send us to kingdom come. The navigator could now be heard directing the pilot and the bomb aimer as we were G.H. Leader, Then it was “bombs away”. I was

observing our followers and saw them release their bomb loads at precisely the same time as us—a few more seconds to allow for photos to be taken by the automatic camera and then we wheeled out of the target area like bats out of hell with our formation still following behind. The flak was still coming up fast and furious and it was getting quite accurate. At times it was too close for comfort. A salvo would suddenly burst just beneath you or under the wing and you would hear the crump, crump, crump and the shrapnel clumping against the fuselage. Besides the firing of the flak now was the time to look out for enemy fighters. Just after leaving the target on the first leg home was the most perilous, although they could be expected at any time and on any leg. I was back in my seat and listening out on one of 3 Group's broadcasts. I'd only been off the wireless for about seven or eight minutes and I hadn't missed any broadcasts. There was nothing for us, just the check number and a timing signal. The steady thrump, thrump of the engines was like a drug making me feel quite sleepy. After flying for about an hour after leaving the target we began to feel a little easier, though nobody was complacent. I had already eaten the flying ration sandwiches and chocolate on the way out so I poured myself the last of the thermos coffee; nice, hot and sweet, it was a lovely feeling once you crossed the French or Dutch coast going home. You would be down to about 10,000 feet, gradually losing height so as to cross the English coast at about 6,000 feet. We would probably cross in at Aldeburgh in Suffolk then we would lose height quickly in daytime and scoot back for home at about 2,000 feet. It would only take fifteen to twenty minutes back to base at Waterbeach and I still had the aerial to wind in. Looking out of my side window I knew we were near home, perhaps just five minutes to go. I knew the pilot was in touch with base flying control so I closed down the radio transmitter and entered it in my log. I then switched myself on to the intercom position with the rest of the crew and heard the skipper calling Waterbeach Flying Control. He was asking permission to join the circuit. Flying Control acknowledged giving him permission to join the circuit giving him barometric pressure also height to fly in the circuit and what our turn was to land. Any aircraft in trouble would be given priority to land. It wasn't long before it was our turn. Flying Control called us up and informed us of the number of runway in use, according to wind direction, and told us to lose height to 1,000 feet. Then the skipper told them when

he had turned into the funnels. This was turning onto the heading to land on the runway gradually losing height all the time. Flight Control would tell him to pancake (land) which our pilot, Hendy, did with expertise. We had great faith in him as a pilot and trust in each other. After landing we taxied round to dispersal and after giving the engines one more run to clear them they were closed down. What a QUIETNESS. The ground staff were there waiting. They gave us the thumbs up sign and put the chocks under the wheels.
The sudden silence was deafening in its intensity. It was strange not to be hearing the roar of those Merlins. I entered in my log the time of landing and signed that all the equipment was o.k. and serviceable. I put all my bits of paper, log and code books into the satchel, picked up my parachute and started to clamber towards the rear door looking to make sure there were no flares in the chute as I passed. I climbed down the ladder, whipped my helmet off and kissed Mother Earth. Our first operation was over. My legs felt strange after being airborne for four or five hours (4hrs 50 mins exactly) and my head seemed tight and ringing. The first thing we did was to pull our cigs out and have one and wasn't it lovely! The transport for us came quickly and we all climbed aboard to go to the de-briefing room for interrogation. On arrival we were offered a large mug of hot sweet steaming tea and also a double tot of rum. We were shown to a table and all seated. There were free cigarettes that were just to smoke at the table. An intelligence officer sat down with us and asked all manner of questions. We all gave him information of what we had seen. It would all be checked and double-checked. This took about thirty minutes. Our escape kits were handed in and then we went to the locker room to take off our flying gear. We then received our own personal belongings in a fabric bag, went on to parachute section and handed in our chutes. Your parachute harness and Mae West stayed with your flying kit. Then it was off to the Sergeants' Mess for our meal of egg and bacon, a smoke and a chat and then off to bed for a couple of hours.

Flight Sergeant Frank Bell,
Wireless Operator / Air Gunner,
514 Squadron 1944-45

1. In the Beginning: Mid 1943

Not a Merlin in sight. A flight engineer's view of the Bristol Hercules engines powering an Avro Lancaster B Mk.II. The aircraft was flown by F/O David Gray, one of the first members of 514 Squadron when it was formed (Gray family).

In 1943, No. 3 Group of Bomber Command was not in a good state. It had been mainly operating the Short Stirling heavy bomber, a type which was rapidly becoming obsolescent compared with the later models of the Handley Page Halifax and, of course, the Avro Lancaster which equipped the rest of Bomber Command. The Stirling was no longer an effective tool against the robust and vicious defences of German-held airspace, so a plan was developed to re-equip its squadrons with Lancasters.

As a stop-gap measure, one of the group's longest standing units, 115 Sqn, was re-equipped with Mk.II Lancasters, the aircraft being powered by four 1650hp Bristol Hercules radial engines rather than the iconic, though less powerful, Rolls-Royce Merlin. The rationale behind the modification of the Lancaster was a concern in 1942 / 43 that there might be a shortage of Merlins. Some 300 Lancaster airframes were equipped with the air-cooled Hercules. Both engines had their strengths and shortcomings. It was generally regarded that the Hercules air cooled engine possessed more torque, though they had a lower service ceiling. This was a distinct disadvantage over the target area, where a low service ceiling had previously exposed the Stirlings to more intensive flak as well as the hazards of 'friendly bombs from higher-flying aircraft. The Mk.II Lancasters possessed greater climbing ability due to their greater torque, and being air cooled, were more resistant to flak damage than their water-cooled Rolls Royce Merlin counterparts.

Warrant Officer Geoff Payne, a 514 Squadron rear gunner who had flown in Lancasters powered by both types of engine, commented, 'I preferred the Hercules like most of the lads did. It was more reliable than the Rolls Royce that suffered badly once the cooling system and radiators were damaged. The Hercs just kept on going even when beaten up, and on top of that, I think they were the sweeter sounding of the two!'

514 Squadron was the only squadron formed specifically to operate the Lancaster Mk.II from the outset. 67 such aircraft passed through 514 Squadron's hands with 59 being lost through enemy action or accident before the type was withdrawn in September 1944, in favour of the Merlin-powered Lancaster Mks I and III. With an operational strength of thirty aircraft, the squadron's fleet was to be lost, along with the crews, nearly twice over in the next eleven months. In all a total of 88 514 Squadron Lancasters were destroyed or written off by the time the war ended.

No. 3 Group itself was moving towards specialisation in blind bombing techniques, in an attempt to improve the accuracy of bombing specific, and quite small, targets. Cloud cover being a regular feature over targets in Northern Europe, a means was needed to ensure that this was not a wasted effort, as earlier, and unachieved, attempts at pinpoint accuracy had been abandoned in favour of area bombing. The requirement had resulted, by

A Gee set installed at the navigator's station. For GH operations, the navigator directed the bomb aimer who released the bombs when instructed, usually through 10/10ths cloud.

1943, in the wider use of H2S radar and the Gee navigation system. Both systems had their known shortcomings; H2S could distinguish only certain specific features of the ground beneath the aircraft, whilst its signals could be detected and tracked by enemy night fighters. Gee, based on a number of radio transmitters in England, was limited by the Earth's curvature and was susceptible to jamming.

Towards the end of 1943, a new location system was being trialled. With an accuracy of 150 feet at 300 miles range from a transmitter in England, Gee-H (GH) could effectively place an aircraft over a relatively small target, such as a large factory, an oil plant or railway yard. The system did not require the bomb aimer to see either the target or markers, and so bombing through ten-tenths cloud cover with sufficient accuracy to hit a

H2S was an air to ground mapping radar which, in theory, allowed prominent features on the ground to be identified. In practice it had many shortcomings, not the least of which was the fact that it could be detected by German night fighters which could then home in on aircraft using it.

high-value target became feasible. The GH system could handle, in theory, up to 100 aircraft at the same time, though in practice rarely more than 70 would use it simultaneously. By late 1943, bombing raids usually comprised several hundred aircraft so seventy bombers would constitute a relatively small force. Therefore the 'GH Leader' tactic evolved. This entailed a GH-equipped aircraft bombing when its receiver said it was over the target; up to four other aircraft would fly in tight formation around the GH leader, releasing their own weapons when they saw bombs falling from the GH Leader's aircraft. The system really came into its own when the Allies enjoyed sufficient air superiority to allow Bomber Command to attack in daylight as well as at night. When it eventually developed the GH tactics to a degree that impressive results were regularly being achieved, 3 Group was allowed the latitude to operate independently of other Bomber Command groups. However the group's aircraft also continued to participate in major raids until the end of hostilities.

2. A Squadron is Born: September and October 1943

514 Squadron was born on 1st September 1943 when HQ No. 3 Group issued administration instruction No. 78 ordering that this be so. The new squadron was to be formed at RAF Foulsham in Norfolk and would have an operational strength of sixteen Mk.II Lancasters with another four in Immediate Reserve. Aircrew would be supplied by 1678 Heavy Conversion Unit. The squadron was to be commanded by Acting Wing Commander Arthur Samson DFC, a native of Newfoundland who had chosen to make his home in the equally damp and windswept environs of Barrow-in-Furness.

Corporal 'Mel' Melluish, who served as an armourer, tells us that the Squadron had an inauspicious start: ‘I was the very first person to be allocated to 514 Squadron, having returned from three and a half years in Iraq in August 1943. I was posted to RAF Foulsham where on arrival I was informed that there must be a mistake as there was no such Squadron. The orderly room made enquiries but told me to report to the station armoury pending further enquiries. The armoury had a corporal and another ranker. The corporal was junior to me and I believe saw me as an intruder into his domain. He didn’t know what to do about me so I solved his problem by going back home on a further seven days leave. On my return I found that several other bods had arrived and a new squadron was forming.’

The first officer of the squadron to show up at Foulsham was the Adjutant, Flight Lieutenant M. Stevens. He arrived on 7th September 1943, but had been beaten in the rush to set up the squadron by the Flight Sergeant - Discipline and various unnamed staff who, it is presumed, got on with cleaning the place up under his steely glare. There now being someone to complete the daily Operational Record Book, the history of 514 Squadron officially began.

Making the place habitable and fit for purpose presented something of a challenge, as the previous incumbents at Foulsham had, according to the ORB, stripped the office accommodation of all furniture including the shelves. Whilst the official record points no finger, it is noted that 320 Sqn, operating Mitchell bombers, made a sharp exit from Foulsham just before 514 Squadron was formed. The Adjutant promptly made a visit to 226 Sqn at Swanton Morley who provided him that absolute essential of service life, a large quantity of paperwork.

Wing Commander Arthur Samson DFC, the first of three COs of 514 Squadron, relaxing at home. His leadership qualities were to be ably demonstrated over the first few months of the squadron's existence.

514 Squadron leaders in October 1943. Wing Commander Arthur Samson (front row, centre) is flanked by (left) S/Ldr Barney Reid and S/Ldr Alan Roberts, 'A' and 'B' Flight Commanders respectively (TNA).

A period of thoroughly miserable weather over following days ensured that everything and everyone was, no doubt, thoroughly wet through as stores, spares and equipment were obtained through the usual official and less official channels. It was necessary, for example, to send crews to different stations to try and obtain spares from crashed aircraft. Eventually, on 11th September, less than a fortnight after 514 Squadron was created, its first aircraft arrived, this being Lancaster Mk.II DS735. She was followed by further arrivals over the next few days.

The arrival of W/Cdr Arthur Samson DFC from HQ 3 Group added a further spur to the frenzied activity, which also involved the transfer of 1678 Conversion and its aircraft. This unit was to provide a steady flow of aircrew to 514 Squadron after conversion to the Lancaster Mk.II. The squadron's leadership was further bolstered by the transfers in of Squadron Leaders Eric 'Barney' Reid and Alan Roberts, Flight Commanders of 'A' and 'B' Flights respectively. Reid brought his own crew but Roberts turned up alone so arrangements were made with Group to find him some suitable colleagues. The hierarchy was further enhanced by the appointment of the section leaders, F/O Harry Beckett RCAF, DFC (Navigation), P/O H Hall

(Flight Engineer), F/O PR Thompson DFC (Signals) and F/O Jackson Pollock (Gunnery) being the first. Meanwhile, the Adjutant, F/Lt M Stevens, picked up responsibility for Security.

To cheer the staff up, either because of the weather or the implementation of such a robust leadership team, a concert by the Entertainments National Service Association (ENSA) was arranged; however the room provided was apparently far too small for the audience. It was noted that those who managed to see the show did enjoy it and the entertainers were taken off to the Sergeants' Mess after the event to celebrate the event. This, perhaps, gave lie to the commonly-voiced opinion that ENSA actually stood for 'Every Night Something Awful'. The ORB noted that Foulsham was at least ten miles from the nearest town, meaning that buses had to be laid on every so often to enable personnel to go into Norwich for an evening out. It was further noted that the buses were pre-payment, nothing coming for free, it would appear.

On 21st September, 514 Squadron became airborne when P/O George Chequer RCAF took to the air at 1650hrs in DS735. His crew was supplemented by the squadron's Radar Officer in order to test the newly-installed GH equipment, which would later define 514's role as a specialist blind bombing outfit. By the end of its first month, 514 Squadron had some seventeen crews and a similar number of aircraft and was making good progress towards becoming operational.

Training intensified as more Lancasters became operational, and crews began to practice using GH. Pilots and navigators doubled up to make the most of breaks in the otherwise miserable weather. The ORB's author noted on 2nd October that crews were 'Up with the lark', to the chagrin of members of the Conversion Unit and others apparently intent on sleeping off the after effects of an evening's recreation. Planning glitches continued to occur; an afternoon training detail had to be delayed for an hour when the aircraft came to be refuelled, only to find that the Conversion Unit and a diverted Stirling from another squadron had accounted for all the fuel in the petrol bowsers.

When not engaged in GH, high level or low level bombing training, often due to wind, rain or visibility so poor it was noted that 'even the birds were walking', other activities were arranged to prevent boredom. Crews enjoyed, or endured, a programme of lectures, such as Escape and Evasion Tactics, from their respective Section Leaders whilst no opportunity was lost to experience other operational essentials. In particular, all air crew personnel were encouraged to visit the Air Sea Rescue station at Bircham Newton. They would later have a vested interest in the effective work of the unit.

Fighter affiliation was another vital ingredient in their training, arrangements being made with RAF and USAAF squadrons to pit the skills of the Lancaster crews against the Hurricanes, Mustangs and Thunderbolts that were thrown against them. Typically such encounters could last for twenty minutes or more, with resultant queasiness for those crews who had earlier complained about hangovers. In reality, encounters with enemy fighters would prove to be shorter and much more brutal.

By the middle of October, the Squadron Commander was well pleased with the training effort, marking the occasion with a general stand down. Fourteen Lancasters were serviceable by now, out of twenty two on the squadron's books. In preparation for full operational readiness, F/O Guy Hinde and F/O Ron Clements were detailed on 19th October to join 115 Sqn crews out of RAF Witchford for a raid, though this was subsequently cancelled. This was not to delay them long however, as they got their chance on the night of 20th October, when Bomber Command visited Leipzig. Tragically, F/O Clements, flying as second pilot with F/Lt John Anderson in DS725, KO-F, lost his life when, at around 2000hrs, the aircraft was shot down by Lt. Paul Fehre of 5./NJG3 at Engersen, near Gardelegen. There were no survivors from the crew. F/O Clements was therefore the first member of 514 Squadron to lose his life in action.

'Bullseye' navigation exercises started to feature more frequently even though poor weather continued to intervene. They were diversionary tactics designed to irritate the enemy defences, and involved flying towards one of the channel ports or coastal towns of Europe. Then, having alerted the defences, the spoof raider would turn for home whilst still out of their range.

The inclement conditions now included widespread fog, which at least made a change from the usual rain. This resulted in the first planned operations being cancelled, two aircraft having been detailed for gardening (sea mining) duties on each of the last two days of the month. Despite this the senior officers were pleased enough with progress, so arranged to have a group photograph taken of themselves.

Meanwhile, on the ground, W/Cdr Samson went off to a special conference, possibly to do with the imminent Battle of Berlin, whilst his aircrew officers were dragooned into rifle shooting. This was doubtless considered beneficial to their life expectancy on operations, and it was also to provide a team to represent the Squadron at the Group Shoot, the unit's pride being at stake as in all such events. The ORB notes, however, that the Squadron Team did very badly *'through being misled in training'*. The reader is left to speculate on what went wrong.

P/O Bob Langley DFC and his crew were the first from 514 Sqn to participate in thirty operations. They were stood down on 27th June 1944 after 34 trips. The crew is shown here early in their career.

Back row, L-R: Sgt RR Smith (MU Gunner), Sgt CF Wakeling (W/OP), Sgt R Parker (Flight Engineer), Sgt H Oliver (Rear Gunner). Front Row, L-R: Sgt FR Jones (Navigator), Sgt Bob Langley (Pilot), Sgt DT Bradsell (Air Bomber). Source: Marilyn Langley.

3. Baptism of Fire: November and December 1943

The weather finally settled down and the squadron was able to offer aircraft for operations on 3rd November. It was a small-scale effort that first night; four Lancasters, led by 'B' Flight' commander S/Ldr Alan Roberts dropped sea mines near the Frisian Islands whilst two others joined the 589-bomber two-pronged attack on Düsseldorf. Sgt Bob Langley flew DS787, JI-F on the 'gardening' trip, as mining sorties were known, and found the experience less fraught than he had anticipated, noting in his log book *'Wizard night. Never saw a thing.'*

Flight Sergeant (later Pilot Officer) Garth Hughes RAAF dropped the first of 514 Squadron's total of 14652½ tons of bombs when he attacked Düsseldorf on 3rd November 1943 (AWM).

F/S Garth Hughes RAAF in DS785, JI-D had an altogether more exciting time on his op to the Mannesmann Steel Tubing Works in Düsseldorf, reporting two combats with enemy aircraft either side of his bombing run on the target. An Me-210 approached from dead ahead, to the consternation of the bomb aimer, passing between 50 and 100 feet beneath 'D', thus allowing the rear gunner a good opportunity to open fire, with possible damage caused to the night fighter. After F/S Hughes and crew had delivered what was the first of many bomb loads to be dropped by 514 Squadron in the course of the war, they saw a Ju-88 on a parallel course, giving the mid upper gunner, Sgt Eric Moorhouse, the chance to use his guns in anger for the first time, along with Sgt George Thornton in the rear turret. The Ju-88 broke away. Neither enemy aircraft had returned fire on this occasion. F/S Hughes, along with his colleague P/O Colin Payne in DS786, JI-E, carried a bomb load of a single 4,000lb 'cookie' with 4,080lbs of incendiaries. P/O Payne, unable to pinpoint the Mannesmann works, elected to join the main attack on Düsseldorf itself.

The attack on the Mannesmann works was a trial run with a small force of 38 Lancasters equipped with GH, in order to assess its effectiveness in a stand-alone raid. Because of faults with the GH sets along with other problems only 15 of the crews were able to locate and bomb this specific target. Of the 589 aircraft participating in the joint raid, 18 were lost. All six of 514 Squadron's aircraft returned safely to Foulsham.

The next operational outing was on 7th November, when two aircraft were detailed for further mining operations off La Rochelle. Such mundane work was necessary to maximise the harassment of enemy U-Boats and coastal convoys and it was deemed to be highly effective. A further such task was carried out off La Tranche by nine of the squadron's Lancasters on 11th November; ten aircraft had been despatched with one returning early due to a navigational error. DS786, JI-E, flown on this occasion by F/S Fred Steed, suffered flak damage to the rear turret and a radio aerial, demonstrating that such sorties were not without their hazards. Sgt Bob Langley in DS787, JI-F, also sustained heavy flak damage to his aircraft over Nantes. All aircraft did, however, return to base.

On 14th November, the squadron received an instruction that it was to relocate from Foulsham to RAF Waterbeach, just north of Cambridge, as part of the reorganisation of 3 Group. RAF Foulsham became home to 192 Sqn, part of 100 Group, with 462 Sqn RAAF, of the same electronic warfare group, joining them later. As with all such wartime unit movements, the whole process was expected to take place in very quick time with the absolute minimum effect on operations. In fact the timescale for this considerable logistical exercise was eleven days from start to finish, and involved the movement of aircraft, transport, ground equipment, spares and personnel. All bicycles, apparently the property of the station rather than the squadron, had to be signed in. No mention was made in the movement order of all the shelves and other fixtures and fittings that the squadron had gone to such pains to acquire two months previously.

Lancasters Mk.II LL679 (main) and LL678 (background). The aircraft have yet to be marked with their squadron codes, suggesting that they were new to 514 Squadron at the time. LL678 flew 36 ops, being shot down attacking Gelsenkirchen on 12th / 13th June 1944. LL679 was lost on 14th January 1944 attacking Brunswick on her maiden operation (WMHM).

In the meantime, operational business continued, subject only to the vagaries of the weather. On 18th November, whilst an advance party set off for Waterbeach, the squadron tried to dispatch twelve aircraft on bombing operations. Three developed major snags preventing their participation whilst one was cancelled as it was no longer required. Two aircraft joined an attack on Berlin, featuring 444 aircraft, of which nine were lost. F/S Hughes in DS787, JI-F noted that it was a scattered raid with PFF late over the target area. He did at least manage to bomb the target indicators with his 4,000lb 'Cookie' and incendiaries, despite the poor visibility and complete cloud cover. The raid was indeed scattered with four industrial premises damaged.

A further six aircraft participated in the diversionary raid on Mannheim. Intended to split the night fighter defences, the attack by 395 bombers was also scattered, though the Daimler-Benz factory was damaged. These aircraft included P/O Stanley Thomas and crew, flying DS784, JI-C on their first and, tragically, only bombing sortie. The aircraft left Foulsham at 1724hrs and was attacked, apparently by two night fighters, exploding at or over Assesse, ten miles SE of Namur, Belgium. The loss is credited to Lt. Erhard Peters, 1./NJG4 but was also claimed by Hptm. Franz Evers, Stab 1./NJG6. The crew had previously carried out one mining trip. The aircraft's two gunners escaped with their lives, mid upper gunner, Sgt HA Lucas, managing to evade capture and remain hidden in Brussels until the city was liberated whilst his colleague from the rear turret, F/S Bernard Haines RAAF, was taken prisoner. Losses from the Mannheim raid totalled 23 including DS784.

Fog prevented further operations until 22nd November when four Lancasters joined a major raid on Berlin, involving 764 aircraft. F/L Colin Payne in DS786, JI-E, commented that a large glow could be seen beneath

F/S Bernard Haines was taken prisoner after escaping from DS784 on the crew's first and only operation (NAA).

Sgt HA Lucas, mid-upper gunner in DS784, JI-C, survived the loss of his aircraft and evaded capture, remaining in Brussels until the city was liberated in 1944 (TNA)

the cloud, with an exceptionally big explosion. The large glow was probably the result of localised firestorms, resulting in high casualties and significant destruction on the ground, F/L Payne having contributed the standard load of 'Cookie' plus incendiaries. The buildings destroyed or damaged included significant landmarks such as the Kaiser-Wilhelm Gedächtniskirche (Memorial Church) which still stands as a testament to the destruction visited upon Berlin during the war. Other notable locations affected were the Unter den Linden, Charlottenburg Palace, Waffen-SS Administrative College and the former British Embassy. Berlin Zoo was also damaged. 175,000 people were rendered homeless whilst casualties on the ground were estimated at 2,000 including an unfortunate 500 people in an air raid shelter which sustained a direct hit. Although all 514 Squadron's aircraft returned safely, 26 others did not.

Berlin featured again on the following night, with the squadron contributing three aircraft to the 383-strong raid. With almost complete cloud cover to around ten thousand feet the target was not easy to see, but fires were still burning from the previous night, and many of these were bombed in error. F/L Guy Hinde in DS738, JI-J reported that the glow through the clouds was visible for a considerable distance. A large number of red and white fighter flares were noted around Berlin and at least one Lancaster was witnessed being shot down. This was apparently carrying red and green target indicators, these being seen to fall from it as the aircraft went down. Again, the squadron escaped without loss, though twenty aircraft from other units failed to return. F/L Hinde made his landing at Waterbeach on return, becoming the first of 514 Squadron's aircraft to use the new base operationally. His colleagues landed at Cranfield, no reason for this being noted.

A 'gardening' operation on 25th November saw F/S Noel Thackray RAAF taking DS824, JI-U to SW France to drop four sea mines before returning to Exeter rather than Waterbeach. Other operations had been cancelled due to poor weather which did, however, clear by the following afternoon to allow Berlin to be visited again.

On this occasion, the squadron dispatched eight aircraft, one of which turned back with engine trouble. Conditions were much improved though haze impeded a clear view of the ground.

F/O David Gray in DS818, JI-Q reported that the target area was, once again, a mass of flames. His controls were, he noted, stiff with ice. Damage included Berlin Zoo again; whilst many animals had been moved to other zoos there were still a number resident and most did not survive the onslaught. Several large and dangerous animals, big cats and apes, took the opportunity to escape, roaming the streets of the city before they could be

Flying Officer Maurice Cantin RCAF, lost with his crew when his Lancaster DS814, JI-M, was shot down by flak leaving the Berlin target area.

hunted down and shot. Defences were seen to be particularly active with the lack of cloud cover assisting fighters and flak alike, not least because the searchlights could be used more effectively. The flak accounted for F/O Maurice Cantin RCAF and his crew in DS814, JI-M, which was coned by searchlights as the aircraft left the target area and shot down by the flak battery of 1.-4./Schw.Abt.148. The aircraft crashed at Germendorf, 4 km west of Oranienburg. None of the crew, on their first op, survived. Parts of DS814 were subsequently salvaged from the crash site and have been preserved by German aviation archaeologists.

On 27th November, the senior leadership was boosted by the arrival of the veteran S/L Ernest Sly AFM, DFC, whose previous exploits had included landing an Airspeed Oxford which was missing most of its starboard wing outboard of the engine. The Oxford had been involved in a mid-air collision with another aircraft but Sly's airmanship had saved the day, not to mention his own life.

Sergeant (later Squadron Leader) Ernest Sly was awarded the AFM for carrying out a successful forced landing of this Airspeed Oxford. The aircraft had lost a large portion of its starboard wing in a mid-air collision with a similar aircraft.

There were no further ops in November, and the month ended with 44 operational sorties credited to the squadron. There were other matters concerning the squadron's personnel, in particular an outbreak of flu which, according to the RAF Waterbeach ORB *'was on a scale less marked than seen in the general population but was serious enough to impair the operational effort. It was energetically tackled with encouraging results.'* The Sick Bay also catered for one casualty and one case of frostbite from the squadron's operations.

Eric Basford was an Engine Fitter attached to 'A' Flight: 'My arrival at Waterbeach in November '43, to join 514 Squadron, coincided with a large scale reorganisation of No. 3 Group of Bomber Command. A new concept of 'the Bomber Base' was being introduced. A base was to comprise three stations (or airfields) each of which would house a heavy bomber squadron. One of these stations would become 'the base station' and an Air Commodore, appointed AOC of the base, would be resident there. Each 3

Group squadron was being expanded to have three flights, A, B and C, instead of just two.
Waterbeach had already been designated as base station for No 33 Base when 514 Sqn moved in, two days before I arrived. The other two stations in the Base were closer to Ely: Witchford with 115 Sqn and Mepal with 75 New Zealand Sqn. Similar arrangements were being set up throughout 3 Group.
A Base Servicing Unit was already being set up in one of the hangars at Waterbeach. This unit, independent of the three squadrons, was to deal with extensive repairs and major inspections on aircraft that had been detached from the squadron. What was previously the Maintenance Flight on each squadron became known as R & I (Repair and Inspection) Flight. The Base Servicing Unit relieved the new R & I Flights of much major servicing work, but in turn the R & I Flights were allocated the task of minor inspections at 50 flying hours, 100 hours, 150 hours etc. plus repairs expected to take three days or more. This resulted in the workload on the ground crew of each aircraft in the flights being reduced, along with that of the other specialists involved, e.g. electricians, instrument repairers, armourers etc. Previously they did the minor inspections and repairs besides the daily servicing routines. It meant that minor inspections would be completed in the relative comfort of a hangar, instead of outdoors on the dispersals where the vagaries of the weather often created problems. That was the theory. It needed some 'give and take' in practice at times, but it worked reasonably well.
The concept of a regular ground crew for each aircraft in a flight and the responsibilities of the ground crew for their aircraft did not change in any way. A Flight Sergeant, universally referred to as 'Chiefy', remained as NCO i/c Flight.'
Another member of the ground crew to arrive early in the squadron's history was LAC Bernard Yeomans: 'I arrived at Waterbeach in late November 1943, to find tradesmen arriving by every train, bus and lorry. Knowing my way around I soon found an empty bed in my old billet. I was assigned to 'B' hangar, to find a hangar full of unassembled trestles. With so many bodies now at the NCOs' command, the physical assembly soon got underway. The hangar was under the command of Squadron Leader Pearce and W/O Blackmoor.

What started as bodies arriving from four corners of the Empire, in a chaotic mass, soon developed into a very good shift system. The hangar was manned 24 hours a day, 7 days a week, with three shifts, two shifts on 5am until 10pm, or 5pm on alternative nights, one shift 10pm until 5am. There was a 36 hour 'Stand Down' at the end of the third week.
Outside the hangar brand new Lancs arrived direct from the Ministry of Aircraft Production. These were then hauled into the hangar, mods checked and / or fitted, flare chutes for example. At one period we were receiving 30 new aircraft a month, these were sent to Witchford and Mepal

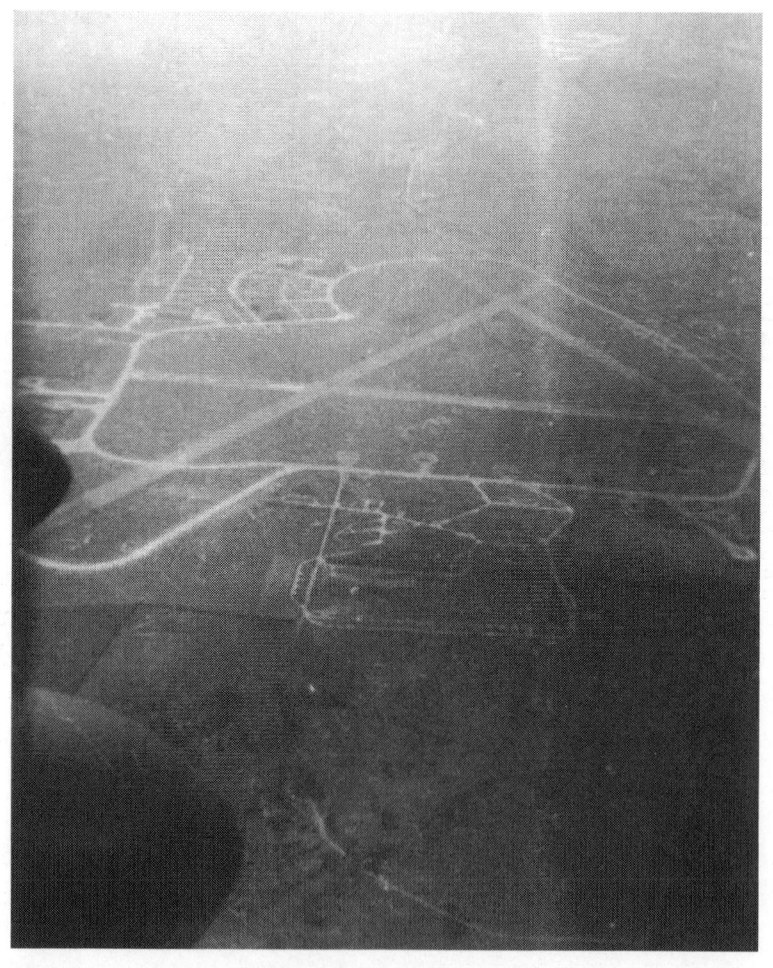

RAF Waterbeach from a 514 Squadron Lancaster flown by F/O Brian Haslam in the second half of 1944. The standard triangular layout of RAF airfields is apparent. The view is towards the south and west with the A10 road just visible next to the perimeter track (WMHM).

as well. During the nine months I served in the hangar Mk Is, IIs and IIIs came through for various mods. With the Mk IIs came the familiar Hercules engines I had earlier maintained on the Stirling.'

By early December 514 Squadron was fully operational, already blooded in the bombing war by the loss of two of its aircraft and their crews. The poor weather, and the visits to Berlin continued unabated. On 2nd December, ten Lancasters left Waterbeach for 'the Big City', three returning early with technical problems, including Sgt Bob Langley in DS787, JI-F. With excessive engine icing, he returned to base but the aircraft's brake linings were iced up and it ran through a fence on landing, fortunately without injury or damage. Patchy cloud covered the target but, once again, fires and smoke featured prominently, being visible up to 120 miles away. Whilst searchlights did not cause too many problems there was fairly intense heavy flak[1], which decreased over the target area to give the night fighters a free run at the bombers. DS738, JI-J was lost over Potsdam as F/L Guy Hinde and his crew approached the target. DS738 was possibly the Lancaster credited to Lt. Alfred Koerver of Stab.II or 7/JG302 at 2011 hours. According to the bomb aimer, F/S John Alford RAAF, the port fin and rudder were shot away, port wing tank set on fire, undercarriage hydraulics damaged and there was possibly damage to the rear turret. It is thought that the rear gunner, Sgt Robert Curle, was killed as he did not respond to the order to bale out. The port wing was on fire and the aircraft entered a dive. F/L Hinde, who was from Rhodesia, was thrown clear. All crew survived as POW except for Sgt Curle. His body was not recovered and he is commemorated on the Runnymede Memorial. Over the target itself, F/S Fred Steed in DS815, JI-N encountered danger from his colleagues in a higher-flying aircraft when a 4lb incendiary bomb fell through the perspex canopy, landing behind the navigator's table. It was promptly despatched overboard. Meanwhile a 30lb incendiary holed the port aileron. Their adventures were not yet over as the crew encountered an Me109 fighter attacking another Lancaster. The fighter crossed over Steed's Lancaster, allowing the mid upper gunner, Sgt W

[1] Flak was described in terms of its intensity (slight, moderate or intense), then by its calibre (light, medium or heavy). Intense light flak was potentially more dangerous than slight heavy flak, though the latter caused more damage if it got too close.

Sweet, to loose off 100 rounds, which he believed struck the enemy aircraft, resulting in it breaking off its attack.

The luck of F/S Steed and crew on this occasion was not shared by Sgt Leo Wilton, the rear gunner in DS783, JI-B. P/O Garth Hughes had bombed from 20,000 feet and was making his way out of the target area when, at 2030hrs, the aircraft was attacked from the port quarter by an Me210 which fired a single burst, killing instantly the unfortunate Sgt Wilton, a Canadian on his first bombing operation. The attack wrecked both turrets and caused fires in the bomb racks, now fortunately empty. These fires in turn set the mid upper gunner's clothing alight which, in the words of P/O Hughes, 'caused him to vacate the turret momentarily.' The Me210 made an immediate follow-up attack from starboard, to which P/O Hughes responded with a corkscrew manoeuvre, which was effective in shaking off the attacker. Sgt Wilton's crew mates were unable to extricate him from his turret until the aircraft, despite its lack of defences, was able to land safely back in England.

This was a bad night for Bomber Command, with forty losses from the 458 aircraft despatched. The bombing was scattered over south Berlin. One of the aircraft lost was carrying members of the press, Captain Grieg for the Daily Mail and Norman Stockton, Sydney Sun.

Hot on the heels of Berlin, the following night saw five of the squadron's aircraft detailed to raid Leipzig, though only three managed to take off. Once again, the glow of fires was noted through the cloud covering the target. After feinting towards Berlin, the attacking force diverted to the actual target leaving few fighters to provide opposition, although the stream was coming under sporadic attack. The TIs were well positioned making this a most successful raid. However this was marred by extra casualties incurred when many aircraft in the stream mistakenly flew over the Frankfurt defences. On this occasion, the squadron escaped without loss though 24 other aircraft failed to return.

The weather then intervened again, giving a fortnight of respite to the squadron as fog shrouded Waterbeach and other bomber airfields. On the ground, on 10th December the squadron was honoured to host a visit by HRH the Duke of Gloucester. According to the Station ORB, the Duke *'visited in the afternoon accompanied by AOC 3 Group, AVM R Harrison CBE, DFC, AFC. HRH visited the Base Operations Room, Flying Control Tower and inspected and talked to an operational Lancaster crew. After tea in the Aircrew Tech Library HRH inspected the new briefing and interrogation rooms. He departed amidst rousing cheers from station personnel. A Guard of Honour was supplied by the RAF Regiment under the command of F/L WE Harper.'*

Meanwhile the squadron's first DFC was awarded to P/O Garth Hughes for bringing home his badly damaged aircraft from Berlin after the attack that killed Sgt Leo Wilton. The citation read: *'One night in October 1943 (sic), this officer piloted an aircraft detailed to attack Berlin. Just as his bombing run was completed his aircraft was attacked by a fighter. Pilot Officer Hughes succeeded in evading the attacker but his aircraft had been repeatedly hit by bullets from the enemy aircraft. The rear gunner was*

Prince Henry, Duke of Gloucester, an early VIP visitor to the squadron at Waterbeach. In 1945 he was appointed Governor-General of Australia.

killed. The mid-upper turret was rendered unserviceable, while the fuselage became filled with smoke which prevented Pilot Officer Hughes from seeing his instruments. The smoke cleared, however, when several small fires in the fuselage were extinguished. Almost immediately another fighter took up the attack but Pilot Officer Hughes was able to evade it and set course for base. Soon afterwards one of the damaged engines became

HRH the Duke of Gloucester has a close look at a 4,000lb 'cookie', supposedly about to be loaded into DS815, JI-N. In fact, the squadron did not operate for a further six days, so this was purely for show (WMHM).

useless. Although the aircraft became difficult to control, Pilot Officer Hughes succeeded in reaching base. This officer, who has attacked Berlin on 5 previous occasions, displayed a high degree of skill, courage and determination.'

On 11th December, Mr Leonard Cotterill of the BBC visited to make arrangements for Lancaster crews to broadcast at USAAF Flying Fortress station at Bassingbourne on a 'Round the World Hook-Up' on Christmas Day. On 14th December, a conference was held by the Station Commander, Gp Capt GIL Saye, and BBC engineers regarding a New Year's Eve broadcast from the control tower.

On 16th December twelve 514 Squadron Lancasters took to the air for their next operation, a return to Berlin. One aircraft suffered engine and undercarriage problems necessitating an early return to Waterbeach while the remaining crews successfully attacked the target. Three crews reported combats with enemy fighters, these being F/S Don Crombie RAAF in

DS820, JI-R, F/S Noel Thackray in LL627, JI-U and F/L Cyril 'Nick' Nichol in DS815, JI-N. No damage was sustained by any of these aircraft, whilst the two gunners in F/S Crombie's crew, Sergeants Edward Jenner and Harold Hill, claimed their FW190 as damaged. Meanwhile their own aircraft was returning to base on three engines, the fourth being out of action, cause unstated. The raid itself resulted in the destruction of railway facilities which in turn disrupted the transport of troops and supplies to the Russian Front, whilst it was assessed by Bomber Command that by now some 25% of all housing in Berlin had been obliterated.

Flight Sergeant (later Pilot Officer) Noel Thackray RAAF. Together with his crew he was one of the original members of the squadron and flew 17 ops, including nine trips to Berlin and the infamous Nuremberg raid. They failed to return from Aachen on 11th April 1944 (Lyn Hammet).

This nght became infamous as 'Black Thursday' because of the atrocious weather conditions that met the returning bombers, their bases being closed due to thick fog. Of the total raid strength of 493 aircraft, 55 were lost. 25 of these crashed or were abandoned on their return to England with a loss of around 150 men in addition to the battle casualties. Once again 514

Squadron was fortunate, all its aircraft returning safely though two diverted to Little Snoring and nine to Downham Market. It was three days before conditions allowed the last of the diverted aircraft to return to Waterbeach. The next operation, on 20th December, saw eleven Lancasters join an attack on Frankfurt, always a fiercely-defended target, one aircraft having failed to participate because its engine cowling would not fit over the new type of coolers being fitted to the Hercules engines. This was another night that saw heavy losses to the bomber force; 41 of the force of 650 aircraft were to be shot down by fighters or flak, or lost to other causes. The toll could have been even worse but for the cloud covering the target, which reduced the effectiveness of the searchlights. Although all 514 Squadron's aircraft reached the target, F/S GJ ‘Roger’ Davis and his crew in DS817, JI-P were attacked by Hptmn Wilhelm Herget of 8./NJG3 at about 2015hrs, having bombed the target. The Lancaster exploded, with only F/S Davis surviving, as he was wearing his parachute when he was thrown clear in the explosion. He fell from 21,000 feet to around 600 feet before he got his parachute open. F/S Davis was captured and spent the next seventeen months as a POW, in Dulag Luft and Stalag IVB, escaping three times and being recaptured each time. Eventually, as a habitual escapee, he was marched along with many others, through Poland, to a secure facility up

Flight Sergeant 'Roger' Davis, the sole survivor when his LancasterDS817, JI-P, was shot down, went on to be a thorn in the side of his German captors with his repeated attempts to escape (Davis family).

on the Silesian Plateau near the Ukraine, Stalag 17. F/S Bob Langley's DS787, JI-F, suffered a double engine failure and bombed an enemy aerodrome before landing at RAF Woodbridge.

Despite the heavy casualties, the squadron record notes that opposition was 'moderate'. In the event, bombing was reported to be widespread with fires burning short of the target. F/S Walter Henry in DS823, JI-M considered that 'shortage of TIs may have had a lot to do with this.' On approaching the target, the Germans set off dummy TIs and lit a fire as a diversion. A wind change forced the smoke to reverse direction and it ended up over Frankfurt by mistake. By the end of the raid, over 23,000 people had been rendered homeless.

The Station ORB noted the approach of Christmas. On 21st *December 'the annual children's party was held in the Officers' Mess for the forty children of station personnel (all ranks). The Entertainment Officer and volunteer officers arranged the party, including a Christmas tree in the ante room, and played games with the children. The highlight of the party was the arrival of Father Christmas in an armoured car, then he distributed toys made by personnel of station workshops in their off-duty hours.'*

Christmas brought no respite to crews or the population of the target areas. On 23rd December 19 of the squadron's Lancasters were detailed for another attack on Berlin, the largest effort to date. This was assisted by 'C' Flight, 514 Squadron's third, achieving operational status under S/Ldr Ernest Sly DFC. 514 Squadron could now, on paper at least, provide nearly thirty aircraft if required. On this occasion, four of the squadrons Lancasters failed to take off whilst two had to return early due to technical problems. On this occasion, four of the squadron's Lancasters failed to take off whilst two had to return early due to technical problems. One aircraft became bogged down whilst taxying out thereby causing another to fail to take off as it was blocked. This still left thirteen to carry out the attack, the pilots noting good fires through the clouds, the glow being visible from a distance of 100 miles. Opposition was described as 'moderate', though F/O Leonard Kingwell's crew in LL625, JI-C survived three encounters with enemy aircraft, these being two Ju88s and an FW190. His aircraft was undamaged although one of the Ju88s opened fire as it past LL625. In return the gunners, Sgt Harry Taylor and W/O Harold Fidge RAAF, engaged the Ju88s driving off both aircraft. LL671, A2-B was not so fortunate. According to F/S John Moloney RAAF, the only survivor, it is believed that the pilot, P/O Kenneth Whitting RAAF, was killed during an attack on the aircraft. The aircraft crashed at Catheim, approximately 10 miles north of Frankfurt. This location has been difficult to pinpoint; however it is likely that LL671 was attacked by Ofw. Walter Mackens of 1./JG300 at 0250 hours or Oblt. Hans-Heinz Augenstein of 7./NJG1 at 0300 hours, both of these unidentified claims being in the Frankfurt area. The crew were on their first operation with 514 Squadron, though they had previously flown some five ops with 623 Squadron from RAF Wratting Common.

379 aircraft, mostly Lancasters, formed the attacking force, of which sixteen failed to return. The PPF (Pathfinders) experienced H2S problems resulting in the TIs being scattered. On a positive note an effective diversion by Mosquitoes temporarily tricked the German Fighter controllers which reduced the amount of fighter opposition. A Ju-88 G-6 of 6.NJG3, D5+HP, was shot down and credited to the rear gunner of a 514 Squadron. Lancaster over Berlin. Fw. Rudolf Frank and his BF (Radar Operator) Uffz. Schierholz, an ace crew with 27 victories, bailed out unharmed. It is likely that this was the Ju88 fired on by W/O Harold Fitch. Christmas itself saw no operational flying, though this was due to poor visibility rather than a festive truce. There was a stand-down for the squadron and football matches, described as 'of a not very serious nature' took place in the morning. The Station ORB noted in some detail the festivities:

'24/12/43 The Station Commander, Senior WAAF Officer and Station Adjutant were judges of the decorations at the WAAF Camp. A very high standard of artistry was displayed by the WAAFs. Mr F Saravanamates, member of the Legislative Council of Ceylon, visited the station. As an expert on the growing of rubber he was greatly interested in the numerous uses to which rubber is put to on an operational station. A Christmas Eve dance was held by the RAF Regiment in the gym where the festive spirit was already in evidence. A piper in traditional Highland dress played reels which were enthusiastically danced. An ankle competition for the WAAF proved a popular novelty.

On Christmas Day ops were laid on but cancelled ten minutes later. A day of varied social activities ensued. The Station Commander stated that sections could stand down from 1030hrs unless employed on essential operational duties. A soccer match was held in the morning, Officers v Senior NCOs; the officers won. The Senior NCOs were entertained by the Officers in the Officers' Mess prior to the departure of all to the Airmen's Mess to wait at Christmas Dinner there. The Station Band played whilst dinner was being served. Officers and Senior NCOs, led by the Station Commander, attended to the needs of a multitude of hungry airmen. The Station Commander also visited the WAAF Mess, No. 2 Sergeants' Mess and Station Sick Quarters. A non-operational night enabled the Officers' Mess to hold an informal party, music being supplied by the Swing Trio led by the Base Signals Officer on the Double Bass. Boxing Day saw an all ranks dance, held in the Station Institute, which was a great success. The Christmas Spirit was very much in evidence on a crowded floor, despite the 'NO beer or other drinks' notice being put up in all messes throughout the camp, including the NAAFI.'

The respite from ops lasted until 29th December when seventeen Lancasters that left Waterbeach, out of the original nineteen tasked with the raid. For one crew this was to prove an exceptionally long, cold and uncomfortable night. F/O Lou Greenburgh and his crew in DS821, JI-S were on their first op with 514 Squadron, though F/O Greenburgh had previously undertaken some operational flying with 620 Sqn at Chedburgh. On arrival at Waterbeach as a Lancaster skipper, Greenburgh related that he was approached by his crew who extracted a promise from me not to volunteer for additional missions. 'I could understand their concern and I didn't want to get shot down any more than they did. My ambition was always to die of old age. "Okay guys," I replied, "I won't volunteer for any missions." On December 29th I met with the CO, Wing Commander Arthur Samson, who welcomed me to 514 Squadron and offered me a cigarette. As I put it to my mouth and took the ritualistic first puffs, he mentioned that he needed one more crew for a raid that night. "It's an undefended target," he added, "Just across the Channel." I remembered my promise not to volunteer but it sounded like a breeze; a short, safe way to get combat experience we so badly needed, so I replied "Alright, sir, we'll do it." My crew hit the roof! Five of them blew up when I told them how brave I had been on their behalf. Fred Carey (mid upper gunner) blurted in his Cockney accent, "My wife's just had a baby. I've got a son I've never seen'. I don't want to go into action yet!"

"I understand," I told him, "but it's an undefended target. We'll be alright. It's just across the Channel."

"Like hell it is!" exclaimed Geordie, the Flight Engineer. "They're going to Hanover or Leipzig or some place. They're loading up those aircraft to full capacity!"

We rushed to find Wing Commander Samson and found that he was in the briefing room. He didn't want to see me. I had to say something to the crew to ease the tension we all felt. "Remember guys," I said. If we go on an operation, we get a free chocolate bar."

"Free chocolate bar?" Strommy, the wireless operator, snorted. "That's all our skin is worth, a free chocolate bar?!"

When the map was uncovered in the briefing room that afternoon and I saw the red circle around our target, I felt sick. There had been a last minute switch. Fred's face was ashen and he gestured to me in desperation, but there was nothing I could do. By now it was too late to switch crews and the 'undefended target just across the Channel' was Berlin.'

Once again, cloud obscured the target but the glow of fires permeated the undercast, and could be seen from 70 miles on this occasion. In the depths of winter an early start was possible, and 514 Squadron's contingent attacked the aiming point at around 2015hrs.

The Greenburgh crew had come under attack from a Ju88 near Meppen on the outbound leg. A prolonged exchange of fire between the two aircraft was followed by the enemy fighter firing a rocket projectile which exploded under the port wing of the Lancaster. F/O Greenburgh's strenuous efforts to corkscrew his way out of trouble paid dividends, and the Ju88 was shaken off, though petrol was now leaking from the damaged Lanc. Undeterred, F/O Greenburgh pressed on to the target and was on the return leg near the site of the first attack when the mid upper gunner, Sgt Fred Carey, saw another Ju88 manoeuvring to attack them. Both gunners fired on the enemy aircraft with commendable, and understandable, enthusiasm whilst F/O Greenburgh once again threw the Lancaster into a corkscrew. The gunners saw a red glow in the centre of the Ju88's fuselage as it broke away, seemingly out of control. Three twin-engine night fighters were lost on the evening and it is possible that Sgt Carey and his rear turret colleague F/S Connie Drake had accounted for one of these.

The defenders of the Reich had not yet finished with DS821 and her crew, however. Quarter of an hour later, by which time the stricken Lancaster, perilously short of fuel, was heading due West some 30km South of Texel, Ofw. Karl-Heinz Scherfling of 12./NJG1 in another Ju88 found and attacked the aircraft. Three times Ofw. Scherfling pressed home an attack but eventually F/O Greenburgh managed to make good his escape. Lou Greenburgh recalled: 'We were about twenty minutes from the coast. Geordie said, "I doubt if we'll make it to the coast, Skipper. We're going to wind up behind enemy lines."

"OK," I acknowledged. "Are you sure? Give us a true picture of what's happening."

"We'll never make England again," he stated, "because we've lost all of the fuel from the starboard outer tank and we're using too much fuel trying to get above the overcast." We were just passing over Holland.

"Well guys," I said over the intercom, "Get ready to bail out."

"What about you, Skipper?" someone asked.

Strommy answered for me. "With a name like Greenburgh?! Would you bail out?"

Connie snorted, "They'd cut his balls off!"

I told them I would try to make it back. Geordie said, "We'll never make it. But if you're going to try, we're with you Skipper."

"Skipper, we've got to get back to England!" exclaimed Don Bament, the bomb aimer. "I've got a date with Susie tonight. If I don't get back there's a damned sailor who will go after her!"

I set course for the East Frisian Islands just off the German coast. It was taking nearly all the strength I owned just to keep the wheel straight. Slowly, slowly we gained altitude. We were over the North Sea. Then the canopy cleared and the turbulence stopped. We were above the storm.

Tracer bullets ripped past the canopy and I cranked the wheel hard to starboard as an FW190 flashed by. Round and round I corkscrewed with a tenacious fighter on our tail. We finally lost him. I don't think he actually hit us, but our fuel shortage was now critical. Geordie told me we only had six minutes' fuel left. That's when Connie in the rear turret began screaming. "An airplane with a beard," he wailed. "It's an airplane with a beard. A Fortress with a beard, it's coming after us."'

Knowing that Flying Fortress aircraft were day bombers and, in any case, were generally clean-shaven, Greenburgh assumed that his rear gunner was suffering from hallucinations and, by now, he was having to cope with a full-blown emergency. As the fuel gauge needles moved to show 'Empty' the engines failed, one by one till only a single engine remained. Greenburgh recalled, 'I forced myself to remain calm. "Strommy," I said quietly, "You'd better get started with your MAYDAY routine. And get a fix."

Strommy sent off the following message: "Petrol low, crossing coast 5235 North, 0143 East." The time was 2310hrs. It was the last message from S-Sugar which anyone would ever receive. I ordered the crew into forward crash positions. Our latest position report had placed us within a few miles of the English coast. We flew on one sick engine for a while and then it failed too. We started down.

I pushed the nose down to keep the aircraft from stalling. We were falling like an enormous brick with seven men aboard and it seemed like we were going straight down. I knew that I would have to pull back at just the right moment; too soon and we would stall and crash, too late and we would explode on impact.

The wind shrieked against the metal. The mid upper's intercom was open; I could hear Fred praying for the son he would probably never see whilst Connie was babbling about the bearded Fortress on our tail.

The wheel ripped itself from my hands and we began to spiral. The shrieking increased as I open my side window panel. I regained control of the wheel and divided my attention between the open side window, the altimeter and the air speed indicator, trying to check everything at once. The vertical speed indicator was off the scale. I knew that I would never see the stormy ocean in that pitch blackness and was almost frantic for some clues about when to pull up. I struggled to remain in control of myself, fighting the urge to pull back on the wheel.

A flash of light radiated through the clouds, spoiling my night vision, and we were buffeted by an explosion. As if I didn't have enough problems, a damn flak ship was firing at us! At 10,000 feet Connie left the rear turret and came forward to his crash position.

The altimeter was unwinding. "10,000 feet, 9,000 feet, 8,000 feet, 7,000 feet..." Another shell burst nearby.

"For God's sake!" I hollered. "Can't somebody do anything?!" I was completely helpless. But I managed to stay in control of myself. As totally absorbed as I was in trying to save the aircraft, I accepted the fact that I was about to die. I even did a little praying.

All at sea. F/O Lou Greenburgh and his crew endured sixteen hours in the North Sea before being rescued unharmed (Harry Dison)

The altimeter showed zero and a shocking face full of salt water burst through the open window panel. I hauled back on the wheel for all I was worth, forcing the tail down. The aircraft skipped through the top of one wave and bounced onto another one. The tail section dragged through a wave top, slowing the aircraft, then broke off. The canopy shattered as Sugar rammed into a vertical wall of water.

I woke up coughing. As my consciousness returned, I found myself up to my chin in heart-stopping cold water. I had no strength to struggle against the waves which pushed me around the sinking cockpit. My head dropped below the surface again and I was helpless. I was trapped in an elevator heading for the bottom of the sea.

Miraculously, the cockpit began to rise and most of the water drained out. Hands unclipped my harness. I was dragged out of my seat and through the upper escape hatch by Geordie and Strommy, who pushed me onto the forward part of the fuselage. I lost my balance and fell into the sea, taking Geordie with me. Somehow we made it to the half-inflated and leaky raft and were helped aboard.'

Lou Greenburgh had achieved his greatest feat of the night, and possibly of his life, by successfully ditching his Lancaster in pitch darkness in the North Sea. Strommy's message had, mercifully, been received at Waterbeach and the squadron was therefore well aware that the aircraft had attempted to ditch. At first light the following morning Wing Commander Arthur Samson refused to leave his crew without hope of rescue. Assembling a scratch crew he flew back along the return route and, seventy miles off the Norfolk coast, on the first leg of the search a Very Light was seen by the rear gunner in the squadron commander's Lancaster. A dinghy in which there appeared to be six men was sighted shortly afterwards. It had been the crew's last flare. Samson's crew kept the dinghy in sight for three hours, giving directions for the Air/Sea Rescue operation, until other aircraft appeared and remained on the scene. Finally a Rescue Launch appeared in the vicinity and was guided to the dinghy and all the occupants were taken on board. It was subsequently ascertained that the dinghy contained all seven of the crew and that none of them was injured. This is the first known case of a 'ditching' in the Squadron and the circumstances of the rescue caused great satisfaction. The aircraft itself was observed still afloat, after nearly twelve hours in the sea. Wing Commander Samson later told Lou Greenburgh, 'I had told you it was an easy target and talked you into volunteering. I wanted to make damned sure you were rescued.'

Lou Greenburgh was awarded an immediate DFC for his calm handling of the situation.

A few years later, whilst flying on the Berlin Airlift, Greenburgh met Taff Richardson, an old friend who had trained with him at Chipping Warden. Richardson told him he had witnessed the ditching, having been flying a 'Radar Fortress', a top secret electronic counter-measure aircraft used to jam German radar. He had followed the ailing Lancaster relaying its position to Air/Sea Rescue. The Fortress had a huge radar dome, called a 'chin dome' under the nose. It looked just like a beard.

This was not the last time F/O Greenburgh's exploits would feature in the annals of 514 Squadron history. Meanwhile Ofw. Scherfling, an experienced combatant for whom DS821 was the 26th victory, would be shot down himself on the night of 20th/21st July 1944 by a Mosquito night fighter, losing his life.

The Station ORB went on to detail some of the events back on dry land, in which the Greenburgh crew were doubtless delighted to have been able to participate: *'BBC New Year's Eve 'Round the World' broadcast took place from the control tower. Mr. Stuart Macpherson acted as a commentator and the Station Commander, Squadron Commander and SFCO broadcast. A Fancy Dress dance was held in the WAAF Quarters in the evening. It was evident by the fancy dresses that the WAAF had spent a great deal of time in preparing them. Air Commodore CB Cayford CBE, DFC, AFC and Mrs. Cayford attended the dance and Mrs. Cayford presented the prizes. The music was supplied by the Station Band and a grand time was had by all. Dresses were excellent, refreshments good and seldom has so much lipstick been transferred by so few to so many in so short a time.'*

On that note, 1943 came to a close. 1944 was to prove no less eventful, and difficult, for 514 Squadron and its crews.

4. Blood, Sweat and Tears: January to April 1944

DS813, JI-H, stands alongside LL624, JI-B. DS813 carries eight ops markers on her nose, dating the photograph early to mid-January 1944. The photo was taken by Sgt George 'Hawkeye' Henry, mid-upper gunner for the crew of W/O Ed Greenwood. DS813 was lost on her 56th op, to Stuttgart on 28th / 29th July 1944, whilst LL624 was struck off charge following a crash whilst taking off for Vincly on 25th August 1944 (Sgt George Henry via Tracy Holroyd-Smith).

New Year's Day 1944 saw yet another trip to Berlin, this time involving 421 Lancasters, of which 15 were from Waterbeach. As so often before, there was complete cloud cover, and the bombing was fairly scattered, although crews reported explosions with smoke rising to over 20,000 feet. 28 Lancasters were lost, though 514 Squadron's aircraft returned safely.

The squadron returned to Berlin yet again the following night, participating in a raid of similar size, with the loss of one fewer aircraft this time. Again, all 514 Squadron's aircraft returned though DS824, JI-K, flown by P/O John Williams, sustained damage following two combats with enemy aircraft. Bombing was again scattered, and regarded as fairly ineffective. 156 Squadron suffered badly with the loss of five of its fourteen aircraft and ten Pathfinder aircraft were also lost.

There then followed a lengthy lay off due largely to the poor weather; low cloud, rain and limited visibility on most days made ops difficult. The twelve days did at least allow Bomber Command's squadrons the chance to replace crews and aircraft after recent heavy losses. There was time for social activity as well. On 10th January the Officers' Mess held a party.

The Officers' Mess at RAF Waterbeach was the location for many a party, according to the station's Operational Record Book (Gary Smith).

Guests included Air Marshal Sir Patrick Playfair, HL, KBE, CB, CVO, MC, Commandant Eastern Area ATC, and Lady Playfair, along with Air Commodore Howard Williams MC, the Daily Telegraph's Air Correspondent.

When ops commenced again on 14th January, the squadron was despatched to Brunswick by way of a change from bombing Berlin. 23 aircraft were detailed from the squadron's three flights, a new record, though three failed to take off and four returned early. This still meant that sixteen aircraft bombed the primary target, in what was the first major attack of the war on Brunswick. 469 Lancasters and two Halifax made up the force, but the small size of the town and the complete cloud cover resulted in a widespread and scattered bombing pattern. This was not the perception at the time however; the ORB comments that this was *'believed to be a good raid.'* P/O Garth Hughes in DS785, JI-D having bombed from

20,000 feet, reported 'well concentrated fires below cloud'. He also commented on the defences, noting 'Fighters appeared to drop red flares and flak opened up on these.

The opposition was, once more, very effective and it was not a good night for the attacking force as a whole or 514 Squadron in particular. Squadron Leader Ernest Sly, DFC, having worked so hard to get 'C' Flight ready for the fray, was flying LL685, A2-G. His Lancaster was intercepted on approach to the target at 1905 hrs by Hptm. Walter Barte of Stab III./NJG3 West of Bennebostel and shot down, crashing 5km south of Celle with the loss of all on board. S/L Sly was the highest ranking officer to be lost by the squadron.

After bombing the target, LL679, A2-J, another 'C' Flight Lancaster, piloted by F/S Paul Mason RNZAF, was shot down at Lauenberg, near Dassel. Other 514 Squadron aircraft had bombed the target at around

Flight Sergeant Paul Mason RNZAF and his crew were lost on their first operation. Their aircraft is thought to have fallen prey to Hptm. Erhard Peters' night fighter (AWMM).

1915hrs. The location of the loss suggests that LL679 was probably shot down between 1930hrs and 1935hrs. Hptm. Erhard Peters of 9./NJG3 claimed a Lancaster shot down at an unstated location at 1933hrs and this is the most likely match for the loss of LL679. There were no survivors from the crew, on their first operational sortie, all of whom are buried in Hannover War Cemetery.

Persistently poor weather returned, forcing the crews to stay on the ground, apart from the odd training flight, and to while away their time in lectures and the occasional football match. In the evening, the Station personnel endeavoured to provide a variety of distractions. The Station ORB relates that on 16th January, *'the Service Concert Party from RAF Newmarket was delayed by the fog and as a result arrived in part only, one hour and twenty minutes late. In spite of this, and in the absence of their orchestra, music, a number of costumes and some members of the cast, they displayed the real 'trouper's spirit' and the show went on. An audience which had been previously entertained by a one-man Concert party in the person of LAC May, showed its appreciation of Newmarket's valiant effort in no uncertain fashion.'*

Mel Melluish provided some additional background: 'In the early years of the war 'the flicks' were the main form of off-duty entertainment on RAF stations. Training stations had purpose built cinemas that were open every evening and, apart from being smaller, were comparable with those in small towns. Admission charges were low, programmes up-to-date, and projection and presentation of a professional standard. Cinemas on operational stations were no match for those on training stations. The cinema at RAF Waterbeach, although located in a room over the airmen's mess, was open every evening, had up-to-date films changed regularly, and was well patronised. We also had the advantage of several excellent modern cinemas in Cambridge.

From the spring of 1944 onwards we also had some top quality live entertainment on the station. These ENSA shows were put on in the NAAFI, where there was a good permanent stage at one end. It meant that the NAAFI would have to be closed for that evening. I recall that we had Stanford Robinson with the BBC orchestra. James Mason (the most recent film and stage star of the day) acted in a play at Waterbeach. Then we had a few variety shows in which some stars of the London stage appeared. Pat Kirkwood, glamorous vocalist, is one name that springs to mind. All in all, we enjoyed some excellent professional live entertainment at Waterbeach in 1944. Perhaps as a consequence of these top showbiz people, an amateur concert party and an amateur dramatic society were formed from airmen and WAAFs serving at Waterbeach in 1944.

The concert party staged some excellent shows for us but I do not remember any production from the dramatic society. General movements, i.e. postings to and from the station, always created major problems for such activities, since the loss of just one key performer could be disastrous.'

The operational inactivity persisted for almost a week, the next call to arms occurring on the night of 20th January with yet another outing to Berlin. On this occasion, nineteen aircraft departed Waterbeach, the squadron's take off being accomplished in an impressive fourteen minutes. Five aircraft subsequently had to return early with the remaining fourteen all making a safe landing some hours later. As usual the target was covered by cloud, through which the fires were seen to glow, these being visible from 130 miles. F/L George Chequer in DS735, JI-A bombed on ETA having arrived before the Pathfinders and noted the target indicators going down as he left, albeit three miles north of where he had bombed.

F/S Alan Winstanley, in LL677, A2-E reported two encounters with enemy aircraft, coming under attack on both outward and return legs. Before reaching the target his aircraft was hit in the starboard inner engine and wing and the mid upper turret was also put out of action as the attacker made two passes. By corkscrewing the Lancaster managed to escape, carrying on to bomb the target before coming under a further onslaught, this time from a Ju-88. On this occasion the rear gunner managed to score hits on the fighter which broke off the attack.

P/O Garth Hughes in DS816, JI-O also had to work hard to shake off a determined pursuer en route to the target, his manoeuvring being successful on this occasion. There was considerable night-fighter activity with fighters harassing the stream until it was well into the return journey, resulting in the loss of 35 bombers from the force of 769.

On 21st January, the exemplary leadership qualities of W/C Samson were recognised in the Station ORB when he *was 'officially cited by the AOC in C for his resource and leadership in finding F/O Lou Greenburgh and crew in the North Sea.'* That night, the squadron was tasked with an attack on Magdeburg, lying midway between Brunswick and Berlin. 18 Lancasters were sent from Waterbeach, one of which returned early. Scattered cloud over the target made something of a change from recent nights over Berlin but even so the marking was scattered over the target area.

The squadron arrived over the city at around 2300 hrs, somewhat later than on previous evenings. Many aircraft had arrived ahead of the Pathfinder force, bombing when their H2S sets indicated that they were over the target. Some crews made more than one attempt to locate the right location to release their bombs, including F/L Len Kingwell in LL681, JI-J whose aircraft found itself under attack as he made a second attempt at a bomb run. The mid upper turret suffered a stoppage in one gun and two of the four Brownings in the rear turret were also unserviceable. The two gunners were forced to fight off the attack with half their armament, this ultimately being successful at the expense of 540 rounds of ammunition between them. LL681 had sustained extensive damage in this attack including damage to the port inner engine, port right hand undercarriage, port bomb door, starboard main-plane and starboard outer oil tanks. The aircraft and her crew managed to survive this trip, but there was a heavy toll from their squadron colleagues on what was to be one of Bomber Command's worse nights. Of the 57 aircraft that did not return from Magdeburg, four were from 514 Squadron, the unit's heaviest loss to date.

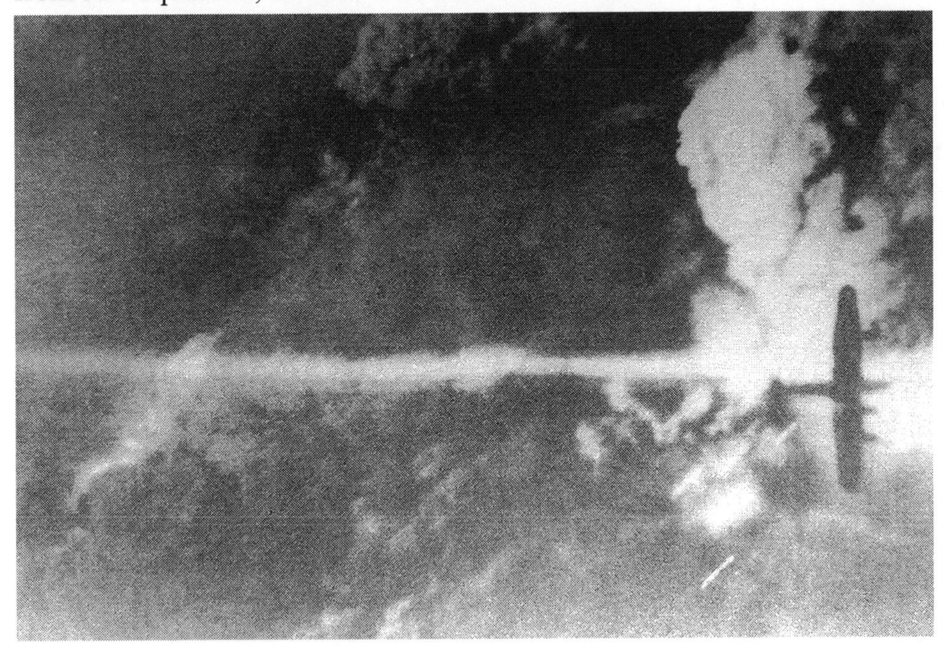

Trailing flames and smoke, and missing its port inner engine, a Lancaster plunges earthwards after being shot down over Magdeburg (Floyd Williston).

Outbound at 21,000 feet LL680, A2-H was intercepted and shot down by an unidentified night fighter. As his aircraft disintegrated, P/O Victor Vizer, on his fifth operation, was thrown clear through the Perspex canopy and survived though badly injured. It is likely that he was saved by wearing the pilot's seat-type parachute. There were no other survivors from the crew. Neither the location nor the time were recorded and there were numerous claims from night-fighter pilots for downed bombers on the outbound leg, so it has not been possible so far to identify which Luftwaffe pilot may have been responsible.

At 2245 hrs, some 25 minutes before they were due over the target, F/L Joe Bourke RCAF and his crew aboard LL672, A2-C, were at 21,000 feet above Perleberg when they had the misfortune to encounter a night fighter, believed to have been that of Hptm. Heinrich, Prinz zu Sayn-Wittgenstein. They were brought down with five of the crew managing to escape. Rear gunner Sgt Albert Williston RCAF and flight engineer Sgt Peter McQueeney were less fortunate and lost their lives. The aristocratic Luftwaffe pilot claimed five allied victims on this night, but it ended as tragically for him as for his victims. The Ju88 was shot down, though it has never been definitely established by whom. One account suggests it was a Mosquito flying an intruder sortie, though the Ju88 came down close to LL672 and it is possible that the night fighter came to grief in a final exchange of fire with Sgt Albert Williston and Sgt Les Brewer[2]. The crewmen bailed out but the prince, who habitually declined to wear a parachute, remained in the aircraft and was killed.

The remaining aircraft of 514 Squadron reached Magdeburg and bombed the target but the danger was not yet past. The return route saw the force turn back towards the North Sea coast and then west towards England. This brought them over the north of Holland and they continued to be harried by the German night fighters who claimed two more of the squadron's Lancasters. DS824, JI-K was flown by P/O John Williams who, along with three of his crew was on his second tour.

They were over the Ijsselmeer when they were shot down by the Me110 night-fighter flown by Oblt. (Later Hptm.) Martin Drewes, another high-scoring ace with 11. /NJG1. Oblt. Drewes' colleague in the unit, Ofw. Heinz Vinke, is believed to have accounted for 514 Squadron's fourth lost

---

[2] Lou Greenburgh in *DFC and Bar* by Ed Greenburgh

Brothers in arms. Flight Sergeant Albert Williston (left) and Sergeant Pete McQueeney (right) flew together, both losing their lives when their Lancaster LL672 was shot down approaching Magdeburg on 21st January 1944 (Floyd Williston).

Lancaster that night, LL627, JI-U which was flown by F/S Richard Bennett RCAF and his crew, none of whom survived the encounter.

23rd January saw the award publicised of a DFC to F/L Colin Payne. The officer completed his tour of operations, 16 of which took place whilst he was with 514 Squadron. He subsequently became a Squadron Leader and Flight Commander with 149 Sqn at Methwold. Meanwhile, poor weather for the following few days appears to have played its part in keeping the squadron away from operational activity until 27th January, when Berlin was, once more, the destination.

Prior to the raid itself, various crews took part in tests of flak suits, an item of kit that was popular with American aircrew. These armoured vests were designed to protect the torso from shrapnel. They were, however, cumbersome, heavy and uncomfortable and, crucially, had to be discarded before the parachute could be attached to its harness. A red toggle, when pulled, allowed the flak suit to be discarded quickly. However, they were not widely used by Bomber Command.

That evening twenty Lancasters left Waterbeach for Berlin, five of these returning early including LL674, A2-D captained by F/S Horace Symmonds. The RAF Waterbeach ORB notes that F/S Symmonds was sick, and the aircraft was flown home by F/S Norman Hall who, fortuitously, was flying as 'second dickey'. On landing LL672 overran the runway, coming to rest in a ditch with the wing obstructing the Ely road, fortunately without injury to the crew or passing motorists.

The remaining fifteen aircraft successfully bombed the target with a mixture of 4,000lb 'cookies' and incendiaries. Although the target was cloud-covered, fires were visible from a distance of 150 miles on the return trip and the raid was later assessed to have been effective, with damage to significant infrastructure and the displacement of some 20,000 Berliners. All 514 Squadron's aircraft returned safely, although many fighter flares were seen and four combats were reported by the squadron's crews. These included P/O Garth Hughes in DS785, JI-D, whose rear gunner Sgt LJH Whitbread fought off an attacking Ju88 claiming many hits on it. In total 33 of the 530 aircraft attacking Berlin failed to return.

Back at Waterbeach, Major General Sharapov and Lieutenant Colonel Rouday, Russian Military Air Attache and Assistant Air Attache respectively, visited the station after dining at 3 Group HQ and were conducted around the Operations Room and Flying Control. They also attended the debriefing of 514 Squadron crews returning from Berlin. F/O Lou Greenburgh was one of the pilots who gave the Russian visitors the benefit of their thoughts: 'The Soviets were pushing for a second front to take the pressure off their guys who, they felt, were fighting the war by themselves. Two Generals were going to interview us to get some idea of what we were doing.

We all gathered in a class room. The senior officer told us to hold nothing back, but to give the Soviets an accurate picture of what we were going through. Our bosses wanted the Russians to know that our raids were not a 'piece of cake.'

It was strange, seeing those Soviet uniforms. The only Soviet uniforms I had ever seen before were in the movies. One of the Generals was quite young and spoke English well. The other one was older and needed some translation. He probably learned what he needed to know by the sound of our voices and the look in our eyes.

Soviet Air Attache Maj. Gen Andrei Sharapov presents a medal to a US serviceman. Sharapov and his assistant, Lt. Col. Rouday, were amongst the VIP visitors to Waterbeach. They had a conversation with F/O Lou Greenburgh which was, no doubt, interesting to both parties.

"Hey," somebody said, "if you want to know about air battles, you should talk to Greenburgh!" With that introduction, I told them about some of my experiences. I think they got the message.'[3]

On the entertainment front, the show went on. In spite of the destruction by fire of the props, curtains and hangings of the NAAFI Canteen Stage the previous weekend, the Station Concert Party was able to give its initial performance in time thanks to the splendid improvisation of S/L J Healey MBE, the CTO, and his workshops personnel. The show, which was produced by LAC May, was generally agreed to be the best yet produced on the station and played to a packed and enthusiastic house on the nights of 27th to 30th January. Another VIP attended briefing and debriefing the following night, 28th/29th January, when Air Vice Marshal Robert Oxland

[3]Lou Greenburgh in *DFC and Bar* by Ed Greenburgh

gave a short talk on enemy radar and counter-measures and inspected flying control and the Operations Room. Oxland had previously been AOC 1 Group and was, by this time, Senior Air Staff Officer in Bomber Command. He was present as fifteen Lancasters took off for Berlin. In the evening, the Station ORB noted, *'discussions continued to flourish on the Station and the two subjects, 'Russo-Polish dispute' and 'Should Women compete on equal terms with Men in the post war world?' made keen and lively debates which were enjoyed by all.'*

AVM Robert Oxland (centre) was a visitor to the squadron on 28th / 29th January. Oxland, pictured here with ACM Sir Arthur 'Bomber' Harris (right), and Mr. M T Spence, Bomber Command's 'Met' man (left), was Senior Air Staff Officer to Harris.

It was the turn of F/O John Laing and the crew of LL625, JI-C to face the ordeal of combat with a Ju88, the gunners, Sergeants Ronald McAllister RCAF and Charles Salt, returning fire and claiming to have damaged their foe. F/S Bertie Delacour RAAF in LL678, A2-L also came under attack twice, on the second occasion Sergeants Spurgeon 'Pop' Williams RCAF in the mid upper turret and Don Savage, the rear gunner, scored hits on their opponent. This raid involved 677 bombers, of which 46 were lost; however there was widespread destruction with a further 180,000 residents de-housed.

The final raid of the month for the squadron took place two nights later on January 30th when sixteen aircraft took off, yet again heading for the Reich capital. Major concentrations of bombs fell on the south-west and centre of the city causing severe fire damage. Over 1,000 casualties were later reported and Josef Goebbels' Propaganda Ministry was heavily damaged, though it is unlikely that Goebbels publicised the fact at the time. There was stiff opposition once more, with some 150 twin-engined and 50 single-engined night fighters despatched to the target area. Although losses overall were fewer than previously, with 33 of the 534 attackers shot down, 514 Squadron did not emerge unscathed on this operation. There were several combats reported. P/O Tommy Penkuri RCAF in DS785, JI-D came under attack but his gunners, Sergeants Ken Peake and J Crawford, drove off the enemy aircraft.

Sergeants Ronald McAllister and Charles Salt had more luck this time, as F/O John Laing's LL625, JI-C once again attracted unwelcome attention. Sgt Salt had spotted a Ju88 silhouetted against the white cloud tops and apparently shadowing their Lancaster at a distance of about 1,000 yards. Visibility was very good, with a bright quarter moon, and two lines of fighter flares illuminating the stream. Closing to 800 yards, the enemy fighter was slowly weaving from starboard to port and back, then took up an attacking position astern of the Lanc. As it moved in, Sgt Salt ordered a corkscrew to port, resulting in the German pilot's shots going wide. Both Lancaster gunners opened fire, hitting the Ju88 in its port engine. The enemy fighter dived away in flames, though a parachute was seen to deploy. The kill was confirmed by the crew of another Lancaster, who noted the Ju88 going down in flames at 2010hrs. The crew of the Ju88 and their fate is not recorded. Meanwhile F/S Paul Ashpitel, flying DS822, JI-T received the unwelcome attention of a light brown Ju88, apparently a day fighter. His rear gunner, W/O Ray Hall, engaged the enemy at close range and claimed it as damaged, as pieces of the fighter were seen to part company with its airframe.

The squadron lost two Lancasters on this operation. Both were flown by Flight Lieutenants, relatively senior officers in the context of day to day ops.

F/L George Boyd, 25 years old, had been awarded the DFC in 1942, whilst at 1651 CU which had been stationed at Waterbeach since January of that year. Whilst he was on only his third operation with 514 Squadron, his age, rank and the earlier award of the DFC suggests that he was on at least his second tour of operations. Had he survived it is likely that he would have become a flight commander when a vacancy arose. His aircraft, DS706, JI-G was lost without trace, probably one of three Lancasters shot down over the North Sea. One was shot down at 1910hrs approaching the Danish coast by Lt. Bruno Heilig, and two on the homeward leg by Lt. Guido Krupinski and Ofw. Heinz Vinke, both of 11./NJG1. The location of recovered aircrew casualties from the other aircraft indicates that DS706 is definitely one of those lost over the sea. There were no survivors amongst F/L Boyd's crew.
The other aircraft lost from the squadron was DS735, JI-A, flown by F/L George Chequer, who had been with the unit since its formation and who had got 514 Squadron airborne when he piloted DS735, JI-A on a test flight. He was flying the same aircraft when he and his crew were shot down at approximately 2030hrs approaching Berlin. The aircraft crashed in flames and the crew bailed out. F/S Alex Robertson RAAF, the rear gunner, walked SW for five nights before being captured near Magdeburg. He stated that the aircraft had been hit by flak. However, the 'second dickey' pilot, F/S RL Gulliford, later stated that the aircraft was hit by upwardly-fired cannon shells which immediately ignited the petrol tank. He presumed, albeit after the event, that this was 'Shräge Musik', especially as he heard a shout from the rear gunner to corkscrew immediately beforehand. It has been suggested by unverified sources that DS735 was shot down by Obstlt. Gunther Radusch of Stab NJG5, who destroyed three Lancasters in the area between 2024hrs and 2030hrs. F/L George Chequer, 22 years old and Sgt John O'Brien RAAF, MU gunner, 23 years old, baled out too low for their parachutes to deploy whilst Sgt Robert Montgomery, the WOP/AG also lost his life after landing in a lake and apparently drowning. They are now buried in Berlin War Cemetery. F/S Ken Mortimer aged 22, the navigator, was subsequently killed on 19th April 1945 when Typhoons shot up a POW column near Boizenburg. F/S Robertson survived the war and was discharged from the RAAF as a Warrant Officer.

At the end of January, the Station Commander's summary appeared in the ORB:

'The previous good record of 514 Squadron was somewhat marred by an unduly large number of failures to take off and 'returned early' sorties during the early part of the month. This tendency was arrested towards the end of the month by a sharp reminder being given to all Senior NCOs and Captains of Aircraft on their responsibilities towards aircraft maintenance and their general standard of discipline.

Outstanding amongst a number of visits was that by a Russian Military Mission. The organisation of a Bomber Station was explained in detail which our allies appeared to appreciate.'

F/L George Chequer (front centre) and crew. Chequer was the first pilot to take to the air in a 514 Squadron aircraft and was a key officer in the squadron (WMHM).

There were no operations for the first half of February, due in part to the full moon period. Whilst on the ground, crews continued to avail themselves of new information. On 1st February, according to the Station ORB *'Mr. Bernard Newman, the famous author, traveller and spy raconteur, gave a most interesting talk in the NAAFI canteen on 'The Balkans'. He packed a wealth of detail about the people and countries of Roumania, Yugo-Slavia, Greece, Hungary and Albania and their historical and political background, into a one hour talk illustrated by lantern slides.' On 4th February, 'Mr W Davis and Mr HA Friburn of the West Herts and Watford Observer, together with a photographer of the Sunday Pictorial visited the station in order to gain a picture for their readers of the activities of a heavy bomber squadron. A very enjoyable dance was held at the WAAF Mess, to which all ranks were invited. The proceeds were given to the newly formed Cambridge branch of the RAFA.'*

'Fanny Firkin II', DS824, JI-F, completed 63 operational sorties, surviving unscathed. She is now commemorated by an Airfix kit.

Meanwhile non-operational flying continued without interruption. On 5th February, for example, crews were tasked with air tests, cross country, high and low level navigation exercises, day and night bombing at Rushforth and Lakenheath, local practice, two-engine flying, three-engined overshoots, beam flying, bomb aimer flying, low flying and four details of fighter affiliation. There was little danger of the crews getting bored. To add further spice to training, F/L Jackson Pollock, the Squadron Gunnery Leader, contacted a local USAAF fighter squadron to arrange for their participation in future fighter affiliation exercises, making a change from the Hurricane previously provided for this purpose. It was subsequently agreed that squadrons from the 355th Fighter Group at RAF Steeple Morden would provide aircraft when not otherwise engaged. Further such arrangements were also made with the 361st Fighter Group at RAF Bottisham.

Berlin was a regular target for the squadron in the first four months of its existence. 203 sorties were despatched in 16 raids for the loss of seven aircraft and six crews. The 3.4% loss rate was actually relatively light by the standards of the time.

On 8th February, Air Vice Marshal Richard Harrison, AOC 3 Group, visited Waterbeach in the afternoon. He was escorted by Group Captain GIL Saye, the Station Commander at RAF Waterbeach and S/Ldr Barney Reid, standing in for W/Cdr Arthur Samson DFC who was away on a tactics course at Bomber Command HQ. It is presumed that the AOC was suitably impressed as the following day the squadron was given a complete stand-down.

On 9th February a successful dance was given by the Sergeants Mess. A cabaret, directed by LAC May, was one of the highlights of the evening. 'The Floats', an amateur dramatic society of undergraduates sponsored by the YMCA gave AA Milne's 'Sarah Simple' in the NAAFI canteen which was brilliantly rendered by a youthful cast and was well received by an appreciative audience. The propaganda film 'Divide and Conquer' was shown in the Station Cinema. Nazi plans and strategy for invasion of the Low Countries and France were well portrayed and excellent photography of the assaults by air and land on these countries made a profound impression on Service audiences[4].

Ops finally commenced again on 15th February with, perhaps inevitably by now, another trip to Berlin. 22 Lancasters were despatched from Waterbeach as part of an 891-strong force. One of the squadron's aircraft returned early with the remainder attacking the target at around 2130hrs through thick cloud. As before there was fighter activity to the north of Berlin with fairly heavy flak over the target. P/O Alan Winstanley was flying LL684, A2-B, having just crossed the Baltic coast at Stralsund, heading SSE towards the target when the aircraft came under attack from an unseen aircraft, the tracer being seen by the gunners however. Some effective corkscrewing was successful in enabling the crew to escape unscathed.

P/O Harry Darby was bomb aimer for the crew of F/S Don Crombie: 'On the night of 15/ 16 February, returning from Berlin, the bomber stream became rather spread out and we strayed over a heavily defended area between Munster and Osnabruck. We were suddenly coned by about a dozen searchlights which created an enormous blob of light from which it was almost impossible to escape, and shells were soon bursting all around us. I could hear the clatter of shell splinters striking us and feared for the safety of my mates. Crombie worked a miracle by putting the aircraft into a terrific dive and we dropped from 20,000 to 14,000 feet in a matter of seconds, enabling us to escape and race for the Dutch coast and comparative safety.'

Losses were again severe with 43 aircraft failing to return, though all 514 Squadron's crews returned safely. The raid set a new record with 2462 tons of bombs being dropped. Although the target was cloud-covered as usual,

---

[4] RAF Waterbeach ORB

the force caused severe damage with over 1100 fires reported and heavy damage to important infrastructure in Siemensstadt. It is considered this raid effectively marked the end of the 'Battle of Berlin' as the city was not attacked for over a month afterwards.

The emphasis now switched to attacking the German aircraft industry, the intention being to degrade the Luftwaffe's strength by the time of the planned invasion of Normandy. The night raids by Bomber Command were part of a combined assault with the USAAF who were striking the manufacturing plants by day, accompanied by their long-range fighters which would attempt to destroy as much of the Luftwaffe in the air as possible. The first in the series of raids in what became known as 'Big Week' was against Leipzig on the night of 19th / 20th February, this being the next operation in which 514 Squadron participated.

The squadron was once again placed in the tender care of S/Ldr Barney Reid, W/Cdr Arthur Samson acting up as Station Commander for the time being. Of the 23 aircraft from Waterbeach originally tasked, four were withdrawn and three returned early, still leaving sixteen to attack the target, part of an initial strength of 823 aircraft. Many aircraft arrived over Leipzig too early, some having orbited off the Dutch coast, others at various points on the route.

P/O Edward Greenwood, in DS813, JI-H reported bombing from 20,000 feet at 0412 hrs, with 'one large fire noticed spreading around'. He also commented that the northern route was 'satisfactory', suggesting that his crew had been fortunate enough to avoid witnessing the carnage that afflicted Bomber Command that night. F/O Ian Hay in LL645, A2-H on his second operation, *reported 'At 0408 hours, 5 miles SW of Leipzig, the rear gunner (Sgt WH Tate) saw a rocket projectile coming towards Lancaster on the port quarter up, which died away before reaching Lancaster, and immediately after saw a twin-engined aircraft identified as a JU-88 on port quarter up at a range of 1,500 yards silhouetted against a fighter flare. The rear gunner gave an order to corkscrew to port. During the corkscrew, the enemy aircraft fired another rocket projectile at the Lancaster from range of approximately 1,200 yards which passed well below the Lancaster on port quarter. Shortly after E/A was lost to view and was not seen again.'*

This turned out to be a very bad night for the attacking force, not least because the defence commanders guessed the intentions of Bomber

Command, deploying a record 294 night fighters against the stream. The Luftwaffe was waiting for the bombers to cross the Dutch coast and harried their quarry all the way to the target. 53 were shot down before they reached the target. Poor weather predictions caused some allied aircraft to arrive ahead of the Pathfinders, and go into a holding pattern. This proved costly as the fighters and flak from ground defences took its toll. A diversionary raid against Berlin by Mosquitoes was ignored by the night fighters. The return trip was less of a bloodbath for Bomber Command's depleted force, mainly because the vast majority of the night fighters had eventually run out of fuel and their controllers had not left any significant reserves. This raid saw the second highest loss to Bomber Command of the entire war. Some 20 aircraft fell to flak, though only five of these were lost over Leipzig itself, and four were lost in collisions. Most of the other 78 losses were claimed by the night fighters. This raid, the last in which Halifax IIs and Vs were deployed to Germany, saw the heaviest loss of bombers to date, a toll that would only be surpassed by the Nuremberg raid of 30/31st March 1944.

514 Squadron lost three Lancasters, no crew members surviving from any of these. DS736, A2-D piloted by F/S Norman Hall and LL681, JI-J flown by F/L Len Kingwell were both lost without trace, the crews being commemorated on the Runnymede Memorial. A number of aircraft are listed as 'lost without trace', whilst four are believed to have been shot down over the sea. It is possible that DS736 and LL681 are amongst those lost over the sea, the alternative explanations being that they crashed in inaccessible locations or exploded in mid-air leaving no discernible trace. It is probable that the aircraft were destroyed by night-fighters.

Meanwhile DS823, JI-M, along with the crew of F/S Walter Henry, was shot down at 0230 hrs en-route to the target, crashing on the south-western edge of Grosses Moor, 11km north-west of Rahden. This was some distance south of the planned route and it is not known if the aircraft was off track when attacked or whether its combat and subsequent struggles took it away from the stream The only verified claim anywhere near where the Lancaster crashed was for an unidentified 4-engined aircraft by Lt. Hans Raum, the details given as '50 km SW of Hannover at 0241 hrs'. It is therefore considered that this is a possible cause of the loss of DS823. Hptm. Erhard Peters claimed five Lancasters this evening, including one shot down at 0233 hrs but these were not confirmed as, the same night,

Peters was killed when he was shot down in error by another night fighter.[5] DS823's crew members are buried in Rheinberg War Cemetery.

Next evening, 20th February, the squadron was again in action, this time despatching thirteen aircraft against Stuttgart, twelve of which attacked the target. There were some clear patches in the target area and visibility was good. Most crews arrived early in the target area, just after 0400 hrs, and had to wait for the markers to drop. The attack was considered by the crews as being well concentrated, falling mainly to the north of the town with scattered fires burning from east to west. Fires gained a good hold as the attack developed and smoke was seen rising to several thousands of feet and the glow was visible from up to 200 miles on the return trip. It was the turn of F/S Ernest Kingham's crew in DS785, JI-D to attract unwelcome attention, this time from an Me210, which opened fire from 4-500 yards. Having given the order to corkscrew starboard, Sgt Dan Davis RCAF in the rear turret fired back and drove the attacker off. There was no damage to the Lancaster.

F/O Bill McGown, DFC and bar, in LL683, JI-P, arrived early over Stuttgart and overshot the target. The pilot, on seeing TIs falling behind him, turned on his course but calculated that he would be too late to hit the markers so bombed an aerodrome on track instead. The bomb aimer, Sgt Lyndon Lewis, observed their 8,000lb bomb burst on a runway.

F/O Bill McGown and crew at RAF Foulsham in the early days of 514 Squadron. Note the wellington boots, not normally part of flying kit.

[5] Nachtjagd War Diaries.

Photographs, plotted as 'Hall Aerodrome', showed their bomb bursting on the airfield, as well as numerous aircraft on the ground. A later assessment showed that, although the bombing of Stuttgart was scattered, the Bosch factory along with other important public buildings were badly damaged or destroyed. The success of the raid was marred somewhat, by five aircraft crashing on return to England. In total fourteen of the 598 bombers were lost.

On 24th February, the day after Group Captain RE Sharp DFC had assumed command of RAF Waterbeach, 21 aircraft left the airfield for Schweinfurt as 'Big Week' continued. The ball-bearing factories had been the target on earlier occasions, the defences exacting a heavy toll on the B-17s of the USAAF when they had attacked by day in 1943. There were two phases to the night raid by Bomber Command and 514 Squadron's aircraft were split between the two, eight Lancasters participating in the first phase and thirteen in the second. F/S Bob Langley in DS842, JI-F bombed at 2311 hrs from 20,000 feet and noted *'Saw large explosion to South. Seemed a very good attack. Barrage of heavy flak moderate. Large factory seen to be hit and set on fire by showers of incendiaries.'*

There were combats for F/O Ian Hay, whose MU gunner Sgt WE Baldwin pitted his Brownings against a Ju88, and F/Lt Ralph Chopping, whose gunners F/O Henry May (Mid Upper) and Sgt PJ Fox (Rear) fought off an Me210. Sgt Fox saw strikes on the rear portion of the Me210's fuselage and claimed it as damaged.

Of the 734 aircraft sent to Schweinfurt, 33 did not return, two-thirds of these being from the first wave. 514 Squadron's DS785, JI-D was part of the second wave and crashed at 0114 hours at Heidingsfeld, near Würzburg. The cause remains unknown, but the aircraft was possibly another victim of Lt. Hans Raum, 9./NJG3, who claimed a 4-engined aircraft west of Würzburg. It is also possible that the aircraft was a victim of flak. There were no survivors from the crew of Sgt Alfred Kay, on their second sortie, all of whom are buried in Dürnbach War Cemetery.

The final operation of the month was to Augsburg on 25th February, involving sixteen of the squadron's aircraft. F/O John Laing was piloting DS842, JI-F and its load of one 8,000lb 'blockbuster' plus incendiaries on this raid. He reported: 'Bombed at 0127 hours at 19,000 ft. Northern part of target solid mass of fire. Monica u/s. Route very good. Pretty good effort. Total searchlights about 60, mostly south and north of the target.

Solid concentration of fires seen from 200 miles.' Bombing caused the damage or destruction of approximately 8,000 buildings and nearly 90,000 people became suddenly homeless. It was assessed as a successful raid in which important infrastructure was damaged or destroyed including the MAN engineering company's buildings and an aircraft component factory. Artwork estimated to be worth approximately £80 million was also believed to have been destroyed in various civic buildings which were destroyed in the raid. In total, 21 bombers from the attacking force of 594 were lost, mostly to fighters but a few also to flak.

F/L Ralph Chopping's gunners were exceptionally busy on this op as their Lancaster LL733 JI-G came under attack on three occasions. Outbound, in the Aachen area, an Me109 moved in to attack but the gunners fought it off, noting strikes on the enemy aircraft as their shots apparently hit home. The Lancaster arrived early and F/L Chopping elected to orbit whilst awaiting the markers, never a particularly popular move with the crews; Sgt PJ Fox in the rear turret spotted a Ju88 on a parallel course and chose to pick a fight with it. He and F/O Henry May in the mid upper turret once again saw strikes and claimed the Ju88 as damaged. Finally at 0222 hours 12 Miles NE of St. Dieder, homeward bound, Sgt Fox reported an Me109 on the port quarter up, range 400 yards, just about to commence an attack. He immediately gave order to corkscrew to port and opened fire with a burst lasting 3 seconds. Hits were once again seen on the enemy aircraft which did not fire but attempted to break away astern and was thrown over on its back apparently out of control as it passed through Lancaster's slip-stream. F/O May, who was waiting for the break away, saw another Me109 at a range of only 30 yards on the port quarter up, closing in to attack. The Lancaster was still corkscrewing, and F/O May opened fire immediately holding it for three seconds. The Messerschmitt did not fire and F/O May saw both enemy aircraft quickly break away, almost colliding in their efforts to avoid the accurate fire from the Lancaster. All attacks had been preceded by a 'Monica' warning, this being a radar device designed to detect night fighters. It was not until later in the campaign that it was realised that 'Monica' could itself be detected by equipment on the German fighters, drawing them towards bombers using the device.

The Station Commander's Summary for February noted:

514 Squadron have maintained a good standard of operational efficiency but there is still room for improvement in the matter of failures to take off

and early returns. A considerable drive was made towards ensuring that all pilots are aware of the measures required to prevent plugs oiling up when awaiting take off.
Mr L Taylor of the ATC Gazette and Mr WS Masters visited the Station and inspected the work of the Flight Engineers of the Squadron. During the month further parties of 'Back Room Bodies' have seen with interest the work of the operational side of the Station. Discussion Groups included the topics 'Should consumption of goods at home be restricted after the war in order to help in the feeding and rebuilding of Europe?' and 'Are strikes justifiable in war time?' and roused a great deal of interest.

March 1944 started with notification of the immediate award of the DFC to F/O Lou Greenburgh, following his successful ditching in December 1943, which is stretching the definition of immediacy somewhat. Also on 1st March, the squadron sent 21 aircraft to Stuttgart, three of these returning early. Perhaps because of the ten tenths cloud cover, the ORB noted that *'it is not the general opinion that this raid was an unqualified success'*, suggesting a degree of understatement of returning crews' honest opinion. F/S Bob Langley's logbook records that two members of his crew faced adversity throughout the trip: *'Bert's oxygen mask U/S. Does trip with tube in his mouth. Fred gets frostbite.'* The crew members are believed to be rear gunner Sgt Herbert Oliver and navigator Sgt FR Jones. The route was apparently well-received by most crews, because it was also described as 'more or less trouble free, fighters being few and far between.' No combats were reported by the squadron.
There was a marked change of fortune for Bomber Command as the heavy cloud cover hampered enemy defences and allied losses were limited to four from the force of 557 bombers. Despite the thick cloud, and contrary to the opinion of 514 Squadron's crews, the bombing effort was considered reasonably effective with the destruction of many houses and key industrial Infrastructure including the Daimler-Benz and Bosch factories.
The monthly 'moon period' intervened once more, the next operation taking place on 7th March. There was a radical change of emphasis with 304 aircraft, eighteen from Waterbeach, being sent to bomb railway yards at Le Mans. The stream concentrated its bombing on the railway yards with overall success. P/O Noel Thackray, in LL734, JI-U noted '...large explosions seen from own bombs. Orange glows seen and occasional

bombs bursting.' Despite careful planning and the best efforts of the crews, a few bombs fell outside the railway yards and 31 local residents were unfortunately killed. Enemy defences were described as 'negligible' and few fighters were seen with the result that no bombers were lost due to enemy action. One night fighter was claimed as 'probably destroyed' by a Halifax crew whilst one bomber was wrecked in a landing accident and another was shot down in error by a Halifax air gunner.

There were no operations for the next week; instead a 'very successful party and sing-song' was given by aircrew to the ground crews in the Briefing Room. A celebration was also in order for PO James Hydes who was awarded the DFC for disposing of incendiaries which had hit his aircraft, flown by S/Ldr Alan Roberts, on the Schweinfurt raid of 24 / 25th February.

On 15th March the squadron was again tasked with attacking Stuttgart, the 23 Lancasters from Waterbeach contributing to an 863-strong force. Strong winds affected the marking by PFF and the attack was scattered as a result. To fool the defences the stream headed towards Switzerland, before turning for Stuttgart. This diversionary tactic worked to a limited extent, delaying the night fighter attack until just before the target. For once the target was not completely covered by cloud and the TIs were clearly visible, although they had been dropped in the wrong place. The squadron bombed at about 2320hrs and, in common with many other aircraft, three of 514's crews reported combats with enemy fighters. At 2314hrs F/O Peter Hood's DS820, JI-A had been fired on by an FW-190 15miles south of Stuttgart. Prompt evasive action, in the form of a corkscrew, along with return fire from the rear gunner, Tech Sgt Maurice Lanthier[6] of the USAAF, ensured that the crew escaped on this occasion, with strikes being seen on the enemy aircraft.

[6] Maurice Lanthier was born in Texas on May 9th, 1924, but moved to Canada and lived in Upper Almaville, Quebec with his parents and sister. He joined the RCAF, subsequently transferring to the USAAF but remaining on attachment to the Canadian service. He was posted to England, and in 1943 was in Bournemouth during an air raid. He rescued a woman who had been badly injured and subsequently lost her left leg. His quick action saved her life.

Less fortunate was Sgt John McNeill RCAF, the mid upper gunner in DS813, JI-H which was flown by fellow Canadian P/O Edward Greenwood DFC RCAF. At 2328 hours, approximately one minute before dropping bombs, trace was observed passing close to Lancaster on the starboard side. Immediately after this, the rear gunner, P/O Bob Bourne, RCAF saw return fire from Sgt McNeill, who had not given the pilot a combat manoeuvre, presumably through lack of time before dealing with the enemy aircraft. P/O Greenwood, however, started corkscrewing to starboard. At this stage P/O Bob Bourne in the rear turret reported an Me-109 with green under surface and gave it a burst lasting one to two seconds as it was banking steeply to break away. Hits were observed as it broke off the attack and it was last seen flying away on the port quarter with smoke coming from its engine. Immediately after the enemy fighter had fired at the Lancaster, the navigator P/O Douglas Nicol, in his compartment saw a brilliant purple flash from the Mid Upper turret. As no response had come from Sgt McNeill despite numerous calls, the wireless operator and flight engineer proceeded to the turret to render assistance, and found Sgt McNeill had been killed instantly by the burst of fire from the enemy fighter. Numerous attempts were made to extricate him, but without

Sgt Howell John whilst training. His duel with a night fighter resulted in the destruction of the enemy aircraft when it collided with Howell's Lancaster, which emerged unscathed (John family).

success. The Lancaster sustained damage to the mid upper turret, around the astro-dome and the main spar. P/O John McNeill RCAF, who was 27 years old, rests in Cambridge City Cemetery. It is possible that he received a posthumous commission to officer rank, as this was not uncommon practice in the RCAF.

F/S John Underwood in DS786, A2-F had an encounter which, though far too close for comfort, had a fortuitous outcome for him and his crew, if less so for their opponent. At 2320 hours a few seconds before dropping bombs, the rear gunner reported what he identified as an FW-190 which opened fire at Lancaster. The rear gunner, Sgt Howell John, returned fire with a four second burst and ordered his pilot to corkscrew to port. The enemy aircraft closed in almost dead astern slightly up to within thirty yards and the mid upper gunner, Sgt RC Sime RCAF, gave it a burst lasting one to two seconds. Many hits were seen on the fighter which at this stage was within a few yards of the tail. It tried to break away underneath, and in the attempt, collided with Lancaster carrying away most of the air screw and exhaust manifold on the port outer engine. The bomb aimer was the last to see it spiralling down out of control on the starboard bow. The fighter was claimed as destroyed. On examination later it was found that Lancaster had sustained severe damage on port side and round rear turret due to a cannon shell. Parts of the fighter's airscrew and perspex cockpit canopy were found embedded in the engine nacelles on the port side.

'Nachtjagd War Diaries' records: '*One Wild Boar attacked a 514 Squadron Lancaster at 2330 hours at 20,000 feet over Stuttgart. The German pilot opened fire on the Lancaster from the port quarter level at a range of 300 yards. Both the Lancaster's gunners returned fire, and hits were registered on the fighter, which they identified as an FW-190. The FW-190's aim, however, was also accurate, the Lancaster receiving numerous strikes. So determined was the attack that the German pilot collided with the Lancaster resulting in damage to the rear turret and port rudder, and wrecking the port outer engine. On the Lancaster's return, part of the fighter's canopy perspex and fuselage were found embedded in the engine. The crew reported the German fighter as destroyed.*'

The incident probably concerns the loss of Ofw. Fritz Nimmisch of 1./JG300, who was killed flying a Me-109 G-6 near Boblingen and which was the only reported Wild Boar loss (other than a second 1./JG300 pilot who was injured by 'friendly' flak fire).

'Tommy' Penkuri RCAF prior to commissioning as an officer. Penkuri was an exceptionally popular member of the squadron.

The squadron did lose a Lancaster on the night; F/O Kaiho 'Tommy' Penkuri RCAF and his crew were flying LL653, JI-E when they were shot down, probably by a night fighter flown by Hptm. Eckart-Wilhelm von Bonin, Stab II./NJG1. The aircraft exploded and crashed between Blondefontaine and Villars-le-Pautel with no survivors from the crew, who are buried in Villars-le-Pautel Communal Cemetery. The occupants of the aircraft included F/S Ken Drummond RNZAF who was on his first outing with the squadron, flying his 'second dickey' trip.

There were to be no operations for the next three nights, but training continued apace. Even so, the risk to aircraft and crews remained ever present. On 17th March, whilst practicing flapless landings at RAF Woodbridge, famed for its very long and wide runway, F/S Charlie Medland suffered a crash landing in LL669, JI-K, though fortunately without injury to the crew. Meanwhile a similar mishap occurred at RAF Martlesham Heath to F/S Edward Shearing in DS820, JI-R.

Frankfurt was the target for the squadron on 18th March, when 17 Lancasters departed Waterbeach, part of an 864-strong force. Despite

LL669, JI-K's service life came to a premature end at RAF Woodbridge after F/S Charlie Medland's attempt at a flapless landing did not go entirely to plan (WMHM).

moderate flak, numerous searchlights and some attention from night fighters, none of 514's aircraft were among the 22 bombers lost on the raid. It was noted that at least some of the force arrived early and had to orbit the target whilst they waited for the markers to arrive. F/O Lou Greenburgh in LL727, A2-C, having survived his ditching in the North Sea, again found himself the subject of unwanted attention as an unidentified twin-engined aircraft followed his Lancaster maintaining its position and distance for some time. Eventually his gunners got bored and fired two or three short bursts each at the mysterious stalker whilst F/O Greenburgh executed a corkscrew to starboard. This activity successfully shook off the other aircraft. It is possible, given the lack of hostile action by the following aircraft, that it was actually one of the seventeen Mosquito aircraft included by Bomber Command in the raid.

The night fighter force had been split with part of it heading north to counter the diversionary mining operations off Heligoland. However the remainder were able to intercept the main force as it approached Frankfurt. There was good marking and serious damage was caused to the city, especially its previously-preserved medieval quarter and the city's Opera House. Nearly 100 industrial buildings and 5,500 homes were destroyed. Meanwhile on 20th March, the Station ORB noted:

Miss Audrey Roussell, BBC Commentator, visited the station in the evening to gather material for a broadcast on the part the WAAF play in the operational effort of a bomber station. As operations for the night had been cancelled she interviewed WAAF of various trades and gathered material and background for the programme which she hopes to complete by a second visit to the Station in the near future.

F/O Harry Bryant (left) and his pilot, F/Sgt Paul Ashpitel (right) at the start of the squadron's operations in November 1943. Bryant was from Dominica in the Caribbean, the region contributing many aircrew to Bomber Command.

The squadron went back to Frankfurt on the evening of 22nd March, 22 aircraft setting out from Waterbeach though one returned early. A slightly smaller force, comprising 816 aircraft, carried out an attack which was even more devastating than four days earlier, though it came at a higher cost. There is a discrepancy between the 33 losses officially recorded by Bomber Command, 28 of which were attributed to the night fighters, and the 42 claims by the Nachtjäger units[7]. However, it is clear that the night fighters did have an effect on the attacking force. For a while the Germans believed that the intended target was Hannover, well to the north of Frankfurt. They did manage to intercept the stream in limited numbers. The attack was, as stated above, accurate and effective with 175,000 people left homeless and Frankfurt effectively destroyed as a city, despite continuing resistance from the ground as well as air defences. Sgt Robert Cole, wireless operator in F/S Paul Ashpitel's crew flying DS822, JI-T, counted 127 searchlights.

It was another difficult night for 514 Squadron. Limited though the night fighter interceptions might have been, a number of the Waterbeach aircraft reported combats, and worse. F/S Ashpitel bombed at 2154hrs from 19,000 feet and his aircraft was promptly hit by two incendiaries from another aircraft which severed the oxygen mask of F/O Harry Bryant in the mid upper turret, to his undoubted surprise and consternation[8]. This operation also happened to be the final trip of F/S Ashpitel's second tour, having completed his first in 1941-2 with 40 Sqn, flying Wellington bombers from Malta. Whilst at Waterbeach, F/S Ashpitel, who eventually left the RAF after the war as a Flight Lieutenant, met a WAAF whom he subsequently married. Ashpitel's crew, who had not finished their tour of operations, subsequently flew with the highly-experienced F/L Robert Curtis DFM. F/L Curtis had previously flown a tour of operations on Handley Page Hampden bombers. The crew was lost six trips later, returning from Chambly on 1st May 1944.

Events were even more traumatic in LL703, JI-L flown by F/S Bernard Windsor on the crew's second operation. The crew had not yet bombed the target when they came under attack from a night fighter. The Flight Engineer, Sgt Frank Dolamore, saw tracer flying over the cockpit canopy from astern and Sgt Leonard Blackford in the rear turret ordered the pilot to dive, which he did almost vertically. There was a second burst of fire from the enemy aircraft which killed both Sgt Blackford and the mid upper gunner, Sgt Lewis Warren, who was nineteen years old. The crew heard a very long burst of gunfire from the rear turret, due to Sgt Blackford

---

[7] Nachtjagd War Diaries

[8] Bryant was born in Dominica, in the Caribbean. His actions in dealing with the incendiaries were to see him awarded the DFC.

refusing to relinquish his guns even though mortally wounded. The Lancaster became uncontrollable for a while, as the elevators had been damaged by enemy fire, so F/S Windsor ordered his crew to bale out. The bomb aimer, Sgt K Attwood and navigator, Sgt GK Hardwick had done so before F/S Windsor regained control and was forced to abandon his mission, struggling back to RAF Woodbridge's emergency runway with only Sgt Dolamore and the wireless operator, Sgt Robert Langford, for company. Whilst over the target P/O Don Crombie in LL645, JI-R, saw his flight engineer Sgt Ben Le Neve-Foster hit in the back of the head by a piece of flak, the injury proving immediately fatal. F/O Harry Darby, the crew's bomb aimer, was asked by P/O Crombie if he could do anything to help his colleague, but quickly saw that he was beyond saving. The crew later escorted Sgt Le Neve-Foster's body back to his family home in Sevenoaks, Kent, for the funeral then, as F/O Darby put it, they 'went into London and got rather drunk - it seemed to be about the only thing to do.'
Other 514 Squadron crews also found themselves under attack; F/S John Hudson RNZAF and his crew were flying LL728, JI-B on their first op when a twin-engined aircraft apparently closed in to attack them. The tried and tested routine of firing at the attacker whilst the pilot threw the Lancaster into a corkscrew manoeuvre was once again successful for them. F/O Lou Greenburgh, who must by now have thought that the Germans had something personal against him, also corkscrewed LL627, A2-L out of the firing line when a Ju88 attacked the aircraft. The 'two or three minutes' this took must have seemed much longer to the crew.

F/S John 'Toppy' Topham and his crew in LL620, A2-G were also on their first operation from Waterbeach and faced three encounters with enemy fighters. Fortunately their alertness and prompt evasive action meant they escaped unscathed on this occasion. They were to have more excitement ahead of them as their tour progressed.

A third debutante to come under repeated attack on this raid was F/S Charles Johnson in LL698, A2-J. There was no exchange of fire in the first encounter at 2147 hrs as they managed to shake off an attacking FW190 before attacking the target, though five minutes later a twin-engined aircraft fired two rocket projectiles at their Lancaster, these passing close underneath. Their guns had apparently frozen up and the gunners managed very few shots in reply, but the crew escaped by the usual corkscrew. A further five minutes passed before the gunners saw another twin-engined attacker which, once again, was evaded by corkscrewing.

Two of the squadron's aircraft did not share the luck of their colleagues. At 2130 hrs, about 5 miles SE of Emmen in Holland, F/S John Underwood and his crew, on their fourth op, were shot down by Oblt. Heinz Rökker of 2./NJG2. The only survivors were the crew's two Canadians, F/O WD McPhee, bomb aimer, and Sgt RC Sime, the mid-upper gunner, both of whom were captured.

Fifteen to twenty minutes after bombing the target, F/L 'Nick' Nichol's DS815, JI-N was in the vicinity of Trier, flying straight and level at 20,000 feet. Wireless operator F/S Arthur Elliott called out 'Aircraft – starboard', it is believed in response to an indication on his Monica set. The pilot immediately banked the aircraft to starboard but as he did so a burst of what was believed to be cannon fire struck their Lancaster. The mid upper gunner, F/S Albert Jackson, was searching to starboard and, immediately after the cannon fire hit, saw what he identified as a Ju88, with a bright silvery finish and without conventional camouflage, at a range of 120 to 150 yards, coming in fast. F/S Jackson got in a two-second burst which he was confident scored hits, and continued to fire at the enemy fighter as it broke away.

The fighter had only fired a single burst lasting two to three seconds, but this caused serious damage to the Lancaster. The starboard fin, elevators and side of the fuselage were extensively damaged, some of the holes being about six inches in diameter. The bomb aimer, F/O Keith Deans, was wounded in the foot and F/S Arthur Elliott, the wireless operator was paralysed by a wound, probably in his spine. . Almost immediately after the strikes the flight engineer, Sgt FC Townshend, reported the starboard outer engine on fire. The navigator, Sgt Percy Stevens-Hoare, reported that the bomb bay was on fire and F/S Jackson in the mid upper turret could see sheets of flame streaming out behind the aircraft. F/L Nichol warned his crew to prepare to bale out and then put the aircraft into a steep dive. After losing 5,000 feet the fires appeared to have been extinguished. As a precaution, however, the pilot repeated his warning so F/Sgt Jackson left his turret. He found the bomb aimer helping the pilot to hold the controls and he could see that the wireless operator was badly injured. The aircraft was flying port wing down, losing height and with considerable damage to

the starboard control surfaces. Three engines were still working, Nichol having feathered the starboard outer before diving.
F/L Nichol chose to attempt to reach the English coast and set course for Calais. The crew managed to keep the ailing Lancaster on course for some time but could not prevent it losing height. Eventually Nichol warned the crew to prepare for a crash landing. Before they could do so, the aircraft landed in a ploughed field, at Nordausques, about twenty miles south east of Calais. Flying level it had made what was, under the circumstances, a good landing. The nose of the aircraft was extensively damaged and the fuselage broke in two at the mid upper turret position. At the time of landing the gunners were at the rear of the aircraft, the wireless operator was lying in the well by his compartment and the bomb aimer, flight engineer and navigator, positioned somewhere at the front of the bomber, were thrown clear, probably through the nose. The bomb aimer was unhurt though the flight engineer suffered injuries to his head and face. The gunners were bruised and shaken, but otherwise unhurt. Nichol, having been strapped in, was unharmed. The wireless operator, F/S Arthur Elliott, could not be extricated from the wreckage as he was trapped and was believed to have been killed, either beforehand or as a result of the crash. Shortly after crashing the navigator returned to fetch his maps and the Lancaster burst into flames but F/S Jackson, who submitted the loss report, did not know whether this was spontaneous or a deliberate act by Sgt Stevens-Hoare to destroy any remaining equipment. Jackson and the rear gunner, Sgt George Fearman were driven from the fuselage by the flames. Even so, Nichol made a further attempt to rescue his wireless operator and had to be prevented by the two gunners from going back into the flames. The crew had to leave the scene when they saw lights approaching and heard voices that they believed to be German. Jackson and Fearman evaded capture whilst their four surviving colleagues were subsequently taken prisoner.
The kill is credited to Hptm. Ludwig 'Luk' Meister of 1./NJG4[9], though the time is given as 0015hrs. Although F/S Jackson identified the fighter as a Ju88 it was, in fact, an Me110. The timing of the incident in Jackson's report suggest it was more likely to have occurred around 2215hrs. DS815 was the last aircraft lost by the Bomber Command force that night. Hptm.

---

[9] Nachtjagd War Diaries

Meister, who was at that time one of the Luftwaffe's leading aces, landed away from base and was flying his Me110 back to his base the following day when he was shot down himself by an American fighter. He sustained significant injuries requiring lengthy recuperation, adding only one further victim to his tally before the war ended.

Whilst the squadron enjoyed the following night off, music lovers on the station were delighted by a visit of the 'Celebrity Concert Party' including Miss Flora Ashe, the well-known soprano. A delightful hour was passed listening to Chopin, Greig and Handel. A request, the aria 'One Fine Day' from 'Madame Butterfly' sung by Miss Ashe was enthusiastically applauded by aircrew members of the audience. In other news in the Station ORB Group Captain CM Heard took command of RAF Waterbeach from Group Captain RF Sharpe DFC.

The ORB went on to relate that Friday evening, 24th March, was a night out for the cooks of the Station when the Mess Staff dance was held at the WAAF site. Everyone apparently had an enjoyable time and Air Commodore HH Down AFC and Group Captain CM Heard were the guests of honour. Needless to say the refreshments were described as perfect.

This was the briefest of respites before the squadron was next tasked; Berlin was the target on 24th March for 883 bombers directed to participate. Nineteen Lancasters left Waterbeach with one returning early. 8,000lb 'Blockbuster' bombs were the order of the day for some of the crews, the others carrying a 1,000lb bomb to penetrate buildings with the rest of their load being incendiaries to set fire to the interior. Opposition was even heavier than the raids on Frankfurt and a total of 72 bombers were destined never to return, one of the heaviest losses to date though even this grim total was to be surpassed within a week. Once again the indomitable F/O Lou Greenburgh was on the Battle Order, flying LL727, A2-C as usual. As had become customary, F/O Greenburgh's presence on the raid did not escape the attention of the Luftwaffe, on this occasion three fighters making separate attempts to kill him within ten minutes as he returned from the target having contributed his 'blockbuster' in his personal attempt to rearrange Berlin. Two Ju88s attacked LL727 at 2235 hours and 2237 hours respectively, their fire not causing any damage to the Lancaster, whilst Sgt Fred Carey in the mid-upper turret claimed strikes against the second fighter. Eight minutes later, the third attack started and it is best described by the combat report submitted by F/O Greenburgh on his return: '*At 2245 hours Engineer reported aircraft making an attack from starboard bow down and immediately ordered Pilot to corkscrew to starboard. As Lancaster made first part of manoeuvre by diving to starboard E/A fired a burst putting Lancaster's starboard engine out of action causing aircraft to turn over into a vicious spiral and it became uncontrollable. All the instruments were completely unserviceable and aircraft was losing height rapidly, completely out of control. At 10,000 feet Pilot gave order to abandon aircraft. The Engineer (Sgt Les Weddle) and Bomb Aimer (Sgt Don Bament) jumped immediately and the Pilot was half way out of his seat but decided to have another attempt to control aircraft when he realised that the Navigator's chute had been thrown out of the Escape Hatch during the spin, and at about 7,000 feet managed to get aircraft on more or less an even keel. At 9,000 feet Lancaster returned to base and Pilot made a safe landing. The mid upper gunner and Wireless Operator (Sgt Gordon Stromberg) were standing by the Rear Hatch almost on the point of jumping when they realised that the aircraft was now by this time under control and returned to their posts. E/A was lost after the Lancaster started spinning and Gunners were unable to get any shots at it. Visual Monica gave warning of approach of E/A on all astern attacks but not from the bow. The Monica caught fire during the spin. No flak was directed at the aircraft, but there were some searchlights and fighter flares in the vicinity. Visibility was very good.*'

By now, F/O Greenburgh was probably wondering if volunteering for aircrew duties had been such a good move.

Flying a few minutes behind F/O Greenburgh was P/O Garth Hughes in LL738, JI-D. At 2239 hours, whilst on the bombing run, both gunners reported a fighter flare, so P/O Hughes put his aircraft into a corkscrew; at that moment trace appeared from behind the flare and struck the mid-upper gunner, Sgt Eric Moorhouse, in the arm, causing a serious injury. However Sgt Moorhouse, along with his colleague in the rear turret, Sgt George Thornton, carried on firing and drove their attacker away. On this occasion, they returned to Waterbeach. Sgt Moorhouse's injury apparently ended his part in the war but, ironically, saving his life. He was awarded the DFM, the citation reading: '*As air gunner, Sergeant Moorhouse has participated in many sorties, including 11 attacks on Berlin. On the last of these occasions, Sergeant Moorhouse was badly wounded in the arm when his aircraft was struck by bullets from a fighter. In spite of his injury he continued to engage the attacker, manipulating his turret and guns with one arm. As the enemy aircraft broke away, Sergeant Moorhouse was thrown from his turret owing to his own pilot's violent evading action. He fell heavily to the floor of the aircraft and was temporarily stunned. On recovery he attempted to re-enter his turret but was unable to do so. He calmly reported the position to his captain, however, and did not request first aid until a member of the crew could be spared to attend to him. This airman displayed great fortitude and his strong sense of duty set an excellent example.'*

F/S Norman Wishart in LL697, JI-E managed to evade a single-engined fighter unscathed. Meanwhile P/O Elmer Protheroe in LL670, A2-K, having escaped the attentions of an FW190 on the outward leg, became coned in searchlights on the way home, managed to avoid some close flak

Flying Officer John Laing and crew ran out of luck on their fifteenth op, Bomber Command's last major raid on Berlin. They were shot down near Dessau, probably by a night fighter. The only survivor was Flight Sergeant Ronald McAllister RCAF, who was captured (McAllister family).

bursts and was then attacked by an Me109 firing rocket projectiles. Fortunately the aircraft and crew were undamaged.

F/S Charles Johnson, piloting LL698, A2-J was also homeward bound when his mid upper gunner, Sgt James Poad, saw another Lancaster, one thousand feet below and silhouetted against a fighter flare, being attacked by a Ju88. Sgt Poad was able to get his sights on the Ju88 and engaged it with his Brownings, causing the enemy fighter to break off its attack. This probably saved the lives of his unknown colleagues.

The experienced crew of F/O John Laing, on their fifteenth op, failed to return. Their Lancaster LL625, JI-C crashed on homeward leg at Wörlitz, 12 km ENE of Dessau. There was intense fighter activity on the return leg with 57 losses as the bombers returned to base. There is no specific information about the loss of LL625 and many RAF aircraft were shot down by flak as well as the night fighter force. However, the Laing crew were lost away from the heaviest flak concentrations, and at a time when night fighter interceptions were at their height. Most 514 Squadron aircraft bombed at between 2230hrs and 2245hrs. There are claims for unidentified '4 motor' aircraft shot down in the rough area of Dessau at around 2250hrs, which is a feasible time for the returning LL625 to have been in the vicinity. It is therefore quite possible that F/O John Laing's crew was one of these. The most likely claim is that of Hptm. Heinz-Horst Hissbach of 5./NJG2 at 2250hrs, 20-50 km west of Berlin. The only survivor from the crew was F/S Ron McAllister RCAF, the mid upper gunner, who was taken prisoner.

This was to be the last major attack on Berlin for the RAF. Five important military locations were hit, including the Waffen-SS Leibstandarte Adolf Hitler barracks. Strong winds scattered the bombers on return, leaving them to the mercy of enemy radar guided flak batteries and the swarms of night fighters that had by now infiltrated the bomber stream. Casualties were accordingly very heavy with 72 aircraft failing to return, Bomber Command's highest loss to date on a single raid.

There was little respite for the crews. On 26th March, the squadron was tasked with attacking Essen, sixteen crews being despatched. Once again, cloud covered most of the route and the target, though the glow of fires and bomb flashes were visible. Although the ORB notes that very few fighters were seen, combats were reported by three crews. F/S Charles Johnson's crew in LL698, A2-J was once again grateful to their gunners, especially F/S Roy Dymott RCAF in the rear turret whose fire drove off an attacking Ju88. F/S Edward Shearing's gunners in LL728, JI-B, Sgt Joe Clinton in the mid upper turret and Sgt MH Smart in the rear, saw an Me210 attacking another Lancaster so engaged the enemy which promptly broke off its attack on the other Lanc and turned on them instead. F/S Shearing executed a corkscrew which shook off the fighter. Sgt Ben Williams, rear gunner in DS669, JI-C flown by F/S Charlie Medland, had a notable success when their aircraft was attacked by an Me109 as they flew home. The single-engine fighter followed the Lancaster into the obligatory corkscrew and the German pilot found himself in a duel with Sgt Williams. Despite the frantic evasive action of the Lancaster, Williams managed to score hits, initially on the fighter's port wing and then on its fuselage and engine. The Messerschmitt burst into flames and dived away through the clouds. The crew then saw a glow which had all the hallmarks

No. 514 Squadron. BATTLE ORDER. Serial No. 50. Date :- 30th. March, 1944.

Officer i/c Flying :- S/Ldr. C. PAYNE, L.R.C.

A/C. PILOT.	NAVIGATOR.	BOMB AIMER.	W.OP/AIR.	M.U. GUNNER.	REAR GUNNER.	FLIGHT ENGINEER.
[illegible] (struck out)	F/S. Cosgrove	F/O. Walton	F/S. Bullings	Sgt. McKenzie	F/S. [illegible]	Sgt. [illegible]
[illegible]	F/O. Gray.	Sgt. Thornber.	Sgt. Turner.	Sgt. Saint.	Sgt. Fairbrass.	Sgt. Cartwright.
G F/S. Medland.	F/O. Walker.	Sgt. Venus.	Sgt. [illegible]	Sgt. Rose.	Sgt. Williams.	Sgt. Sealtiel.
F [illegible]	F/S. Newman.	F/S. Deans.	Sgt. Cringle.	Sgt. Henry.	P/O. Bourne.	Sgt. Thornton.
J [illegible]	Sgt. Constable.	Sgt. Goddard.	W/O. Ralph.	Sgt. Campbell.	Sgt. Granbois.	Sgt. James.
B F/S. Shearing.	F/S. Taylor.	Sgt. Rigden.	Sgt. Marshall.	Sgt. Marson.	Sgt. Smart.	Sgt. Blundon.
[illegible] (struck out)	F/S. Smith	F/S. [illegible]	[illegible] Goddard	F/S. Whitebread	Sgt. Thornton	Sgt. [illegible]
[illegible] (struck out)	Sgt. [illegible]	P/O. Darby.	Sgt. [illegible]	Sgt. [illegible]	Sgt. Hill.	Sgt. [illegible]
K P/O. Woods.	F/O. [illegible]	Sgt. Shanks.	Sgt. [illegible]	Sgt. [illegible]	Sgt. Doherty.	Sgt. Coles.
C S/L. Roberts.	Sgt. Bell.	Sgt. [illegible]	F/L. Hydes.	F/L. Clewlow.	F/S. [illegible]	Sgt. Bannister.
[illegible]	F/S. Durham.	Sgt. Lewis.	F/S. Bryan.	F/S. [illegible]	Sgt. [illegible]	Sgt. Clarke.
[illegible]	Sgt. Fox.	Sgt. Pattison.	Sgt. Pratt.	Sgt. Shepherd.	Sgt. Guy.	Sgt. Ive.
[illegible] F/O. Thackray.	Sgt. Watts.	F/S. [illegible]	Sgt. Hughes.	F/S. Heron.	F/S. Bromley.	Sgt. Banfield.
[illegible] F/S. Johnson.	Sgt. [illegible]	Sgt. Leah.	Sgt. Green.	Sgt. [illegible]	Sgt. [illegible]	Sgt. Whitmore.
[illegible]	Sgt. Reid.	W/O. Parker.	Sgt. Beal.	Sgt. Pitt.	Sgt. McLean.	Sgt. Chandler.
[illegible]	F/O. Baxter.	Sgt. [illegible]	Sgt. Gilmore.	Sgt. [illegible]	Sgt. Reid.	Sgt. [illegible]
[illegible]	F/O. Picton.	F/S. Palamountain.	Sgt. Benham.	Sgt. Williams.	Sgt. Savage.	Sgt. Martin.
[illegible]	F/O. Davey.	F/O. [illegible]	F/O. [illegible]	F/S. Marshall.	F/S. Clubb.	Sgt. Bristow.
[illegible] (struck out)	Sgt. McDonald	Sgt. [illegible]	Sgt. Ford.	Sgt. [illegible]	Sgt. [illegible]	Sgt. [illegible]
[illegible]	Sgt. Kellock	F/S. Sach.	Sgt. Law.	Sgt. [illegible]	Sgt. Tate.	Sgt. Proctor.
[illegible] F/S. Harrison.	Sgt. Wilde.	F/O. Kirkpatrick.	Sgt. Nash.	Sgt. Wilson.	Sgt. [illegible]	Sgt. Norris.

MEALS : 19.00 TRANSPORT : 20-25. MAIN-BRIEFING : 17.50 PRE-BRIEFING : 17.00

Distribution :
O.C. 514 Sqdn. — Sqdn. Armoury.
O.C. 'A' Flight. — N.C.O. i/c Cloakroom.
O.C. 'B' Flight. — RADAR Officer.
O.C. 'C' Flight. — C.T.O. (2).
Officers Mess. — Base Messing Officer.
Sergeants Mess. — Station Operations.
Flying Control. — Intelligence.
Sqdn. Photo. Sectn. — Transport Officer.
Nav. Officer. — Medical Officer.

[signature]
[illegible] STEVENS.
Flight Lieutenant, Adjutant,
for Wing Commander, Commanding,
No. 514 Squadron R.A.F.

The Squadron Battle Order for Nuremberg on 30th / 31st March 1944. Four of these crews would be shot down and two others would crash on their return. Only seven of these crews survived their tour of operations. (Sgt Len Venus via WMHM).

A very narrow escape for F/O Douglas Woods and crew, who survived no fewer than five night fighter attacks whilst outbound on the Nuremberg raid. Unsurprisingly, they were not able to complete the mission (Linda Miles).

of a mid-air explosion. The crew had no time to rest on their laurels as they immediately saw an Me210 attacking from the port quarter, but they were again able to evade their foe. The crew claimed the Me109 as destroyed. No single-engine fighters were apparently deployed by the Luftwaffe that night; however a total of twenty night fighters were destroyed[10] and it is probably a misidentification in the
heat of the moment; there was little doubt on the part of the crew that they had shot down an enemy night fighter.

The force had carried out an effective raid on the oft-targeted city of Essen and losses were light for once, with only nine bombers failing to return of the 705 sent out. This was, however, just the calm before the storm.

On the night of 30th / 31st March, 514 Squadron contributed 21 aircraft to the infamous Nuremberg raid. The day had got off to a sombre start, with the funeral of Sgt Len Blackford aged 24, killed on 22nd/23rd March. His crew mate Sgt Lewis Warren 19 yrs. had been buried the previous day. The

[10]Nachtjagd War Diaries

night was to be an unmitigated disaster for Bomber Command which suffered its heaviest losses of any single operation of the war. It was a clear, moon-lit night and the aircrews were slaughtered as they fought their way through the massed ranks of enemy night fighters. In total 82 aircraft were shot down over the target and outbound. Due to the intensity of the battle, German fighters had to land, re-fuel, re-arm and return to the air. This left the surviving allied aircraft a safer run on the route back to base, though a further fifteen were lost on the homeward leg and eleven crashed on their return to England. The results of the raid itself were almost an afterthought; TIs were scattered and the raid was considered unsuccessful. Much has been written about this operation, the subject of much opinion, speculation and controversy. The combination of contrails, caused by the cold air and were highly visible in the bright moonlight, along with a long straight outbound track that took the stream perilously close to night fighter beacons, combined to make matters particularly favourable for the German night fighter force. They fell upon their prey with alacrity. The enemy's response was so devastating that the suspicion formed amongst some crews that the Germans must somehow have known the route and its timings in advance. This has, however, never been proved.

S/L Alan Roberts in DS816, JI-O reported after the raid, with masterly understatement, that the route was 'badly chosen', though he considered the attack itself to have been good. The operation proved to be a short though chastening, night out for P/O Douglas Woods RAAF and his crew in LL739, JI-M whose Lancaster was attacked no fewer than five times on the outbound route. Woods returned early due to the significant damage sustained by his aircraft, landing at the emergency airfield at Woodbridge. He then submitted a typically concise combat report that downplayed the undoubted drama of their ordeal: *'Outward bound (bombs not dropped), flying on a course of 083 degrees T, IAS 155. At 0027 hours, rear gunner reported Me210 on starboard quarter down at 600 yards. Rear gunner immediately gave order to corkscrew to starboard and pressed triggers but guns failed to fire. E/A was then temporarily lost to view. Approximately 2 minutes later, rear gunner reported Me-210 on starboard quarter level at range of 700 yards. Rear gunner gave order to corkscrew to starboard but again, guns failed to fire and enemy was lost to view. About 7 minutes later, E/A was again seen on starboard quarter down at 500 yards. Rear gunner immediately gave order to corkscrew to starboard and at the same time, mid upper gunner reported a fighter flare dropped by FW190 on starboard bow level. Me210 then came in to attack from starboard quarter below, closing to range of 400 yards and opening fire on Lancaster. Mid upper gunner fired a few rounds in direction of trace, before his guns failed. Lancaster sustained several hits on starboard wing. Me210 then broke away to port quarter up and was lost to view. About a minute later, rear gunner reported Me210 attacking from starboard quarter level at a range of 300 yards and gave order to corkscrew to starboard. mid upper gunner fired a 2 second burst from 1 gun, but did not observe any hits on E/A which closed to 150 yards and opened fire scoring hits on Lancaster starboard tail unit before breaking away. Lancaster went out of control in a spiral dive and recovered at 6,000 feet. No flak was observed at the time, but there was numerous fighter flares on the port side. Visibility was very good with half-moon.'*

In his operation report, P/O Woods noted that his crew had seen fifteen to twenty aircraft shot down by fighters by the time they had reached a point south of the Ruhr. Had he continued in his badly-damaged Lancaster, Woods would have seen many more go down and, in all probability, he would have joined their number.

F/S Charles Johnson in DS633, A2-B once again came under attack, from a Ju88 over the target which he successfully evaded by flying into the contrail laid by another aircraft. Meanwhile P/O Noel Thackray's bomb aimer, F/S John Moulsdale, had seen another Lancaster being attacked by a Ju88 over Nuremberg and had manned the front turret, firing at the enemy and claiming it as damaged as it dived away almost vertically into clouds. Another Good Samaritan crew was that of F/S Charlie Medland, on this occasion in LL733, JI-G. Mid upper gunner Sgt Charles Rose saw another Lancaster being attacked so intervened, firing at the German night fighter and diverting its pilot's attention to his own aircraft. F/S Medland was able to corkscrew his way out of trouble, to the undoubted relief of his crew.

LL738, JI-D with the crew of P/O Garth Hughes RAAF were intercepted whilst holding course at 21,000 feet near Sinzig, south of Cologne at about 0020hrs, possibly by Lt. Hans Raum. Their aircraft crashed at nearby Westum, with the loss of all on board other than the bomb aimer, W/O AD Hall RNZAF. Also lost on the outbound leg was LL698, A2-J flown by F/S Fred Gregory. The aircraft was also brought down a by night-fighter, possibly that flown by Uffz. Lorenz Gerstmayr of 4. /NJG3 at 0038 hours,

near Oberpleis, 12 km ESE of Bonn. There was a single survivor from this crew as well, the navigator F/S CG MacDonald RCAF managing to escape the crashing aircraft but being captured on the ground.
The third 514 Squadron Lancaster to fall was DS836 JI-L flown by P/O Don Crombie RAAF. The crew had witnessed many of their colleagues in other aircraft falling victim to the rampaging night fighters, sometimes three or four being visible simultaneously. Whilst approaching the turning point on to final leg at 22,000 feet, the gunners, Sgt Claude Payne in the mid upper turret, and rear gunner Sgt Roy Hill, observed what they believed to be a Ju88 flying parallel to their own aircraft with its navigation lights on[11]. They alerted P/O Crombie and aimed a short burst at the German aircraft, which turned its lights off. For the next half minute, calm was restored but suddenly there was a succession of loud bangs and the starboard inner engine caught fire. Despite Sgt Jim McGahey, the new Flight Engineer replacing Sgt Ben Le Neve Foster, trying to extinguish the flames, the fire could not be contained and indeed it was soon spreading towards the fuel tanks. P/O Crombie ordered the crew to bale out; F/O Harry Darby, the bomb aimer, heard Sgt Hill say he couldn't free himself from the rear turret, but was unable to make his way the whole length of the Lancaster to try and help his comrade. As F/O Darby was right on top of the escape hatch in the nose, P/O Crombie ordered him to get out to allow access to freedom. F/O Darby and F/S Andy McPhee, the navigator, managed to get out of the aircraft but none of their five mates were able to join them. The Lanc was probably intercepted by the fighter flown by Lt. Wilhelm Seuss of 11./NJG5 at 0056 hours, coming down at Eichenhausen, in the Bad Neustadt district. The crew members who lost their lives are commemorated on the Runnymede Memorial. F/O Darby had, whilst at Waterbeach, submitted a design for a squadron crest in a competition held by the squadron commander. Whilst W/Cdr Samson, born in Newfoundland, had wanted the squadron emblem to be a caribou, he had magnanimously invited suggestions from the members of 514 Squadron. F/O Darby's submission, a cloud pierced by a sword, symbolised the use of GH to allow the squadron to strike through clouds and this design was

[11] Use of such lights was possibly a deliberate ploy to attract the attention of crews in the hope that they would be distracted and would fail to notice another, unlit, aircraft creeping up on them.

judged the winner. By the time this became known, however, F/O Darby was in captivity.

F/O Peter Hood was flying LL696, JI-A, the aircraft being shot down while on final leg to target. It has been stated that this was by the Ju88 of Fw Emil Nonnenmacher, III./NJG2, crashing near Memmelsdorf', which is 6.5 km NE of Bamberg[12]. However Fw. Nonnenmacher, who was actually with 9./NJG2, made no verified claim in that area. Lt. Achim Woeste, Stab III./NJG3 was credited with an unidentified 4-engined bomber in the Schesslitz area, 10 km NE of Bamberg at a time consistent with 514 Squadron aircraft being in the vicinity[13]. It is therefore considered more likely that LL696 was shot down by Lt. Woeste. Mid upper gunner Sgt Fraser MacKenzie was the sole casualty, the remainder of the crew being taken prisoner. The rear gunner, T/Sgt Maurice Lanthier, was apparently injured in the incident and was detained in hospital rather than a POW camp.

The fates had not yet done, even as the remnants of the force, some battered, many remarkably unscathed, returned to the comparative safety of English skies. LL645, JI-R was flown by P/O Walter Chitty and had dropped an 8,000lb 'blockbuster' plus a few incendiaries for good measure. On return to base, they were baulked on finals by another Squadron aircraft and crash-landed two miles south west of Waterbeach while attempting a go around. The impact was severe and the main undercarriage was ripped away, with serious injuries to the crew along with two fatalities. The bomb aimer, Sgt Allen Pattison RCAF is buried in Brookwood Military Cemetery whilst mid upper gunner Sgt Joseph Shepherd lies in Heywood Cemetery, Lancashire.

W/O Bill McGown had brought his aircraft LL683, JI-P back to England but was instructed to divert to RAF Stradishall, but this airfield was fog bound. Subsequently, and after three crew members had out, he made a forced-landing in a field near Sawbridgeworth, Hertfordshire. W/O McGown's report notes one injury, but no further details were given.

Six empty dispersals at Waterbeach on the morning of 31st March marked the low point of the squadron's fortunes in terms of aircraft lost on a single

---

[12] Bomber Command Losses 1944

[13] Nachtjagd War Diaries

raid, though the toll of twenty crew members killed would be exceeded within a few months. On that sombre note, March 1944 drew to a close.
The Station Commander's Summary for March 1944 related:
514 Squadron took part in eight major attacks during the month. There were only three failures to take off but a total of fourteen early returns which although due to technical causes is too high a number. Eight aircraft are missing from these operations. In addition on two separate occasions two members of the crew baled out of an aircraft out over enemy territory on their Captain's order, while the aircraft was out of control; later control was regained and the aircraft brought back to base.

The first week in April brought something of a breather for the squadron, following its mauling on the Nuremberg raid. Medals were awarded to F/O Harold Bryant, who received the DFC, along with F/Sgt Bernard Windsor and Sgt Frank Dolamore, both of whom were awarded the DFM for their heroics on the night of 22nd-23rd March attacking Frankfurt.
On 6th April the monthly dance given by the WAAF was as crowded and cheerful an affair as ever. The following day, Good Friday, was a quiet day on the station, the squadron enjoying a stand-down in the afternoon. Mr. Geoffrey Smith of Ministry of Production visited the station. His purpose was to obtain materials for a propaganda tour of the United States. Accompanied by the Station and Squadron Commanders he talked with crews who had dropped 8,000lb bombs on Berlin. S/L NF Vincent DFC RAAF, Liaison Officer, HQ Bomber Command had a chat with Australian members of aircrew.
The first operation of the month was on the night of 9th - 10th April, as the attention of Bomber Command moved away from German industrial targets towards locations in France as the Allies prepared to launch the invasion. The first such operation for the squadron saw two aircraft, LL697, JI-E flown by F/O Lloyd Taylor RAAF and DS822, JI-T flown by F/Sgt Bernard Windsor DFM, attack railway marshalling yards at Villeneuve along with 223 other bombers. No aircraft were lost on this apparently successful raid which took place just after midnight. Loads for such targets in occupied territories generally comprised smaller bombs, typically 1,000 lb, in order to reduce the risk of casualties amongst the local civilians.

The following night, the squadron sent nineteen aircraft to attack railway yards at Laon in France. The target indicators were concentrated and the squadron considered the raid to have been a success, though a later assessment showed that the destruction was largely to one corner of the yards. P/ O Maurice Morgan-Owen's gunners in LL732, A2-H sighted a Ju88 night fighter apparently manoeuvring to attack their aircraft; however they drove it off by opening fire. All but one of the 163 aircraft deployed returned safely, though F/S 'Toppy' Topham in LL677, A2-E noted two bullet holes in the fuselage of his aircraft, from an unknown cause. Several of the squadron's aircraft noted potential conflicts with other bombers over the aiming point, meaning that they were unable to obtain photos to prove the accuracy of their attacks.

The night of 11th April saw a larger raid on Aachen in Germany, the 350 bombers despatched including eleven from Waterbeach. This was, in fact, the largest raid of the war on Aachen. The attack took place between 2230 and 2300hrs through broken cloud and F/S Norman Wishart in LL728, JI-B reported 'many good fires'. Overall this effective and accurate raid caused much damage, including to the transport infrastructure. F/S Les Petry RNZAF and his crew in LL620, A2-G, were attacked by an unidentified twin-engined aircraft on the return leg which they evaded by corkscrewing and returning fire. Although opposition was less than expected, nine aircraft failed to return, including LL645, JI-R, flown by P/O Noel Thackray RAAF and his crew. They were intercepted returning from the target and shot down, probably by an Me110 night fighter flown by Uffz. Hans Fischer of 12./NJG1, or by flak. An engine fire led to the separation of one engine, making the aircraft uncontrollable, the aircraft crashing at 2315hrs, 10km West of Roermond. P/O Thackray ordered the crew to bale out but the sole survivor was the navigator, Sgt Edward Humes, who was captured.

This was followed by a week of operational inactivity, though non-operational flying and ground training continued unabated. On 13th April Sir Edmund Richards, Governor of Nyasaland, accompanied by F/L Dickinson of Air Ministry, visited the station. Unfortunately operations were cancelled but he was conducted around the Station and shown Sections of general interest to him by the Base and Station Commanders.

The WAAF social evening on 16th April was well attended by all ranks. Everyone, according to the Station ORB, 'entered into the party spirit and three officers of the RASC, who were guests, obviously enjoyed the games which formed a novel part of the evening's entertainment.'

On 18th April Miss Audrey Russell of the BBC returned to complete her commentary on the WAAF and their part in the work of an operational station. She was on hand to see the squadron participate in its next effort on 18th April, when 20 aircraft joined 269 other bombers attacking Rouen. Once again, the French railway infrastructure was the target, the attack taking place shortly after midnight. F/S Richard Pick in LL696, JI-A had a brush with an unidentified single-engined aircraft as he approached the target, Sgt W Aston in the rear turret driving it off without the enemy getting a shot in. Continuing to the target, F/S Pick dropped his 11,500 lb bomb load from 12,500 feet. Noting that there was 'too much conversation by the M of C', (Master Bomber, also known as 'Master of Ceremonies') Pick felt that the attack had fallen too far west, though the subsequent raid report indicated that the attack had been successful, causing widespread damage without loss to Bomber Command's force. Other pilots, however, felt that the Master Bomber had been helpful and effective. Not all the bombing was perceived as accurate; F/S Geoffrey Clewlow, rear gunner in LL731, JI-U flown by F/S Bernard Windsor, observed bombs falling across buildings including a church. F/S Bob Langley, in DS842, JI-F *'Fanny Firkin II'*, found that there were hazards to be encountered even on his return, his logbook recording: *'Bandits. Circled base for an hour.'*

On 20th April, Hitler's birthday, the squadron marked the occasion with another outing to Germany, the city of Cologne being selected for attention. 22 aircraft left Waterbeach, all of them carrying out their allotted task, despite PFF turning up late. Comments on the elite Pathfinders were often less than complimentary, and this was probably not just inter-unit rivalry. A delay in marking could mean that bombers arriving at the head of the stream faced a few minutes circling in the target area whilst they awaited their aiming point, a situation which reduced the crews' life expectancy even further. The alternative was for the main force crews to drop their bombs based on their own estimated time over the target, and this is what many 514 Squadron crews did on this occasion. Although crews described the bombing as scattered, it was noted that some good fires were started, some of which were visible from the English coast on their return. In fact the 379 aircraft that comprised the force carried out what was described in the records as a devastating raid with widespread destruction and severe casualties on the ground. Over 190 industrial buildings were destroyed along with heavy damage to seven railway yards and stations. There were nearly 1300 fires and 46 churches were destroyed. Deep penetrating bombs destroyed many underground bomb shelters. It is speculated that as many as eighty percent of the 660 people killed on the ground were in those shelters. Four bombers were lost on the raid.

Two nights later, on the 22nd, it was the turn of Düsseldorf, with 22 of the Waterbeach Lancasters deployed amongst the total of 596. Two 514 Squadron aircraft returned early, whilst a further three did not return at all. F/O Lou Greenburgh was flying, as usual, in LL727, A2-C and was one of the 'early returns', though not for any technical reason: 'We took off at dusk and joined the main formation as the sky got dark. Once darkness fell, each plane had to rely on its own navigation because you couldn't see well enough to formate on someone else. Although we were flying the same route from the same departure point to the same target, and usually wound up being together, each plane was making its own way.

We were heading on a course of 180. Ronald and I had an ongoing dialogue.

"Checking the course," I said.

"One eight zero," he confirmed, "One eight zero."

"Okay," I acknowledged, "One eight zero."

We carried on for a while before the navigator said, "Skipper, make it 'eighty-seven." I made a minor course adjustment and steadied up on course, replying "One eighty seven".

After a while, we began to draw quite a bit of flak. I hadn't expected so much at this stage of our journey and I was concerned that nobody else seemed to be drawing any. If you're on your own, they can single you out.

Ronald Fox explained what happened in a letter dated November 11 1944

'We were flying a short leg due south (180 degrees, approximately). At the time to turn east, I gave the pilot a course of 087 degrees (east) which he mistook for a slight alteration to 187 degrees. I failed to check the course as I was busy catching up on the plot. After ten minutes or so. I checked the course and was horrified to find we were travelling due south instead of east.'

"Jesus Christ!" I cursed when I realized our situation, "There's no way we can turn back!" We had been flying at right angles to our proper course with a one hundred miles per hour tail wind.

"No! No!" he concurred, "We're a hundred and forty miles off course now!"

The anti-aircraft flashes were all aimed at us. I wondered where the hell we were.

"Skipper..."
I interrupted him. "How far are we from Dusseldorf?"
"I don't know, Skipper, but we're outside of Paris." "Jesus Christ! Well, what are we going to do? We've got our bombs. We can't waste them and we can't take them back." I decided that there was nothing for it but to jettison the in the North Sea and go home. I turned the plane around and began heading north.
There were still plenty of lights on in this area. I guess nobody was expecting the Allies to bomb Paris. Sitting about forty miles outside of Paris was the distinctive form of an aerodrome. I decided to head towards it.
The flak died down and then stopped. As we circled the aerodrome in preparation for our attack, I saw that it had its own airplanes flying around. They probably figured that we were one of theirs.
"Listen," I said to the navigator and the bomb aimer. "Get ready. We're going to bomb this enemy airport." I pulled the lever to open the bomb doors and began an approach which would line us up with the runway. Then I saw some large rectangular buildings by the side. "It's no use bombing the runway," I said to the bomb aimer, "because they can take off and land in the field beside it. Aim for those buildings."
I made another circuit to line up with the new target and began to take direction from the bomb aimer. "Left, left, left we're coming on to the buildings," he said. Then I felt the aircraft heave and heard Eric say. "Bombs gone!"
An instant later we saw one or two explosions smack in the middle of the buildings. All of the lights went out for miles around and the sky was suddenly full of anti-aircraft flashes
I pushed the wheel forward and gunned the throttles, swooping down to 150 feet off the ground. I was afraid that I might hit a mast or something but I was more afraid of fighters. They would be after me like nobody's business.
I stayed at a low level until we hit the coast, then began to climb a little bit. We still had to be careful because there was flak coming up at us from flak ships.
At last, we saw the beacon from our own aerodrome. I came in and requested permission to land. We were all alone and way ahead of schedule. The air traffic controllers were surprised.
Since we were the only ones back, we had our own private debriefing. I told the officers what had happened and was worried about possible repercussions. They didn't seem to mind though. And the next day, Intelligence confirmed that a German training station had received a direct hit. We must have killed quite a few young pilots.

I made a note in my log book, *"April 22, 1944. Ops Düsseldorf. Bombed Airfield NE Paris."*'[14]

In what was, despite the absence of F/O Greenburgh, a successful attack, TIs were seen to go down on the marshalling yards and the bombing was concentrated, with 56 large buildings damaged and seven industrial locations reportedly destroyed. Bob Langley, now promoted to Pilot Officer, commented laconically after the operation in DS842, JI-F: *'Happy Valley in all its glory.'* Searchlights were very active, but flak was moderate over the target, possibly to allow the fighter force free rein. The Luftwaffe had already infiltrated the bomber stream to deadly effect, with

Lancaster Mk.II LL624, JI-P in the background at RAF Woodbridge after being damaged over Düsseldorf by falling bombs on 22nd April 1944 (Crown).

29 of the attacking aircraft destroyed. Nor were the German defences the only hazard. LL624, JI-P, being flown on this trip by W/O Bill McGown, was just about to drop its bombs on the target when the aircraft was struck from above by bombs from another aircraft. This resulted in damage to its wings and the starboard outer engine cowling, but did not prevent the crew from carrying out their mission.

---

[14] Lou Greenburgh in *DFC and Bar* by Ed Greenburgh

F/O Maurice Morgan-Owen's crew in DS682, JI-N crashed in the North Sea on their return from the target. The circumstances are not known. An SOS message was sent out by wireless operator Sgt Sunny Gledhill and received at 0256hrs giving its position as 5236N 0351E. No night-fighter claim is recorded so it is likely that the aircraft sustained damage earlier in the raid and failed to make it home. The bodies of Sergeants Henry Sadler, the Flight Engineer and Alfred Tetley, mid-upper gunner were recovered later and are buried in Sage War Cemetery. The rest of the crew are commemorated on the Runnymede Memorial. No sign of aircraft or dinghy were found in the subsequent ASR search in which the squadron's aircraft took part.[15]

DS669, JI-C, piloted by F/S John Harrison, and DS828, JI-D, which was flown by F/S John Hudson RNZAF, were both lost over the target area. The Lancasters were either hit by flak or collided with each other, crashing in the target area. DS669 came down at the junction of Ecke Rethel and Schubertstrasse. The crew members are buried at Reichswald Forest War Cemetery, with the exception of the wireless operator, Sgt Frederick Nash, who is commemorated on the Runnymede Memorial. The crew of DS828 are buried at Reichswald Forest War Cemetery, except F/S Hudson and W/O Henry Rolph, who are commemorated on the Runnymede Memorial. There were no survivors from any of the three aircraft that failed to return to Waterbeach that night.

The Düsseldorf raid was the first operation for F/S Ted Prowles and his crew, flying DS826, JI-L. The crew's Flight Engineer, Sgt Harry Osborne, recorded their first trip shortly afterwards[16].

'It was on the morning of Saturday, the 22nd of April, 1944 that my report begins, the time being about 10 o'clock. Myself and the rest of the crew were all standing around in a group outside the flight office chatting, while we were waiting to see what we had been detailed for that day. We had heard that there were ops on that night but we did not know if we would be on the battle order, we would not know until 10.30. At last we saw the skipper coming from the Flight Commander's office, yes we were detailed to fly, this was to be our first op. It gives you a peculiar feeling when you are first told, I would not say so much fear as of curiosity and expectancy,

[15] RAF Waterbeach Station ORB

[16] Part of the Story of 514 Squadron – Harry Dison

although I must admit I was a bit scared but then the rest of the chaps are feeling the same so you don't worry about it.
The next thing on the programme was to check the aircraft over and give it a Night Flying Test (NFT). The gunners were cleaning and checking their guns while the pilot and myself test the oxygen, intercom, saw that fire extinguishers and oxygen bottles were in position, also that the aircraft is not damaged in any way etc. Then we went up on test, this is to see that the kite flies OK and to check a few other things while in the air. After this came dinner. After dinner we got what things we would be needing for the trip and then got in a few hours' sleep. Tea was at 4.30 and at 5.25 or 17.25 hours the navigator and bomb aimer had to report for Pre-briefing. The Skipper is not allowed into their briefing until half an hour after the start. While they were doing this I had a bath and shave, and got changed into my flying underclothes. At 1955 hrs we had our flying meal. This is quite some tum out, the boys arrive in all manner of queer get ups, the most striking thing being the assortment of different coloured scarves, others have civvy shirts, white roll top polo jerseys, flying boots on and an assortment of good luck charms. In fact to see them one would think that they were going to a Sunday School treat rather than a raid. The meal consisted of egg, bacon and chips and as much bread and butter as you wished for. At 20.35 we all had to report for main briefing. Here we have all the crews that are taking part in the night's operation, navigators are plotting the courses on their maps and writing down winds. There is the C.O. of the Squadron, the Group Captain and a host of other officers of the various sections. Then the C.O. takes the platform and we hear that so commonly known phrase "The Target for Tonight". Our particular target being 'Düsseldorf'. Next the Met. Officer gives the gen on what the weather will be like, height of cloud, the temperature where icing is likely to be encountered etc. Next the Intelligence Officer says his part, when the target was last bombed, what we are after hitting, type of defences liable to be met, if any other raids are going on. Then the C.O. tells us what speeds and height to fly, at what wave of bombers we are in, fuel load, bomb load, time of take-off time to set course, time over target.
After briefing we collect our flying rations and walk over to the cloak room to get our flying kit and get dressed. Here we have a Medical Officer and he gives us two 'wakey wakey' tablets to take before we reach the target, also he has an ointment which the gunners smear on their faces to prevent

frostbite. At 21.25 hrs transport arrived to take us out to the aircraft. Then the pilot and I make a final check on the aircraft, while the wireless operator tests his set. The boys then lay around smoking and chatting till 10.30 when we all get into the kite and start engines and then give them a run up. We then taxi out to the runway ready for take-off. We got the green 'Go' from the caravan and took off at 22.50 hrs. We then had to circuit round the drome for 40 mins before setting course and at last we were on our way.

As we neared the enemy coast we were all on the lookout for fighters and other bombers in the stream. We crossed the coast at 20,000 feet. As we flew on towards the target we started to see a few searchlights and bursts of flak. Every now and again we would see fighter flares also a few scarecrows. These come up at you in the form of a small ball of fire, then it would burst throwing out showers of sparks and clouds of black smoke which gives it the appearance of an aircraft which has been hit. As we came into the target area we could see the vapour trails of other aircraft and sometimes the aircraft themselves as dozens of searchlights were now searching the sky. Every now and again we would feel a bump in the aircraft as we would be caught in the slipstream of another kite or some flak burst near us. Just ahead of us lay the target lit up by fires caused by the bombers before us, also by flares and hundreds of incendiary bombs. We could now see the marker flares dropped by the Path Finder boys, so we started to make our run up on the target. Here we were cornered by about half a dozen searchlights so the Skipper took a bit of evasive action and we had soon shaken them off At 0102 hrs we dropped our bombs and now we were flying straight and level over the target so that we could get some good photos. It seemed hours before the bomb aimer said OK photos taken, this was because we had been caught again in the searchlights, but now at least we were heading for home. You feel as if you just want to sit back and relax but you know there are fighters to contend with so you keep a good look out for them.

As we neared the Dutch coast the Skipper said the kite was handling badly and she was pulling round to starboard. So I made a check on the gauges and found that the oil pressure had fallen off the gauge and also the boost and R.P.M. had dropped considerably so I had to feather this engine; that was at 0203 hrs. Later I found out that the main bearing had gone on this engine, so we flew the remainder of the trip home on three engines.

As we came near the English coast we could see searchlights flashing and they certainly gave you a feeling of relief The Skipper decided that we would land at an emergency 'drome, which has an especially long runway and is for all aircraft to land on when in trouble. So we called them up and asked them if we could land. They told us to go ahead and that transport would be waiting for us at the end of the runway. The Skipper made a really wizard landing and the transport was already waiting to take us to the medical room where we were given rum.
Next the Skipper and myself were taken to a hut where we had to make out a report on what was wrong with the kite. Then we were all taken down to the cookhouse where we were given fried egg, bacon and chips, after this a place to sleep and we certainly did appreciate that bed that night. Next day we were picked up by an aircraft from our own Station and flown back to base. Here we had to go for interrogation where we were asked all sorts of questions, and at last our first operational flight had come to an end, resulting in slight damage by flak and one engine unserviceable.'
At 1100hrs on 24th April, whilst taking off for a cross country flight, Lancaster Mk.II DS623, flown by F/O RW Mann of 1678 CU, crashed at RAF Waterbeach, owing to premature raising of the undercarriage by the Flight Engineer. It was established that the pilot and Flight Engineer had arranged a sequence of hand signals so that they could avoid the need to shout. The pilot's goggles slipped slightly and, when he lifted his hand to move them the Flight Engineer mistook this for the sign to raise the undercarriage. It is believed that there were no injuries.
Later that night the squadron detailed sixteen aircraft to raid Karlsruhe, one crew returning early. The cloud cover was complete and extended above 17,000 feet so sky markers were used. While many crews believed that they had bombed accurately, in fact the cloud and high winds had conspired to make the bombing scattered. A number of aircraft from the 637-strong force actually bombed Mannesheim, thirty miles to the north, in error. W/O Bill McGown in DS822, JI-T reported a 'very successful attack' but then found on his return that his aircraft's flaps would not deploy, so he had to divert to the emergency runway at Woodbridge. The enemy defences were much less effective than on the previous few raids, and only two of the squadron's crews reported combat. F/S Thomas Gibson in LL786, A2-F repelled a single-engined FW190 whilst F/S Charles

Johnson in DS633, A2-B fought off an Me210. Neither Lancaster actually came under fire. Overall 19 bombers were lost from the attacking force.
Festivities continued on the evening of 26th April, the venue on this occasion being the invariably hazardous target of Essen, home of the Krupps armament works. Eight Lancasters were sent from Waterbeach, one returning early. The returning crews claimed an accurate attack, which was borne out by the post-raid assessment. It was also noted that opposition from flak and fighters was much less than expected, but searchlights were very numerous. One pilot who doubtless disagreed with the latter assessment was F/S William Gibson, this time in LL732, A2-H, who had four encounters with enemy aircraft. The first, while the crew were outbound at 0106hrs, was a sighting of a single-engined fighter with its navigation lights on which approached from the port bow. Combined fire from the front and mid upper turrets forced a rethink on the part of the enemy pilot and the fighter was not seen again. At 0135hrs, two minutes after bombing the target, LL732 was coned by searchlights and would have been easy prey for a prowling Ju88 had it not been spotted by the alert rear gunner, Sgt Gallagher. He ordered a corkscrew and fired at the German aircraft which promptly lost interest and went off in search of easier prey. The Lancaster was also apparently successful in escaping the clutches of the searchlights. At 0142hrs another Me109 approached and was driven off by Sgt George Kemp in the mid upper turret. Finally, and only three minutes after the previous encounter, two twin-engine aircraft were seen, both with navigation lights on. These were once again repelled by Sgt Gallagher.
The attacking force, comprising 493 bombers, had escaped with very light losses, only seven crews failing to return.
The following evening, ops were on again at Waterbeach, eighteen crews being briefed to attack the distant target of Friedrichshaven, on the Swiss border. The location of important factories making engines and gearboxes for tanks deep inside south Germany, this target was of considerable strategic importance. German defences were hampered as the target was on the fringes of Luftwaffe coverage. The night fighter response was delayed, although they eventually intercepted the bomber stream over the target, accounting for eighteen of the 322 aircraft in the attacking force. Assisted by a clear and moon-lit night and well placed TIs, the attack proved devastating, with approximately two thirds of the town being

destroyed. After the war's end, this attack was described by German officials as 'the most damaging attack on tank production of the war'.
F/O Ian Hay, in DS633, JI-R managed to evade an FW190 without coming under attack, whilst P/O Doug Woods in LL731, JI-U was fired upon by trace from an unseen aircraft underneath his Lancaster. His gunners returned fire and the enemy aircraft did not return. They subsequently found two holes in the wings of LL731.
There were no further operations during April 1944 but the month had a sting in its tail. On the night of 30th April, three aircraft were detailed to carry out a 'Bullseye' navigational exercise. These included LL691, A2-D, flown by F/S Norman Turner. LL691 which crashed at 0015 hours in the English Channel off Dover. The crew of seven was supplemented by a member of the ground crew, being carried as a passenger. AC1 George Robinson lost his life along with the rest of the crew and their bodies were not recovered; their names are commemorated on the Runnymede Memorial. It is possible that the aircraft was shot down by local anti-aircraft defences, having presumably been mistaken for an enemy raider.
Eric Basford, Engine Fitter with 'A' Flight, explained the carriage of ground crew on non-operational flights: 'If any member of a ground crew wished to fly in one of the Squadron's aircraft, usually his own, there was

LL691, A2-D shown here with the crew of P/O Les Petry RNZAF. The aircraft was lost whilst in the care of the Turner crew, after which F/O Petry flew her replacement (WMHM).

an official procedure to follow. Assuming that the pilot agreed to take him on a particular flight, his name would be recorded as being on the flight and he would be issued with helmet, oxygen mask, parachute and harness for the trip.

In spite of this facility, it was not unusual for ground crew members to persuade their pilots to take them along unofficially, if the flight was only for an hour or so. That meant foregoing the helmet and parachute, but that was the price of short cutting official procedure. As no serious attempt was made to stamp out this out, it was assumed to be acceptable practice.

However, unofficial flying over this country in daylight (on officially approved flights) was one thing, but to do it at night and beyond our coastline was something else.'

The Station Commander's Summary for April 1944 noted:

During the month the tempo of operational activity increased slightly. 514 Squadron provided 146 sorties in the course of eight night operations. Attacks were delivered principally on marshalling yards, though Berlin, Essen and Friedrickshaven were also attacked. In the course of these operations, four aircraft were lost.

Ronald Spencer RAAF was a wool sorter from Tasmania before he joined up. F/S Spencer was the bomb aimer in the crew of F/S Ted Prowles and was to lose his life returning from Valenciennes (ANA / Andrew Porrelli).

5. Overlord: May to July 1944

From the beginning of May, and with the grudging acquiescence of Air Chief Marshall Harris, Bomber Command's efforts were finally diverted from its efforts to destroy German war industries as the war planners focused on the forthcoming invasion of Normandy. The strategy ahead of D-Day was for the bomber force to cripple the transportation system in France, thereby preventing the Germans from easily bringing reinforcements to the battle front. The planners' rationale went further; bombing railway lines was a temporary inconvenience to the enemy as these could be repaired, rolling stock and locomotives could be replaced and makeshift loading and unloading facilities put in place. Far more damage could potentially be caused by destroying repair and maintenance centres first of all, thereby delaying any efforts to restore railway communications.

It was with this intent that, on the night of 1st - 2nd May, nineteen aircraft were sent out from Waterbeach to attack the railway depot at Chambly. Although the depot was in France, and opposition in the target area itself was slight, the German defenders were still able to deploy night fighters in considerable force, on this occasion these intercepting the bombing force on its return. The weather was clear over Chambly and crews noted bomb bursts and fires apparently in the target area. Notably, the bombing height was around 5 - 9,000 feet, less than half of the usual altitude, with aircraft returning at relatively low level to the French coast. On this occasion, an extremely successful raid was carried out by a relatively small force comprising 120 aircraft on what was considered the largest stores and repair depot in the North of France. Some 500 HE bombs hitting the mark, causing heavy damage which rendered the site inoperable for almost two weeks. Five bombers failed to return including LL732, A2-H from Waterbeach, which was shot down on the home leg by a night-fighter flown by Oblt. Jakob Schauss of 4./NJG4. There were no survivors from the crew. The pilot, F/L Robert Curtis DFM, had previously flown a tour on Hampdens with 144 Sqn. and was on the 17th trip of his second tour. .

After the raid, F/S Ted Prowles in DS816, JI-O commented on the chatter from the 'Master of Ceremonies', making it difficult for him to hear the instructions from his own bomb aimer as they attacked the target at

0023hrs. It had already been an interesting op for the Prowles crew; eight minutes before they bombed the target, the rear gunner, Sgt John Porrelli, had seen an FW190 tailing their Lancaster and, choosing his moment, had opened fire. Mid upper gunner Sgt Bert Holmes had joined in with the firefight, as their pursuer had shown a degree of persistence, until the enemy pilot decided to give up and find a less alert victim. Sgt Porrelli had expended 1,000 rounds and Sgt Holmes an additional 200. At 0038hrs the gunners in DS786, A2-F, flown by F/S WM Watkins, outgunned even the Prowles crew, firing 1800 rounds as they came under repeated attack, also from a Ju88. Sergeants Peter Dawson and B Ferris were ultimately successful in driving away the enemy aircraft but their own plane had its radio and intercom equipment, along with other electronics, shot away.
F/S Charlie Medland, in LL695, JI-A was leaving the target area at 0029hrs when his aircraft had the first of three encounters with enemy fighters that night. A Ju88 had been spotted by the rear gunner, Sgt BR Williams, who then fired at the enemy as it came towards them. The German fighter moved in towards the Lancaster, opening fire at a range of about 650 yards, and Sgt Williams was joined by Sgt Charles Rose in the mid upper turret in fighting fire with fire. The Ju88 closed to within fifty yards, still firing, and the starboard inner engine was described by the crew as 'shot out of the Lancaster' and the aircraft fell out of control. F/S Medland ordered his crew to bale out but countermanded the order as he was able to regain control. The port outer engine was also vibrating badly, so it was feathered, leaving the Lanc with two working engines. At 0043hrs, LL695 was fired at by an unidentified single-engine aircraft, the trace passing underneath the Lancaster. F/S Medland desperately corkscrewed the aircraft whilst the gunners tried to repel the night fighter and ultimately their combined efforts were successful. Shortly afterwards, at 0048hrs, another unidentified single-engine fighter closed in and opened fire from the port beam. Sgt Rose, by now operating his turret manually, returned fire and the enemy aircraft broke away. Almost immediately there was a further attack from a single-engine aircraft, possibly the same one as previously, this time from ahead. Another corkscrew manoeuvre was again successful in allowing the Lancaster and her crew to escape and this time they were left in peace of the remainder of their trip. F/S Medland's courage and leadership were marked by the immediate award of a DFM, the citation

concluding that 'he proved himself to be a skillful, courageous and resolute captain and pilot.'
There then followed a lull in operations, at least for a few days.
On 3rd May the Station Concert Party under its producer, LAC OB May, gave another successful show, 'The Lido Follies'. Amongst the many members of the Concert party, F/O H Portway of No. 1678 Conversion Flight, proved a most clever and versatile comedian. This was attended the following day by AVM R Harrison, AOC 3 Group, Air Commodore HH Down AFC, Base Commander and Group Capt CM Heard, Station Commander.[17]
The next outing was on the very early morning of 8th May, coinciding with the full moon, when ten 514 Squadron Lancasters were sent with 89 others to bomb the airfield at Nantes. Bombing was accurate with many hangars destroyed and runways damaged. This was achieved with the loss of only one aircraft from the overall force. Once again the raid took place from a relatively low altitude, in order to maximise accuracy and reduce collateral casualties amongst the French population.
P/O Cedric Thomson RAAF and his crew were on their first op: 'l remember the 'Bulls Eye' to the North German coast in Lancaster Mk.II DS 622, and our last training flight which involved night tactics with F/L Prager. He certainly taught us the extreme limits of the Lancaster Mk.ll in the corkscrew because our aircraft was put out of action for some time as the ground crew had to replace some fractured parts.
Seven days later we started life in A Flight. On 7th May **we** went on our first official operation in LL 733, 'G' George, under the guidance of F/Lt Chopping; his name did not give us confidence although his guidance was very valuable. The target was Nantes Airfield. We bombed at lower level than most, because we were told to, and bombs raining from above impressed upon us that we were on ops.'
The following night saw the deployment of ten of the squadron's aircraft amongst a small force of 38 attacking gun emplacements at Cap Gris Nez. The operation had two purposes; the gun emplacements could potentially threaten shipping movements in the English Channel supporting the D-Day landings and any attempts to bomb them might also help the Germans believe that the forthcoming invasion would be in the Pas de Calais area,

---

[17] RAF Waterbeach Station ORB

rather than further south in Normandy. There were, on this occasion, no enemy fighters and very little flak; as a consequence all aircraft returned unscathed. Unfortunately the target does not appear to have been hit effectively, if at all. Therefore a much larger force comprising 414 bombers, nineteen of which hailed from Waterbeach, set out the following night 9th - 10th May, tasked with obliterating seven separate gun emplacements. 514 Squadron was sent back to Cap Gris Nez. Opposition this time had risen from non-existent to merely negligible, with two or three bursts of heavy flak reported by 514 Squadron crews. P/O Bob Langley in DS842, JI-F reported on landing: *'Bomb load 1 x 1000 GP, 13 x 1000 MC. Primary target: CAP GRIS NEZ. Clear conditions, and visuals of red and green TIs were obtained. On instructions of Master Bomber, bombs were aimed to left of red TIs at 0413 hours from 6400 feet. For a small target, markers appeared scattered at beginning of raid but concentrated towards the end. Bombs were seen to burst in centre of TI concentration. Attack improved later and bombs appear to burst in area marked.'*

No combats were reported by 514 Squadron crews, and only one aircraft was lost from the overall force, that being a Lancaster from 550 Sqn based at North Killingholme, with the loss of all crew. Four of the seven targets were claimed as hit.

Courtrai's railway yards were the destination the following night for fifteen aircraft of 514 Squadron, as part of a combined attack on five separate targets by 506 aircraft. The raid was considered to be successful, with favourable comments forthcoming from the Master Bomber. There was slight heavy flak and a few enemy aircraft were seen, but no combats with the squadron's Lancasters. None of the 13 aircraft lost were participating in the Courtrai raid. P/O Cedric Thomson recalled: 'On our third trip, to Courtrai, still in LM733 'G' George, again we were bombing at a lower level, because we were told to do so. I clearly remember a stack of bombs coming at our aircraft from the port bow and the last of them passing me about ten yards away, and reading the word 'FUSED' along the side of the last bomb.'

The pace was picking up by now, with operations on for the third consecutive night, as 11th / 12th May saw ten of the Waterbeach contingent visit more railway yards, this time at Louvain in the company of one hundred other aircraft. In contrast to the previous couple of nights, there was more opposition to the attacking force. Target marking was scattered and opinion varied as to the success of the raid, the result being difficult to assess as smoke obscured vision in all cases. Flak was slight though the defences of Brussels and Antwerp were noted to be in action. DS813, JI-H, flown by P/O Edward Greenwood suffered flak damage to the fuselage. F/O Cedric Thomson, in LL733, JI-G twice evaded enemy aircraft, the first being a Ju88 whilst the second was unseen, its presence being signalled by a Monica warning. He later commented: 'We were attacked by night fighters and for the first time put the teaching of F/L Prager into use in a very serious way. We had completed four trips in five days. It was an exhausting introduction to operations, but think of the longer hours the ground crews endured in all weathers.'

The original Cunningham crew, shot down on their ninth op. Back row from left: F/O Reg Brailsford (Bomb Aimer), Sgt Fred Brown (MU Gunner), Sgt Gordon Hay (Flight Engineer), F/S John Stone (WOP). Front row from left: Sgt Taffy Roberts (Rear Gunner), F/S (later P/O) Bruce Cunningham (Pilot), F/O Bob Ramsey (Navigator) (WMHM).

P/O Bruce Cunningham RNZAF and his crew were on their ninth op, flying LL739, JI-M. Their aircraft was attacked by a FW190, possibly flown by Ofw. Vinzenz Glessübel, while they were leaving the target area. The starboard inner engine caught fire which, within five minutes, spread to entire wing. LL739 crashed in the Brussels area. P/O Donald Winterford, the flight engineer, was shot in the leg by a German patrol who initially thought he was a saboteur. P/O Cunningham was also quickly captured. Navigator F/O Robert Ramsey and Sgt Fred Brown, the mid upper gunner, evaded for a while but were arrested by the Gestapo whilst bomb aimer F/O Reginald Brailsford, Sgt John Stone, wireless operator and rear gunner Sgt Bob Roberts were more successful, managing to elude their captors completely. All the crew members survived.

On 12th May 1944, the squadron's first commander, W/Cdr Arthur Samson DFC, gathered together all crews who were not sleeping off the fatigue of the previous night's ops. This was to bid the squadron's personnel farewell as he left to take command of No. 1657 Conversion Unit[18].

Whilst the squadron awaited the replacement for W/Cdr Samson, it was commanded temporarily by S/Ldr Barney Reid. In the meantime, a high-flyer visited the squadron on 16th May. W/Cdr Hamish Mahaddie, DSO, DFC, AFC of the Pathfinder Force gave a lecture to all squadron aircrew personnel upon the techniques and methods adopted by the PFF. It is not known if the previously-recorded comments from returning crews about the late arrival of the PFF markers on several occasions were passed on to the Wing Commander on this occasion.

On 17th May, The Station Commander addressed the Station at a Muster Parade and spoke of the necessity for longer working hours and a 100% effort by each person, when intensive operations begin. He was confident that everyone realising the big issues at stake, would respond cheerfully and willingly. Mr AH Whyte, Air Ministry Horticultural Adviser, inspected the unit gardens and gave some useful advice on land cultivation. Meanwhile on 19th May, Group Officer C Woodhead, Deputy Director of WAAF and Group Officer LM Crowther OBE of HQ Bomber Command, arrived on the station in order to judge the Waterbeach WAAF contingent who were representing 3 Group in the final of the Sunderland Cup[19], presented by the Mayor of Sunderland to the best WAAF Station in

---

[18] Although W/Cdr Samson survived the hostilities he lost his life on September 8th 1945 in the Far East, when the Dakota of 117 Sqn he was flying exploded. The aircraft was ferrying sick POWs recently liberated from their Japanese captors.

[19] The Sunderland Cup in 1944 was won by RAF Snaith of 4 Group.

Bomber Command. They were, the Station ORB records, accompanied by Squadron Officer BS Mitchell of HQ No. 3 Group and Flight Officer EB Smith. After dinner in the Officers' Mess they inspected the various activities of WAAF engaged on a domestic evening at the WAAF site. The Deputy Director had a word with girls who were busy gardening and admired the gardens and the artistic rockery-cum-air raid shelter. The party accompanied by the Base and Station Commanders, the Base WAAF 'G' Officer and the Station 'G' Officer admired the needlework and handicraft classes, the cookery class and the lessons given in drawing, poster work and beauty treatment.

Two instructors and twelve students from the RAF Staff College visited Waterbeach during the day to study the operational organisation of the Station. PA Productions Cambridge visited the Station for the third time and gave an excellent play, 'Painted Sparrows' which was well received. The Station Concert Party, led by S/L J Healey MBE assisted the 'Salute the Soldier' campaign at Ten Mile Bank.

The brief interlude ended that evening with a raid against railways at Le Mans, with 22 crews from the squadron participating amongst the 116-strong force. One returned early for technical reasons whilst two others were unable to clearly identify the target, so brought their bombs home rather than risk the lives of French civilians. Once again the bombing height was reduced to improve accuracy, in this case to below the cloud level at 8,000feet. This was considered to be a very successful raid, with a large explosion as an ammunition carriage blew up. Two of the main lines were disrupted with trains and sheds also destroyed. It was marred, however, when the Master Bomber and his deputy's aircraft collided in the air over the target. The ORB contains a combat report from F/O Alex 'Red' Campbell, RCAF, flying his initial 'second dickey' trip with F/S John 'Toppy' Topham in DS842, JI-F. The combat report states that at 0015hrs, in the vicinity of the target, the crew spotted a Ju88 taking an interest in their aircraft which they drove off by firing at it. P/O Cedric Thomson put LL690, JI-J through a tortuous 35 minutes of corkscrewing in an ultimately successful attempt to shake off predatory night fighters. Meanwhile a hitherto successful evening's work for F/S Ted Prowles in DS822, JI-T was somewhat spoilt when they landed at RAF Bourne by mistake.

There was a more tragic outcome for LL641, JI-K, flown by F/S Edward Shearing. Having bombed the markers at 0030 hours from 7,500 feet, a

1,000lb medium capacity bomb hung up and was jettisoned safely in the English Channel near the French coast. Unfortunately the aircraft crashed on return near Newmarket, trying to effect a forced landing after having earlier suffered battle damage. No night-fighter claims related to this loss; it is believed that the damage was due to flak. Bomb aimer, F/O J Peake, RCAF, baled out successfully and rear gunner Sgt MH Smart RCAF was thrown clear, but sustained injuries. All the other members of the crew were killed. Two aircraft were also lost from the contingents of other squadrons.

Life on the Station continued the following day as Group Officer C Woodhead and Group Officer LM Crowther visited various station sections and saw WAAFs at work. A PT display was given by sixteen WAAFs under Sgt CM Fox on the sports field and there was an exhibition of drill later in the morning. In the afternoon they made a more detailed inspection of the WAAF camp. Air Commodore L Dalton-Morris, Chief Signals Officer of Bomber Command, visited the Station. Three contingents of aircrew, airmen and WAAF took part in the parade which marked the opening of the 'Salute the Soldier' week at Waterbeach village. Music was provided by the Station Military Band and the salute was taken by Lieutenant Colonel W Jayne, the Station LDA. A dance was held in the gymnasium in aid of the week, the Station Dance Band being in attendance. A Lancaster aircraft on exhibition was one of the highlights of the Waterbeach 'Salute the Soldier' Savings campaign. F/L SP Wand and members of the CTO's staff acted as guides and raised £70/0/0[20]. Duisburg was on the agenda two nights later, 21st / 22nd May, with 23 crews sent out from Waterbeach as Bomber Command returned to Germany with 532 bombers. The clouds blanketed the target area and extended to 20,000 feet meaning that sky markers were used; these soon disappeared from view into the murk. Despite this the marking and the bombing were good and the target was severely damaged. The outward route was described as 'uneventful' for the squadron, though there was moderate heavy flak over the city itself, and some crews had to orbit the target area waiting for it to be marked, which would not have gone down too well. F/O Cedric Thomson in LL690, JI-J was one pilot who found himself going around more than once: 'Our first German target was Duisberg. My wireless

[20] RAF Waterbeach ORB.

operator's diary called it 'Dante's lnfemo'. The loss rate of 6.1% was too high. 514 lost three aircraft. Having a very accurate bomb aimer we went round the target twice, each time a few thousand feet lower in order to avoid oncoming aircraft. The second time round I made it quite clear that we were not going around again!'

A combination of factors, including a delay by the controllers in directing night fighters to the main force, poor visibility with no moon and high cloud, as well as static interference on their radios, meant that the German pilots were mostly unable to intercept the stream until it was on the return route. Fighter activity was noted along the homeward leg as far as 4 degrees East, near the Dutch coast, with one crew reportedly attacked by a fighter thirty miles off the coast. This was S/Ldr Ralph Chopping, who had replaced S/Ldr Sly as 'B' Flight commander after the latter's sad demise. His aircraft LL733, JI-S was well out to sea when at 0204hrs his rear gunner F/S EJ Fox reported trace passing 200-300 feet behind the Lancaster, having been fired at what he considered to be extreme range. S/Ldr Chopping carried out a precautionary corkscrew and there was no further sign of the enemy fighter.

Meanwhile F/S Ted Prowles was back with his usual mount, DS816, JI-O, the aircraft christened 'Feodora'. At 0120hrs and again at 0204hrs his Lancaster was fired at by unidentified enemy aircraft but without ill effect. This would put DS816 in the vicinity of LL733 and there is a possibility that one fighter had fired at, and missed, both the 514 Squadron aircraft. However the night fighters had a number of successes off the Dutch coast as they pursued the bombers[21]. Notwithstanding their late arrival, the German night fighters had made up for lost time and brought down 29 of the attacking force, including three from Waterbeach. The first to fall was LL695 JI-A, flown by F/S Charlie Medland near Eindhoven. There was a subsequent disagreement between F/S Medland and his bomb aimer, F/S Les Venus, over why they were shot down, which occurred at 0138hrs after bombing the target. F/S Medland believed that they were hit by flak and set on fire but F/S Venus maintained that they had been brought down by a night fighter. In fact their loss is credited to Hptm. Martin Drewes, Stab III./NJG1, who claimed five victims that night. The aircraft apparently exploded after F/S Venus, along with the navigator, F/O Johnny Walker

[21] Nachtjagd War Diaries

and the wireless operator Sgt Les Shimmons, had managed to bale out. F/O Walker and Sgt Shimmons evaded capture with the help of the Dutch Resistance. It was believed by the surviving crew members that the flight engineer, Sgt Tony Sealtiel, had managed to get out but that his parachute failed. Neither of the gunners, Sgt Charles Rose and Sgt Benjamin Williams, survived. Remarkably, F/S Medland, who had lost consciousness, then regained it to find himself alone and trapped in the wreckage of the cockpit. He thought he was back at base and wondered why the crew had left without him. Unable to free himself, he joined F/S Venus in captivity. .DS781 JI-R, flown by P/O Bernard Windsor, crashed in the North Sea with the loss of all the crew. There are several claims by night-fighter crews for unidentified Lancasters shot down as they left the Dutch coast and it is most likely that DS781 fell victim to one of these. The only body recovered was that of the mid upper gunner Sgt Ernie Haigh, who is buried in Kiel.

The circumstances of the loss of DS633 A2-B, flown by F/S Thomas Gibson are unclear, but the squadron ORB states *'aircraft is believed to have crashed in The Wash. A fix was obtained at RAF Waterbeach at 0303 hours and the crew was ordered to jettison its bombs.'* The aircraft was possibly shot down by the Me410 intruder of Fw. Johann Trenke, who claimed three aircraft over Northern Norfolk between 0305 and 0322 hours. The aircraft shot down at 0305hrs is verified but not identified and its location is close to The Wash. There were no survivors.

Sixteen Lancasters were tasked the following night with attacking Dortmund, the first such raid for a year, though it was severely affected by the poor weather, in which icing caused problems for many aircraft. Nine of 514 Squadron's aircraft were unable to carry out their task, leaving seven to press home the attack. Fortunately all the squadron's Lancs landed safely, though three had to divert to Woodbridge. One, LL733, JI-S, flown by 'B' Flight's commander, S/Ldr Ralph Chopping, suffered damage from icing, presumably dislodged from the aircraft's propellers which smashed the cockpit canopy Perspex. Unable to climb, S/Ldr Chopping ordered his crew to bale out which all did, leaving S/Ldr Chopping to land his Lancaster at Woodbridge unassisted. Unfortunately his mid-upper gunner, Sgt Thomas Combe, was found dead on the ground, his parachute having failed to open for an unknown reason.

The weather was clear over Dortmund itself and the squadron's crews all identified and bombed the markers, noting numerous fires and occasional explosions. In fact the raid was scattered and most bombs fell in the south-eastern suburbs. The defences were described as 'slight heavy flak, with numerous searchlights acting aimlessly.' Fighters were noted over the target area only, though fighter flares were seen over most of the outbound route. Although no combats were experienced by the squadron's returning pilots, F/O Alex Campbell in LL727, A2-C had to take evasive action after an unidentified enemy aircraft was detected by Monica equipment and seen by his rear gunner, Sgt Sam Harvey. All told, eighteen aircraft were lost from the total of 375 deployed. The large-scale 'Wild Boar' activity which saw many single-engine fighters finding their own prey over the target was the final time that this tactical option was used by the Luftwaffe.

F/O Alex 'Red' Campbell RCAF was to have an interesting time while on the strength of 514 Squadron (Bruce Johnston).

The new squadron commander, W/Cdr Mike Wyatt, took up his post on 24th May. He had previously served in XV and 75(NZ) Squadrons, the latter as its commander. Returning from an operation to Turin whilst with XV Sqn, he had crash-landed his Short Stirling in Spain and had to make his own way back to England. Mike Wyatt had earned the respect of his fellow airmen every bit as much as his predecessor in 514 Squadron.

Meet the new boss. Wing Commander Mike Wyatt (second row, left) accompanies His Majesty King George VI on a visit to Waterbeach. Like his predecessor, Wyatt was a popular figure with his crews (Linda Miles).

W/Cdr Wyatt's first task was to send 17 aircraft to attack gun batteries at Boulogne. The squadron's aircraft were part of a 224-strong force which divided its efforts amongst four separate coastal gun positions. The attack on Boulogne took place between 0113hrs and 0120hrs. There was only slight flak over the target and no fighters were noted. No aircraft were lost from any of the four raids. F/O Thomas Lever, in his debrief, commented 'Request more trips like this one.' There were no results noted from any of these raids, though the attack on Boulogne cannot have been conclusive as the squadron was directed to return three nights later, on 27th / 28th May. The Station Armament Section broke all records when they managed to bomb-up successfully in spite of certain delays and difficulties in unloading bombs at the railway station. They were the only Armament Section in 33 Base to complete the process in time for the night's operation.[22] This time nine aircraft were despatched, all of which carried out the attack successfully, in the face of slightly heavier flak and the presence of night fighters. F/O Alba Fowke, flying DS826, JI-U on his third op, had an encounter with a single-engine enemy aircraft along with an Me210, the location being near Dungeness. The fighters had apparently been tailing his aircraft for some time. Two aircraft were lost from this combined raid involving 272 aircraft against five gun emplacements.

On the same evening, ten aircraft from Waterbeach were also tasked with joining 160 others to attack railway yards at Aachen. The weather over the target was clear though hazy, and dense smoke soon obscured the yards. However, crews obtained good sightings of the river, built up area and target indicators. The attack was considered a success, with the railway yards being severely damaged and traffic unable to pass through them. To further complicate matters for the defenders, a large proportion of delayed action bombs was used. The suburb of Forst was locally described as being 'razed to the ground'. The whole raid was of twelve minutes duration. There was slight to moderate light and heavy flak, though only one searchlight was seen. There was fighter activity, with flares noted from the target back to the enemy coast. F/S Ted Prowles in DS816, JI-O was approached by an unidentified twin-engine enemy aircraft at 0215hrs, shortly before bombs released. Other than that, F/S Prowles described it as a trouble-free trip. P/O RR Harvey in DS795, A2-C had a similar encounter, shaking off an FW190.

Their thirteenth operation with the squadron proved desperately unlucky for F/L Lloyd Taylor and his crew flying LL652, JI-C. Having bombed the target they were shot down at Ophasselt, near Geraardsbergen, possibly at 0256hrs by Hptm. Hans-Karl Kamp of Stab.III, NJG4, one of three victories that night for the German pilot. There were no survivors from the crew. In total, twelve Lancasters failed to return from the Aachen raid.

---

[22] RAF Waterbeach ORB

A more routine mission awaited the squadron the following evening with 21 aircraft leaving Waterbeach to attack more railway yards, this time at Angers. Crews managed to see sufficient markers to bomb despite the haze but unfortunately many bombs fell outside the target area and a total of 254 French people were killed. A Lancaster of 622 Sqn was the only bomber lost from the 126 sent out, its whole crew surviving as prisoners.

A return to Boulogne featured on the night of 30th May as fourteen aircraft from the squadron attacked the gun position with 36 other bombers. TIs were well concentrated, with most bombs landing on them, but they tended to be slightly to the North of the intended aiming point. There was a fair amount of smoke and no visuals were obtained, except of the coastline. Heavy and light flak was slight but a little more than on the previous occasion. Only three fighters were seen, two twin-engined and one single-engined. However the squadron reported no combats, and no aircraft were lost from the attacking force.

The final operation of a busy month saw sixteen Lancasters set out from Waterbeach to bomb the marshalling yards at Trappes. Crews reported their bombs as straddling the yards. However, whilst the flak was slight but accurate, fighters were much in evidence and several aircraft were reported as shot down in the area. In fact a total of four bombers were lost from the 219 deployed. On this occasion, 514 Squadron's luck held and no combats were reported, all the unit's aircraft returning unscathed.

Over the course of the month, seven Lancasters had been lost.

The Station Commander's Summary for May commented on the attrition suffered through losses and the departures of tour-expired crews: '*Operations have continued through the month at a steady pressure – even through the moon period. No. 514 Squadron has lost most of its more experienced Captains and crews, including its Commanding Officer and three Flight Commanders on posting and several others missing from operations. The squadron is getting short of Lancaster II aircraft for which replacements are no longer available and is awaiting re-equipment with Lancaster III aircraft.*

On the administrative side, efforts have been directed towards preparing the Squadron and Station for an intensified effort in the vent of the 'Second Front' opening in the near future. A comprehensive scheme for night and day operations and quick turn round of aircraft has been evolved – though some concern is felt at the shortage of armament personnel in the bomb dump.'

The beginning of June saw a continuation of Bomber Command activity over France in the final few days before the invasion. In order to ensure the squadron could deliver the goods, Air Commodore GNR Bilney OBE, Senior Armament Officer at HQ Bomber Command, visited the Station to inspect the Armament Section and the bomb dump on the first day of the month.

On 2nd June, nine aircraft were sent out as part of a 271-strong force targeting four gun positions, 514 Squadron being tasked with attacking those at Wissant in the Pas de Calais. The weather remained cloudy, though the cover was lower and thinner than the squadron had so often encountered through the winter. One aircraft descended through the cloud, breaking cover at 4700 feet, despite the odd burst of heavy flak. Only four of the squadron's aircraft felt confident in bombing, because of the desire to avoid casualties amongst the population they were trying to liberate. S/L William Devas, 'A' Flight Commander in LL728, JI-B, felt that the success of the attack had been difficult to ascertain but he thought that the red Target Indicators had been too far inland. All 514 Squadron's aircraft returned safely though there was one casualty amongst the overall force.

In the early hours of 6th June, D-Day, 21 Lancasters left Waterbeach to attack gun batteries at Ouisterham, in Normandy. In total, 1012 bombers were sent to a number of targets guarding the beaches that were about to be occupied by Allied ground troops. The Station ORB recorded: *'W/C G Bray of the 'Daily Express' and Mr. Normacott of The Times flew on squadron aircraft on the Ouistreham op on the early morning of 6/6/44. Their aircraft flew below cloud to enable the crews to have a good view of the D-Day shipping movements. Aircraft were turned round and held on four hours readiness. The news of the opening of the Second Front was received in the Station with great enthusiasm. The Station Commander read out General Eisenhower's message from Supreme Command Headquarters and the tonic effect of the news was reflected in the work of all sections on the Camp.'* P/O Cedric Thomson RAAF reflected on the events of 6th June: 'June began with the D-Day landing. I remember that all aircrew were given revolvers to wear. Then we were briefed in the evening of the 4th June, but shortly afterwards the trip was delayed whereupon the station was closed and the RAF Regiment deployed their troops around the aerodrome preventing anyone leaving. We all guessed that the raid was part of D-Day attack as we had never seen so many senior RAF Officers at a briefing before.

ln addition we noticed that all aircraft had black and white stripes painted on their wings and we had never been on a trip when the target was to be bombed at dawn. We were not told that this trip was the invasion but that if we saw a large number of aircraft and ships around we weren't to be surprised. Twenty one 514 Squadron aircraft took part. After final briefing and a flying supper of greasy eggs and bacon, we took off at 0335hrs, set course at 0409, and crossed the coast just east of Beachy Head at 0435. We crossed the French coast at 0507hrs and bombed a minute later at Ouistreham where we destroyed some gun emplacements. We turned east round Le Havre and crossed the coast at 0526hrs on the way home. We were privileged to see a massive display of ship of all shapes and sizes and a huge number of aircraft including gliders being towed. The gunfire on and around the beaches was spectacular.'

The bombing height was around 9,000 feet with the markers seen to be concentrated, although some were slightly east of the aiming point, possibly in the sea. Reports from returning crews indicated that the bombing had been good, though the misplaced markers had also attracted some bombing. The force dropped some five thousand tons of bombs on the night of 5th / 6th June, a new record. Only one enemy fighter was seen in the target area. Three aircraft were lost though all the Waterbeach crews returned safely.

F/S Bob Armit was bomb aimer in LL716, A2-G flown by 'C' Flight Commander S/Ldr Derek Stewart: 'The fifth of June 1944 seemed to me just like any other day on the squadron at Waterbeach. Our crew had been detailed on three operations during the last week of May, but strangely, nothing in the last five days. I was lounging on the grass outside the flight hut with a cigarette and the dog-eared daily paper when our mid-upper gunner came over and sat down beside me.

"We are on tonight, Junior..." he said quietly. "Briefing is at a quarter past one."

"That's a bit early in the afternoon," I answered. "It must be a blooming long one. Any idea where we're going?"

"No idea. And it's in the morning!"

"Crikey! Briefing half past one in the morning .... we will just about be airborne when the sun comes up. It will be like doing a daylight."
Briefing didn't seem the same as usual. The various officers that came onto the dais and said their own particular piece seemed to be energised and bubbling and yet somehow vague. Instructions at times were not as specific as they were normally. The target was to be Ouistreham which was right near the French channel coast.
There were no details of any precise aiming point or what the quarry would be. The navigator would tell us en-route. Our operational height was to be ten thousand five hundred feet. This was pretty low. We would normally go in at twice that height.
My job as the air bomber during the journey to and from the target was to try to obtain visual fixes by map reading, that is, if it was possible to see the ground. I collected my maps which were issued at briefing and were only enough to cover the route. I pencilled in the route and realised that the only map reading that I would be able to do would be over Blighty. This certainly seemed to be a piece of cake. Take off was to be at 03.45 am.
Over the Channel I concentrated on checking the sky for fighters. We must have been about ten or twelve miles out from the French coast when I saw a small break in the cloud showing a circle of dark, dark sea. As it passed beneath the aircraft, just slightly to port, I wondered what the white spots were. I looked hard at it and then realised that they were not spots, but more like tadpoles and were the wakes of a flotilla of small boats, all on a zig-zag course. Then it was gone. The gap had closed. I was about to switch on my intercom to ask if any others of the crew had seen them, when it dawned on me that this was an invasion fleet. That would explain a lot of things. I still thought, in my excitement, that I would tell the lads and give them something to cheer about, but my second thought was that if we got shot down, and survived, then Jerry would have seven of us as a possible source of information. So I kept quiet.
A few minutes later the navigator gave the pilot the details of the time and distance from the target, and he started to lose height gently to come down through the cloud. It was my clue to start to get things organised for the bombing run. As we broke cloud I looked around to see where we were and spotted two ships slightly ahead and to port and assumed that they were just rounding the headland from Le Havre. They would make a good target, I thought, but a heck of a job to hit them from this height. However,

it seemed that someone down there had exactly the same thoughts about us, for as I looked at it the whole of the deck of one ship started to twinkle as they opened fire and the flak started to climb slowly, slowly up towards us. It came slowly closer and closer, then suddenly appeared to change speed and shot past us like an express train. By the time that the first shots were closing in the second ship had opened up on us too. The skipper did not need any advice from me about evasive action. "I'm going back up" he called over the intercom and as he said it the nose of the Lancaster lifted as if in disdain and within seconds the cloud enveloped us again.

This iconic image shows Bomber Command's contribution to Operation Overlord, as more than one thousand bombers attack gun emplacements guarding the Normandy beaches.

By now we were too close to the target to stay up in cloud. We dropped down below once more by which time the flak ships were paying attention to someone else. This was the moment when all my thoughts had to be concentrated on the shoreline. My mind started to rapidly take in the detail. The first thing, of course, was to see where the flak ships were, so I looked east into the wide mouth of the river Seine but could not see them. My gaze followed the coastline slowly towards the west searching for a suitable target. The navigator told me that this was what we would do a little earlier.

I became somewhat puzzled as I looked along the beaches a little to starboard because they seemed to be obscured by a parallel line of fog or smoke. I followed this along to the western end where I saw, protruding from the smoke, bow first, almost the whole of a major warship, with all guns firing at the shore. A closer look at the scene showed that there were another four or five other warships within the smoke, in line astern, and all firing at the beaches as fast as they could load. It was an incredible sight but no time to watch it, even though it took only a few seconds. It had to be back to the business in hand.

We were so close to the coast that it was imperative to pick a target so that I would have enough time and distance to manoeuvre onto it for an accurate run. It was not a good idea to go around again, for I would not be popular with the rest of the crew.

Slightly to port I picked out a river, or canal, which ran into the sea through a series of locks and I thought that that would be appropriate. I gave the pilot directions for a turn to port and then a gentle turn to starboard so that we were running up to it quite nicely. It needed only a small "left ..... left..." to bring the aircraft square onto it. “Bomb doors open." Straight and level for a few long seconds, "steady.....steady... ..." and the approach was good. I pressed the bomb tit just ahead of the locks and the first bomb exploded in the sea, dead in line. The second was just in front of the first lock gates and the next was spot on target. The rest went straight down the waterway. I was exhilarated by the success, and have often wondered since how useful that was to the oncoming battle. We carried on straight and level long enough to get a photograph and then did a gentle climbing turn to port, up into the cloud again and onto course for base.

We landed at 06.37 am. With everything switched off we gathered our kit and climbed out, walked a short distance from dear old 'G' George, sat down on the grass and lit a cigarette while we waited for the crew bus. The first cigarette was sheer bliss.

Back at the briefing hut we collected our mug of coffee and tot of rum, and waited for a table to be free for our de-briefing. It was soon our turn and it was at this moment that l decided to tell what l had seen on the sea and on the target. Standing behind our Intelligence Officer was a tall Squadron Leader who never spoke at all during the session but took a keen interest in everything that we had to say. After our de-briefing was completed, as we started to walk away, he came over to me and asked me to repeat what

I had seen. He then asked my name and where I lived. And that was that. I must say that I wondered, with some trepidation, what it was all about. But now it was bacon and eggs and straight into the pit.
On my way to the mess before lunch, one of the lads saw me wandering along and shouted out "Hey, Junior, you are in the paper." He told me that I had got myself in The Times. With almost complete disbelief, I had a little chuckle and carried on to the mess. I found the Times and saw it on one of the inner pages as he had said. That Squadron Leader this morning was obviously a war correspondent, and this was his story.
With the usual reporter's flair for making the items sound better, he had put me in as being the first man across. I laughed but was very pleased to accept the accolade.
Forty five years later, on the anniversary of that event, The Times produced a souvenir print of the 6th June 1944, but it was obviously a later edition. As more facts had come in on that day, the story had begun to fall into place, so I could no longer be the first man across. I didn't mind, but it had been lovely while it lasted. 1 have been to the Newspaper Museum at Colindale to see if that first edition is on file but no such luck, and now I don't suppose that I shall ever see again that version where 1 was the first man across on 'D' Day.'
The crews had little rest that day, preparing for a night raid that evening, which saw seventeen of the squadron's number attack railway facilities at Lisieux, just behind the beachhead. As was becoming the norm, the fleet of 1065 bombers was tasked with a number of different targets as Bomber Command adapted to its new role in tactical support to the ground forces. All 514 Squadron aircraft landed at base on completion of their duty. There was broken cloud down to 6,000 feet at the target and crews bombed below cloud. Red TIs were seen until 0142 hours. Most of the time the Master Bomber was unintelligible because of other aircraft transmitting on the intercom. Many bomb bursts were seen on the town along with a few fires. A little light flak only was seen and no searchlights, some light flak on the coast and from the sea. One Ju88 and 2 unidentified fighters were sighted. LL677, A2-E, flown by F/S CS Johnson, reported assisting in the destruction of an Me110. *'Immediately after Captain had seen cannon fire to starboard beam and Mosquito in same direction, front gunner (F/S E Lush) reported Me110 on starboard bow level at a range of 300 to 400 yards with port engine on fire. As E/A crossed in front of Lancaster from*

starboard to port, both Front and Mid Upper Gunners (Sgt J Poad) opened fire and strikes were observed on E/A by Gunners, W/Op and Captain. E/A was immediately enveloped in flames and exploded just before crashing in the sea where it continued to burn for a considerable period. E/A claimed as destroyed.' With varying weather conditions over the different targets accuracy was always going to be compromised. Unfortunately this resulted in a number of civilian casualties in several locations. Six aircraft were lost in the attack on Caen alone, from a total of eleven that failed to return from the combined raids. Complications with TIs delayed the attack and gave time for defences to be readied. The crews were forced to bomb from 3,000 feet and so experienced extraordinary amounts of flak and the losses that came with it. The railway yards in Lisieux were badly damaged.

On 7th June 337 aircraft, including 18 from Waterbeach, went to Massey Palaiseau, a suburb of Paris, railway facilities once again being in their sights. The strategy was to deny the Germans an easy way of bringing reinforcements to the invasion area, and this was to prove decisive. It was not without considerable cost, as this night was to show; 27 bombers would not return, representing 8.3% of the force. The marking was reported to be concentrated, as was the bombing, despite the light-calibre flak which was described as 'particularly vicious' in the target area. There was also a great deal of fighter activity, and combats were numerous. P/O Ted Cossens RNZAF in LL624, JI-R had bombed at 0216hrs, sustaining flak damage to the Lancaster's starboard wing when, a minute later, an Me109 was seen by the gunners, F/L Herbert Wright in the mid upper turret and Sgt Peter Brown in the rear. As P/O Cossens desperately tried to evade the fighter, it fired a burst into the rear turret, resulting in Sgt Brown losing his leg and the turret being rendered unserviceable. P/O Cossen's debrief report noted that he was 'too busy elsewhere to pay attention to the raid.' Unwelcome attention was thrust upon P/O Herbert Delacour RAAF at an even earlier stage, as he was still outbound at 0205hrs in LL678, A2-L when his aircraft came under fire from an unidentified single-engined assailant, the crew noticing trace passing underneath their aircraft from the port bow. P/O Delacour was able to dive into cloud and the fighter was not seen again.

Another New Zealander pilot whose Lancaster came under fire was P/O LM Petry in LL677, A2-E, homeward bound at 0240hrs. On this occasion, the enemy aircraft was reported to be a Do217, rather than one of the more common fighter types, though this unusual distinction was probably at the front of the crew members' minds at the time. Not least of their worries was the serious injury to their rear gunner, F/S A MacLean, sustained when his turret was rendered unserviceable by a flak burst. It is believed that F/S MacLean lost his leg as a result of wounds.

Also busy was F/S WM Watkins in DS842, A2-F who had two encounters. Whilst on the bombing run at 0212hrs, the mid upper gunner Sgt P Dawson was doubtless mortified when he saw a Ju88 in an attacking position some fifty to one hundred yards away. Shouting for an immediate corkscrew, Sgt Dawson, along with Sgt B Ferries in the rear turret, returned fire as the night fighter tried to bring them down, its own trace passing very close to the latter crew man. The Ju88 was unable to follow the Lancaster which therefore evaded its foe. At 0258hrs, having managed to bomb, Sgt Ferries spotted an Me410 trailing them at a distance of 300 yards. Again, a relatively uncommon type in the night fighter role, the Me410 was more frequently used as an intruder, a point which again would not have been at the forefront of the rear gunner's mind as he fired on the stalker. The fighter broke away without pressing home its attack.

On his 24th operation the irrepressible F/O Lou Greenburgh was flying LL727 A2-C, joined on this occasion by a 'second dickey' pilot, W/O Les Sutton. Lou Greenburgh had enjoyed a relatively quiet few trips since his earlier endeavours and on this occasion made a good bombing run in what was considered exceptional visibility, with a full moon and no cloud. As the bomb aimer, F/S Eric Rippingale, called 'Bombs about to go', Sgt Fred Carey in the mid upper turret called 'There is a fighter on our tail, corkscrew to port, go!' F/O Greenburgh waited two or three seconds to allow the bombs to fall, despite the continued urging from Sgt Carey to take immediate evasive action. With the bombs gone, Greenburgh put the aircraft into a violent corkscrew, seeing tracer going past his head and heard strikes on the fuselage. He put the aircraft into a steeper dive just to be on the safe side. But further strikes hit the starboard outer engine which cut out. Immediately a fire broke out behind the starboard inner engine. This spread rapidly in both directions and the pilot could see the bare ribs of the wing, leading him to fear an explosion from the petrol tanks. None occurred, but the hydraulics had been damaged and the mid upper turret was unserviceable as was Sgt Carey's intercom.

F/O Greenburgh pulled the Lancaster out of its dive at between six and seven thousand feet having successfully shaken off the fighter. The fire

The indomitable F/O Lou Greenburgh with his original crew. Clockwise from left: F/S Connie Drake, F/S Gordon Stromberg, Sgt Les Weddle, Sgt Fred Carey, Sgt Pat Butler, F/O Lou Greenburgh, Sgt Don Bament (Ed Greenburgh)

was still burning in the wing, flames licking back just behind the cowling of the inner engine which, remarkably, was still functioning satisfactorily. Greenburgh began to climb and, when a fighter flare was dropped ahead he made a detour round it. He saw that some of the crew had put their parachutes on whilst W/O Sutton had left his seat and was standing next to him. Greenburgh remarked 'I think we shall have to be getting out of this, fellows,' though he did not intend this to be an order to bale out. However, and perhaps understandably, the crew interpreted it accordingly and did precisely that. As the fire appeared to be abating slightly, Greenburgh called out 'Hold it!' but by this time F/S Rippingale, W/O Sutton, F/S Ronald Fox the navigator and Sgt Frank Collingwood, the flight engineer, were already earthbound.

F/O Greenburgh flew on without them, trying to avoid defended areas as much as he could, applying full aileron to correct the swing to starboard. He was about to feather the starboard outer engine, its drag contributing much to the aircraft's enthusiasm for turning right, when the Lancaster was coned in searchlights. He saw a wall of light flak rising to meet him and heard one of his remaining crew ask 'Do we bale out or don't we?' He told the crew to hold on and dived straight towards the searchlights, the flak passing the aircraft without striking home. The searchlights could not

keep track and at about five thousand feet he emerged into darkness and tried to regain some altitude.
Ten seconds later the Lancaster was coned again so he repeated his previous manoeuvre, which had served them so well. This time, the flak was even more intense, coming from all directions as he levelled out at three thousand feet, and the fuselage and one rudder were hit. With no rudder control now he tried to climb even though the Lancaster was vibrating badly. On a more positive note the fire in the starboard wing appeared to be burning itself out, so he told the crew that he would take them home. He told F/S 'Strommy' Stromberg, the wireless operator, to send out an emergency signal and obtain a fix, in case they had to ditch. He then trimmed the Lancaster, feathered the troublesome starboard outer engine and headed roughly north east. Sgt Andy Woosnam in the rear turret then called out that they were being followed by a Ju88 fighter showing a red navigation light. F/O Greenburgh immediately put the aircraft into a steep dive and heard strikes on the fuselage, which filled with smoke.
The Lancaster obstinately swung to starboard and the starboard inner engine started to belch smoke. At that point. Strommy told his pilot that it might be a good idea to get out. Greenburgh ordered him back to his post but Strommy persisted, so he was given permission to bale out, which he did. With his aircraft still drifting to starboard despite his valiant efforts, Greenburgh decided that the time had come to stop trying to control it, so immediately ordered his gunners to bale out as well. Sgt Woosnam did not hang around to argue and left straight away but there was no response from Sgt Fred Carey in the mid upper turret and it appeared that he had left the scene as well. The fighter made another pass, tracer flying over Greenburgh's head, so he undid his seat harness and, wearing a seat type parachute, wasted no time in diving through the escape hatch at a height of about 1,200 feet. He pulled the ripcord at once, losing his boots and escape kit in the process and landed very shortly afterwards, about ten miles north of Froissy, one hundred yards from the wreckage of the Lancaster. He later found the two gunners safely on the ground.

The Ju88 night fighter was flown by Hptm Herbert Lorenz, of 1./NJG2 who was credited with shooting down LL727 at 0255hrs. Lou Greenburgh, W/O Sutton, F/S Fox and F/S Rippingale all evaded capture. Sgt Carey (mid upper gunner, Sgt Collingwood, the flight engineer, Sgt Woosnam and F/S Stromberg were all captured. Sadly, having escaped the burning Lancaster, Strommy Stromberg was apparently caught up in telegraph wires and sustained injuries from which he died the following day. The crew members who successfully evaded capture returned to England around the end of August. F/O Greenburgh was promoted to Flight Lieutenant and posted to No 1332 Heavy Conversion Unit at Longtown near Carlisle and then Nutts Corner, Northern Ireland. His adventurous tour with 514 Squadron was concluded. Les Sutton's time with the unit continued, having been promoted to Flying Officer on his eventual return from his somewhat extended 'second dickey' trip. He resumed ops on 30th October 1944 with a trip to Wesseling and subsequently completed 39 operations, surviving the war.

F/O Les Sutton and some of his crew on his return to the squadron after his prolonged and arduous 'second dickey' trip with his friend F/O Lou Greenburgh. They survived the war.

P/O Bill McGown, in DS822, JI-T, was approaching the end of his tour of operations, which had included the squadron's first attack on 3rd November 1943. The aircraft is believed to have been coned and hit by flak leaving the target area. The Lancaster was then shot down by an Me110 flown by Major Walter Borchers. German soldiers attempted to shoot at P/O McGown as he descended by parachute, but he survived and, indeed, evaded capture. On his return to England, he transferred to another squadron, flying Mosquitoes.
Sgt Jack Clarke, the flight engineer, initially evaded capture but was betrayed to the Gestapo and sent to Fresnes Prison in Paris. He was amongst 168 allied aircrew who were sent to Buchenwald from French prisons. Sgt Jack Clarke and his colleagues were spared and transferred

LM734, shown here in July 1944 bearing code JI-O, survived 57 operations with the squadron. She survived the war (WMHM).

to Stalag Luft III as well. His health was greatly affected, probably by TB. A full account, involving three further crewmen from 514 Squadron, is given later in this book.
The crew's rear gunner, F/S Charlie Guy, was one of twins, his brother Bert being rear gunner for F/L Walter Chitty. He was killed, along with the wireless operator, W/O Kenneth Bryan and the mid-upper gunner, F/S John Boanson. P/O Lyndon Lewis, the bomb aimer, was on the run for a month prior to being captured. He survived the war and remained in the RAF, retiring in 1969 as a Wing Commander.
A change of executive responsibility occurred on 8th June with F/L LC Blomfield taking over as Adjutant from his colleague F/L M Stevens, who had carried out the role since the squadron was formed. That night the squadron was in action attacking more railway facilities at Fougeres.

Waterbeach contributed ten Lancasters to the attacking force of 483. The weather was clear over the target and crews were able to see and bomb the TIs. However these ran out at about 0025hrs and the Master Bomber ordered the remaining crews to bomb a large yellow fire instead. P/O Douglas Woods RAAF, in LL620, JI-T reported bombing from 4,000 feet, seeing trucks blown into the air as bombs fell on the railway tracks. Crews reported that flak was negligible and the squadron emerged unscathed from the raid, although four other aircraft failed to return.

9th June saw W/C PH Alington AFC and a party of five officers from the Empire Central Flying Training School, Hullavington, visited the Station to study the operational activities of 514 Squadron and to discuss flying training requirements of operational aircrew.[23]

After a night off, offensive activity resumed on the night of 10th June with various railway targets again being selected, as Bomber Command continued its task of disrupting the reinforcement of German defences. 514 Squadron's task was to attack facilities at Dreux, west of Paris. Nineteen aircraft were despatched from Waterbeach and attacked the target. It was noted that flak was light and there were no searchlights. There was, as at Massey-Palaiseau, considerable fighter activity and several crews submitted combat reports on their return.

At 0106hrs, on the return leg, F/O Henry Chapman, the squadron's Gunnery Leader, was in the mid upper turret of LL734, JI-G, flown by F/S John Whitwood when his colleague in the rear turret, Sgt Thomas Birch saw an unidentified single engine fighter two hundred yards behind their Lancaster. Both gunners fired on the enemy aircraft as F/S Whitwood threw the Lancaster into a corkscrew and both gunners, along with Sgt D Cargill, the wireless operator, saw a ball of fire fall to the ground and explode. They claimed the enemy aircraft as destroyed.

Three minutes later, F/S Arthur Dymott, rear gunner in LL677, A2-E, flown by F/S Charles Johnson, saw a nearby Lancaster come under attack from an Me410, which he fired at. The enemy pilot broke off his attack to concentrate on F/S Johnson's aircraft instead. F/S Dymott exchanged fire with the night fighter, scoring hits and starting a fire in its port engine. Joined by F/S James Poad in the mid upper turret in firing at the enemy, the Lancaster's gunners scored more hits on the Me410 which was

---

[23] RAF Waterbeach ORB

resolutely continuing to attack. It became enveloped in flames and was seen to explode on the ground by members of the crew in LL677 as well as other bombers.

P/O Ronald Harvey in DS795, A2-J and crew also came under attack, from a Ju88 which caused damage to the starboard flap, wingtip and tyre. The mid upper gunner, F/S DF Acaster, had been dazzled by trace so was unable to see but W/O ED Reid in the rear turret fired 400 rounds at the Ju88 which decided that discretion was the better part of valour, and left the scene.

Meanwhile, at about the same time as the above combats, W/O Cyril Williams in LL492, JI-A took evasive action when he saw an unidentified twin-engined aircraft which opened fire. His gunners opened fire but no hits were claimed.

The final event of the night for 514 Squadron's crews was at 0153hrs when, in the vicinity of the Channel Islands, Sgt W Aston and Sgt AW Hanson, respectively rear and mid upper gunners in LL666, JI-D, saw an Me109. They opened fire, believing that they hit the fighter, but lost sight of it in the ensuing corkscrew, laid on for their benefit by their pilot, F/S Richard Pick.

'Nachtjagd War Diaries' states that a Ju88, one Me410, one Me110 and 'two Me109s' were claimed as destroyed by bomber gunners with five other unspecified night fighters claimed as possibly shot down or damaged. Fifteen bombers were lost in total.

On 11th June, with Bomber Command again tasked with attacking several railway facilities, Nantes was the target for fifteen Waterbeach aircraft, on what was a cloudy night. Despite the mixture of light and heavy flak, the Master Bomber instructed crews to bomb below the cloud base, which was given as 2,500 feet, which over more strenuously defended targets would be deemed suicidally low. From the total attacking force of 329 bombers, only four were lost, none from Waterbeach, though W/O Cyril Williams had to bring LL692, JI-A home on three engines.

On the evening of 12th June, seventeen apprehensive crews watched the Waterbeach briefing room curtain draw back to reveal the target as Gelsenkirchen. This raid marked the start of the Oil Plan, which was to feature prominently in the squadron's plans in the future. The Nordstern plant, known in German as Gelsenberg, was a synthetic oil production plant using forced labour from Buchenwald Concentration Camp. The oil plant was extensively damaged with local reports estimating some 1,500 bombs hit the target. This caused the loss of around 1,000 tons of fuel per day, for a period of several weeks. The refinery was robustly defended, with heavy-calibre flak moderate to intense, along with much searchlight activity. Locals reported that six German schoolboy 'Flakhilfers' were killed, the Nazis having resorted to using teenagers to man the anti-aircraft defences. Whereas the stream had been relatively unmolested on its way to the target, circumstances conspired to put the bombers in the path of hordes of night fighters on their return, resulting in the loss of seventeen bombers in total.

Two combats were reported by returning pilots. The first of these was F/L William McFetridge in LL694, JI-E at 0047hrs whilst en route to the target. Sgt Ron Britnell in the rear turret saw an Me410 by the light of fighter flares and opened fire as the Lancaster corkscrewed desperately. Sgt WH Corney in the mid upper turret joined in, and the fighter broke away.

At 0141hrs, half an hour into the homeward journey, Sgt Peter Dawson, mid upper gunner in LL670, A2-K reported an unidentified twin-engines aircraft 300 yards to starboard and ordered his pilot F/S William Watkins to corkscrew starboard, opening fire as the Lancaster dived away. The enemy aircraft followed the Lancaster through three complete corkscrews, during which time Sgt Dawson fired at it as much as possible, though the fighter did not itself shoot at the Lancaster. Sgt Dawson was reduced to one gun, the other having suffered a stoppage, whilst rear gunner Sgt Bernard Ferries was mostly unable to bring his own Brownings to bear as the fighter was too far above, though he did manage to get one short burst in. Both gunners saw bullets strike the enemy fighter, which started to trail smoke and fall away into the sea where it crashed in flames. The official Luftwaffe records of fighter losses have not been found so it is not possible to verify the claims made by the gunners for the destruction of the aircraft stated.

Two of 514 Squadron's crews were amongst the seventeen lost from the 303 sent on the raid. P/O Bertie Delacour RAAF and his crew in LL678, A2-L were shot down at 0124hrs at Zuid Loo, 3 km south east of Bathmen, Netherlands. 'Nachtjagd War Diaries' credits Hptm Gerhard Friedrich of I/NJG6 with shooting down LL678. P/O Delacour's crew were approaching the end of their tour, having completed 25 operations with five others aborted, whilst F/O Alex Phillips was on his 'second dickey'

trip. The Lancaster was attacked by a night fighter and set on fire. Ordered by P/O Delacour to bale out, Sgt Gerry Martin, flight engineer, saw that the bomb aimer, F/S George Palamountain, was no longer in the nose of the aircraft and presumed that he had managed to escape, and went through the hatch without further delay. Of the other crew members, only Sgt 'Pop' Williams, the mid upper gunner, manage to get out of the blazing aircraft alive. It crashed minutes later with at least four of the crew still inside. P/O Delacour, from Queensland, Australia, was twenty years old.
DS818, JI-Q, which bore the name 'Maggie', was hit by flak, possibly over the target, and damaged. As a result the aircraft was a relatively easy target for one of more than one hundred marauding night fighters which had been directed into the bomber stream as it made its way home over Holland. There has been no verification, but Dutch sources consider that Lt Ewald-Werner Hittler of 3./NJG1 was the most likely German pilot to have claimed DS818. The Lancaster was flown by P/O Derek Duncliffe, another comparative veteran about two-thirds of the way through his tour. The pilot along with bomb aimer, F/S Harry Bourne, and flight engineer Sgt Peter Cooper, were able to escape the aircraft which was on fire. F/S Bourne broke his leg when he landed in a beech tree whilst Sgt Cooper insisted on going to the wreckage of the Lancaster in the forlorn hope of rescuing his mates. He was taken prisoner when the Germans also turned up. P/O Duncliffe was able to remain hidden by the Dutch Resistance until the country was liberated, and he eventually returned to England.
On 14th June, the squadron went back to France, tasked with bombing the harbour at Le Havre, the base for German E-boats and other light naval forces which potentially threatened the supply convoys supporting the Normandy beach head. The raid was in two waves, the first, in the evening, being carried out in daylight as the summer solstice approached. It was the first daylight operation for Bomber Command since May 1943. 514 Squadron's aircraft participated in the second wave, which bombed at around 0115hrs. Both waves were escorted by Spitfires of 11 Group, ensuring that only one Lancaster was lost. All crews bombed on markers, chiefly red and green as instructed by Master Bomber. The dock area was illuminated by fires started in the northern part of the harbour earlier in the attack and by numerous explosions which lasted throughout the attacks, bombs were seen falling in the dock area. Flak was negligible and confined to light tracer.

At 0115hrs, F/L Marcus Dods was flying LL731, JI-L over the target when his rear gunner, Sgt RK Redfern, saw an Me110 approaching very fast from behind and below. He opened fire and shouted for the Pilot to corkscrew. The Me110 also opened fire whilst the rear gunner continued to engage it. Having passed the Lancaster, the enemy fighter then turned and came back for another go, once more coming under fire from Sgt Redfern, who noted numerous strikes on the Messerschmitt. The enemy pilot then gave up on LL731 as a bad job and left the scene.

Another senior pilot to get uncomfortably close to the action was 'B' Flight's commander, S/Ldr Ralph Chopping in LL733, JI-S. His gunners saw a FW190 six hundred yards away and opened fire on the enemy as S/Ldr Chopping took the usual evasive action. Both measures were effective as the fighter was not seen again.

F/S Charles Johnson, in LL677, A2-E found his aircraft under attack, notwithstanding the presence of escorts. At 0124hrs, whilst over the English Channel, his rear gunner, F/S Arthur Dymott, saw an Me110 attacking a Lancaster behind their own, so fired at the night fighter. The Luftwaffe pilot promptly forgot about his target and climbed to attack LL677 instead. His trace passed very close to the Lanc with F/S Dymott firing back. On Dymott's fourth burst of fire, the enemy aircraft burst into flames and headed back towards France. F/S Dymott continued to fire at the fighter which then dived into the ground and exploded. Whilst the enemy fighter was falling away in flames, Sgt James Poad in the mid upper turret, who had been unable to bring his own guns to bear in the combat, saw another twin-engined aircraft, type unknown, 250 yards off to starboard. This new foe fired at LL677 so Sgt Poad returned fire as F/S Johnson immediately corkscrewed out of harm's way. The enemy aircraft was not seen again. Once again, no records exist to corroborate or disprove F/S Dymott's claim of one enemy fighter destroyed.

The unrelenting pressure continued on the night of 15th June, as did the crews' ordeals by combat . Seventeen aircraft of 514 Squadron attacked the railway yards at Valenciennes, in Northern France. As the cloud cover was ten tenths, the Master Bomber ordered crews to descend below it to bomb. Although the markers were scattered the Master Bomber coordinated activities to achieve a concentrated attack. There was an absence of flak and searchlights over the target, but fighters featured once again. F/O Robert Jones in LL734, JI-G found his aircraft was the target of a rocket

Experience gained in 26 operations could not save P/O Ernie Kingham and his crew, who were shot down returning from the raid on Valenciennes (Kingham family).

projectile between Valenciennes and Cambrai, but prompt manoeuvring meant that he was able to avoid catastrophe.

The force of 224 bombers, divided between Lens and Valenciennes, was to lose eleven of its number, five from the Valenciennes raid including two from 514 Squadron. P/O Ernie Kingham and his crew were on their 26th operation, mostly in LL790 JI-J in which aircraft they were this night. They were attacked, probably at 0052hrs by an Me110 flown by Oblt. Peter Ehrhardt of 9/NJG5. The aircraft came down between Iwuy (Nord) and Rieux-en-Cambresis, 9 km from Cambrai. There were no survivors from the experienced crew. The Germans allowed six members of the crew to be laid to rest in local cemeteries, but denied even this courtesy to F/S Ben Bloom, the wireless operator, who was Jewish. It is believed that his body was disposed of unceremoniously in local woodland and it was never located.

DS816, JI-O, christened 'Feodora' was the favoured mount of F/S Ted Prowles and crew, who were shot down at much the same time and place as the Kingham crew were lost and F/O Jones' aircraft came under attack.

It was probably the Me110 flown by Hptm Hubert Rauh of Stab II/|NJG4 that accounted for the Prowles crew, on their sixteenth op, and DS816, which crashed at Croisilles.

The only survivor was the navigator, F/O Arnold Morrison RAAF, who later wrote to the parents of his friend Sgt Harry Osborn, the flight engineer. His letter gave an account of the incident: *'We had, as you know, bombed the railway marshalling yards at Valenciennes in the north of France. We hit the target very solidly, as usual, having an Al bomb aimer, and had turned for the run out of the French coast. It was a very dark night with no light at all below us and just a very small amount in the northern sky. Ted, the pilot, said that there was a small layer of cloud just above us then, and he was going to climb just above it so that the gunners would have some little reflected light from the clouds to assist them.*

Just then a night fighter, which must have been following us for a fair while, opened fire and hit us in the port wing (the left hand one, looking forward). Ted took immediate action to avoid it, but he had hit us too hard and the whole wing was a mass of fire. Ted then said that he could not maintain height, and said 'Bale out chaps. I'll see you later'. Harry helped Ted on with his chute, and then put his own on. I put my pack on also and stood behind Harry. Meanwhile, the bomb aimer was struggling to get the escape hatch open and then he turned around and looked up at us with his palms upwards, telling us that it was jammed - apparently by cannon shells, or splinters from them. We were then very low and losing height quickly and the fire was getting worse, and we realised that we hadn't much chance. Ted, Harry and I looked at each other and gave the thumbs up sign - our farewell. Then we hit the ground and all I remember is a red flash in front of my eyes - I didn't feel any pain and I'm quite positive that Harry and the rest of the lads did not feel anything either. I don't know how I escaped with my life – I had only cuts and scratches and a slight concussion. I woke 2 hours later, right in the middle of a field, and set out to find the other lads, but because of the concussion, I was very light headed and wandered around until daylight, when there was no sign of the aeroplane.

The French people I met later told me that the lads were given a beautiful funeral, and 2,500 people attended. They were buried in the British cemetery at Croiselles, in the Pas de Calais, the only servicemen from the Second World War buried there. They held a special mass in Arras

Cathedral also, for our lads, and the same number of people came to pay their last respects and tributes.
I was gratified that the last observances on the chaps who were my best friends, were carried out by the wonderfully grateful and very kind French people. They were, I think, as grief stricken as I was about the lads' deaths - their regard for the lads or the RAF was really something wonderful to see.
I shall never completely lose the sense of loss that I have had since it happened - I know that I shall always feel proud to have flown against the Hun with Harry and the other lads - they were as fine a crew as the RAF has produced - they were thought very highly of by the Wing Commander - he had complete faith in them. I honestly think that Harry was the coolest member of the crew. On our first trip - to the Ruhr - we ran into some trouble and had to come home on 3 engines, and Harry's prompt and efficient handling of the matter undoubtedly saved us from having an engine on fire. He was always such a great source of help to the pilot, particularly during landings, that Ted never had to worry about or question the engine settings etc., and believe me that was very important.'
F/O Morrison evaded capture and eventually returned to the UK. He was discharged from the RAAF as a Flight Lieutenant and received the DFC for evading capture. Montdidier's railway facilities provided the next target for the Waterbeach contingent when, on 17th June, thirteen aircraft attempted to bomb through ten tenths cloud. The Master Bomber was described as indistinct, and no clear orders were given, with the result that only three of the squadron's aircraft were able to bomb before fleet was ordered back to base after only a dozen aircraft in total had released their bombs. On this occasion there was little or no resistance over the target. Only one aircraft was lost from the 317 deployed against Montdidier and another target in this combined raid. Several crews reported sightings of flying bombs on the return leg.
Of particular note was the squadron's first deployment of a Packard Merlin-powered Lancaster Mk.III, PB143, JI-B which was flown by W/O Norman Jennings and his crew. Following the realization that there would be plenty of Merlins to go round, production of the Mk.II had, by now, ceased. Replacement Mk.II Lancasters were accordingly scarce, so the

F/O David Gray and crew were one of the squadron's original crews. The morning after the Rimeux raid of 24th June 1944, they celebrated the end of their tour of operations with DS813, JI-N, 'Marg'. Sadly 'Marg' was not so lucky, being lost on 28th July en route to Stuttgart with the crew of F/L Alba Fowke (WMHM).

squadron would gradually re-equip over the coming months, starting with 'A' Flight.

After a break of three days, the squadron returned to action on 21st June with a marked change of strategy. The flying bombs noted by crews on their previous outing required a prompt and effective response, which meant a new onslaught by Bomber Command. Raids were now to be carried out in broad daylight, this now being feasible because of the Allies' effective air supremacy, at least over Northern France by day. As it was the middle of summer darkness was, in any event, of very limited duration. So it was that eighteen aircraft left Waterbeach in the early evening, heading for V1 flying bomb installations at Domleger. In total 322 bombers were to attack three separate aiming points. Unfortunately the long daylight hours had not brought improved weather and the TIs were not visible. As a result the Master Bomber cancelled the attack on two of the locations, including that allocated to 514 Squadron, sending everybody home after only seventeen aircraft had bombed. No aircraft were lost.

Two days later, on 23rd June, twenty aircraft were despatched amongst 412 attacking four separate V1 installations, the squadron's Lancasters targeting L'Hey. This was a night raid, with the attack taking place just after midnight. The glow of red TIs could be seen through the clouds and all the squadron's crews bombed the target. Flak was described overall as slight in intensity, a mixture of light and heavy guns being brought to bear with some accuracy. S/L Philip Clay in the still-new PB143, JI-B, which he had christened 'Black Bess' after his Labrador dog, noted that it was intense heavy flak as far as he was concerned. Five bombers were shot down though the Waterbeach aircraft were unscathed.

The strategy was repeated on the following night, 24th June, in even larger measure. 739 aircraft attacked seven V1 targets, the twenty from Waterbeach being despatched to Rimeux. The raids caused fresh damage to the flying bomb installations, but at a higher cost than before with 22 aircraft failing to return. Whilst there was only slight flak there were numerous searchlights and fighters were much in evidence. No combats were reported by 514 Squadron crews, though some were seen at a distance, and the squadron's aircraft all landed safely. However, other crews were not so lucky, twenty Lancasters and two Stirlings being shot down by the night fighters that were assisted by clear conditions, bright moonlight and the searchlights. Five of the losses were from the Rimeux raid.

Despite the continued night time deployments, daylight operations were very much on the agenda and the COs of 622 Sqn and XV Sqn, Wing Commanders Swales and Watkins respectively, visited Waterbeach on 26th June to share the joy with W/Cdr Wyatt. Waterbeach was now beginning to resemble a magnet for senior officers as it hosted two distinguished visitors the following day. Wing Commander (later Air Chief Marshal) Lewis 'Bob' Hodges, a former Special Operations Executive pilot who had escaped from German captivity earlier in the war, was now Tactics Officer for Bomber Command. He attended the briefing and watched the take-off, landing and de-briefing of the crews, nineteen of whom paid their own visit to a V1 site at Biennais. At the debriefing of crews Wing Commander Hodges was also joined by Air Commodore Herbert 'Jimmy' Kirkpatrick, Senior Air Staff Officer at 3 Group. The returning crews were able to tell their interrogators and the two eminent guests that the target was cloud-covered, but they had bombed the glow of red TIs. P/O Les Petry, RNZAF was also able to relate that his aircraft, DS787, A2-D, had been approached by a single-engined enemy fighter which had been driven off by rear gunner Sgt WB Watt's fire whilst the Lancaster corkscrewed away from trouble. The Biennais raid was one of six against V1 targets, the 721-strong force losing only three of its number. The raid was the final operation of their tour for the crew of P/O Bob Langley, who had taken part in 34 sorties. Bob Langley was awarded the DFC, the citation mentioning his earlier attack on an airfield despite having lost two engines. He survived the war and became an airline pilot for BOAC and subsequently Freddie Laker. Whilst with BOAC he endured a forced landing in the Sahara Desert.

The fifth birthday of the WAAF was celebrated on 29th June by a special luncheon at the WAAF site. Nearly all the WAAF personnel on the Station were in the Dining Hall to sample the birthday cake and other good things, and they were waited on by WAAF and RAF officers. The Base Commander, Air Commodore HH Down AFC referred in his speech to the good work done by the WAAF in the past five years and the way in which their presence had brightened the lives of the RAF. The Station Commander, G/C CM Heard was loudly applauded when he cut the cake with Flight Officer DJN Percy, the Station WAAF 'G' Officer.

The Station Sports took place in the afternoon. In spite of the heavy operational commitments of the Station and the inclement weather, there was a good turn-out of competitors and spectators. Rain and wind could not prevail against the good spirits and enthusiasm with which the competitors tackled the main events. Highlights of the afternoon were the High Jump, won by S/L DWA Stewart who cleared 5ft 5ins, the Half Mile won by LAC A Hoyle, the Tug-of-War won by Base Major Servicing Unit and the Officers' Race ('Yards for Years') won by F/L VJ Chapman. A successful afternoon concluded with Mrs. WJ Armstrong of Cambridge presenting the prizes.

The final raid of the month saw the squadron's biggest effort to date, with 29 Lancasters setting out in the early evening, intent on supporting Allied ground forces by bombing German troop concentrations at Villers Bocage. The raid got off to the worst possible start for the squadron. At 1925hrs PB178, JI-P, flown by F/S Jack Hanneson RCAF, collided with Lancaster ME695 of XV Sqn and exploded at 5,000 feet, crashing at Pittsham Farm, near Midhurst in Sussex. The XV Sqn aircraft landed safely at the airfield at Ford. The only survivors from PB178 were Sgt Tommy Colbeck, the bomb aimer and Sgt Bert Brown, wireless operator. The subsequent Board of Inquiry later concluded:

'Lancaster aircraft PB178 took off from Waterbeach at 18.18 hours on the 30th June, 1944. The Pilot F/Sgt. Hannesson signed the form 700 accepting the aircraft as being serviceable. F/Sgt. Hannesson was briefed to fly in the No.2 position in the leading vic of No.514 Squadron, this Squadron leading the attack. Duo to a late change in bomb load F/Sgt. Hannesson who was detailed to take off at 18.00 hrs did not take off until 18,18 hrs. Due to this late take off, F/Sgt. Hannesson was unable to join his formation in the forming-up area. He therefore decided to fly above his briefed airspeed in order to make up for the loss of time. (see evidence of 3rd Witness). At Luton, which was the rendezvous point, he circled but did not see his formation. However he saw a formation ahead and decided that it might be his. On catching up with this formation he found that they were Halifaxes of an earlier attack. At this point he was just about to cross the English Coast when he was informed by the Navigator that they were about 10 minutes ahead of D.T.A. F/Sgt. Hannesson then decided to orbit in order to wait for his formation. He then turned to Port and as he turned he saw two formations coming towards him on his Port side. He continued to turn and crossed between the two formations flying across them from left to right. (East to West). After he had crossed he turned to starboard as he thought he saw one of his squadron aircraft. While he was turning, F/Sgt. Hannesson was informed by the Air Bomber that there were two aircraft ahead. The Pilot saw these aircraft and asked the Engineer to increase his engine power, he managed to avoid the first aircraft but hit the second. The aircraft hit was Lancaster aircraft MD695 of No.15 Squadron piloted by F/Sgt. French. The wreckage of Lancaster PB178 and Lancaster MD695 which landed at Ford have been investigated and the results of the investigation are contained in the Investigation Officer's report.

The primary cause of the accident was an error of judgment on the part of F/Sgt. Hannesson when he was turning into the formation. F/Sgt. Hannesson managed to avoid the first aircraft by diving underneath it and it appears that he tried to avoid MD695 in the same manner. From the evidence available it seems that the top portion of the Pilot's Cockpit (PB173) hit the underside of the Fin of MD695, immediately afterwards the Port Inner propeller, part of the starboard fin and the Port Outer removed the turret, As. PB173 was turning to starboard it is possible that after the first impact it "slipped on" and the Port Inner propeller cut a portion off the starboard wingtip of MD 695. Thereafter the aircraft dived away and after falling a few thousand feet exploded. The crew of MD695 is not entirely blameless; not one of the members saw the aircraft approaching them until it had almost hit their aircraft. To prevent accidents of this type recurring it would appear necessary for pilots to have more practice in formation flying, and for crews to be warned to keep a good look out at all times. The Gunners should arrange their search so that all fields of vision are covered the whole time. Had this aircraft taken off on time this accident would not have happened, therefore briefed time of take-off for this type of operation should be strictly adhered to.'

The remainder of the force had been tasked with bombing a vital road junction, in order to halt the advance of a German panzer division. Broken cloud cloaked the target area at 6,000 feet, and smoke added to the poor visibility. Aircraft were ordered to bomb from 4,000 feet in order to achieve the necessary accuracy, which was demonstrated by the 1100 bombs that hit their mark, putting an end to the panzers' attempts to join the battle. There was much heavy flak, however, which caused damage to some aircraft. LL635, JI-M 'Minnie the Moocher' was flown by P/O Bert Sandland, who reported hits to the nose and port and starboard sides of the mid upper turret. The crew of LL635 also looked on as horrified spectators as the aircraft just behind them sustained a direct hit from flak. LL620, JI-T was flown by P/O Douglas Woods, RAAF on his 27th operation. The Woods crew had survived five combats on the night of the disastrous Nuremberg raid, described earlier, as well as other uncomfortably close encounters with night fighters. The flak burst broke the tail off LL620, which was seen to crash without any likelihood of survivors. The two 514 Squadron Lancasters were the only aircraft lost from this highly successful raid. F/O Cedric Thomson was flying PB142, JI-A: 'On the 30th June we bombed Villers Bocage where the army was closing around the enemy. Two out of three aircraft lost were from 514. Although we were bombing fewer German targets than in the winter of 43/44 the chop rate was still fairly high. The enemy fighters were very strong and well organised.'

At the end of the month, the Station Commander's Summary noted:

The principal event of the month was the opening of the Second Front on 6th June 1944. Preparation had been made in advance to operate the Squadron at greatly increased intensity. It was expected that the squadron might be employed in both large and small scale attacks against tactical targets at all hours of the day and night, and some reorganisation of the station had been effected to provide for this. In the event the squadron continued to operate at little more than its average intensity over the preceding month during the first fortnight of the attack, and only by night. To some extent this had a slightly lowering effect on morale, since it came as something of an anti-climax to most of the personnel on the station. During the latter part of the month, however, daylight operations were instituted and although the squadron operated little, owing to adverse weather, they were standing by for the greater part of the time for either day or night attacks. This was very tiring to aircrew and rather demoralising. The day attack on Villers Bocage was outstandingly successful, however, and raised tremendous enthusiasm for daylight bombing. The Command Armament Officer visited the Station to inspect working conditions of Armourers employed in bombing up. In view of the frequent changes of target and of bomb load, these personnel are the hardest worked of any on the Station. The principal difficulties are shortage of personnel and shortage of suitable handling equipment.

July started with rain and low cloud. The first operation for the squadron was on 2nd July, with a return to V1 sites, the 'P-planes', as F/S Geoff France referred to them in his log book, which were still menacing the

HM King George VI presents a medal to a member of 514 Squadron, believed to be a Flight Lieutenant (WMHM)

South of England. 26 aircraft left Waterbeach at lunchtime bound for Beauvoir, though one had to return with engine trouble. There was broken cloud over the target and crews could see the yellow TIs, bombing being concentrated on these though with some other bombs being scattered as far as they decoy airfield. Clearly it was not a very convincing decoy as the other crews were not fooled. There were no losses from the total force of 374 aircraft attacking three separate aiming points.
There was then a hiatus for the squadron until 5th July. However, before the intrepid fliers took to the air on that day, Waterbeach excelled itself in its ability to attract important visitors, as the station played host to His Majesty King George VI, along with Her Majesty the Queen and Her Royal Highness Princess Elizabeth. There were, naturally enough, plenty of high ranking officers in attendance, including the AOC No. 3 Group, Air Vice Marshal Richard Harrison. The Royal Party appears to have been visiting a number of airfields in the locality as RAF Witchford, just down the road, was similarly honoured. No doubt due to the recent rain, the Station Commander directed the personnel to parade in a hangar where a Guard of Honour presented arms and the station band played the National Anthem. His Majesty then invested various officers with the DFC and DFM as appropriate to their rank. These included the DFC for the squadron commander, W/Cdr Mike Wyatt, and his three flight commanders, Squadron Leaders Barney Reid, Alan Roberts and Ralph Chopping amongst others. The Station ORB described the occasion: *'The Station was honoured by the visit of Their Majesties the King and Queen and Her Royal Highness Princess Elizabeth. At 1500hrs in the afternoon, His Majesty held an Investiture in 'A' Hangar where Base, Station and Squadron personnel were on parade. One Bar to the Distinguished Flying Cross, eight DFCs and one DFM were presented to past and present members of 514 Squadron. After the Ceremony their Majesties inspected the parade and spoke to many RAF and WAAF personnel. The Royal Party accompanied by the Base and Station Commanders then made a brief tour of the station, visiting the Squadron H2S Trainer which greatly interested the King; the MT Section and the Station Information Room which aroused the admiration and keen interest of the Queen.*
Their brief visit concluded, the Royal Party drove away amidst the cheers of hundreds of airmen and airwomen who had congregated outside the Camp gates to wave farewell to Their Majesties.'

Sgt Bob Chester-Master recalled 'During the inspection when the King stopped, Princess Elizabeth stopped in front of me and asked my name. As I replied she astutely recognised by my accent that I was an Aussie.' W/O Geoff Payne recalled: 'I remember the day very well. Princess Elizabeth's hat was blown off by the wind with one excited officer running about to rescue said chapeau.'
Having departed so soon, the royal visitors were therefore not able to witness the 22 aircraft leave for the Watten constructional works, where V2 missiles were to be actually fuelled. The massive bunker, which was to be part of the launch site for the supersonic rockets, was nearing completion and would represent a clear and present danger if it became operational. There were four targets for the 542 aircraft tasked with attacking various flying bomb facilities and the clear moon-lit conditions helped in what was a successful attack. The Master Bomber for this attack was Group Captain Leonard Cheshire VC, flying his North American P51 Mustang, a gift to him from the USAAF. At the opposite end of the operational spectrum, this was the first operational sortie for F/S Geoff France and his crew. Rather than waving their pilot off on a 'second dickey' trip with an experienced crew, the France crew found that they were all in it together, with their squadron commander, W/Cdr Mike

V2 rockets continued to menace the Allies, and particularly the population of south east England, until the end of the war. Unlike V1s, the rockets could not be shot down once airborne.

Film star Edward G. Robinson visited 514 Squadron whilst undertaking research into the life of bomber crews for a film for the Ministry of Information. Robinson's visit was extremely popular with the crews, who considered him to be 'a grand personality'.

Wyatt, coming along with them to offer advice and guidance. There was slight heavy flak but no combats noted by 514 Squadron crews, though overall four aircraft did not make it home from another V2 launch site at Wizernes. One was shot down by flak and three were lost without trace. On the following day, the Station ORB was delighted to record the visit of another distinguished guest. *'Mr. Edward G Robinson, the well-known American film star, accompanied by Mr. G Archibald of the Ministry of Information and S/L A Lloyd of Air Ministry visited the station to gather material for a new Ministry of Information film. Mr. Robinson attended the Squadron Briefing with the Station Commander and was afterwards entertained in the Officers' Mess. He proved to be a popular guest and a grand personality, and the shortness of his stay was regretted.'*

The marshalling yards at Vaires, Paris, came under the Bomber Command cosh on 7th July. Twenty aircraft were despatched from Waterbeach though two returned early with engine trouble. Whilst outbound at 11,000 feet, F/O Alba Fowke in DS826, JI-U was three miles starboard of the bomber stream in the vicinity of Luton when he saw a stream of red tracer fired vertically for approximately two to three seconds into the main body of aircraft. The report submitted by the Station Intelligence Officer, S/L ME Clarkson, noted that no enemy aircraft were reported as being in the area. It is not known if the tracer was fired by an unknown intruder or local anti-aircraft defences.

This was the first op with 514 Squadron for experienced air gunner W/O Geoff Payne, assigned to the 'spare bods' pool. He noted: 'Reporting to the Gunnery Office on July 7th, to my delight was informed that I would be flying that night with F/Sgt Whitwood's crew as M/u gunner, as their own gunner was off sick with a bad stomach. Target for the night was Vaires railway marshalling yard Paris and was part of the plan to disrupt the German supply route to the Normandy battlefields. Take off time was 22-30 just as darkness was falling. Flying as a mid-upper gunner was a new experience for me with great views all around. It was a fairly direct route to the target, plenty of searchlight activity but the flak was nowhere near as heavy as my experience of German targets. A well concentrated attack without the loss of aircraft possibly due to another attack on a flying bomb storage depot at St-leu-d'esserent north of Paris where enemy fighters claimed thirty aircraft. Landed back at base after a 4hr 45min flight.' The attack on Vaires, by 128 aircraft, was thought to be accurate. There was, however, night fighter activity either side of the target. At 0030hrs Sgt Bill Meredith, mid upper gunner for the crew of F/S Geoff France in ME842, JI-K, saw an FW190 approaching from starboard. When the enemy fighter had closed to 300 yards Sgt Meredith opened fire, causing it to break off its attack. F/S France described this as 'a good trip' otherwise.

The attack on the marshalling yard at Vaires was a good example of a concentrated GH attack by 3 Group squadrons. The bomb craters can be seen clearly (TNA).

S/L Ralph Chopping's crew, in LL733, JI-S, had two similar encounters in which enemy aircraft approached his aircraft and were deterred by the quick response from his gunners. Meanwhile F/O Alba Fowke's adventures continued as he weaved to avoid the Paris defences. A burst of trace was seen to pass between the mid upper and rear turrets, which drew the attention of the rear gunner, F/O Gordon Murphy, to a twin-engined aircraft which was closing in from starboard. Ordering a corkscrew to starboard, F/O Murphy opened fire, hitting the enemy fighter, the wing of which burst into flames. F/O Henry Chapman, the mid upper gunner, joined in, as the Ju88 dived away, flames now enveloping the front of the fuselage as well. The crew saw the aircraft hit the ground and continue to burn for some time. On their return to Waterbeach the crew found that the nacelle of the port outer engine had been short away by a cannon shell, damaging the oil system. The crew was unscathed.

A Lancaster over the aiming point at Nucourt, photographed by F/S S Bryant, bomb aimer in DS786, A2-F, flown by F/L Ian Hay (Bryant family).

The final skirmish of the night for the squadron was at 0224hrs when P/O Bruce McDonald RCAF in LL728, A2-L encountered another Ju88 as the crew crossed the English Channel on their way home. The fighter was subjected to fire from both turrets and broke off its attack. Despite all the encounters recorded in the ORB, no aircraft were lost from the raid on Vaires.

Shortly after dawn on 10th July 223 aircraft, including 25 from Waterbeach, attacked constructional works at Nucourt. The facility was for the storage of V1 flying bombs. There was ten-tenths cloud cover and bombing was inaccurate. For the second raid running, no aircraft were lost.

The squadron returned to the marshalling yards at Vaires on the evening of 12th July, 23 of its aircraft joining 136 others. Unfortunately the target was covered by cloud and the Master Bomber ordered the mission to be aborted after only twelve aircraft had bombed, including PB142, JI-A flown by P/O Cedric Thomson. All aircraft returned to base safely.

Chalons-sur-Marne was the next railway centre on the list, and it was visited on 15th July 1944. 24 Lancasters from 514 Squadron participated amongst the 229 aircraft tasked in total. Eighteen of the Waterbeach contingent successfully bombed the primary target, another major part of

Scattered bombing is apparent in this photo of the flying bomb site at Nucourt following the raid on 10th July 1944.

the French transport infrastructure. The attack took place around 0130hrs. S/L Phillip Clay, 'A' Flight's Commander, demonstrated the 'press on regardless' spirit typical of Bomber Command crews when his Lancaster, PB143 JI-B, 'Black Bess' suffered failures of an air speed indicator and a starboard engine whilst en route to the target. A painting of his subsequent landing at Waterbeach was presented to S/L Clay after the war. In conversation with the author, S/L Clay's son mentioned that his father had been extremely protective of his personal bomber and was mortified when another crew borrowed 'Black Bess' and returned her with flak damage.
F/O Geoff France suffered what was, for him, a rare early return in LM627, JI-D. The wireless operator, Sgt Ron Harding, saw fuel pouring off the starboard wing. The crew tried, at the behest of Waterbeach Control, to jettison fuel before landing but the petrol cocks would not open. Geoff France later recalled: 'We had to land with the bombs aboard. We got the thing down on the runway, stopped it and you've never seen an aircraft empty so quickly, easily beating our drill record for abandoning an aeroplane. The aircraft did not catch fire and the ground crew said that the number one tank on the starboard side had slipped and fractured a line. Next day the whole of Bomber Command was at panic stations, checking all petrol tanks in the wings and practicing jettisoning fuel[24].
Three combats were reported by 514 Squadron crews. F/O Alex 'Red' Campbell RCAF, in LL692, A2-C was told to corkscrew by his rear gunner, Sgt Sam Harvey, who opened fire on an Me410 which was getting a little too close for comfort. Meanwhile, Sgt EM Temple, the rear gunner in W/O Don Beaton's LL677, A2-E, had an even busier time, fighting off enemy aircraft on two occasions. None of the enemy fighters fired on the Lancasters, though after the two-pronged attack on railway targets, three bombers were missing.
The Station ORB relates that on 17th July an inspection of the Station was made by Air Chief Marshal Sir Edgar Ludlow-Hewitt, CBE, KCB, CMG, DSO, MC, Inspector General of the RAF. The following day Mr AH Whyte, Air Ministry Horticultural Adviser, inspected the Station Gardens. The list of such visits lengthened further on 20th July when Group Captain DE Williams, MBE, MA, Senior Education Officer, Bomber Command, accompanied by the Group Education Officer S/L ET Lewis, visited the

---

[24] Geoff France in *'Hell on Earth'* by Mel Rolfe, Grub Street Publishing 1999

Station and inspected the Information Room and other educational facilities.

While all the painting of fixtures, weeding of flowerbeds and sharpening of pencils helped RAF Waterbeach pass muster, for 514 Squadron the war went on. Another change of tactics on 18th July 1944 saw Bomber Command and the USAAF direct their assets to support Operation Goodwood, a major British Army attack in Normandy, which was to last three days. By the raid's end, it was considered one of the most effective bombing operations in support of the Army of the whole war. The weather was clear for the raid, which included American aircraft in the early morning attack. Support from Navy gunfire and Army artillery meant there were few reports of flak as they suppressed the AA guns. In total, Bomber Command delivered 5,000 of the 6,800 tons dropped during this raid. The result was that two whole German enemy divisions were severely affected. Bomber Command's contribution was 942 aircraft, including an impressive 26 from 514 Squadron. Six bombers were lost in total, none of these being from Waterbeach.

That evening, many of the squadron's crews were in action for a second time in 24 hours as eighteen Lancasters were detailed to attack the railway centre at Aulnoye. As was becoming standard practice, the 263 bombers sent out were divided between two targets, the other being Revigny. F/L Malcolm Head RNZAF and his rear gunner Sgt Albert Beckford in LL697, A2-B subsequently submitted the following account in a combat report: *At 0105 hours the MU Gunner reported an unidentified aircraft with navigation lights burning on the starboard beam up. A minute later the rear gunner reported a S/E fighter (later identified as an ME109) coming in from the starboard quarter down range about 300 yards. The rear gunner gave orders to corkscrew starboard, and at the same time the E/A opened fire, his trace passing well behind our A/C. The rear gunner returned fire with a 3 second burst, there was a small explosion and the E/A dived to the ground enveloped in flames where it was seen to burn for a considerable period by the mid upper gunner and Rear Gunner. During the combat the aircraft burning navigation lights was kept under observation by the Mid Upper Gunner. As the ME109 dived to the ground the other aircraft switched off its lights and was not seen again.*

Two aircraft were lost from the Aulnoye raid, one from each of 514's sister squadrons, 75(NZ) and 115. Meanwhile the contingent attacking Revigny was savaged by night fighters, 24 aircraft being shot down, over a fifth of the attacking force.

20th July was to be another dark day in the history of 514 Squadron. For the first time, the unit's crews were tasked with attacking the Rheinpreussen synthetic oil plant at Meerbeck, Homberg, part of a 148-strong bombing force. 24 Lancasters departed Waterbeach after 2300hrs and crossed the enemy coast over the Schelde estuary, swinging south-east before turning to the north east for the run in to the target. Eighteen of the

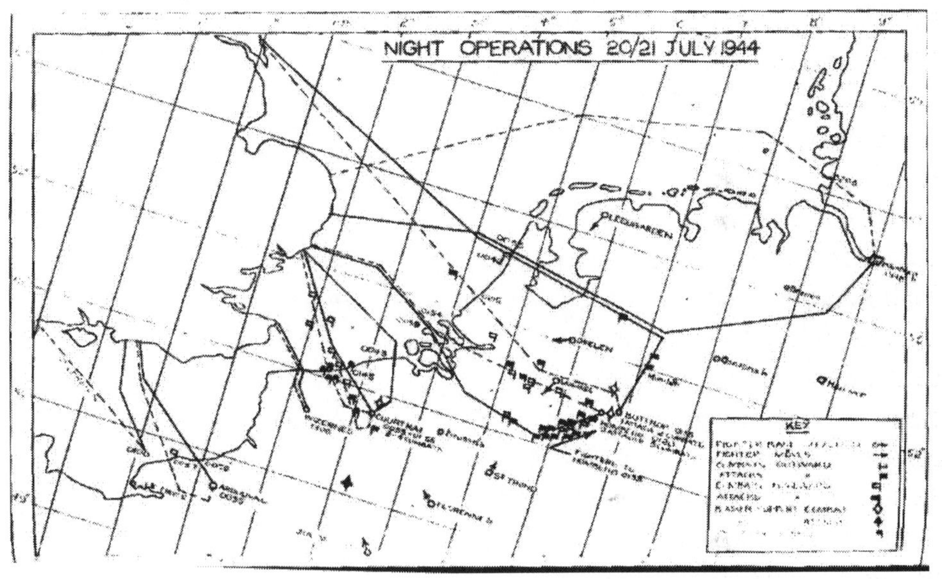

Combat plot from the Bomber Command Night Raid Report of 20th / 21st July 1944. The white flags indicate combats and the black flags show losses to the bomber force (TNA).

squadron's aircraft attacked the primary target, two having returned early whilst P/O William Watkins in LL726, A2-H was compelled to jettison his bombs in the target area when his aircraft came under attack from a fighter. The weather was clear with slight haze over Homberg and the red TIs were reported to be very concentrated. However there was moderate heavy flak and fighters were very active, the Nachtjagd force having infiltrated the bomber stream as it passed Brussels and remaining with it until it was well out to sea on the return leg. Crews returning from Homberg reported, between them, a total of 42 combats with enemy fighters, and lost twenty of their number.

As their aircraft ran in to the target, Sergeants Don Gardiner RCAF and 'Ben' Bentley, mid upper and rear gunner respectively with F/O Bruce MacDonald in LL697, A2-B, engaged an attacking twin-engined fighter. They saw their tracer strike home and the fighter fell away in flames.
P/O William Watkins' LL672, A2-H came under attack from a Ju88 which had been spotted by rear gunner Sgt Bernard Ferris, who expended 800 rounds in trying to deter the attacking fighter. This was a worthwhile investment of effort and ammunition and he was delighted to see the Ju88 pull up, roll onto its back and spin down in flames, the fighter's fiery return to earth being corroborated by other members of the crew.
Another enemy aircraft claimed by a 514 Squadron gunner was an FW190 which attacked DS787, A2-D, flown by F/S Arthur Holland RAAF. This was the second encounter of the night for the Holland crew, rear gunner Sgt Bill MacDonald having previously driven off a Ju88 shortly after leaving the target area. At 0147hrs the Lancaster was attacked by the single-engined fighter, Sgt Charles O'Brien in the mid upper turret joining his colleague in firing at the assailant. The Fw190 opened fire itself, without scoring any hits and Sgt O'Brien claimed strikes on the enemy aircraft as it burst into flames and dived away into the clouds.
Claims by the Homberg force for two Ju88s and an unidentified fighter destroyed along with three other probably destroyed and one fighter damaged are noted in 'Nachtjagd War Diaries'.
Four other crews also reported having fired at enemy aircraft. F/L John Timms in DS786, A2-F and F/S John Lawrie RNZAF in DS826, JI-F had one encounter each. W/O Don Beaton's gunners had already noted tracer fired at them by an unseen foe when they were intercepted by an Me109 whose fire fortunately missed their Lancaster. The fighter did not press home its attack. Even busier was the crew of DS813, JI-N, flown by F/S Edgar Richardson. Outward bound, they had come under attack shortly after seeing a FW190 flying past them in the opposite direction. As they neared the target, mid upper gunner Sgt Bernard Vince reported a twin-engined fighter attacking them so gave it a short burst as the Lancaster corkscrewed away. Five minutes later, and whilst they were still in the target area, F/S Richardson saw an enemy aircraft attacking from dead ahead, firing rockets at the Lancaster as they corkscrewed away again.

The wreckage of ME858, JI-J lies in a Dutch field after being shot down by Uffz. Gustav Sarzio during the first of several visits by the squadron to Homberg. F/O Douglas Millar and his crew were lost on their fourth op (Ton Bosmans).

Having left the target area, they were attacked again at 0130hrs, another frontal assault with the enemy firing two rockets which again missed.
The first of 514 Squadron's aircraft to be lost on the night was ME858 JI-J, flown by F/O Douglas Millar. The aircraft was shot down at 0114 hours by the Me110G-4 of Uffz. Gustav Sarzio, 6./NJG1, crashing at 0116hrs at Limburg as it approached the target. Only a few bombs exploded in the open field outside the village of Hunsel. The Lancaster was also carrying a 4,000lb HC 'Cookie' which did not detonate. According to an eye-witness, 'the aircraft was hit in one of the wings and exploded high in the air. None of the crew members was able to leave the Lancaster. Parts of the plane are laying in a circle of 500 metres around the crash site.' There were no survivors from the crew whose four ops had taken place in the space of ten days. Two of 514's Lancasters came to grief in the target area. F/O Lamont McLean RNZAF and his crew were all killed when LM181, JI-E was shot down at about 0122hrs, probably by Fw. Klaus Moller, 12./NJG3, or Ofw. Heinrich Schmidt, 2./NJG6. No further details have come to light.

F/O Douglas Millar spent a brief ten days as an operational pilot at Waterbeach, before being killed with his crew.

Two minutes later, P/O Stanley Anderson and his crew also failed to survive when HK571 JI-L fell prey to a night fighter, probably that of Hptm. Hermann Greiner, 11./NJG1, crashing at 0124 at Daubenspeckhof one kilometre West of Moers, of which Homberg is a suburb. Finally, W/O John Lassam and his crew in HK570, JI-P came to grief over the North Sea, on the return leg, shot down, possibly by either Hptm. Heinz-Martin Hadeball, 3./NGr.10, or Hptm. Ernst-Wilhelm Modrow, 1./NJG1. HK570 crashed at 0159 in the sea off the Dutch coast with the loss of the entire crew. The operation had cost the squadron four Lancasters and twenty eight aircrew. Bad as the night was for 514 Squadron, it was even worse up the road at RAF Mepal where 514's sister squadron, 75(NZ), lost seven aircraft. Twenty aircraft had been lost from the 158 taking part in this raid. Heavy damage was caused to the oil plant which caused disruption to the supply of fuel from 6,000 tons, down to under 1,000 tons per day. Homberg was to feature significantly on the casualty lists of both squadrons in the future.

The squadron was back on its feet after two nights respite when, on 23rd July, twenty two Lancasters set out from Waterbeach to bomb warehouses and other harbour facilities at Kiel. Two aircraft had to return early, F/S John Lawrie with intercom problems and F/O Bruce McDonald RCAF with the rear turret unserviceable, whilst the remainder bombed successfully. 629 aircraft took part in the raid, the bombing itself being completed within thirty minutes. Sergeants Charles O'Brien and Bill MacDonald, mid upper and rear gunners in F/S Arthur Holland's PB185, A2-F, joined several other Lancaster gunners in firing at an unidentified single-engined fighter which was attacking one of their number. The enemy aircraft was seen to be shot down whilst only four bombers were lost. Damage to the target was extensive with the U-Boat facilities and port being heavily bombed. 500lb delayed action bombs ensured that recovery operations were made more difficult for the enemy.

Attention now switched to the city of Stuttgart with three raids in quick succession. On 24th July eighteen aircraft were despatched from Waterbeach but five had to return early. The total force was 614 bombers, attacking through ten tenths cloud, into which the red TIs quickly disappeared. However, as F/S Geoff France reported on his return, they were able to bomb the south east corner of green and yellow star sky markers and could see the glow of fires beneath the cloud. It transpired that the attack was very effective, despite the poor visibility, proving to be the most devastating raid so far on the city of Stuttgart.

Two of the squadron's crews had to take evasive action to get away from enemy fighters, these being W/O Norman Jennings in ME841, JI-H and F/O William Watkins in LL716, A2-G. 21 bombers failed to return, including PB185 A2-F, flown by F/O Thomas Middleton. The aircraft was probably shot down at 0233 hours by Hptm. Paul Zorner of Stab III./NJG5 in the vicinity of Trier, returning from the target. All the crew, on their fifth operation, were lost. Despite Sgt Stafford being identified at the time he, along with the rest of the crew, are commemorated on the Runnymede Memorial.

The following night, the squadron again tasked eighteen crews with the second successive trip to Stuttgart. On this occasion, seventeen actually took off and four returned early with technical problems, the intensive operational schedule by now taking its toll on airframes and engines as well as the crews. F/O R Harvey returned early when his port inner engine suffered a rapid drop in oil pressure and caught fire. On what was not a good night for port inner engines, F/S Holland's aircraft also suffered a failure and landed at Ford, where it overran the runway sustaining damage to the fuselage. F/S Wilson's engines were all working correctly but unfortunately his mid-upper turret wasn't, also necessitating an early return.

Most of 514 Squadron bombed between 0150hrs and 0155hrs, apart from P/O PF Carter RNZAF and F/S Eric Williams RAAF[25] who turned up some twenty minutes later. The cloud cover, complete once more, extended to 22,000 feet though fortuitously it broke over the target. There was slight to moderate heavy flak and, once again, fighters were present. A large fire was seen in the centre of the target, and a red glow could be seen from eighty miles away, according to F/L Marcus Dods.

F/S Maurice Oliver RNZAF in LL697, A2-B found that his Lancaster was the target of choice for the Luftwaffe on this night, as he and his crew were attacked on three occasions in the space of eighteen minutes. It was doubtless of only academic interest to the crew that the attacks were by three different aircraft types, being an Me110, Ju88 and unidentified single-engined type respectively. Of more immediate note was that their Lancaster was undamaged in all three encounters. Twelve bombers were lost of the 550 sent to Stuttgart. This was the final trip of the month for F/O Cedric Thomson in PB142, JI-A: ‘This trip had everything, searchlights coning us, fighters all the way home, heavy flak over the target, and going around again at the target. The crew were most efficient throughout and the two gunners kept the fighters at bay. The running chart of Ron Cooper on this trip is displayed at the RAAF School of Navigation at East Sale, Victoria, so the flight of one aircraft of 514 is honoured in a far off place.’

A flying bomb launch site at Les Catelliers in France was the squadron's target on the early evening of 27th July. Twelve Lancasters from Waterbeach joined sixty others in the first attack to use the 'GH Leader' technique. This involved each GH-equipped aircraft having up to five followers, who released their bombs when they saw the GH Leader doing so. With close formation and good synchronisation the force could achieve

---

[25] Eric Williams completed his tour with the squadron, finishing as a Flying Officer. He survived the war but died in an air crash on 18 February 1948 at Amberley, Australia with his five crew members and ten passengers.

unparalleled accuracy, the GH sets being accurate to 150 feet at a range of three hundred miles from the transmitter. This was good enough to allow an effective and highly concentrated attack on specific military and industrial targets. However, as it could only be carried out in daylight, it depended on local air supremacy and the availability of fighter escorts. It was this technique that was to become No. 3 Group's hallmark, meaning that the group was able to act independently of the rest of Bomber Command on many raids. All aircraft returned safely on this occasion.

The following evening saw the squadron deployed once more to Stuttgart, with seventeen crews taking part, though F/S Oliver was forced to return with engine trouble. The bombing was thought by the returning crews to be scattered, some complaining that the Master Bomber had not been specific as to which markers should be bombed. In the event, it was hard to tell new damage from that caused a few days previously. W/O Geoff Payne was now with the crew of F/O Ted Cossens, having replaced Sgt Peter Brown in the rear turret. 'We were detailed to attack Stuttgart which was to be the third heavy raid by Bomber Command against Stuttgart in seven days. In fairly clear moonlight, fighter flares began to illuminate the sky as we approached the French/German border with a number of combats taking place north of our track. It seems as though the German radar had correctly forecast our target owing to the amount of searchlights waving about in the target area. Very heavy flak as we went into bomb with usual buffeting about. Turning for home I spotted a number of Me109s scurrying about, silhouetted against the fires. The return journey was uneventful although these were the times that a marauding fighter could catch you unawares. After an eight hour flight we landed back at base at 04-00 hrs. Later we were to learn that 39 aircraft had been lost on this raid from the five hundred that had participated.'

The Luftwaffe would consider this to be a good night out, 39 of the 596 bombers attacking Stuttgart being brought down. Bright moonlight and new precision radar assisted the 200 night fighters sent out to intercept the Stuttgart raid, which was carried out in parallel with other bombing operations. F/S John Whitwood in LM180, JI-G managed to evade a Ju88 but others were less fortunate. The first of the squadron's aircraft to be lost, and the first from the attacking force that night, was LL692, A2-C, flown by F/L Alex 'Red' Campbell DFC on his twenty fifth op. He was carrying a second dickey pilot, F/O Bob Giffin for whom this was his first taste of operations. Giffin had, in fact, been rostered to fly with another pilot but had swapped crews as he was friends with Red Campbell from their time in training.

The night was initially dark with low cloud and, having crossed the coast, F/L Campbell descended to 8,000 feet to seek cloud cover, as the crews had been instructed. Just before midnight the Lancaster had broken cloud, which was by now patchy, and was flying straight and level at 7,500 feet when it was attacked without warning by a night fighter. Rear gunner F/S Sam Harvey had been monitoring another suspicious aircraft, which had crossed from port to starboard below and behind the Lancaster, when a twin-engined fighter came in from the port quarter below and opened fire with tracer from about 350 yards. F/S Harvey returned fire with two short bursts and saw his tracer hitting the enemy aircraft.

The Lancaster sustained numerous hits in the port wing and a number of gaping holes appeared extending from the root to beyond the outer engine. A big fire started in the wing immediately behind the inner engine and spread along the leading edge to the fuselage. The fuselage was also hit in the vicinity of the mid upper turret, causing injuries to the legs of mid upper gunner F/S Earl 'Jonesy' Jones. The turret itself was put out of action though he was still able to depress his guns manually and gave a defiant five-second burst towards the attacker.

F/L Campbell attempted to dive for the cloud whilst feathering the port inner engine and pressing the fire extinguisher button, though to no apparent effect. He ordered the crew to put their parachutes on. Before the aircraft could reach the safety of the cloud there was a second attack, tracer entering the port wing and one or two bullets entering the cockpit. The port outer engine also stopped at this point. The Lancaster, port wing low and with apparent rudder damage as well, was by now very difficult to control and the fire showed no sign of abating so Red Campbell ordered his crew to bale out.

The bomb aimer, F/O Jack Chapman, removed the escape hatch cover and stowed it in the nose compartment but after he had baled out it fell back into the exit. The flight engineer, Sgt 'Jock' Donaldson, managed to partially shift it but could not remove it completely. F/O Giffin was having trouble exiting and was thought to be wounded. His parachute deployed in the nose compartment, snagging on the bombsight, but Sgt Donaldson was able to disentangle it, gather it up and help Giffin through the hatch. The rest of the crew successfully exited the burning Lancaster, leaving F/L Campbell at the controls.

As he left his seat, his parachute straps twice got tangled in the throttle controls, taking him precious seconds to free himself. He then found the hatch cover had once again blocked the exit and he struggled to manoeuvre it to make a gap large enough for him to wriggle through. Although he managed this, head first, his parachute harness was forced off his shoulders and down his arms, eventually becoming entangled around his knees and legs. Campbell eventually worked himself through the hatch and found himself falling free. He could see his ripcord on the pack about two feet from his body, but was able to bend his knees and pull himself back up his own body hand over hand. Reaching the ripcord he pulled it and was jerked out straight, ricking his neck. He thus descended by parachute upside down, his head narrowly missing the edge of the roof of a cottage. He was able to bend his body just enough to land shoulder-first rather than on his head. He was fortunate enough to avoid serious injury. This was related by

F/O Bob Giffin failed to survive his 'second dickey' trip with F/O Alex Campbell when his parachute malfunctioned (Bruce Johnston).

F/L Campbell in conversation with the author seventy years later. His memory of the event, perhaps understandably, was still crystal clear. His crew mates all landed comfortably, with the exception of Bob Giffin who apparently died of injuries the following morning. The Lancaster was shot down by a JU-88 G1 4R+AK flown by Lt. Johannes Strassner of 2./NJG2, crashing 4 km. East of Chateaudun.

F/L Robert Jones and his crew in LM206, JI-C were on their ninth op when they were intercepted at 0117hrs over Domremy by the Ju88 of Oblt. Heinz Rökker of 2./NJG2. Having survived one pass by the night fighter, the Lancaster was attacked again, losing an engine. Two of the crew, flight engineer Sgt Thomas Harvell and navigator Sgt George Robinson managed to get out, Sgt Harvell being blown out of the aircraft, hitting his head and losing consciousness. He was even more fortunate in that he was wearing his parachute and came to in time to deploy it. Sgt Harvell recalled: 'On 28/29 July we went to Stuttgart but never arrived. At about 01.30 hours over eastern France, which was still occupied by the Germans, we flew out of cloud into brilliant moonlight. Alf, the rear gunner, reported fighter flares and the next moment two bursts of cannon fire struck us.

The port inner engine caught fire and our Lanc started to go down. An explosion blew me out through the bomb aimers' observation window. I steered my parachute sideways to avoid burning debris. This took me away from the crash area of the burning wreckage of our Lanc, but the only other survivor, Robby the navigator, fell near it and was taken prisoner.'

Sgt Harvell was able to link up with the French Resistance, with whom he fought until liberation. Harvell found himself fighting alongside a former unit of the Ukrainian SS who had defected en masse to the Resistance. He was therefore one of a very few members of the RAF to have fought alongside members of the notorious SS. He later recounted:

'On the 10th September 1999 at Neufchateau, I had the unique experience of meeting the night fighter pilot of the Junkers 88 who shot down our Lanc. He is 83 year old Heinz Rökker, ex highly decorated air ace with 64 kills to his credit. He spoke English well and we relived that fateful night which he clearly remembers. He had been traced by a friend of mine who is in the aviation business in Germany and who was able to gain access to Luftwaffe wartime records. Heinz told me the following that goes a long way to explain Bomber Command's high losses. Most of his many 'kills'

were carried out using 'Shräge Musik'[26] (slanting music), the upward firing guns fitted to the top of the fuselage of his Junkers 88. Attacking unseen, from the blind spot beneath a bomber, he was rarely fired at by gunners and not once in his 64 combats was his fighter hit by return fire. Regarding the 'corkscrew' manoeuvre, he said that he did not follow a bomber into this manoeuvre but just slackened speed and maintained his heading. Invariably the bomber would surface ahead of him in his sights and as it did so it would be despatched by his nose cannon. He stated that he was grateful for H2S and MONICA that gave off signals that allowed his radar operator to home in quite easily on a bomber.
I suppose, all in all, it feels better to have been shot down by a highly skilled night fighter ace than some novice pilot. We paid homage to my crew members buried in the town cemetery and attended a civic reception hosted by the Mayor who looked on the meeting as a reconciliation of former enemies and their respective homelands.'
The third of the Waterbeach aircraft to be lost was DS813, JI-N, a veteran of 52 successful operations and one of the first aircraft to arrive at 514 Squadron. On this sortie the aircraft was flown by 26 year old F/L Alba Fowke RCAF, on his twentieth operation. The circumstances of the aircraft's loss are not known other than that it came down at Deinvillers, near St. Die. However a Lancaster, possibly DS813, was shot down in the St Die area at 0130hrs by Offzr. Walter Swoboda, 2./NJG6, this being his only successful combat. All onboard DS813 were killed, including F/L Henry Chapman who was Gunnery Leader for the squadron.
The final operation of a difficult and sometimes traumatic month was on the morning of 30th July, seventeen Lancasters being deployed against Aiming Point 'B' at Caen, in support of Allied ground forces. W/O Geoff Payne recalled the flight. 'This was a daylight raid to Normandy in support of our ground troops who were ready to advance against the stubborn resistance of a German mechanised division. Caen target area B was our aiming point, orange smoke was deployed at the British front line, and we were to bomb east of that line at 4,000 ft. Going in to attack we were met

[26] In conversation with the author in 2014, Sgt Adge Boal, a wireless operator in the crew of F/O Les Petry RNZAF, said that crews were never told by Bomber Command about Shräge Musik, nor about the murder of bomber crews by German troops and civilians. He believed that this was to 'preserve morale'.

by a lot of light flak which subsided appreciably as the Germans took cover. I don't know how anyone could have survived such a concentrated battering as that I had witnessed.'

The weather included low cloud over the target, the cloud base being as low as 2,000 feet, this being the bombing height by F/S Geoff France in LM180, JI-G. This was so low that F/S France's aircraft sustained damage from its own bomb blasts and then had to land at the emergency airfield at RAF Woodbridge due to poor visibility at Waterbeach on the crew's return. F/L Bruce McDonald in LL728, A2-L had the misfortune to suffer the loss of port and starboard inner engines on the return leg and diverted to RAF Bassingbourne. 377 of the 692 aircraft sent to six aiming points in the Caen area, and four failed to return including LL733, JI-S. The pilot was F/L Walter Chitty RAAF who had, along with his rear gunner Sgt Bert Guy, survived a serious crash after the Nuremberg raid on 30th March[27]. The aircraft is recorded as 'lost without trace' with all her crew. However a 75(NZ) Sqn Lancaster, HK558, AA-D, was seen to crash in the sea off Caen after colliding with another, unidentified, Lancaster, which was believed to have returned safely to base. A body identified as that of Sgt Guy was recovered from the English Channel by the Royal Navy, and then reburied at sea. It is therefore possible that HK558 collided with LL733, both aircraft crashing into the sea.

F/O Cedric Thomson and his crew also took part in a special attack on a building in France. The operation is not recorded in the squadron's ORB. He later recalled: 'This was carried out by a lead Mosquito and two Lancasters. The differing aircraft speeds caused formating problems but we accomplished the task, bombing from about 2,000 feet. On another occasion the outward flight to a target near Paris was not much above ground level, as we were instructed not to fly above 150 feet over England. The first part of the route was to Lands End and I remember looking up at cars at one time, as this force of 100 plus Lancasters careered along the Cornish valleys. We continued at low level over the sea to the west of

[27] Bert was one of twin brothers serving with 514 Squadron, Charlie Guy having lost his life on 8th June. There was one other set of twins known to have served with the squadron. Flight Sergeants Jack and Fred Blandford, from Surrey, were the air gunners in the crew of F/O Les Adams RNZAF. At 31 years old, they were well above the average age of bomber aircrew and significantly older than Adams, who was aged twenty

Brittany, crossing the French coast further south, and eventually climbing in the dusk to at least 20,000 feet as we approached the target. The ruse may have avoided radar detection on the way to the target but fighters were around after we had bombed.'

F/L Thomas Lever and crew, including F/S Max McLaughlin RAAF (3rd from left), flew their tour of thirty ops between May and August 1944 (McLaughlin family)

The Station Commander's Summary for July was unusually lengthy:

No. 514 Squadron operated on fourteen occasions during the month. During the remainder of the time they were standing by almost continuously. Targets, bomb and petrol loads were changed frequently, before operations were cancelled for the day. This imposed a considerable strain both on aircrew and technical personnel, and general fatigue was obvious. Aircraft serviceability also tended to drop towards the end of the month. Apart from the fatigue referred to above this is attributed to aircraft being bombed up and standing by for long periods so that maintenance crews were allowed no leisure time in which to ensure perfection of maintenance, as opposed to routine inspections of essentials. The further necessity for marshalling 'C' Flight aircraft on a runway, to simplify take-off, also contributed to the Flight's lower efficiency.

The Squadron had many unfortunate losses of crews who were halfway through their tour during the month. Most of the crews now remaining are

comparatively new and inexperienced, having arrived during the past six weeks. There has been 100% turnover of aircrew since the 15th March 1944 i.e. in 4½ months, some crews having completed their tour in little more than three months.
Administration: The principal event has been the attempted registration of RAF personnel as Parliamentary voters. Despite strong appeals when registration cards were issued, the response has been apathetic, less than 50% of all personnel having returned their card. The value of the vote and the responsibilities of the electorate have been stressed throughout the month. Many discussion groups have been devoted to the purpose and these meetings have made it clear that the subject is not fully understood. The number of registrations has, however, now risen to 75%.
Towards the end of the month arrangements have been made to reorganise the Station on a more centralised basis. The scheme, in which all maintenance personnel are established on the Station Headquarters and the Squadron is reduced exclusively to its aircrew personnel and Adjutant, is due to become effective on 1st August 1944. It is expected that the system will remove many anomalies and make for better administration.
Mr. Black and Mr. Williams of MGM Film Corporation visited the Station to gather material for a Ministry of Information film. Discussion groups have expressed themselves in lively terms on such subjects as 'The Vote' and the Far Eastern Question has been studied quite seriously if a trifle vaguely.
The scheme for the stimulation of interest of ground personnel into the operational side of the Station has continued this month. Thirty tradesmen of the Instrument and Electrical Sections have flown during this period and airmen of the Base Servicing Unit have been allowed to fly on air tests wherever possible.

6. The Opposition: Luftwaffe Night Fighters and Pilots

Messerschmitt Bf-109 (Me109), single Daimler Benz engine, armed with machine guns and / or 20 mm cannon dependent on mark. The Luftwaffe's iconic single-engined fighter won fame in the Battle of Britain in which it was a regular adversary for the Spitfires and Hurricanes of Fighter Command. In the night bombing war it was frequently used in the freelance 'Wilde Sau' role.

Messerschmitt Bf-110 (Me110) powered by twin Daimler Benz engines. Armament was two 20 mm cannon and four machine guns (forward firing), supplemented by one machine gun for defence. Often augmented by twin upward-firing 20 mm cannon in Shräge Musik configuration. A relative failure in the Battle of Britain, the Me110 came into its own as a night fighter, proving a deadly foe to Bomber Command's crews and aircraft.

Messerschmitt Me 210. Twin Daimler Benz engines. Armament two 20 mm cannon, two 7.92 mm machine guns. Intended to replace the Me110, the Me210 suffered from chronically poor handling and did not live up to initial expectations, meaning that the Me110 remained in service until the end of the war.

Messerschmitt 410. Powered by twin Daimler Benz 603 engines. Armament two 20 mm cannon and two 7.92 mm machine guns. A redesign of the Me 210 led to the vastly improved Me 410. The aircraft featured regularly in combat reports though was primarily intended as an intruder. The two types were so similar as to lead to understandable misidentification when be attacked by one at night.

Messerschmitt 262 powered by two Junkers Jumo turbojets. Armament was four 30 mm cannon, occasionally augmented by R4M rocket packs. Me262s were occasionally noted in combat reports by 514 Squadron crews. Though very much faster than their prey, this required new tactics by the night fighter jet pilots and the evidence suggests that they were more effective fighting the USAAF in daylight operations.

Junkers Ju 88. Powered by twin Junkers Jumo or BMW engines. Armament was typically three forward-firing 20 mm cannon with a further two Shräge Musick upward-firing 20 mm cannon mounted in the fuselage. Along with the Me110, the Ju 88 was a very effective night fighter and accounted for numerous 514 Squadron Lancasters.

Dornier Do 217. Powered by twin Junkers Jumo, Daimler Benz or BMW engines, according to variant. Photo shows Do 217 with Daimler Benz DB 603 in-line engines. Armament was four 20 mm cannon and four machine guns (various calibre). There was only one combat with a Do 217 reported by 514 Squadron's crews.

Focke Wulf Fw 190. Powered by single BMW 801 radial engine. Armament typically two machine guns and four 20 mm cannon. Like the Me109, the single-seat Fw 190 was usually deployed in the freelance role when night fighting.

Major Walter Borchers flying an Me110, shot down DS822, JI-T flown by P/O Bill McGown on 7th June 1944. Borchers was shot down and killed on 5th / 6th March 1945 by a Mosquito. 27 or 28 night victories.

Hptm. Hermann Greiner probably shot down HK571, JI-L and the crew of P/O Stanley Anderson on 20th July 1944. Greiner survived the war with 47 night victories.

Hptm. Heinz-Martin Hadeball possibly shot down W/O JL Lassam and his crew in HK570, JI-P, returning from Homberg on 20th July 1944. Hadeball survived the war with 27 night victories.

Hptm. Paul Zorner probably destroyed PB185 A2-F, flown by F/O Thomas Middleton on the Stuttgart raid of 24th July 1944. Zorner claimed 59 night victories and survived the war.

On 22nd March 1944 Ludwig 'Luk' Meister brought down F/L 'Nick' Nichol's DS815, JI-N near Trier. Another survivor of the conflict, Luk Meister claimed 35 night victories.

Hptm Heinrich, Prinz zu Sayn Wittgenstein possibly shot down F/L Joe Bourke RCAF and his crew aboard LL672, A2-C, attacking Magdeburg on 21st January 1944. Wittgenstein was killed very shortly afterwards, possibly shot down by Sgt Albert Williston, rear gunner in LL672. He had 83 night victories.

Ju 88 pilot Oblt Heinz Rökker accounted for two 514 Squadron Lancasters. On 22nd March 1944 he shot down LL684, A2-B, flown by F/S John Underwood. F/L Robert Jones and his crew in LM206, JI-C then fell victim to Rökker en route to Stuttgart on 28th July 1944.

Hptm Hubert Rauh survived the war with 32 victories, including DS816, JI-O, which he shot down returning from Valeciennes on 15 / 16th June 1944.

Ofw. Heinz Vinke, is believed to have accounted for LL627, JI-U with F/S Richard Bennett RCAF and crew on 21st January 1944 and, possibly, F/L George Boyd's DS706, JI-G on 30th January 1944. With 52 victories, Vinke was himself killed on 26th February 1944

Hauptmann Martin Drewes in his Me110 accounted for at least two of the squadron's aircraft. He shot down DS824, JI-K, flown by P/O John Williams, over the Ijsselmeer returning from Magdeburg on 21st January 1944. On 21st / 22nd May 1944 Drewes shot down five bombers, including LL695, JI-A flown by F/S Charlie Medland. Drewes survived the war with 43 night and 5 day victories. He was later described by RAF men who met him after the war as 'a true gentleman'.

Left: Feldwebel (later Leutnant) Rudolf Frank had 27 allied bombers to his credit when he was shot down by W/O Harold Fidge in 514 Squadron's first combat victory. Frank survived this incident, but crashed and was killed on 27th / 28th April 1944 after his aircraft was hit by debris from his final victim.

7. Germany Calling: August to October 1944

The poor weather of July continued into August with fog and drizzle welcoming the new month to Waterbeach, though it faired up enough to allow eighteen aircraft to take off for the flying bomb constructional works at De Nieppe on 1st August. There was complete cloud cover at 3,000 feet over the target area, which contained multiple aiming points, meaning that only 79 of the 777 aircraft deployed were able to bomb. Amongst these was F/S Don Gordon RAAF[28] in PB142, JI-A whose bomb aimer was able to pick out smoke from the red TIs from 12,000 feet. The Master Bomber cancelled the attack shortly afterwards and all aircraft returned safely to their bases. Whilst the squadron was out and about bombing things, the Station ORB noted that '*...four members of TRE Defford visited the station in connection with experimental flying. The WAAF held their monthly dance in the Airwomen's Mess. Once again the RAF were provided with a gay social evening by their Hostesses in uniform.*'

Another raid against the flying bomb menace was undertaken two days later with a massive attack on various sites involving 1,114 bombers. The contribution of nineteen Lancasters from Waterbeach was sent to Bois de Casson where the target was a supply depot. On this occasion, cloud over the target was scattered, all crews bombed visually and good photos were obtained.

Six aircraft were lost overall, the only one from the Bois de Casson target being LL716, A2-G. The crew had just bombed the target when it was hit by several bombs, believed by the navigator, F/O Stuart Baxter, to have been from a Halifax of No. 4 Group, whose attack time coincided with that of No. 3 Group. One bomb passed through each of LL716's wings with a third removing an engine, making the aircraft almost impossible for the pilot, F/O John 'Toppy' Topham, to control. Bomb aimer, F/O John McGlenaghan and Sgt John Scully, mid upper gunner, escaped by parachute but insufficient time was available for any other crew members

---

[28] Don Gordon survived the war but was killed in a flying accident shortly afterwards when his Spitfire crashed in Australia.

French civilians Claude Danis and his father pose next to the wreckage of LL716 after its crash-landing (Claude Danis via Colin Pateman).

to jump as the Lancaster plummeted towards the ground. Topham managed to crash-land successfully, the aircraft coming down at about 1410 hours, some 10km South of Beaumont (Oise). LL716 split into two main sections and eventually slewed across a roadway. On one side of the road there were fields and on the other side was woodland. This proved to be significant for the remaining crew members as those in the rear section were quickly located by the Germans while those in the front section were quickly able to escape into the trees. F/S William Egri, from the rear turret, along with F/S Harry Gilmore, the wireless operator, were able to get away from the crash site but were captured shortly afterwards. Sgt John Reid, the flight engineer, was more successful, being found by the Resistance who reunited him with McClenaghan and the navigator, F/O Stuart Baxter. Topham had sustained serious injuries to his legs in the crash landing. F/S Dennehy was flying as mid-under gunner, a role unique to the Mk.II Lancs, and one of the very few occasions when this happened in 514 Squadron service.

The crew's wireless operator, F/S Harry Gilmore, later recalled: 'This raid on the 3rd August 1944 was our 27th trip and we were as a crew, I believe, feeling rather good and optimistic about finishing our tour of 30 bombing trips. However this was not to be. As I recall, we had reached the target without any undue trouble, and had just dropped our bombs and were leaving the target area when things happened very quickly. There were sudden shouts of "We're going down - a bomb's gone through our wing". I clearly remember going down with the aircraft for what must have been of course only seconds, when I seemed to remember John, our pilot, shouting "Hold on".

Obviously he must have managed to regain control of the aircraft, for we were next coming down to crash land close to some woods. Our pilot obviously crash landed our Lancaster very well, for we all survived the crash, and managed to get out of the aircraft quickly. However the pilot broke his leg in the crash, and had to be left at a farmhouse.

Three of us, flight engineer, mid upper gunner, and I, were picked up in a wood by German troops within minutes, ending up prisoners of war. However the bomb aimer and navigator who were with the pilot at the farmhouse managed to get to Paris, only to be picked up five days later, also ending up prisoners of war. Three days after we crashed, that same area including the farmhouse was over-run by our troops having pushed back the German troops. As a result our pilot was eventually flown back to England.

I must say that I was always aware of the possibility of being 'shot down', but never being 'bombed down' by one of our own aircraft.'

F/O Topham was hidden by the Resistance and, when the SS arrived in the vicinity of his hiding place he was buried in a makeshift 'grave' with a breathing tube whilst they searched the house in which he had been staying. He was protected from the weight of the soil by wooden boards. Flowers were placed on the grave for effect. Topham was told this would be for thirty minutes or so. The householder, a Monsieur Duval, told the SS that he had buried a shot down British airman, showing them the grave. The two SS officers, somewhat unexpectedly, saluted the grave and left. Unfortunately they posted two sentries close to the property, so M. Duval could not release Topham until they left, some 36 hours later. Eventually he was dug out, in a poor state, and returned to the house. At that point, an SS officer came back and demanded entry. The occupants tried to persuade the pilot to get back in his 'grave' but he was having none of it. Topham borrowed a pistol from one of the Resistance members and shot dead the SS officer when he entered the room in which he was hiding. The SS man was buried in the makeshift grave which by now aroused no suspicion. Topham was liberated later the same day when Allied troops arrived[29].

Gilmore and Egri were sent to the Luftwaffe interrogation centre and thence to a POW camp at Bankau, where they were reunited with Scully. Under the circumstances they might have considered themselves more fortunate than their crew mates Reid, Baxter and McClenaghan. The latter trio were sheltered together by the Resistance before being moved to Paris where they were betrayed and handed over to the Gestapo. From there matters went rapidly downhill. They were thrown into Fresnes jail, along with some of the Resistance members who had helped them. Inside Fresnes were a number of other RAF airmen. All had been shot down over occupied France and some had been captured in civilian clothing and had false papers, the Germans therefore treating them as suspected spies. Others were simply designated 'Terrorflieger' (terror fliers). Fresnes was notorious as an interrogation centre for members of the Resistance, who were usually, and brutally, tortured before being executed at the abattoir at Mont St Marsin or sent to a concentration camp.
The latter sanction was to be the lot of the three crewmen from LL716 as they were amongst 2,000 prisoners evacuated from Fresnes, including 78 RAF evaders. Tightly packed into cattle trucks, they endured a horrendous journey lasting over eight days, in which several men were shot at while trying to escape, one being killed. When anyone tried to escape the SS would take it out on the occupants of the truck concerned, beating the prisoners and removing their clothing. They arrived at Buchenwald on August 20th 1944 to be confronted by the sight of their emaciated fellow prisoners and realised that they were in serious trouble. The aircrew were subjected to the same evil and brutal regime as other inmates. The consignment of prisoners arrived at Buchenwald, to be assailed by the smoke and fumes emanating from the chimney of the camp crematorium. 25,000 wretched prisoners were in the camp, grievously abused by their Nazi captors. The 'terrorfliegers' had their heads shaved, any wounds from the blunt clippers being washed with a purple liquid, before being issued with the infamous striped concentration camp uniform.

---

[29] F/O John Topham DFC transferred to Transport Command on his return to England, survived the war, and went home to Newcastle where, tragically, he died aged 58 when run over by a lorry.

The senior officer amongst the RAF airmen was S/Ldr Phil Lamason RNZAF, who was inspirational in pulling the group together. Lamason was told by one of the German Communist prisoners that orders had been received by the commandant to exterminate the 'terrorfliegers'. Lamason was able to visit another part of the camp where he managed to contact Wing Commander Yeo-Thomas, a captured agent of the British Special Operations Executive (SOE). Between them they managed to pass a message to the Luftwaffe, possibly via the Red Cross. There followed several exchanges between the Luftwaffe and SS, as a result of which the Allied airmen were released from Buchenwald into the hands of the Luftwaffe. Most were transferred to Stalag Luft III at Sagan, of Great Escape fame. Luftwaffe personnel supervised the subsequent rescue of those who were unable to move with the rest on 19th October 1944. Although some airmen died through the abuse they had endured, the Luftwaffe had saved them all from execution at the hands of the SS. Their travails were not at an end as, like many POWs, the trio from 514 Squadron had to endure forced marches as the Allies closed in on the Nazi regime. All three survived.

W/Cdr Yeo-Thomas MC was also transferred out of Buchenwald, having exchanged his identity for that of a dead French prisoner. He wound up in a camp for French POWs at Marienburg, from which he led a breakout of twenty prisoners. Ten were shot dead in the attempt but Yeo-Thomas survived again. Recaptured only 500 yards from Allied lines he then escaped once more, this time leading a group of French prisoners past German patrols to the American positions. He later received the George Cross for his bravery whilst serving as an agent with the SOE and for his excellent work at Buchenwald.

F/O John Topham was awarded an immediate DFC, not least for evading capture. Baxter, Reid and McClenaghan compiled intelligence reports on their return. They received no recognition for the incredible hardship they had endured at Buchenwald and elsewhere[30].

On 4th August another French target was selected, sixteen Lancasters attacking the oil tanks at the Bec d'Ambes depot on a clear early evening. After bombing from 8,000 feet, F/S Richardson in JI-T HK572 reported

[30] The account of the Topham crew's experiences is taken from *Unshackled Spirit* by Colin Pateman (Fonthill Media 2013) with kind permission of Mr. Pateman.

'Aircraft orbited target after bombing. Rear gunner and mid upper gunner fired burst at two tankers in the river at 2,000 feet.' The gunners were Sgt RR Smith (rear) and Sgt B Vine (MU). This was a rare example of the Lancaster being used in a ground attack / anti-shipping role and reflected apparent confidence on the part of the crew that they would not themselves become a sitting duck for the ground defences, even though light flak had been noted. In the event there were no losses from the 288 aircraft participating in the attack. For the first time, Serrate-equipped Mosquitoes were used as escorts. Serrate detected and homed in on the Liechtenstein radar fitted to German night fighters, turning the hunters into prey. No combats were reported. W/O Geoff Payne, in LL624, JI-R, enjoyed the flight. 'Take off time was l330hrs. To avoid being detected by the German radar we were detailed to fly out below 4,000 ft. Setting course in close formation, we joined up with other squadrons at Falmouth, Cornwall then out to sea heading for the Bay of Biscay, an area notorious for patrols of Ju88s. Nearing the French coast we climbed to our bombing height then went into bomb. The attack was extremely successful as I could see the storage tanks on fire and a tanker alongside the jetty listing badly. Very strange that there was only light flak in the vicinity, it being obvious that we had caught the defences unawares. It was a relatively pleasant journey on the way back but it must have been quite a strain for our pilot flying at that low level. A couple of our Mosquito escorts buzzed us on the way home which was gratifying. Back at base after an eight hour flight and ready for a 48 hour pass.'

A further attack on oil storage facilities was laid on for the following evening, as 309 aircraft carried out a combined raid against three targets along the River Gironde. The target for the fourteen aircraft of 514 Squadron was Bassen oil depot, near Bordeaux. Thirteen carried out their task successfully, S/L Philip Clay in his usual PB143, JI-B noting two large explosions seen with flames up to 1,000 feet followed by dense black smoke. P/O PF Carter in LM627, JI-D and F/S Leslie Drew in LM277, JI-F both reported their aircraft damaged by flak over the target. LM627 sustained a holed wing whilst LM277 suffered damage to the rear turret, hydraulics and oxygen system. Both aircraft returned safely to base. P/O Frank Hebditch in DS786, A2-H followed the Master Bomber's instructions to bomb the yellow TIs from 8,000 feet, noting flames and smoke in the target area. Unfortunately, altering course as the TIs went down resulted in his crew bombing the wrong target, hitting the airfield at Blaye et St Luce rather than the oil depot. One aircraft failed to return from the combined raid, which otherwise achieved excellent results.

Bomber Command was called upon to attack troop concentrations on the night of 7th August, these being in the vicinity of Mare de Magne, south of Caen. The operation was to support an attack by Canadian ground forces. Major General KN Crawford CB, MC of the War Office, accompanied by Group Captain RR Nash, visited the station again. He was flown by F/L Tony Prager of No. 514 Squadron in ME841, JI-H, one of the fifteen Lancasters sent from Waterbeach, and viewed the night's operation on a target in Northern France. Major General Crawford commented, 'On approach to target I noticed gun flashes and gun fire on ground and Bofors tracer very clearly. Searchlights appeared after bombing, Red TIs dropped in identical position as red star shells. Bombing very concentrated.'

Fighters were much in evidence on this operation; the night fighter controllers were faced with five separate streams, each of some two hundred aircraft. Shortly before midnight the Mare de Magne force was intercepted by enemy aircraft with 24 combats being reported.

At 2351hrs and again six minutes later F/S Maurice Oliver's crew in DS826, A2-C encountered hostility, rear gunner F/S JT Maphan and mid upper gunner F/S WJ Larler exchanging fire with incoming fighters after warnings from their wireless operator, Sgt CF Bolton. On both occasions the Lancaster escaped unharmed. LM265, JI-E flown by P/O Don Gordon came under attack from an unseen fighter at 2353hrs, Sgt B Robinson firing back from the rear turret. The enemy pilot gave up first.

A successful combat was reported by F/O John Harland and his crew in LL728, A2-L whose mid upper gunner Sgt Stanley Lucas spotted an FW190 closing from 400 yards to port. He 'reported it to the rear gunner', probably an understatement, and ordered a corkscrew to port. He and rear gunner Sgt Leonard Slocombe opened fire, the fighter bursting into flames and diving into the sea where its destruction was verified by the crew of F/S Oliver in DS826, A2-C. The victory, one of two successes claimed by the attacking force against fighters on the operation, was confirmed and credited to F/O Harland's crew.

The last of the squadron's air combats that evening was at 0020hrs when LM286, A2-F flown by F/O Frank Hebditch evaded an Me410, mid upper gunner Sgt Cecil Clarke opening fire on the other aircraft which was lost in the ensuing corkscrew.

All 514 Squadron's aircraft returned to Waterbeach safely, though ten others were lost, mostly to the fighters. Only 600 aircraft bombed, the attack being very carefully controlled to avoid collateral damage. The results were good with German positions being significantly damaged.

The intensive schedule continued on 8th August, on the morning of which three aircraft were flown to Farnborough for unspecified 'special equipment' to be fitted. That night seventeen aircraft were detailed to attack petrol storage at Foret de Lucheux. The target was left well ablaze. There was some fighter activity, notably over the target area. F/S Stanley Wilson in LM265, JI-E was in the target area when his rear gunner, Sgt J Golden, opened fire on an approaching FW190. Strikes were seen on the enemy fighter and, though no claim was initially made in the combat report, one was subsequently noted in the squadron ORB and Luftwaffe records showed that a single engine fighter was shot down[31]. Of the 180 bombers taking part only one, Lancaster LM166 from neighbouring 115 Sqn was lost.

Petrol storage at Fort d'Englos was the target the next night, 9th August, in an operation that was very similar though, with 311 bombing participants, somewhat larger than before. Twelve aircraft from Waterbeach took part. Only one combat was reported, that being by W/O Norman Jennings in ME841, JI-H, whose rear gunner Sgt C Haslam reacted swiftly when he spotted a Ju88 seven hundred yards away, firing at it as he shouted for a corkscrew. All participants in the raid returned safely to England.

More railway facilities were targeted on the afternoon of 11th August, thirteen of 514's crews being tasked with bombing the marshalling yards at Lens. There was patchy cloud over the target area and flak was negligible. The Master Bomber's clear and concise instructions also helped in bombing being very concentrated. Of the 459 aircraft tasked, only one was lost, this being from another squadron. However LL697, A2-B was hit by bombs from above. The pilot, W/O William Brickwood

---

[31] Nachtjagd War Diaries

reported: *'Bombed at 1633hrs, 14,000 feet. Bomb Aimer had given 'Steady' when Lancaster was hit in nose by bombs from Lancaster above. The bomb aimer and equipment were hurled from aircraft. Pilot tried to jettison bombs but believed already gone. All instruments on panel u/s except altimeter. Aircraft was assisted back to Woodbridge by 'E2'.'* The bomb aimer, F/O Harold Crampton RNZAF, was not wearing his parachute and was killed. Whilst the other Lancaster is not identified, the ORB includes a record showing that PB142, JI-A flown by F/S Thomas Charlton released its bombs at 1633hrs from 14,500 feet. It is therefore a distinct possibility that it was bombs from PB142 that hit LL697, the lower Lancaster not being visible to the bomb aimer in the higher-flying aircraft as he concentrated on his own bomb sight. F/O Crampton is buried in Loos British Cemetery.

Another of Bomber Command's, by now occasional, forays into Germany was ordered on the night of 12th / 13th August with a split raid being carried out on Brunswick and Rüsselsheim. Five crews from ‘A’ Flight were sent to attack Brunswick, amongst 379 carrying out an experimental raid using only H2S. W/O Norman Jennings had to jettison his bomb load and return early when PB143, JI-B suffered from insufficient fuel pressure to the starboard outer engine. Heavy flak, moderate in intensity, damaged ME641, JI-H flown by F/L Tony Prager. Flak also damaged the fuselage and hydraulics of PB142, JI-A whose pilot F/L George Bradford found that the bomb doors would not open over the target though they did so when he attacked the last resort target of Terschelling instead. By way of consolation the crew managed to obtain a target photo of Brunswick to prove that they had actually attended the event. LM288, JI-C flown by W/O Cyril Williams suffered a seized engine which was feathered after leaving the target. F/S Geoff France’s LM286, A2-F was the only Waterbeach aircraft to successfully bomb the target whilst emerging completely unscathed. He noted that the bombing appeared to be rather scattered, though there was black smoke up to between six and eight thousand feet. Unfortunately the tactic of relying solely on H2S with no other marking was not a spectacular success with towns up to twenty miles being bombed in error. Losses totaled 27 so were relatively high, the night fighters having arrived over the target area at 0028hrs having initially been misdirected to Bremen.

Meanwhile, a second raid was being carried out against Rüsselsheim, twelve of the squadron's crews being tasked amongst 297 attacking the Opel motor factory. Nine of the Waterbeach contingent bombed the primary target. Amongst these was W/O Geoff Payne in LL635, JI-M. 'We went back to the German industrial towns with a night operation to Rüsselsheim near Frankfurt. The target was the Opel factories who were manufacturing aircraft and military vehicles. I was very apprehensive as, this was my third visit to Frankfurt and it held many unpleasant memories. It was a clear night with heavy flak and many searchlights and fighter flares. Overall, an incident free trip but losses were high; thirty aircraft, a loss rate of 6.7%'

Markers were scattered and numerous fires sprang up. The weather was clear and the Master Bomber was able to instruct crews to bomb the centre of the fires, though F/S Arthur Holland in LM285, JI-H noted that the Master Bomber just appeared to be talking to his deputy rather than anyone else. Whatever the reason the attack was very scattered with many bombs falling in open fields. There were many fighters active, with the result that

F/L Malcolm 'Mac' Head RNZAF, DSO and crew with PD324, A2-B, possibly to mark the completion of their tour on 30th October 1944. Sgt Albert Beckford (2nd from left) received the DFM for shooting down two enemy aircraft.

twenty aircraft were lost from the attacking force. F/L Malcolm Head claimed an FW190 destroyed by his rear gunner, F/S Albert Beckford. 315 night fighters had been sent up to intercept the raids; of these seven were confirmed as lost.
Two of the squadron's aircraft were amongst those failing to return. LM180, JI-G was flown by F/S John Lawrie RNZAF. The aircraft was shot down at 0130hrs by a night-fighter, probably that flown by Uffz. Hermann Möckel of 2./NJG4. This was Möckel's only victim in his career as a night fighter pilot. He was himself shot down by an Allied night fighter on 29-30/12 1944, surviving as a POW. The aircraft bombed the target from 18,000 feet at about 0015hrs, returning at 10,000 feet. Just before 0200hrs, over south central Belgium, the wireless operator, Sgt George Durland, was preparing to receive a Group Broadcast when LM180 was attacked by a fighter. Although the Lancaster was equipped with 'Fishpond', designed to detect night fighters, the operator was not trained in its use so the set was switched off and the attack came without warning. The Australian rear gunner, F/Sgt Bob Chester-Master, saw tracer coming from an aircraft which he identified as a JU88 closing in from about 300 yards range. He immediately ordered 'Corkscrew Starboard!' and returned fire, being joined by the mid-upper gunner, F/S Sam Burford RAAF. F/S Chester-Master claimed that the starboard engine of the fighter caught fire and the aircraft dived away, though he did not see it crash.
It appeared that the Lancaster was hit by cannon fire on both wings and the starboard inner engine, causing a coolant leak. F/S Lawrie ordered his crew to put their parachutes on. The flight engineer, Sgt Tommy Young, feathered the starboard inner engine, and Lawrie asked for a course to the emergency airfield at Manston. The aircraft was losing height, becoming harder to control and then the starboard outer engine also failed. When the Lancaster was at one thousand feet Lawrie ordered the crew to bale out, which they did, whilst he remained at the controls allowing them to do so. The crew landed safely, although Sgt Durland broke his ankle. All six crewmen successfully evaded capture. The body of F/S John Lawrie, who had sacrificed his own life to save his crew, was found in the burnt out wreckage of his Lancaster. F/S Chester-Master gave the following account: *'Rüsselsheim, the target, was a town in the south west of Germany, where the local Opel factory was making wings for the Vl (buzz bomb), which was wreaking havoc in London and the surrounding areas.*

Our job was to 'knock it out' of production. Each aircraft would be loaded with 13,000 lbs of high explosive bombs, plus canisters of fire bombs. A total of 297 aircraft would participate, comprising 191 Lancasters, 96 Halifaxes and 10 Mosquitoes.
The ground crew were making their final checks. A few brief moments of banter, good luck, safe return wishes and now it was our turn. Each man climbed into the plane to take up their positions, as I crawled to the rear. Before opening the turret doors, it was necessary for me to stow my parachute in the rack on the port side of the fuselage, as there was no room inside the turret. In my bulky outfit, I settled in and carried out my pre-flight checks, turret rotation, depressing and elevating the guns, checking mechanisms and searching for oil leaks from the firing rams. With a check of the reflector sights and a final wipe of the inside of the perspex, which was my only protection from the elements, I was ready for whatever the night would bring.
One by one, the crew reported all systems go and we were ready for takeoff. The four throttles were gradually opened and we were on our way to the main runway. We were number three for takeoff, 30 secs behind number two. The green light shone steady and we were on our way to the night's adventure. Gradually speed increased -ninety-five, one hundred, one hundred and five as the tail lifted. (I was always first off and last down). The skipper lifted from the runway and started the climb. The wheels folded away and we became a clean, dark and brutal shadow, loaded with fuel, fire and explosive.
We had joined the stream at 7,000 feet and began the slow climb to operational height. At 10,000 feet, all crew connected to oxygen, to prevent altitude sickness and unconsciousness. I turned on my heating system and gradually felt the warmth flowing through, but as we climbed higher, it would be barely sufficient.
Our track would take us across the enemy coast in a south easterly direction, thus avoiding the heavier anti-aircraft fire along the Dutch coast. We also knew that the German defences would now be alerted to our coming and it would only be a matter of time before we met the opposition. The Germans had very sophisticated radar and could quickly alert all anti-aircraft batteries, as well as the Luftwaffe, who, in this area, were using JU88's with very heavy fire power - 7.62mm machine guns and up to five 20mm cannon. Ahead, the horizon was brightening and tonight

the moon would arise to near full and we realised that this would help the enemy fighters when it came time to turn homewards.
As we left the target area under the orange lit cloud of smoke and dust, I could not help but wonder what carnage we had caused. Time over target had been 0015 hours, which meant a very high state of concentration for 4 hours and we still had a long way to get home. The eyes were getting very tired and it was becoming difficult to focus as there was only the framework of the turret and the guns and the darkness.
Suddenly, the night sky was aglow with green tracer bullets snaking towards us - we were under attack. Quickly ordering "corkscrew starboard - go", I opened fire at the dark object at about 300 yards - it was the dreaded JU88 night fighter. He had come from below and as he came closer and then broke away to port, he gave me a wonderful opportunity to rake his fuselage. A fire started and even in the darkness I could see pieces breaking off his plane. He then rolled over and went into a dive, trailing smoke and fire. He was mortally wounded - a victory to us (later confirmed).
The mid upper gunner came on the intercom to report - "Skipper, starboard inner hit - it's on fire". The engineer reached for the graviners to work the fire extinguishers - "Engine feathered, skipper". The mid-upper gunner now reported that he could see fuel flowing over the port wing, but a check of the panels, indicated it was more likely to be engine coolant, so the port outer was also shut down. The skipper reported loss of control of the aircraft and ordered "Bale out, bale out, we are down to 2,000 feet". This did not give us much time, as I still had to centre my turret, open the doors, crawl out and take my parachute from its storage rack. Ripping off my gloves, I fumbled with the clips as I crawled to the rear door. Up front, the skipper was trying to hold the plane level, as the engineer, bomb aimer and navigator, dropped through the hatch. By doing this, the skipper did not have time himself and as I found out much later, he went down with his plane.
Meanwhile we kept losing height and I could see the rear escape door open and realised that I was the last to leave from this exit. Reaching the door, I could see the ground below and flung myself into the night. It was theoretic practice to count to seven before pulling the ripcord, but there was no time for that and I pulled as I jumped. I felt the parachute open, but almost immediately hit the ground very heavily and felt a surge of pain

shoot up my left foot. I estimate that I had jumped from about 700 feet and that the 'chute had not fully opened. The pain in my leg now became intense, so I opened my escape 'kit' and swallowed a couple of pain killers. As soon as some of the pain was relieved, I crawled to the nearest haystack and burrowed into the base, where I fell into an exhausted sleep.'

LM265, JI-E flown by F/S Edgar Richardson was lost to an unrecorded cause. The aircraft crashed at 0030 hours, in the village of Engegstadt, about 10 miles south west of Mainz, Germany. It was possibly shot down by Lt. Otto Teschner, 11./NJG1, who claimed a 4-engine aircraft at 0030 hours in the Bad Kreuznach area, which is in the vicinity of where the Lancaster crashed. The only survivor was Sgt GM Holt, the flight engineer, who was taken prisoner.

14th August saw 805 aircraft, including eight from Waterbeach, attack troop concentrations at Hamel. The clear weather allowed a good view of the target indicators and effective bombing. Tragically, mid-way through the raid Canadian ground forces in a large quarry set off yellow flares which were confused with target indicators by 70 of the bomber crews. The ensuing bombing led to the deaths of thirteen of the soldiers. This incident detracted from the otherwise successful raid which saw the loss of only two aircraft.

On 15th August, Headquarters staff found something else to come and inspect at Waterbeach as Air Commodore AW Mylne of HQ Bomber Command visited the Station to study the Flying Clothing Cloakroom system. That evening, as the spell of fine weather continued, St. Trond airfield was the target. Twelve of the squadron's Lancasters took part in the raid which consisted of 1004 aircraft, the crews' flying clothing presumably being suitably organised. Bomber Command's AOC was preparing for a sustained assault on Germany once more and this operation was to attack nine Luftwaffe airfields in Belgium and Holland. It would have been a matter of no little satisfaction to the crews that night fighters from St. Trond had brought down twelve aircraft from the Rüsselsheim raid two nights earlier. The raid on St. Trond was carried out just after noon as Allied air superiority over the western part of Occupied Europe was now sufficient to allow heavy bombers to attack Luftwaffe airfields in the middle of the day. Only three bombers were lost from the multiple attack on the Luftwaffe's night fighter crews as they slept.

Of note was a highly creditable attack by P/O Len Saltmarsh in LL624, JI-L. Whilst still fifteen miles short of the target his aircraft experienced engine trouble including a failure of the starboard outer which was feathered. He pressed home his attack, aiming for the intersection of the runways. Having released his 13,000 lb bomb load, P/O Saltmarsh then flew his ailing Lancaster home, with the three remaining engines all giving trouble. He was recommended for a DFC following his exploits over St. Trond, and earlier raids on Vaires and Emieville when he had specifically stayed close to other damaged bombers to escort them home. The citation for the award of his DFC was published in the London Gazette 3 October 1944. It read: *'Flying Officer L. J. Saltmarsh has so far completed 17 successful sorties as Pilot and Captain of Lancaster aircraft, and has been most conspicuous at all times for his extremely high standard of courage and resoluteness. On two difficult occasions during daylight attacks on Vaires on 12 July 1944 and on Emieville on 18 August 1944, he observed a crippled bomber proceeding at a very much reduced speed away from the target. On both occasions he dropped behind the main bomber stream in order to escort the damaged bomber safely back to England. On 15 August, during a daylight attack on the airfield at St. Trond, one of his engines became unserviceable on the way to the target and the propeller had to be feathered. But in spite of the fact that he was getting behind the main stream, owing to his reduced speed, he pressed on and bombed the target, and secured an aiming point photograph. On the way back from the target another engine became unserviceable but did not deter Flying Officer Saltmarsh from proceeding to and bombing an alternative airfield target with a bomb that had failed to be released over the primary target, and once more he secured an aiming point photograph. He eventually arrived safely over base and made a perfect two-engined landing. It was not until after he had landed that he reported the fact that two engines had become unserviceable during the sortie. This very gallant Pilot is strongly recommended for the award of the Distinguished Flying Cross.'*

His first tour of operations commenced with a strike against L'Hey on the 23 June and ending with another against Emmerich on 7 October, the intervening period witnessing him attack numerous French targets in support of the Allied invasion, but also a number of heavily defended German targets, including Bremen, Dortmund, Saarbrucken, Stettin and Stuttgart. As confirmed by the recommendation for his DFC after 17 sorties, several of these trips were not without incident, his flying log book further stating that his Lancaster received flak damage during strikes against enemy panzers and transport at Villiers Bocage on 30 June and against a supply depot at Beauvoir on 2 July. He also sustained similar damage during a visit to Bremen on the night of 18-19 August[32].

There was more variety the following night, 16th August, with the briefing room map's ribbons leading the squadron to and from Stettin. Ten aircraft left Waterbeach, one of which returned early with generator trouble, this being LL677, A2-E flown by W/O Don Beaton. In total 461 Lancasters attacked industry and the docks in the Baltic port. P/O Gordon Smith in LL624, JI-Q, suffered the loss of two engines, one whilst over the target and the second whilst far out over the North Sea, making for a nervous return to England, where the crew landed on two engines at Woodbridge. Successful counter-measures, including a 'Mandrel' screen and radio silence were assisted by the absence of moonlight and the presence of a thin layer of clouds. As a result the few encounters with the Luftwaffe occurred by chance, only five bombers being lost from the Stettin force. Other raids, to Kiel and mining sorties, experienced similarly low losses. The Stettin raid was a success with five ships sunk and eight damaged, along with much destruction to the port and surrounding industrial area. W/O Geoff Payne, in LL635, JI-M, remembers that this was not a popular choice of target. 'Loud groans rose from the assembled crews as the target - Stettin – was revealed, a Polish port away in the Baltic. We were to adopt the same tactics as employed in the successful daylight raid on Bec de Ambes and to fly out below 4,000ft under the radar screen. A diversionary raid would also take place against Kiel in an attempt to confuse the German defences. Take off time was 2100hrs; we set out over the North Sea, crossing over the northern tip of Denmark. To the north we could see the lights of Stockholm with one or two searchlights waving about, accompanied by a few bursts of flak. I think they were warning us to keep clear although I knew that some of our aircraft had wandered into Swedish neutral airspace.

---

[32] P/O Len Saltmarsh subsequently transferred to the PFF and survived the war as a Squadron Leader. He was awarded the bar to his DFC following the end of his second tour, by which time he had completed 53 operations, 25 of which had been with 514 Squadron. He subsequently returned to his previous career as a police officer.

Continuing on over the Baltic we began to gain height in preparation for the attack. Not too many searchlights about with a moderate amount flak we bombed and turned away, dropping very quickly down to almost sea level for our flight back home. Uneventful trip back to base after eight and

Engine problems and flak damage did not hinder PB419, JI-N too much as she completed 32 operations. Seen here on an operation to the Ruhr Valley, she was finally struck off charge in 1947. The photo was taken by the crew of F/O Brian Haslam (WMHM).

a half hours' flight. It seemed as though the tactics employed on that raid were successful, with Stettin being very badly damaged, unfortunately our squadron lost one aircraft crashing in Denmark on the return flight. Five aircraft were lost on that raid.'

The German night fighter controllers' anticipation that Bremen would be attacked was fulfilled within the week. The city was the target for 288 bombers, including seventeen from 514 Squadron, on the night of 18th August. The ORB summarised the raid afterwards: *'16 aircraft attacked the primary target, one aircraft attacked Emden. There was no cloud over the target but slight haze. The Aiming Point was well marked with flares and TIs and bombing was well concentrated around markers, the whole area left a mass of flames with smoke rising up to 10,000 feet. All aircraft returned safely to base.'*

The errant crew was that of W/O Don Beaton in LL677, A2-E, who suffered 'navigation trouble' meaning that the crew arrived late over the target, never a palatable prospect. There was nothing to see so he moved on. As soon as his aircraft came under fire from a flak battery he promptly released his bombs. This happened to be over Emden at 0042hrs, some 25 minutes after his colleagues had bombed Bremen. As the city was in enemy, rather than occupied, territory, the Lancaster Mk.IIs taking part were able to make the most of their ability to carry 8,000lb 'blockbuster' bombs, contributing to the mayhem on the ground. F/O Frank Hebditch in LL728, A2-L commented that fires could be seen from eighty miles away. With excellent marking and fine weather conditions, the end result was the most destructive attack on Bremen of the war. A fire-storm was started and over 8,500 homes and apartments were destroyed. More than sixty ships were damaged and eighteen sunk. 1,100 tons of bombs were dropped by the attacking force and Bremen was devastated.

The squadron enjoyed the luxury of a long operational stand down after Bremen, the next assignment not arising until the evening of 25th August. Before flying commenced there was more administrative excitement on the Station as Group Captain LS Scott-Edeson and members of the Air Ministry's Establishments Committee visited the Station 'for the purpose of collecting data relating to the establishment of personnel for Stock Recording duties.'

Earlier in the day, several of the unit's long-serving Mk.II Lancasters were shipped out to Bottesford as they were replaced by Mks. I and III variants, though a limited number of the old workhorses still remained on the squadron's strength. A split operation was ordained that evening, nine crews tasked with participating in a 161-strong GH raid on a flying bomb site at Vincly whilst twelve were despatched on a repeat visit to the Opel factory at Rüsselsheim, part of an attack comprising 421 Lancasters. Two aircraft failed to join the Vincly raid, including LL624, JI-R flown by P/O Len Saltmarsh. On take-off the aircraft's starboard tyre burst causing the wing to drop and the propellers to ground. The Lancaster, laden with bombs and fuel, skidded across the airfield out of control. According to

The end of the line for venerable Lancaster Mk.II LL624, JI-R. A burst tyre led to damage that was no longer economical to repair. She was struck off charge after 36 ops with 514 Squadron and an unknown total before that with 115 Sqn (WMHM).

F/L John Wake DFC, the flight engineer who was onboard that day, the crew chose to abandon the aircraft even before it had come to a stop, fearing a massive explosion. Luckily there was no fire and the munitions remained intact. However that was the end of LL624 which was struck off charge.

The Vincly raid itself, dependent on GH leaders, took place in the mid evening, bombing being around 2030hrs. There was flak over the target area, and three aircraft were lost from the raid though all those from 514 Squadron returned safely. F/O Ted Cossens brought LL635, JI-M home with flak damage and the aircraft, a veteran of 39 sorties, was deemed to be damaged beyond repair. She was, however, kind to her crew, returning them uninjured from her final sortie. Sgt Geoff Page, rear gunner in LL635, saw an unidentified Lancaster spiral into the ground with only two parachutes deploying.

The Rüsselsheim raid was a success with accurate marking and the bombing completed in ten minutes. It was traumatic for two of the squadron's crews; F/S Ian Campbell RAAF in PB419, JI-N had to cope with a lack of oil pressure in the starboard inner engine, resulting in that power plant being shut down, the aircraft also being coned by searchlights on the run up to the target. Meanwhile F/O Gordon Smith in HK572, JI-T, having been promoted overnight, had the Perspex blown from the mid upper turret by flak over Rüsselsheim, fortunately without apparent injury to the gunner, F/S Lewis Shaw RAAF. Fifteen of the Lancaster force failed

'C' Flight commander S/L John Timms occasionally preferred a slower means of transport than his Lancaster (Bruce Johnston)

to return, though all 514 Squadron's crews were spared.

A further outing to Kiel on 26th August was the next trip for seventeen crews. Fires created from heavy bombing were fanned by strong winds and smoke obscured the PFF markers, but bombing was fairly concentrated none the less. The town hall as well as many other public buildings were destroyed. Local reporting described the attack as a very serious raid, suggesting that it was effective.

F/O Alfred Uffindell RNZAF in HK577, JI-P, was attacked on the run in by two Me109s. He subsequently submitted the following combat reports, claiming the destruction of one of the enemy fighters by rear gunner F/S Max Clark:

1st Encounter: At the target area (bombs not dropped), course 012 degrees, height 19,000 feet, IAS 180. At 2308 hours, the M/U Gunner reported an Me109 flying on opposite course, range 300 yards port beam level. The E/A turned in to attack and the M/U Gunner gave order to

corkscrew port and opened fire with a 5 second burst. The rear gunner noted position of end of trace, and fired a one second burst. E/A closed to 150 yards, then broke away starboard down and was not seen again.
2nd Encounter: As the first E/A broke away the rear gunner sighted another E/A, recognised as an Me109 attacking from the fine port quarter down range 600 yards. Pilot was still corkscrewing from first attack and was going down port in this instance. The rear gunner opened fire immediately, firing until a burst of flames was seen coming from the nose of the E/A. The E/A continued to close in, rear gunner firing throughout attack. The E/A then dropped away on its port wing and dived to the ground in flames. The M/U Gunner and rear gunner saw the E/A burning on the ground.
Fighter activity was quite intense, and LL728, A2-L failed to return with F/O Frank Hebditch and his crew, the only survivor being F/O Kenneth Robinson, the bomb aimer. The aircraft was shot down by the night-fighter of Fw. Gottfried Schneider, 1./NJG3, crashing near Kleve at 2345hrs, 10 km SSE of Friedrichstadt. LL728, one of three successes for Fw. Schneider that night, was lost on its return from the target area. Seventeen of the attacking force was lost overall.
F/O Robert Hardwick in DS620, A2-D could not bomb, due an electrical fault causing his bombs to hang up, though he subsequently managed to jettison the 4,000lb High Capacity bomb over the North Sea. This was a more popular outcome with the crew than trying to land with the 'cookie' as well as a full load of incendiaries. 'C' Flight's commander S/L John Timms in LM286, A2-F also found he was unable to get rid of eight of his 30lb incendiaries, whilst F/O Gordon Smith, this time in PB426, JI-J, suffered additional problems for the third trip in a row, losing an engine over the target area once again, which caused his bombs to undershoot.
Fitter Eric Basford later explained the procedures for dealing with bomb hang-ups. 'Occasionally, it happened that the crew of an aircraft having bombed the target would find that they had a 'hang up', i.e. a bomb still in position on its rack. Attempts would then be made to shake it clear on the way home. Sometimes they were successful, sometimes not. However, the vibrations on landing often dislodged the bomb and the aircraft would taxi round to its dispersal with the bomb resting on the bomb doors. In such circumstances, the pilot would not open the bomb doors before shutting off the engines, as was the normal practice with Lancasters. The aircrew

invariably left the aircraft smartly and the bomb could usually be discerned through the joint of the two bomb doors.
The armourers would be called to deal at once with the potential hazard. They would arrive with a bomb trolley, one of their hand winches and several old bedding biscuits (small mattresses). After positioning the biscuits under the bomb doors, one would go into the cockpit and everyone else would stand well clear. As the man in the cockpit put the bomb door lever to 'open', the bomb would slowly emerge and suddenly fall onto the soft bedding underneath. The other armourers would then return to the aircraft and winch up the bomb, lower it onto the trolley and tow it back to the bomb dump. The whole procedure was simple, if crude, but it never failed as far as I know.
Dealing with a hang-up could be more complicated if the bomb happened to be a delayed action type. In that event, the armourers would examine the bomb for signs of staining, which would indicate that the acid bottle had broken and the bomb was set to explode, after a certain time interval. If the bottle had broken, the bomb was winched back onto its rack in the bomb bay. One of the senior pilots, often a Flight Commander, would take-off with it as soon as possible accompanied by only one other senior aircrew member. They would fly out to a designated area in The Wash to dump the problem bomb. That routine never failed either as far as I am aware.'
A further couple of nights off was then followed by another trip to Stettin on the night of 29th August. Ten Lancasters took off from Waterbeach, eight of which attacked the target just after 0200hrs. No combats were reported, though S/L Clay's former mount, PB143, JI-B flown by F/S Thomas Charlton, was shot down at 0012 hours en route to the target, by Oblt. Fritz Brandt of Stab II./NJG3. PB143 crashed into the sea off the village of Estruplund, Denmark. There were no survivors amongst the crew, who were on only their second op. 23 aircraft were lost from the 403 making up the attacking force. Despite these losses, several ships were sunk and further extensive damage was caused to Stettin, much of it to areas previously untouched.
The final operation of the month took place in the early evening of 31st August as sixteen aircraft, four of them GH leaders, attacked what was believed to be a V2 storage facility at Pont Remy. Six crews bombed on GH with the remainder doing so visually despite the cloud cover. In total 601 bombers attacked nine such sites, eight being found and hit, for the

loss of six of the force. All 514 Squadron's aircraft returned safely on this occasion.

F/ Sgt Hugh 'Richie' Richford with his all-NCO crew, including Sgt Harry Dison, co-author of this book, had arrived at Waterbeach early in August 1944. The operation to Pont Remy was their seventh: 'Pont Remy, near Abbeville, was stated to be defended by four heavy guns. We were allotted A2-F, a new paddle bladed Mk 1 Lanc, 'C' Flight's first replacement for the old Mk.IIs. As might be expected it was the Flight Commander's aircraft. He was at pains to tell me to take great care of it. I did not like to remind him that we had flown it to Stettin and back two nights before without a blemish.

We were at No 3 (port aircraft) in the vic and I closed up as we ran into the target at 15,000 feet on that clear summer evening. Just before we got there something went wrong with the GH run and round we went for another attempt. We bombed, but by then we were the only three aircraft around and the four guns of Abbeville, which had not previously been in evidence, decided to shoot. The shells burst just off our port wing and close enough to be heard above the noise of four Merlins and through the thickness of a flying helmet. A quick check produced rather breathless replies, but all was well and there was no vital damage. The rear gunner kept a wary eye on a hole in the starboard elevator, which enlarged slowly in the slipstream as we journeyed home but we landed without incident.

Back at dispersal, the CO and an unhappy looking Flight Commander were inspecting the damage before I had climbed out. A thin stream of fuel was dribbling from the port wing, there were some twenty five to thirty holes down the port side of the fuselage and the elevator hole was large enough to stand up in. The rear gunner showed us his flying boot torn by a splinter and the mid-upper marvelled that he had been facing starboard and the back of his turret had taken the blast. It was a salutary lesson that going round again could be a threat to one's health and we avoided doing so until our penultimate operation.'

The Station Commander's Report for August summarised activity:

During the early part of the month operations continued at a fairly heavy pressure, the targets being of a tactical nature including tactical reserves of oil. Later several attacks were delivered against main German targets and this provided a completely new experience for many of the Squadron crews who had not previously undertaken such sorties. It is interesting to note, at this stage, that one crew which completed its tour towards the end of the month had only undertaken four attacks against main German targets. Bad weather interfered with operations towards the end of the month. Re-equipment of the Squadron proceeded slowly but the Squadron still had eight Mk.II aircraft at the end of the month. A Flight of the squadron was stood down for the equipping of aircraft and the training of crews in the use of GH equipment. This has curtailed the Squadron's effort during the month.

Administration

The most popular feature of the month has been the commencement of normal leave, including leave to Ireland. This has meant a big reduction in available staff in all Sections, and although there has been little complaint it is apparent in a number of minor respects that less work is being done. The 29-11 runway has been unserviceable throughout the month for repairs to the concrete and tarmacking of the surface.

'Le Havre: Troop concentration. 1st wave of the daylight attack on the 5th September 1944showing TI falling at 18.08 hours and bombing concentration at 18.42½ hours (1, 3 & 8 Groups)' Bomber Command photo and caption (TNA).

On 3rd September the fifth anniversary of the outbreak of the war was marked by a series of heavy raids against six Luftwaffe airfields in Southern Holland. 514 Squadron's crews were amongst those targeting Eindhoven, seven of the ten aircraft from Waterbeach attacking the primary target with one having to settle for Gilze-Ripen airfield instead. Two aircraft had returned early. According to the ORB, *'the opinion is that the airfield was well pranged.'* The attack took place in the early evening, once again reflecting Bomber Command's confidence in daylight operations, and this was borne out when only one of the 675 bombers was shot down.

On 5th September, the squadron went back to Le Havre, on this occasion to attack the beleaguered German garrison which was holding out against the relentless Allied ground assault. Nineteen of 514's aircraft were part of the 348 that attacked the port. No fighters were noted but there was some flak. This was the first of four raids against the garrison in six days, no aircraft being lost on either 5th or 6th September, when the 344 bombers included sixteen from Waterbeach. After the first two relatively uneventful raids 333 aircraft, including fourteen from Waterbeach, were tasked with attacking Le Havre again on the morning of 8th September. On this occasion there was slight to moderate flak but ten-tenths cloud cover down to 3,000 feet meant that the attackers were compelled to bomb from low level. The attack was scattered and eventually was called off by the Master Bomber after only a third of the crews had bombed. Five Lancasters were reportedly seen to be shot down, though in fact only two were lost.

One of the squadron's crews had already returned to Waterbeach with its starboard outer engine out of action, and F/L Tony Prager's aircraft ME851, JI-H had been hit by flak, the ORB recording that the bombs were jettisoned short of the target when flak started a fire in the bomb bay. The flames were promptly extinguished by the navigator and mid upper gunner. It appears that the ORB did F/L Prager a disservice as he received the DSO, his award being published in the London Gazette on 19th January 1945, by which time he had completed his tour, left the squadron and been promoted. The citation read:

This officer has completed very many sorties since being awarded the Distinguished Flying Cross. He has displayed outstanding qualities of leadership, great skill and unfailing devotion to duty. On one occasion in September, 1944, he took part in a bombing attack on Le Havre. In the run-in the aircraft came under heavy antiaircraft fire. The bomb bay was hit and set on fire. In spite of this, Squadron Leader Prager held to a steady run to enable his bomb aimer to release his bombs on the target. Other members of the crew succeeded, with great difficulty, in extinguishing the flames and Squadron Leader Prager flew the aircraft safely to base. His coolness and resolution in dangerous circumstances were most commendable.

F/O Don Beaton in LL677, A2-E then carried out his bombing run. His aircraft was very badly damaged, F/O Beaton and his flight engineer Sgt James Sherry were seriously injured and navigator P/O Alfred Nye slightly injured. Notwithstanding his wounds and the problems he encountered in keeping LL677 under control, Beaton and his crew struggled back across the English Channel. They landed at Tangmere, which had four years earlier achieved fame in the Battle of Britain. For his heroic action in saving his crew, F/O Don Beaton was awarded the Distinguished Service Order, that award being outranked only by the VC. The final attack on Le Havre took place on the late afternoon of 10th September. On this occasion, Bomber Command threw 992 bombers into the fray including twelve from 514 Squadron. Eight aiming points were marked and the defences were apparently much less effective, all aircraft returning safely. The raid was seemingly successful, the German defenders took the hint and surrendered the following day.

Meanwhile, on the ground at Waterbeach, on 6th September the Motor Transport Section came second in the competition for the Bomber Command Cup in which it represented No. 3 Group. Two days later the Waterbeach Amateur Dramatic Society (The WADS), under the management of F/L N Pascall, gave their opening performance in the NAAFI. The comedy 'Quiet Wedding;' directed by Sgt P Levy was their first production and was very well received on its first night. The sets designed by Sgt LA Addison, LAC VU Hepworth and LAC TW McLaughlin received favourable comment.

Bomber Command having seen off the German ground troops in Le Havre, tasking returned to its normal diversity on 11th September. Thirteen of the squadron's crews participated amongst 379 attacking various oil targets including, for 514 Squadron, the synthetic oil plant at Kamen. Bombing was reported to be exceedingly good in this first attack on the Bergkamen works, with several very big fires, a large explosion and much smoke rising to 12,000 feet. The ORB notes that the fires were *'possibly oil'*, perhaps not a surprising deduction given the nature of the target.

The Bergkamen synthetic oil plant was the target on 11th September for 514 Squadron with devastation the result. There were secondary effects as the bombing set off a major gas explosion in an adjacent coal mine. DS787, A2-G was lost with W/O Robert Thornton RNZAF and crew after being hit by bombs from another aircraft.

Local reports state that 609 local residents were killed, there was much damage to the plant and 90% of the houses, schools and churches were also destroyed. A secondary disaster occurred when power supplies in the local Grimberg coal mine resulted in a gas explosion, killing 107 miners. Three aircraft were seen to go down, one of which was hit by a bomb. The only aircraft lost from the Kamen raid was from 514 Squadron. DS787, A2-G flown by W/O Robert Thornton RNZAF, crashed at 1842 hours onto a road at Lerche, 5 km from the centre of Kamen; it is believed to have been hit by a bomb from another aircraft. The crew were on their sixth op. mid upper gunner Sgt Charlie Robinson, rear gunner F/S DR Burns and flight engineer Sgt GF Good all managed to get out of the aircraft and survived as POWs; three of their four colleagues are also believed to have got out but, along with the crewman who remained in the aircraft, they did not survive. In total eight aircraft were lost from the various simultaneous raids.

On 12th September a Class 'A' Post Office, to transact all classes of postal business, opened on the Station. Personnel were, however, still restricted in what they could say about ops as, for example, Frankfurt was targeted in one last major attack, the city receiving the unwelcome attention of 388 bombers. Fourteen were from Waterbeach, one of which returned early, according to the ORB, though no such details are contained in the Events log. With clear weather over the target, markers were easily visible and bombing was concentrated accordingly. Crews noted that the target area was one large mass of fires and palls of black smoke when they left. It was subsequently determined that considerable damage had been caused in the west of the city. Flak was a slight to moderate barrage of heavy flak with numerous searchlights stretching as far south as Mannheim. Fighters were very much in evidence on this night raid against such a major target, with four combats and a near-miss being reported. P/O Don Gordon in PB142, JI-A filed a report stating*: 'At 2239 hours the Wireless Operator warned the Captain and Gunners of an E/A closing from dead astern. A minute later the rear gunner reported a red glow astern. The Captain immediately commenced to corkscrew and the rear gunner opened fire with a 3 second burst. As the glow closed in the M/U Gunner fired a 4 second burst and the rear gunner another burst. The glow then seemed to glide down to the ground and burst into very white flames.'* No further details are given of this malevolent red glow, though the ORB noted that *'a jet-propelled fighter was believed destroyed'*. This claim is also noted in 'Nachtjagd War Diaries', which states that at least two Ju88s and four Me110s were destroyed, though at least four of that total were brought down by British intruders, these mainly being Mosquitoes.

F/O Geoff France was flying his favourite Lancaster, LM277, JI-F and showing the ropes to a second dickey pilot, P/O Don Parks when an FW190 fighter passed within a hair's breadth of their cockpit canopy. Miraculously there was no collision and F/O France and his crew completed their duty successfully. F/L George Bradford had his aircraft LM275, JI-E coned in searchlights at 2253hrs so he immediately took violent evasive action. As he did so, his mid upper gunner Sgt AC Potipher warned him of trace coming in, which continued for some three seconds, after which nothing more was seen. Unfortunately the rear gunner, W/O WS Nicol received head injuries which ended his operational career with the squadron, and rendered his turret unserviceable. There were also numerous holes in the fuselage and tail plane, which bore testament to a very narrow escape for the aircraft and crew.

F/O Robert Hardwick in DS786, A2-L had made his contribution to the rearrangement of Frankfurt and was leaving the target area when his bomb aimer and, for now, front gunner F/O TB Searles RCAF, saw a single-engined enemy aircraft attacking another Lancaster 400 yards on the starboard bow. F/O Searles loosed off fifty rounds which caused the night fighter to break off and dive away. It is not known if this was the aborted attack on F/L Bradford's aircraft.

F/O Bill Coyle in LL666, A2-K and his crew were particularly fortunate to emerge from a six-minute ordeal, remaining coned by searchlights, corkscrewing for the duration and coming under fighter attack five times. In two attacks the fighter was identified as an Me109. Throughout all the attacks the gunners were blinded by the searchlights and could only see their attackers at close range. No injuries or damage were reported by the doubtless relieved crew.

Tragically it was the end of the road for W/O William Brickwood and four of his crew, as their Lancaster LL731, JI-U was shot down by Lt. Fred

Flight Sergeant Ron Rigden, bomb aimer in LL731, JI-U was one of only two survivors when W/O William Brickwood's aircraft was shot down during the last major Bomber Command raid on Frankfurt (Peter Rigden).

Hromadnik of 9./NJG4. LL731 crashed at 2330 hours at Kordel 8km NW of Trier. The two survivors were the bomb aimer F/S Ron Rigden and flight engineer P/O Colin Turner who were taken prisoner. Sixteen aircraft from other squadrons were also lost.

A V2 storage facility at Wassenaar was the squadron's target on 14th September as ten aircraft were detailed for a small-scale raid, involving a total of forty five bombers. The attack was timed sociably, taking place just after lunch. The ORB notes that the various aiming points were *'duly bombed by our aircraft without sensational incident.'* Although one flak gun had the temerity to aim its fire at the raiders as they crossed the enemy coast and the Rotterdam defences were in action, there was no excitement over the target and a complete absence of fighter opposition. As a result, no aircraft were lost.

15th September was already being commemorated as Battle of Britain Day. A Colour Hoisting Parade and short service were held in 'A' Hangar. The service was taken by the Station Chaplain, S/L the Reverend G West and was followed by a March Past at which Group Captain GM Heard took the salute.

After a couple of days' break, the squadron was directed to attack another German garrison, this time in the port of Boulogne. Twenty aircraft took part amongst the total of 762, targeting multiple aiming points. Seventeen of 514 Squadron's crews were tasked with Aiming Point 2, five of which bombed before the Master Bomber called off that particular attack. Meanwhile three were sent to Aiming Point 3, all of whom bombed from around four thousand feet. One unspecified aircraft received slight flak damage to its starboard fin. Two aircraft were lost from the large force deployed whilst all 514 Squadron's crews returned safely. The Germans in Boulogne decided shortly afterwards that the war had not been such a good idea after all, so they surrendered.

Back at Waterbeach, the latest in a long series of inspections occurred on 19th September when F/L WJ Taylor and F/O PM Bridge of Headquarters Bomber Command visited the Station to discuss Physical Fitness matters affecting RAF and WAAF personnel.

Calais was the final French port to remain, at least in part, in German hands. It was accordingly scheduled to receive the attention of the heavy bomber force. The first raid took place on 20th September, with a large contribution of 25 aircraft from Waterbeach making a total of 646 overall.

Some crews had to orbit the target to await their turn due to congestion over the target. One crew noted that the defensive trenches they had seen on their first run over the target had been reduced to craters by the time they came round for a second attempt. The only aircraft lost on the raid was LM277 JI-F which was seen to spin into the sea off Calais, with its wings on fire preceded by bombs which exploded before the aircraft. It is not clear whether LM277 was in fact hit by flak or bombs from another aircraft. Sadly there were no survivors from the crew of F/O Leonard Arkless, who were on their sixth op. LM277 had become the usual mount of F/O Geoff France who was not detailed to fly on this raid. He was, however, tasked by the squadron CO with visiting the widow of F/O Ian Partington, the navigator who was killed in LM277, to inform her of the death of her husband.

Germany beckoned on 23rd September with 22 Lancasters from the squadron participating in an evening raid by 549 aircraft. The target was Neuss. Visibility was not particularly good with ten tenths cloud and crews could only bomb on the glow of markers as they disappeared into the murk. This also meant that the results were difficult to assess. Heavy flak was light to moderate in intensity, bursting at around 15,000 feet which did not affect the squadron's aircraft which were some 5,000 feet above that level. There were some fighter flares seen and an Me109 was spotted, but no combats were reported by the squadron's crews, all of whom returned safely though seven other aircraft failed to return. Fourteen public buildings and 617 houses were destroyed or seriously damaged as the bombing fell in the docks and factory areas. The raid was the last time 514 Squadron deployed its Mk.II Lancasters. 'C' Flight's DS826, A2-C (F/O Maurice Oliver), DS842, A2-J (F/O Thomas Marks) and LL666, A2-K (F/O William Coyle) all returned safely, after which the type was retired by the squadron.

On 24th September F/O CH Simon of Headquarters Bomber Command visited the Chief Technical Officer to discuss the salvage position at the Station. The Station ORB fails to note the outcome of their deliberations.

The following day the Calais area was visited again, the squadron sending 21 of the 872 aircraft taking part. However the raid was cancelled after 287 aircraft had bombed, none of which were from Waterbeach. This was due to the low cloud and in order to avoid civilian casualties. A further attempt was made the following day, this being more successful as all nineteen 514

Squadron aircraft bombed the primary target. A total of 722 bombers took part, two of which failed to return. On 27th September the operation was repeated on a smaller scale, this time the squadron offering thirteen aircraft for a raid involving 341 bombers. All the squadron's crews bombed the target, on this occasion from around 5,500 feet, and returned safely, the only aircraft lost in this raid being from 115 Sqn at Witchford. Crews reported seeing one Lancaster hit by flak, turn on its back and hit the ground in flames. One parachute was seen in the water. A final effort was launched against the Calais area on 28th September, the 494 aircraft including twelve from the squadron. Six of the Waterbeach crews had bombed by the time the Master Bomber cancelled the attack at 0928hrs. All aircraft returned safely to their various bases. Despite the limited success in bombing on this occasion, the German garrison followed in the footsteps of their comrades in Boulogne and surrendered to Canadian ground forces shortly afterwards. The Station Commander's Summary for September was relatively concise:

Pressure of work has not been excessive, but crews have been standing-by much of the time for attacks which did not materialise. The re-equipment of 514 Squadron with Mk.I and Mk.III Lancaster aircraft was completed by the end of the month.

Administration: Shortage of personnel has been very marked owing to heavy postings and to large numbers on leave. Normal leave facilities have been re-introduced and the first rush appears to have exhausted itself during this month. The perimeter track adjacent to the Flying Control building has been made usable by aircraft by filling in the right angled bend of the track and removing obstructions. This will facilitate operational take off on runways 29 and 33. The 11-29 runway has been completely tarmacked and is now awaiting asphalting of the surface.

The French ports were now in Allied hands but were far from being usable due to the destruction wrought in the fighting. The Allies were, therefore, becoming more vulnerable to their supply chains being inadequate to support the advancing troops. One port that could more easily become fit for purpose was the Belgian city of Antwerp. Its facilities were capable of handling 40,000 tons of cargo a day and, although the port itself was soon liberated, access was denied by German troops continuing to hold out on the Dutch island of Walcheren. Their guns were able to cover the estuary

of the River Schelde which provided access to Antwerp. Much of Walcheren comprised reclaimed land below sea level, the area being protected by sea walls.
On 3rd October nineteen aircraft left Waterbeach to join 240 others in an attack on the sea walls at Westkapelle. The cloud was patchy with its base around 5,000 feet. F/O Geoff France in LM733, JI-F carried a bomb load consisting of one 4,000 lb Medium Capacity, six 1,000 lb and, to make things interesting for the defenders, a 500lb long delay bomb. He bombed from 5,700 feet. There were numerous waves of aircraft and the target proved quite difficult to acquire. It was noted that most crews made dummy runs before identifying the target, described as a 'large brown embankment', as cloud obscured visibility. At one point, with bombs falling into the sea or either side of the embankment, the Master Bomber described the efforts as 'lousy', which seems to have had the desired effect, with accuracy improving after that. One of the squadron's aircraft made no fewer than five dummy runs then flew along the wall, reporting several craters but no breach at the time. In fact a major breach did occur, flooding a German gun battery at the extreme Western end of the island as well as the village of Westkapelle itself. No aircraft were lost in this first raid against the sea walls of Walcheren though tragically this resulted in the loss of 180 lives amongst the local population. In the late Sixties the author visited the island on a school trip at which time local buildings still bore the marks of seawater well up their walls. W/O Geoff Payne was in LM728, JI-U. 'We were informed that the target was strategically important as the Germans were denying the Allies the use of the port of Antwerp and was required for the supply of material for our advancing armies. The object of the raid was to breach the dykes and to flood the island purposely to neutralise the German forces established there. I was feeling rather disturbed that we were going to flood vast tracts of land that had taken years to establish and concern for the population who had suffered four years of hardship and deprivation during the German occupation. Take off time was 1207hrs. Reaching our rendezvous point there seemed to be hundreds of four engined aircraft converging before heading out over the North Sea. Dropping down to our bombing height we approached our target and dropped our 4,000 lb bomb which according to our bomb aimer, got a direct hit on the dyke. Passing over the target I saw that the dyke had been breached with the sea gushing through the gaps.

Due to the concentration of German forces on the island there was an enormous amount of light and heavy flak as we tumed for home, however it was thankful that no enemy fighters were seen over the target area but we still had to keep a watchful eye open as there were many enemy fighter airfields in Holland. Back at base after a two and a half hours flight. After " interrogation" we repaired to our mess for a meal and a pint to celebrate our mid-upper's 20th birthday. Some time later I was to learn that my best friend, a Marine, was killed during the assault on the island of Walcheren at Westkapelle. They attacked through the breaches that we had made in the dyke.'

On 5th October the US Third Army asked for Bomber Command support to attack German supply lines at Saarbrucken. Accordingly 551 aircraft carried out the first bombing raid since September 1942 on the town which lay on the Siegfried Line. 514 Squadron was able to offer 27 Lancasters, its highest total to date. However, there appears to have been some confusion despite the clear visibility, as the Master Bomber said that the target was not clearly identified despite red and green TIs being seen and bombed by various crews. He called the operation off because of the proximity of Allied troops to the target; however some aircraft continued to bomb, including F/O Arthur Holland RAAF in NG141, A2-J who heard the instruction not to bomb as his own bombs were released. Despite the apparent confusion and the raid being aborted, the attack was, in fact, very successful with severe damage to the main town area through which the railway lines ran. Two crews, S/L Marcus Dods in LM685, JI-Q and F/L Tony Prager in NG121, JI-H were designated as supporters to the Pathfinder Force, something of an accolade. F/L Prager orbited the target for sixteen minutes before the raid was called off, an unnerving experience given that the defences were described as fairly heavy with slight to moderate heavy flak. F/O Geoff France attacked an alternative target, railway tracks five to six miles east of Saarbrucken. Three Lancasters were lost, two as a result of a mid-air collision near Bitburg. These were from 514's sister squadrons, 75(NZ) and 115. There were no survivors from either crew. The third aircraft, a Lancaster of 101 Sqn, was shot down by flak, again with no survivors. Amongst its crew was F/S LK Robson RAAF, at 19 years of age one of the youngest navigators to be lost by Bomber Command.

The following night another large raid was arranged, this time upon Dortmund. Again Waterbeach was able to offer a record 29 Lancasters, though three of these were subsequently unable to take off due to unspecified reasons. 25 of the squadron's aircraft attacked the primary target. All crews identified the target with red and green TIs and the bombing was reported as concentrated amongst the markers. Numerous large fires were seen along with much smoke. The raid was considered successful by the crews, although none could identify ground details. Flak was moderate in intensity, a heavy barrage with no searchlights active until 2028 hours. They were then exposed to the searchlights from the Bochum-Castrap Rauxel area north of the target, but these were described as aimless. On this occasion, fighters were much in evidence. F/O Robert Vickers RAAF in NF968, JI-L reported bombing without use of his bomb sight due to evading a fighter. Two combats were reported, both on the homeward journey. F/O Alfred Uffindell in PB482, JI-P was at 20,000 feet when at 2038hrs he was warned to corkscrew by his rear gunner F/S Max Clark. F/S Clark, along with Sgt JF Wilson in the mid upper turret, then engaged an attacking Me410 in combat. They saw a small fire break out on the port wing of the fighter which then broke away. The gunners claimed it as damaged. At 2100hrs, F/O Frederick Stephens and his crew in LM728, JI-U were on their third op. rear gunner Sgt PE Steele saw an unidentified single engine fighter approaching so ordered his pilot to corkscrew starboard, at which the enemy fighter opened fire with a short burst which passed harmlessly behind their Lancaster. The fighter was not seen again. The raid, which marked the start of what became known as The Second Battle of the Ruhr, was very accurate and caused severe damage, especially to industrial and transport facilities. Of the 523 aircraft deployed, only five were lost despite the flak and fighter activity. On a clear night over the Ruhr, such a low loss rate was remarkable by earlier experience. The 26th Lancaster of 514 Squadron was LM288, JI-C flown by F/O Ron Limbert. He had somehow become involved in a totally separate raid by 246 Lancasters and seven Mosquitoes of 1 and 5 Groups against the northern German port of Bremen. It is not clear why, or indeed if, F/O Limbert's crew were specifically tasked as the sole representative of 514 Squadron or whether it was an error of navigation. Whatever the reason, the attack was an outstanding success with 1,021 tons of bombs dropped. F/O Limbert's contribution to proceedings was a 4,000lb 'Cookie' and 12 clusters of incendiaries.

A local report described the conditions as clear with a three-quarters moon, making conditions ideal for the bomb aimers. Nearly five thousand houses were destroyed, in addition to the destruction caused on earlier raids, the

Whilst the rest of 514 Squadron attacked Dortmund, F/O Ron Limbert and his crew joined forces with 1 and 5 Group squadrons to bomb Bremen instead. The crew was lost over Homberg on 21st November 1944 (family of Sgt Roger Scott, flight engineer in the Limbert crew).

transport network was seriously disrupted and there was severe damage to the shipyards, two Focke-Wulf aircraft factories, a Siemens electrical plant and other sites. The devastation of this important industrial and transport target was now complete after 32 major raids by Bomber Command and the city would in future only be targeted in relatively minor attacks.

A third consecutive maximum effort for 514 Squadron followed on the afternoon of 7th October, the target this time being the town of Emmerich. The town lies on the border of Germany and The Netherlands and was seen as a staging post for German supplies and reinforcements which threatened the Allies at Nijmegen after the failure of Operation Market Garden at Arnhem. 25 Lancasters took part from 27 originally tasked by the squadron with a total attacking force totaling 350 aircraft. Although the weather was relatively clear with high cloud over the target, the ground was obscured by smoke so the raid was guided by the Master Bomber. Fires were seen to spread over a large area including the railway yards west of the harbour. 2,424 buildings were destroyed and 689 damaged, according to raid reports, whilst 689,000 cubic metres of rubble had to be cleared away after the raid. It is estimated that 91% of the town was destroyed by the bombing raid.

Loss of a Lancaster from the Emmerich raid, photographed from W/O Geoff Payne's aircraft. It is likely that it was PB407, AR-U of 460 Sqn from Binbrook. F/L ER Greenacre RAAF and his crew survived to become POWs (Geoff Payne).

W/O Geoff Payne in LM728, JI-U commented: 'This was a daylight operation to Emmerich, a German town on the border with Holland. Synthetic oil installations and German supply lines were to be attacked. It was the first time that we had been been ordered to fly in formation, with our two sister squadrons, 115 ahead of us and 75 New Zealand behind. Other groups and squadrons had made similar arrangements. As we neared the German / Dutch border very accurate flak opened up which immediately dispersed the bomber stream. The lead Lancaster of 75 Squadron who was following us took a direct hit and completely disintegrated, the wreckage slowly drifting to earth, a very disconcerting sight.

There were clear skies over the target and we bombed the PFF flares accurately but as we closed our bomb door an enormous 'crump' shook our aircraft and shrapnel rattled along the fuselage, putting my turret and the mid-upper out of action. The hydraulics had been severed somewhere leaving us to operate our turrets by hand, not a good position to be in, although we were supposed to have an escort of Mosquitoes. Arriving back at base there was some concern that we would be unable to activate the undercarriage owing to the problem with the hydraulics, however, the wheels dropped down perfectly. We delivered U for Uncle to the hanger for repair and said a fond farewell to the lady. That was my 29th op and I was keeping my fingers crossed that number 30 would be an easy one!'

Emmerich had the misfortune to stand alongside the Rhine and was a hotly-contested strongpoint facing the Allies trying to cross the river. Obliteration by Bomber Command was the preferred tactical option.

Of the four Lancasters lost one was from Waterbeach. LM735, A2-G was flown by F/S Thomas Gilchrist, this being the second op for the crew, all of whom lost their lives. The location of the crash site is not recorded but the bodies of six of the crew were recovered and lie in Reichswald Forest War Cemetery, suggesting that the aircraft came down in the vicinity of the target. Three other Lancasters were also lost in known circumstances, at least one to flak and another to incendiaries from another aircraft. Laurie Woods was a bomb aimer with 460 Sqn, flying in Lancaster AR-K2. As he released his bombs and awaited the obligatory aiming point photo he saw another Lancaster below him. In correspondence with the author he said, *'The Lancaster was possibly about 150 feet below us and was hit in*

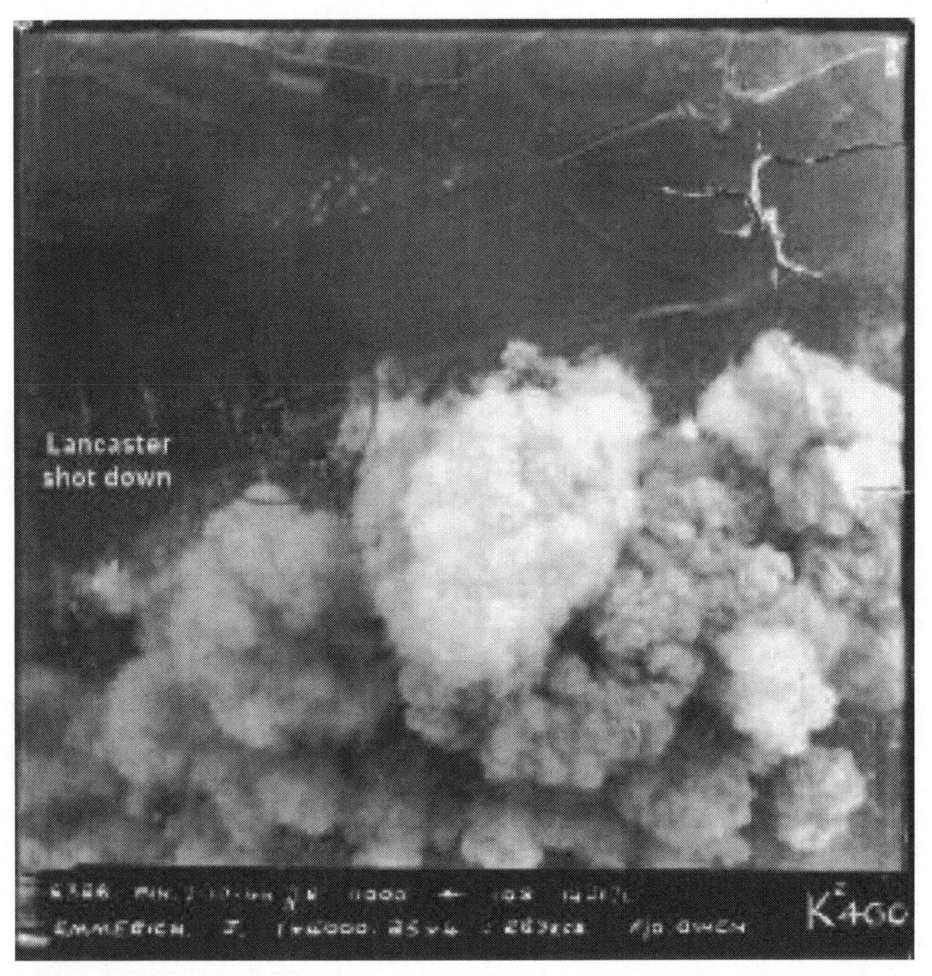

A Lancaster can be seen diving away trailing smoke after being hit by flak over Emmerich. It is believed that this is LM735 of 514 Squadron. The photo was taken by 460 Sqn bomb aimer Laurie Woods who provided this image.

the port inner engine and immediately went into a dive. There were no survivors and the plane finally crashed on the south bank of the Rhine river.' It is believed that this Lancaster was LM735.

The intensive operational activity of the past few days was followed by a respite as the squadron was not tasked for the following seven days. Ops recommenced however on 14th October with its participation in another initiative by Bomber Command and the USAAF. The raid, against Duisburg, was part of Operation Hurricane, intended to demonstrate to the Germans the overwhelming superiority of the Allied Air Forces over Europe. The first attack was mounted at around 0900hrs, with a new record

At full strength, 514 Squadron could put thirty Lancasters into the air for operations. These five Lancasters were almost certainly part of a much larger group preparing to leave Waterbeach.

of 29 of the squadron's crews taking part amongst the total force of 1,103 bombers and a fighter escort. The weather was patchy cloud with gaps for bombing, some scattered TIs were seen, but the Master Bomber gave crews a free hand and all crews bombed visually except one which bombed on H2S. The bombing was concentrated on the built up area from the docks to the airport. A direct hit was seen on a barge on the river with an ensuing large explosion whilst a bridge to the east of the docks was straddled. No enemy aircraft were seen. All the squadron's aircraft returned safely though fourteen others fell to flak. 3,574 tons of high explosives and 820 tons of incendiaries were dropped on Duisburg on this early morning raid. The US Eighth Air Force followed up with a daylight attack on Cologne by 1,251 of their own bombers escorted by 749 fighters. Five American bombers and one fighter were lost. The Luftwaffe did not attend the event. This was the final op of W/O Geoff Payne's tour. 'Briefing was at 0500hrs. I was taken aback when the target was revealed, a daylight attack on the Ruhr town of Duisburg one of the most heavily defended areas in Germany, and dangerous enough at night! This was me going out with a bang one way or another.

As we were to have a fighter escort, the flight out was uneventful until we were approaching the target area, there were nearly a thousand heavy bombers converging towards then passing through what seemed to be a black haze intermingled with deep red flashes of exploding flak shells. As we dropped our bombs, I looked down to see the fires and the ground erupting, a truly awesome sight. Soon we were out of the Ruhr defences heading back to Waterbeach feeling slightly more relaxed but still scanning the skies for the unexpected fighter to jump us. Landing back at base I felt that the weight of the world had been lifted off my shoulders and what a relief to be looking forward to a fortnights leave in a couple of days' time.'

Bomber Command then immediately repeated the raid with 1,005 aircraft carrying out an attack that night. The squadron excelled itself by deploying its maximum of thirty Lancasters, twenty four of the crews having already attacked Duisburg that morning. All the Waterbeach contingent returned safely though F/O Frederick Stephens in NF966, JI-R reported two encounters with enemy fighters. The first was an Me410 whose only burst of fire missed. A further combat was carried out with what the mid upper gunner Sgt MH Hanley described as 'an unidentified enemy aircraft with a greenish blue flame coming from underneath'. The aircraft attacked very fast and it was presumed in the ORB that this was a jet aircraft. There was no damage to the Lancaster from either attack. Only seven aircraft in total were lost on this raid whilst 9,000 tons of bombs had fallen on the city in less than 24 hours. The attack was reported as good and concentrated, with fires visible from 100 miles after the raid.

William Troughton, a correspondent from the Daily Express, flew with 514 Squadron crews on the two Duisburg raids. In the morning he flew with F/O John Whitwood in PD265, JI-G, returning to the city that night with S/L Phillip Clay in LM724, JI-B. Troughton filed the following article.

Daily Express Oct. 16, 1944

I FLEW BACK TO SEE DUISBURG DIE

by William Troughton

William flew on both raids on Saturday, and is the first War Correspondent to make a day and night raid in the same day.

At an RAF Station, 5 a.m. Sunday
The Medical Officer had just asked me to take a sleeping tablet – and I'm almost asleep on my feet. It sounded so silly that I had to laugh.
But the boys who have just come back from Duisburg are all milling around him with their hair dishevelled and their eyes heavy with the need for sleep, and they are taking his tablets. Funnier still, because only seven hours ago we were taking "Wakey-wakey" tablets from him to ward off sleep.
We were pretty tired then, for most of us were setting out to bomb Duisburg again for the second time in 18 hours. Now we are back - and we have left Duisburg dying. We have dropped more than 10,000 tons, including 500,000 fire bombs on the city – one ton for every 45 of its inhabitants – delivered in two great raids of more than 1,000 planes each. Twenty of those planes have not come back. That was inevitable for Duisburg is still one of the most heavily defended cities of the Ruhr Valley. But our losses are surprisingly small, only .9 per cent.
This is what happened in the two attacks.

By Day.
Yesterday morning when we saw at last the great waterways of Duisburg gleaming in the sunshine, the sky ahead of us was full of the aircraft that were going in with the first wave. They looked like a cloud of gnats. Behind us hundreds more were stretched across the sky.
Flying Officer J. Whitwood, of Norwich, stockily built, fair haired, put on his best guide manner and said over the intercom, "and there, Bill, on our Port bow, is the great big 'Happy Valley'."
But ahead of us ugly black smudges of smoke appeared among the gnats and slowly expanded into big, black blobs. And suddenly a pale blue smoke trail spiralled down from the cloud of gnats in front.
"Somebody's got it," came some one's voice over the intercom.
Down in the dock area behind Duisburg's waterways that lie to the east of the winding Rhine the bombs were falling. And far down to the right I saw the little red flashes of an ack-ack battery opening up on us at the end of a straggling village. I pointed this out to the engineer, P/O Ken Thomas, of Swansea. "Jerry never could take a joke," he cracked back.

Just ahead, much nearer, quicker, blacker, and more vicious – new smoke puffs appeared. There was only a few minutes now before we were due over the target. The layout of the city was as clear as a map. The bombs were raining down on it and the sky around us was filling with smoke smudges – hundreds of them. They appeared from nowhere as if they had been painted by an invisible paint brush. Our Bomb Aimer, F/O D.J. McEwen, of Gridrod, British Columbia, Canada, planted the bombs well on the target.

The rest of us had our noses flattened against the Perspex. The Navigator, F/O P. Lankester, of Bexhill, Sussex, pointed to four or five great black balls of smoke right across the dockside. "Looks like an oil dump," said the Mid Upper Gunner, Flight Sergeant J.V. Gillespie, a Canadian from Toronto, "Duisburg had it."

There was the radio operator, Flight Sergeant D (Jock) Cargill, of Arbroath, who, an hour or so earlier, when we were waiting in the darkness to take off, had kept us laughing with his description of a murder film he had seen that made him "sweat with fright".

And there was Sergeant Tommy Birch, of Hendon, N.W. who had pulled Jock Cargill's leg about his birthday – "Friday 13th." Tommy Birch, at

This small map showed Daily Express readers where they could find what remained of Duisburg after the destruction witnessed by the paper's correspondent Bill Troughton (Daily Express).

the end of the trip tumbled out grousing cheerfully: "I've never been so cold in all my life." The rear gunner's cockpit is the coldest place in the kite.

War Correspondent William Troughton

Daily Express correspondent Bill Troughton (3rd from left) with the crew of F/O John Whitwood after their return from Duisburg. Troughton then promptly went back to Duisburg that evening with S/Ldr Philip Clay and crew. The aircraft, JI-G, PD265, was lost over Homberg on 21st November 1944 with the crew of F/O Geoff France.

By Night

This night's work has been much grimmer. There was for me, a bad few minutes when the first searchlights on enemy territory began feeling for us, coning and creeping nearer.

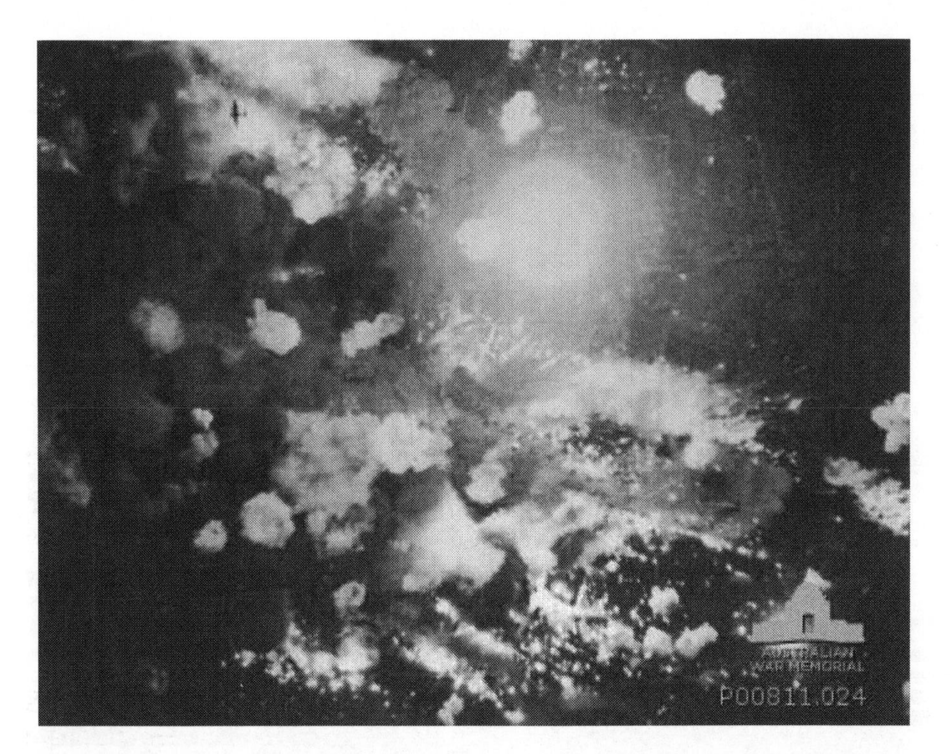

Duisburg comes under intensive attack from Bomber Command once again (AWM).

This time we were a new crew with S/L P.B. Clay of Sowerby Bridge, Yorks, as Skipper. He is a tall young fellow with fair hair and a nonchalant manner, but a brain as cool as ice when he sits behind the joy stick. When the flak began to flash around us I thought of the great cloud of smoke puffs we had left behind us in the sky the previous morning. But Duisburg and a great cylinder above it, stretching four miles into the sky, was ablaze. It was too fascinating for fear.

Markers showered down and lay on the city like shimmering flower beds, others were lost in the fires. Flak of all kinds shattered the darkness. Then as we left this fantastic scene, the boys who followed us sent down thousands of incendiaries. The sky was red and angry above Duisburg when we were 100 miles away.

We could not see our boys in front of the Siegfried Line a we passed over on our way home – we were too high for that – but we drew great comfort in the knowledge that they could see the glow from the city, only 30 miles away, where thousands of tons of supplies to have been used against them were going up in flames.

The night attack on Duisburg was made in two waves. The first began bombing at 1:30 a.m. and the second nearly two hours later.
Later Sunday Now I know why the M.O. wanted to give me sleeping tablets. So many impressions have entered my mind and I saw so vivid the flashes and the colours of the flak, when I finally got into bed, I could not sleep. But the boys who do these trips – the crew of my Lancaster, G for George, was typical of them – night after night were wiser, especially after this, when the greatest weight of bombs that has ever been dropped on one city fell within 24 hours. They took the tablets and slept. They were still sleeping, most of them, when I left the Station later this morning.
There was no flying on 17th October so the Station Cinema had a full house both in the morning and the afternoon when W/C GP Kerr of Air Ministry lectured on 'The Far Eastern Campaign'. The lecture was both entertaining and instructive and all personnel who attended came away with a far clearer idea of the menace of Japan to Western civilisation.
There was more innovation by Bomber Command on 18th October, when 3 Group commenced its new role as a largely-independent force, focusing on its specialism in blind bombing with GH. Bonn had so far been fortunate in that it had been considered unimportant and had remained mostly unaffected by air attack so far in the war. It is likely that Bomber Command considered that the results of a GH raid would show up much more clearly as virtually all bomb damage would be new. The raid, by 128 aircraft including sixteen from Waterbeach, was extremely effective with 700 buildings destroyed and one thousand damaged. The heart of Bonn was destroyed and the former home of the composer Ludwig van Beethoven was only saved by the actions of its caretakers.
The sole casualty sustained by the squadron was the bomb aimer of LM724, JI-B, flown on this occasion by F/O Eric Williams. F/O Kenneth Pritchard RAAF was preparing to bomb as LM724 approached the target when the aircraft was hit by heavy flak. There was much damage to the fuselage, wings, rudder trimmers and engine instruments whilst the unfortunate F/O Pritchard suffered serious leg injuries. F/O Williams aborted his attack and immediately made for the emergency airfield at Woodbridge where he and the crew arrived without further trauma.

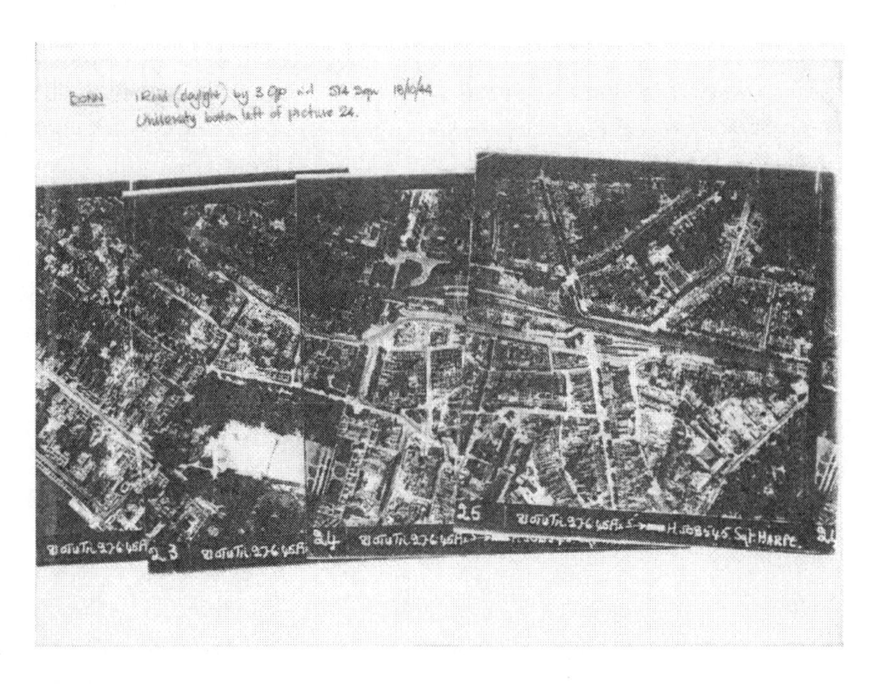

Overlaid aiming point photos show the concentrated bombing in the city centre of Bonn (WMHM).

LM684, JI-O, flown by F/O Gordon Smith was also hit by heavy flak fifteen miles short of the target, causing its 4,000lb 'cookie' to dislodge when the bomb doors were damaged. The aircraft landed at Lille Vendeville owing to flak damage, severe icing and shortage of petrol.

After this brief spell of independence, No. 3 Group contributed to a Main Force effort on the evening of 19th October as 24 aircraft from Waterbeach formed part of 583 in total attacking Stuttgart in two waves. The squadron's Lancasters were divided equally between Aiming Points 'D' and 'E' in the first and second waves respectively.

F/O Irvine Bittner RCAF had to bring LM728, JI-U home early when the oxygen supply failed to the rear turret, leaving the gunner, Sgt EA Mason, feeling somewhat short of breath. F/O Bittner jettisoned his bombs safely in the sea. The remaining eleven aircraft from the squadron's first wave bombed Stuttgart, mostly on sky markers, at around 2030hrs, returning safely to Waterbeach, though air to air tracer was seen and four aircraft from the stream were seen to be shot down.

The second wave arrived over Stuttgart at around 0100hrs, F/O Geoff France bombing from 20,000ft at 0110hrs. His bomb aimer, F/O Ken Barker RCAF had to estimate the position of the 'Wanganui' flares as they died out half a minute before he was in the right position to bomb through them. The results were difficult to assess for all 514's crews as there was complete cloud cover. It was noted that the flak was heavier than usual, and the defences of Saarbrucken-Strasbourg and Karlsruhe were also in action.

Sgt (later F/O) Geoff France was a stalwart of the squadron in the second half of 1944, before being shot down on the penultimate operation prior to ending his tour, ironically in PD265, the aircraft in which Bill Troughton had flown to Duisburg (France family).

Once again, fighter activity was noted. F/O Don Parks in PB426, JI-J reported that his aircraft was approached by a FW190, both his gunners dissuading it from coming too close. Over the target PB426's port inner engine was hit by flak, severing the hydraulic connection powering the mid upper turret and wounding the mid upper gunner, Sgt Henry 'Tich' Taylor. The navigator, F/O Don Forwood RAAF, later gave an account of the operation: 'The outward route was the usual circuitous approach to keep the enemy guessing the destination. The return route was also indirect and

F/O Alfred Uffindell RNZAF with his air crew and ground crew next to their regular mount, PB482, JI-P 'Princess Patricia'. The occasion was the end of their tour of operations, Princess Patricia's 32nd operation, which was to Hamm on 5th December 1944. She completed 57 ops and survived the war.

they were instructed to lose height in a shallow dive to 6,000ft on leaving the target, to give a speedy departure and to put night fighters off the scent. The return route was to pass between Nancy and Metz, described as inner artillery zones to be avoided at all costs.

The outward trip passed without incident apart from bumping about in slipstreams all the way. As navigator, I welcomed such conditions, knowing that we must be on track or at least in good company.

The bombing went well except for the usual Ack Ack (flak) and the shallow dive down to 6,000ft was very bumpy. The winds calculated at 20,000ft were of no use at 6,000ft. I was unable to get a reliable fix as the H2S was not performing well, so I had to rely on the forecast winds. We finally reached a point where we should be over friendly territory, staying alert for fighters but without fear of flak. I was looking forward to a drink of tea from the wireless operator's flask when, without warning, we were hit by a string of four Ack Ack shells, the third one bursting right under the tail.

The aircraft was thrown into a steep dive; I was up against the roof clawing at anything to try and regain my seat. The skipper, at first unable to pull out of the dive, gave the order to bale out, but then managed to pull the nose up with such force that some of us were thrown against the floor. The bomb aimer told us later that as we pulled out of the dive he had seen tree tops racing past below.

A port engine was on fire and in the semi-darkness the engineer feathered and doused the port outer engine. Almost as he did so, he realised his mistake and shut down the correct engine. The skipper would not restart the port outer engine, as its extinguisher was exhausted and therefore potentially unsafe.

The gyro in the distant reading compass had toppled, the Elsan contents spilled, and the hydraulic oil lines of the mid-upper turret had been severed adding to the mess. 'Titch', the mid-upper gunner had been hit by shrapnel just above the knee. The wireless operator got him onto the couch and applied sulphur drug powder to the wound, bandaged it and gave him morphine to ease the pain. There were over 120 holes in the aircraft, including one near the tail as big as a soccer ball, and the tail had suffered damage. The aircraft flew badly as well as uneconomically with two engines out on one side giving a yaw of seven degrees. Unsure the fuel supply was intact, the skipper asked for a direct course home and took the risk of re-starting the port outer engine. It performed well, but we were the last one back by quite a margin. 'Tich' Taylor was in hospital for several months but happily regained the use of his leg, albeit with a slight limp. The rear gunner overstayed his six days 'survivors' leave, so two replacement gunners were needed to finish the tour. The new gunners were from a crew split up by a crash. Both had been burned about the hands and face but their morale was excellent and we felt lucky to have them aboard.'

Don Forwood later checked his log using positive fixes and winds obtained after coming within Gee range, carefully back-plotting the track to where the action had taken place. It transpired that they had been about 12 miles off the intended track in the vicinity of Nancy. Don agonised over the thought that had he been more persistent with the uncooperative H2S screen he may have avoided the trouble. But he would never know. Nor with the fluidity of the front line would he ever know whether they were hit by 'friendly' or unfriendly fire.'

Meanwhile F/O Alfred Uffindell in PB482, JI-P was also over the target when, at 0110hrs, his rear gunner P/O AE Clark sighted a twin-engined aircraft approaching from the port quarter. He ordered his pilot to corkscrew and the trace from the incoming fighter passed behind the Lancaster. The fighter was shaken off in the evasive manoeuvre and was not seen again. In fact, the two crews reporting combats were unfortunate to have encountered enemy aircraft as only five combats were reported by the Nachtjäger crews trying to intercept the second wave of the attack. Diversionary tactics and jamming had been effective in preventing an effective response by the night fighters. In total, six aircraft were lost from the two waves of the raid. Despite a lack of concentrated bombing, there was serious damage to the central and eastern parts of Stuttgart and the Bosch factory was hit.

PB426 survived 51 ops. Between August and October 1944 she bore code JI-J, whilst with 'A' Flight. (Crown).

Back at base, yet another inspection took place when the Catering Officers from RAF Mildenhall, RAF Chedburgh and RAF Stradishall visited the Airmen's Mess on 20th October to see the organisation of 'The Choice of Meal' system. The ORB does not tell us if the personnel at those stations were subsequently offered something other than a rigid set menu.

On 21st October the squadron participated in another attempt to subdue the gun batteries covering the River Schelde. On this occasion the targets were in the vicinity of Flushing on the island of Walcheren. Whilst 514 Squadron had been focusing on German targets, bombers from other groups had continued to pound the defences of the island and by now crews noted that the land was largely flooded. One Waterbeach aircraft, which is not identified, was hit by flak on the run up and its bombs fell on a local oil refinery.

A ship berthed at the northern end of Haren was also hit; the ORB describes the vessel as both *'small'* and *'large'* in the same sentence, the recording officer apparently unfamiliar with the size of ships generally. The flak was slight though two of the squadron's aircraft were damaged, both returning safely however. A total of 75 aircraft from 3 Group took part in this raid, 25 of which were from 514 Squadron. One Lancaster, HK596, AA-O flown by F/O J Johnson of 75(NZ) Sqn at Mepal, was hit by flak and crashed in the target area. Although five parachutes were seen, no crew members survived the descent. Overall, the bombing effort was described as accurate.

F/O Stan Wright RCAF (3rd from right, back row) with his air and ground crew at RAF Waterbeach (Ken Ridley).

Another GH raid was staged by 100 aircraft from 3 Group on the town of Neuss on 22nd October. Ten aircraft were provided by 514 Squadron. All these attacked the primary target through ten tenths cloud cover. Formations of bombers appeared to be flying in all directions with bombing scattered as a result. Five of the squadron's aircraft bombed on GH and three on the GH leaders. No aircraft were lost, though P/O Trevor Trask RAAF in LM627, JI-D had to contend with the loss of his GH and H2S equipment, DR Compass and Air Speed Indicator (ASI) in the run up

to the target. Fortunately he was able to bomb by following another GH leader. Two aircraft sustained small holes in their mid-upper turrets, fortunately with no injuries to the gunners.
That night at Waterbeach the WAAF held the first of a series of combined social evenings and dancing classes for their RAF guests. This innovation proved a great success, perhaps reducing the number of bruised toes sustained by the WAAFs.
It was back to Germany yet again the following evening, 23rd October, as

Krupps Armaments Works at Essen was frequently targeted by Bomber Command. The after effects can be seen clearly in this photo, taken by bomb aimer W/O Ken Staveley on a 'Cooks Tour' trip after the end of hostilities (Ken Staveley).

26 Lancasters left Waterbeach for Essen in what was Bomber Command's largest effort to date with 1,055 aircraft involved. F/O Robert Vickers in NF968, JI-L had to abort with his ASI and port inner engine unserviceable. Weather en route was described as most appalling, with cloud up to 23,000 feet and severe electrical storms. Sky markers were used and the crews with GH considered them to have been accurately placed. There was little evidence seen of the bombing itself, which was considered to be fairly concentrated by the crews. Flak was moderate though it was joined by the defences of Düsseldorf and Cologne. There were a few sightings of Me109s. F/O Stan Wright RCAF in LM719, JI-B was homeward-bound

having just left the target area at 1940hrs when P/O 'Curly' Maynes RCAF in the mid upper turret saw a twin-engined fighter approaching. P/O Maynes fired at the attacker whilst ordering a corkscrew, whilst fellow Canadian rear gunner P/O Jake Stansbury joined in, having to operate his turret manually, the hydraulics having been rendered unserviceable by flak damage over the target. The enemy pilot chose not to return for another go. Overall only eight aircraft were lost, a very light toll for a raid on this most notorious of targets. The bomb loads were now mostly HE rather than incendiaries, conventional wisdom being that most burnable buildings had by now been destroyed. This raid accounted for a further 607 buildings being flattened.

After a night off, 514 Squadron returned to Essen on the afternoon of 25th October, demonstrating the Allies' growing confidence in their ability to control the skies over Germany itself. 26 aircraft were detailed by the squadron as part of the 771 bomber raid. F/L Bruce McDonald had to bring NG118, A2-E back early when his starboard outer engine failed. The target was cloud covered though early crews were able to see the built up area through a clear patch and red TIs were dropped. The bombing was concentrated though considerable haze and smoke accumulated and the raid was described as successful. A further 1,163 buildings were destroyed and there was severe damage to the remaining industrial plants in the city, including the vital Krupps steelworks. Much of Essen's industries had by now dispersed and the city lost its important role in German war production. Only four aircraft failed to return, presumably due to flak as no enemy fighters were seen.

On 26th October a GH raid by 105 aircraft was launched by 3 Group against a chemical plant at Leverkusen. Ten Lancasters were from 514 Squadron, all of which attacked the target, eight using GH and two following their lead. The formation and bombing were reported to be very good, all bombs falling within a radius of 200 yards. It was not possible to assess the actual results due to the complete cloud cover. There were no losses on this raid.

On the morning of 28th October twelve of the squadron's crews took part in another assault on coastal gun batteries at Flushing by 277 bombers, eleven of the Waterbeach contingent bombing the target. LM734, A2-C, flown by F/O Maurice Oliver, was hit by heavy flak, its wing petrol tank being holed and intercom rendered unserviceable. As he considered that it would not be possible to bomb accurately, F/O Oliver elected to jettison his bombs forty miles off Southwold and return to base. None of his crew were injured. Two aircraft from 76 and 90 Sqns were lost to flak. Four parachutes were seen to deploy from the 90 Sqn aircraft, two landing in the sea and two amongst bursting bombs. None of the crew members survived.

Post-raid reconnaissance photograph showing the extensive flooding around Westkappelle after the attack on Walcheren Island.

Following the early morning raid on Flushing a second wave of twelve Lancasters left Waterbeach in the early afternoon, this time bound for Cologne as part of a force of 733 bombers conducting an area attack. The attack was conducted in two waves and there was massive destruction including 2,239 blocks of flats, 15 industrial premises, eleven schools and three police stations. There was also damage to power stations, railways and harbour installations. This time, weather over the target was clear and markers were considered scarcely necessary. On leaving, the target was described as one large concentrated mass of brown smoke rising to 1,000 feet. The flak was moderate to intense, predicted and accurate for height with tracer to 10,000 feet. Fortunately the bombing height was around

20,000 feet. No enemy aircraft were seen and, although seven aircraft failed to return, 514 Squadron's crews were unscathed.
The campaign against Walcheren Island's defences was still continuing and on the morning of 29th October the squadron was called to arms once again, ten crews taking part in a raid of 358 aircraft. There were eleven different German positions earmarked for attention. F/O Geoff France in NG203, JI-A reported bombing from 7,000 feet at 1137hrs. All crews reported circling for four to five minutes before identifying the markers which were dropped in a line along the coast. The target was re-marked as the first markers were not considered accurate. The Master Bomber was on hand to offer advice and guidance and, although the bombing was fairly scattered it was believed that the actual gun position assigned to 514 Squadron was hit, as were all the German positions. There was no flak and no fighters were seen. The only aircraft that failed to return, a 582 Sqn Lancaster sent to mark the target, was lost without trace.
The following morning, 30th October, the squadron sent 24 aircraft to attack an oil refinery at Wesseling as part of another 3 Group GH effort, this one involving 102 aircraft. The target was covered by cloud and bombing was scattered with at least two separate areas developing. However some black smoke was seen rising above the first aiming point and it is believed that the bombing was accurate. No aircraft were lost despite the slight to moderate flak.
The final op of the month was on the afternoon of 31st October, when 23 of the squadron's Lancasters carried out a GH attack on an oil refinery at Bottrop making a total force of 101 aircraft from 3 Group. Nine of the squadron's crews were GH leaders, the rest followers. F/O Geoff France bombed on GH at 1500hrs from 18,000 feet releasing a 4,000lb 'cookie' and fifteen 500lb GP bombs along with a marker flare. Flak was moderate, predicted and four of the squadron's aircraft were damaged. F/O Ronald 'Eddie' Edmundson's LM275, JI-M was hit in the mid upper turret and starboard outer engine. F/O Robert Vickers reported damage to the starboard fin and rudder of PB423 A2-G, F/O Irvine Bittner brought back LM728 JI-U with damage to her fuselage whilst NG142, A2-H flown by F/O Frank Heald, was hit in the bomb aimer's panel. This was one of four occasions when NG142, christened 'The Lancashire Lass' returned with

F/O Eddie Edmundson and crew with LM725, JI-M 'Mick the Miller'. Despite being hit by flak over Bottrop, crew and aircraft survived the war (WMHM).

flak damage. A painting by renowned artist Don Breckon, titled 'Coming Home' commemorates one such occasion and adorns the cover of this book. The only aircraft lost on this raid was a 90 Sqn Lancaster, the cause being unknown but flak is a likely culprit.

So ended a very busy month for the squadron with 395 sorties delivering 1,946 tons of bombs to a wide variety of targets for the loss of a single aircraft. 514 Squadron was now at the peak of its strength and effectiveness as it prepared to mark the first anniversary of its operational status. This was commented upon in the Station Commander's Summary: *The month has been outstanding for the intensity of the operational effort. The base has sent out over one thousand sorties of which No. 514 Squadron has contributed 386, despite difficulties at the beginning of the month. In the latter half of the month, bombing on GH has been resorted to on a large scale and the Squadron has led aircraft of the Base on a number of these attacks. The attack on Leverkusen on the 26th and Köln on the 28th were particularly successful. The strain on armourers and on the MT Section personnel has been excessive but there has been little complaint and, so far, no great increase in sickness. This must be attributed, in some measure, to the attachment of fifty u/t (under training) aircrew cadets who, though inexperienced, have shown great willingness and have helped to make good the scarcity of labour.*

514 Squadron Lancasters en route to Wesseling on 30th October 1944. NG121, JI-H, nearest to camera, was flown by F/O Stan Wright RCAF. The photo was taken by another squadron pilot, F/O 'Art' Wark RCAF in PD325, A2-L. Photo courtesy of F/O Ken Ridley, navigator in NG121.

P/O Bert Sandland (back row, 2nd from left) with his crew and their usual aircraft, LM735, JI-M 'Minnie the Moocher'. The Sandland crew survived but 'Minnie the Moocher' was not so lucky. As A2-G, LM735 was shot down over Emmerich on 7th October 1944 (Wendy Flemming).

8. Oil and Transport: November 1944 to February 1945

November 1944 was to see an intensifying of the bombing campaign against German oil production as this was increasingly recognised to be the Achilles ' heel of the Nazi regime. One target in particular, the Rhein-Preussen synthetic oil plant at Meerbeck near Homberg, was to exact a further toll on the squadron and indeed 3 Group as a whole. Lying just across the Rhine from Duisburg the plant was ferociously defended and had seen the demise of four of the squadron's aircraft and their crews in July.

On 2nd November it was to attack this target that the squadron deployed 23 Lancasters, part of a force of 184-strong 3 Group force. The cloud was variable but clear for bombing, at least until a column of smoke rising to 10,000 feet obscured the target. The flak was as hostile as ever, moderate to intense, heavy and accurate. At least four of the squadron's aircraft were damaged. NG141, A2-J, flown by F/O Arthur Holland, suffered damage to the mid upper turret and port wing flap. F/O Christopher Nicholl RCAF in PD233, A2-K struggled home with his windscreen and the bomb aimer's panel damaged along with the tail plane. F/O Robert Vickers was in the wars again as the bomb doors of PB482, JI-P were hit by flak whilst F/O Don Gordon in LM719, JI-B suffered unspecified flak damage to his aircraft. Five of the Group's Lancasters failed to return. 195 Sqn, newly formed at 3 Base's Witchford from 'C' Flight of 115 Sqn, lost two aircraft on this raid whilst XV Sqn lost two of its Lancasters in a mid-air collision, only two of the fourteen crewmen surviving. A 186 Sqn aircraft made a crash landing in friendly territory after being hit by flak over the target, there being no injuries to the crew.

After a day off to get over the horrors of Homberg, the squadron returned to action with nineteen aircraft making a trip with 157 others to Solingen, which was a major steel-manufacturing centre. Bombs were seen to fall in the built up area as well as open country, so the crews thought the attack generally satisfactory. There was no flak reported over the target and no fighters were seen, however a number of reports were submitted of scarecrow shells. 'Bomber Command Losses' notes that two aircraft

Solingen suffered at the hands of Bomber Command with two raids on successive days attacking the steelworks. The second raid was particularly effective.

exploded over target area, which would almost certainly account for the 'scarecrow shell' sightings. These Lancasters were HK458, A4-C and NG219, JE-T, both aircraft being with 195 Sqn, which lost three of the four Lancasters that failed to return from this raid. In the absence of flak it is likely that these Lancasters either collided or were struck by bombs from other aircraft. The bombing was, in fact, badly scattered and this raid was not successful. However, it was repeated the following lunchtime, involving 23 of the squadron's aircraft amongst the 173 total force. One crew had to return to Waterbeach, this being F/O Geoff France when the supercharger in PB423, A2-G disintegrated. There was one burst of flak over the target but otherwise nothing to bother the squadron's crews. Only one aircraft was lost, that being a XV Sqn Lancaster. No explanation was given as to the cause. On this occasion the force achieved much better accuracy and concentration. German records show this raid to have been an outstanding success, though it is doubtful that is exactly how they phrased it. It appears that the devastation was not fully made good until 1950.

Koblenz was next up on 6th November, with another GH raid by 128 Lancasters from 3 Group. 514 Squadron contributed nineteen aircraft though two of these returned early. F/O Ian Campbell in PB419, JI-N experienced a failure of his port inner engine whilst F/O Maurice Oliver brought NG236, A2-C home early with a defective rear turret. For the aircraft that did function well enough to reach the target, the weather was clear and the crews were enthusiastic about the results, with marking concentrated. The ORB even commented that the marking was *'better than PFF'* which was laying down the gauntlet to the Pathfinders. Large fires were seen to be spreading over a wide area in the loop of the river junction. Over 300 acres were destroyed by fire, this representing 58% of the town's built-up area. There was slight to moderate flak but few fighters were seen and no combats were reported by the squadron. This being an evening raid it occurred after dark and no searchlights were noted. Only two Lancasters failed to return, both being from 622 Sqn out of Mildenhall.

The attractions of Homberg could not be resisted for long and the next visit by 514 Squadron was on 8th November. Eighteen aircraft were despatched in 3 Group's latest attempt to eradicate the plant, this time with 136 Lancasters. As ever there was a less than cordial reception from the defenders, with moderate to intense predicted flak. Bombing was initially accurate causing two large fires, but then smoke obscured the target and bombing became more scattered.

A record eight of 514 Squadron's aircraft sustained flak damage and, from the force as a whole, PD374, HA-C of 218 Sqn at Methwold, was lost. LM684, JI-O, flown by F/O Gordon Smith was hit in the port inner engine and front turret; F/O Hubert Merrett had to fly LM685, JI-Q home half power after three of his Merlins were hit, two being rendered useless; NF966, JI-R flown by F/O Ian Campbell sustained a damaged windscreen; F/L Ron Pickler's PB423, A2-G was hit on the bomb doors and rear turret; F/O Maurice Oliver in NG326, A2-C had his mid upper turret damaged; NG142, A2-H (The Lancashire Lass) was hit again, F/O Frank Heald having to fly her home with a smashed windscreen whilst both F/O John Harland in PD333 A2-K and F/O Irvine Bittner in LM728, JI-U suffered unspecified flak damage to their aircraft. Remarkably there were no reports of injuries to any of the crews.

Amidst all the aerial activity, ground staff had endured another series of visitors arriving to have a good nose around the workings of the Station. On 5th November F/O HK Vickerman of RAAF Overseas Headquarters visited the Station and advised RAAF personnel on their pay queries. The following day Major G Halle and Major H Vikajo of the Norwegian Air Force visited the Station Senior Works Officer. Then on 7th more distinguished overseas guests turned up in the guise of General Ahmed Nakjtchvan, Chief of the Iranian Air Force and Colonel Bayendur, the Iranian Air Attache.

The squadron was not required for the following two days, though this was undoubtedly a busy time for the fitters with the heavy load of repairs. On 11th November the squadron provided eighteen Lancasters for an operation to another synthetic oil plant, this time at Castrop Rauxel. 3 Group had mustered 122 Lancasters for the customary GH daylight raid, these carrying out a concentrated and accurate attack through the complete cloud cover. F/O 'Eddie' Edmundson in PD419, JI-N had to return early with an unserviceable port outer engine. The remaining aircraft were met by slight to moderate heavy predicted flak but no damage was reported by the squadron's crews on this occasion, and no aircraft were lost. There was also heavy flak from the Siegfried Line and some Ruhr towns. F/S Frank Bell was with his crew in PD324, A2-B: 'Once again we were a GH Leader with three Lancasters formating on us. There would be a fighter escort but they would fly way above us at 30,000 feet while we kept at our usual 21,000. The fighters were Spitfires and Mustangs and the usual German fighters they met in daylight were FW190s and Me109s. Flak was always present especially if we passed close to a heavily defended town or city. Sometimes it was quite thick and accurately predicted. We noticed Lancasters in trouble. One running on three engines, one being feathered and still on fire, another with its port wing on fire and going down. A bit further along on our starboard side a formation of Lancasters being victimised by the radar-predicted flak and getting hell knocked out of them over the target. I got the screaming hab dabs. There were too many aircraft above us and we were on our bombing run. There they were fifty feet above us with their bomb doors open; they were also on their bombing run. I nearly had kittens. I yelled at Hendy, our pilot, over the intercom alerting him to the danger and to edge over to port. We gradually moved over and flip me if they didn't do likewise! I told the skipper and he moved quickly back to starboard. Just seeing those blockbusters and the other bombs hanging above us, waiting to be released at any moment wasn't doing me any good at all. Thankfully we got clear of them just as they fell away at the same time as we released our load. I had a last look round in the astrodome and what a sight it was to see all those Lancasters and Halifaxes, some still in formation like us whilst others were on their own. Once over the Suffolk coast Hendy reduced height and flew in at low level at 200 feet with our three colleagues formating on us. We weren't supposed to fly this low but some of us did now and again. It gave us a lift when people in the villages and fields stood waving to us.'

The original sketch by F/O Harry Darby which he entered into the squadron competition for an official badge. Minor changes were required by the College of Arms before the badge was approved by HM King George VI in August 1944. By that time, Harry had been a POW for four months (WMHM)

On the same day, and presumably to help the crew with the spiritual preparations they would doubtless make every time they ventured over enemy territory, the Reverend Canon SJ Marriott, the Archbishop of Canterbury's visitor to the Royal Air Force, arrived on the Station for a week's stay.

12th November saw a particularly notable occasion for 514 Squadron. The Station ORB records: *'At a general Station Parade in 'A' Hangar, Air Vice Marshal R Harrison, CB, CBE, DFC, AFC, Air Officer Commanding No.3 Group, presented the Squadron Badge to W/C M Wyatt, DFC, Officer Commanding No. 514 Squadron. In a short speech the AOC referred to the exploits of the squadron since it was formed twelve months ago and said that this honour was well merited and that the Squadron had earned the right to have its badge along with other units of the three services. Afterwards the AOC, accompanied by Air Commodore HH Down, AFC and Group Captain CM Heard took the salute at a march Past of the Station Personnel. The Badge, which has been approved by His Majesty the King, shows a sword piercing a cloud, symbolising the squadron's operational function, and bears the motto 'Nil Obstare Potest', meaning 'Nothing Can Withstand'*[33]*. The Station Military Band attended the Parade. The Reverend Canon SJ Marriott gave an address on 'Religious Problems Today' to assembled aircrew in the Briefing Room.'*

The occasion was also marked by all available members of the squadron posing with a Lancaster for a group photograph.

On 13th November the High Commissioner for New Zealand, Mr WJ Jordan, accompanied by Air Commodore EG Olsen, DSO, RNZAF, had lunch at the Station and interviewed New Zealand personnel, according to the Station ORB. Unfortunately most of the New Zealand aircrew personnel were flying, though it is noted in the Squadron ORB that ops were cancelled and that H2S training and air tests took place.

As it happened the squadron next took to the air operationally on 15th November with another 3 Group GH attack on an oil plant, on this occasion involving 119 Lancasters and the Hoesch-Benzin facility in Dortmund. It was another maximum effort from 514 Squadron with thirty aircraft detailed, of which 29 actually took off. The attack was concentrated and accurate through the ten tenths cloud. Flak was slight to moderate, though it accounted for two Lancasters, HK595, KO-A and

---

[33]This is believed to be the technical translation from the Latin; however, squadron members have assured the author that they intended the motto to mean 'Nothing Can Stop Us', the title of this work reflecting their wish. This is also corroborated by Lou Greenburgh in 'DFC & Bar' by Ed Greenburgh.

NN706, KO-B, both of 115 Sqn. at Witchford. These were lost with their crews whilst formating on their GH Leader, 514 Squadron's LM627, JI-D flown by F/O Leslie Drew. LM627 was also hit, with bomb aimer F/S RS Williams sustaining a head injury. Fortunately for him it did not appear to be too serious as he returned to ops five days later. Meanwhile F/O Ron Limbert in LM288, JI-C had to return on two engines to Woodbridge after his Lancaster was struck by falling bombs which hit both port engines and the starboard outer. He was able to keep one going and limped back to the emergency airfield on two engines. Another bomb had fallen through the fuselage and lodged alongside the main spar which would have made the trip home even more fraught for the crew who, the ORB notes, behaved admirably.

The following day, 16th November, the role for the squadron switched to army support as they were tasked with bombing German supply lines at Heinsburg, which was to be attacked by the American First and Ninth Armies. This is the first occasion on which the RAF had bombed a tactical target in front of the US Army. 25 aircraft from Waterbeach formed part of a massive raid numbering 1,188 bombers attacking three targets. There was no cloud over the target but slight haze. The squadron's aircraft attacked the town visually or on the upwind edge of the smoke. The attack was considered successful and the target left one mass of smoke and flames. The raids caused massive damage to the three towns targeted; however the American attack then suffered from problems unrelated to this operation. Flak was slight to moderate heavy and three aircraft were damaged. LM733, JI-F flown by F/O Ray Foreman RCAF, was hit by flak which damaged the mid upper turret. The same thing happened to PB419, JI-N flown by F/O Ian Campbell who brought home yet another damaged aircraft. On this occasion he also suffered a hang up so had to bring his bombs back with him, though fortunately he was able to jettison them safely forty miles east of Southwold. There is no record of the third aircraft damaged on this operation.

Homberg was still there and two further raids were to be carried out, albeit at considerable cost. On 20th November the squadron sent 26 crews as part of the 183-strong GH raid on a stormy day. F/O Eric Williams in PB423, A2-G had to abort his sortie, jettisoning his bombs when his elevator controls jammed and the rear turret became unserviceable. F/O Christopher Nicholl in PD333 A2-K also had a wasted trip as his crew was unable to identify the target accurately so he took his bombs back home.

Many aircraft were unable to formate on GH leaders and the bombing was scattered. Flak was slight though crews reported seeing scarecrows. These possibly referred to the explosion of 75(NZ) Sqn's PB689, AA-X, near the target, one of three aircraft lost by that unit on this raid. F/O Geoff France in his favourite Lancaster LM733 JI-F submitted what would be his final post-op report which stated succinctly: *'1 x 4,000 HC, 12 x 500 MC, 4 x 500 GP. Primary target: HOMBERG. Bombed at 1514½ hours from 19,000 feet on GH Leader.'* The squadron lost the entire crew of F/O John Harland when LM286 A2-F exploded and crashed in the target area, believed to be as a result of a premature explosion of its 4,000 lb 'cookie'. F/L Leo Currie RCAF in NF966, JI-R reported that his aircraft was damaged due to another exploding; this may well have been LM286. F/O Trevor Trask also reported his own aircraft, NG118, A2-E diving steeply to starboard out of control, the reason not stated, ten seconds before he was due to bomb on GH. It is likely that this was caused by a close explosion, though luckily F/O Trask was able to regain control after jettisoning his bombs.

F/O Ron Goulding was the bomb aimer in LM727, JI-S, flown by F/O Jimmy Parnell: 'Our most dicey trip was to Homberg on 20th November when just after dropping the bombs the aircraft on our port side exploded (we were in the box with a vic of three a/c in front of us). Our aircraft, S Sugar, flew through the explosion and we appeared to lose control for a time. Thinking that we were hell bound for earth, I tried to put on my parachute but the G force prevented me from doing so. However the skipper managed to regain control after a struggle, only to discover a large hole in the nose of the bomb aimer's position. The front turret had pieces of the other a/c wrapped around it and both gunners were slightly injured. We regained height and formated on several other Lancs as there were German fighters around. I therefore stayed in the front turret and to my surprise found it was working. It was however bitterly cold. The slight injuries to both gunners were patched up and they resumed their duties. On nearing the English coast the skipper's windscreen started to give way and the engineer held a large board over the screen to prevent it caving in. The difficulty was on landing, so I lay in the nose and guided the skipper down (some of my training as a pilot proving obviously useful). When we landed the aircraft was found to be extensively damaged and I understand it was a write-off.'

F/S Frank Bell was also on the op, once again flying in PM324, A2-D: 'It was another trip to the Ruhr, to a town producing synthetic oil. We did not know at briefing that this was to be the raid we lost friends on. They were to blow up over the target on the run in, formating on us. The pilot was Australian and the crew were our special friends. We were third in line for take-off with a five ton bomb load. Our engines were throbbing, just waiting, then Hendy's voice said 'Here we go.' The engines roared and we were belting down the runway, then we were airborne. After orbiting for a few minutes we rendezvoused with our three followers. After thirty minutes we reached 20,000 feet and I looked out of the astrodome; everywhere I looked I could see little formations of Lancasters. I returned to my seat and tuned in the receiver to get the group broadcasts. Five minutes from the run in to the target I returned to the astrodome as observer watching our followers. I heard the navigator say "We are on the bombing run." Next thing we heard was "Bombs away." The followers to our port and rear dropped theirs with us but those to starboard hadn't released. I informed the skipper and we continued to fly straight and level a little longer. I kept my eyes on them, then I saw three black shapes drop away. The next moment, there was a hell of an explosion and the blast threw us all over the place. When we sorted ourselves out and looked back there was only a huge black cloud hanging in the sky where our friends had been. Blown up and just vanished; it was unbelievable. Where our other two followers were, we had no idea. We just kept plugging on for home. We had no idea if we had sustained any damage but the aircraft seemed to be flying straight. We were a shaken crew when we landed at base and told the ground crew what had happened. They were upset because they had known that crew very well. Their dispersal was next to ours.

At the de-briefing each of us had to describe what we had seen and nothing more. There was an inquiry in which every aspect was explored. It concluded that there was a fault in the electrical circuit in the bomb aimer's panel and the crew therefore had to jettison the bomb load. But a mistake had been made. Instead of dropping the blockbuster (4,000 lb 'cookie') on its own, either first or last, and the 500 lb bombs separately, the bombs had been released together and a 500 lb bomb had cannoned against the blockbuster as it was leaving the bay, causing the explosion. The crew wouldn't have known a thing about it.'

The following day, 21st November, the 22 crews chosen for the day's ops were undoubtedly dismayed when the briefing curtain drew back to reveal that, yet again, they were to brave the defences of Homberg. They were told to expect the target to be overcast, which was supposed to make life more difficult for the flak batteries. This conveniently ignored the fact that the anti-aircraft defences had so far shown a remarkable ability to wreak havoc even through complete overcast. Departure was delayed and the crews had no option but to sit in their bombed-up Lancasters at Waterbeach waiting for the signal to go. This only added to the tension felt by F/O Geoff France and his crew in PD265, JI-G. They had just been told that after their 35th trip they would be screened from ops having completed their tour. This would be their 34th.

Eventually, some two hours later than planned, the squadron was airborne. The met forecast, as happened with monotonous regularity, turned out to be wrong. The bomber stream arrived over the hotly-defended target of Homberg to find clear skies, which gave the flak crews a clear view of what was heading their way.

The bombing was scattered at first but then became very concentrated, culminating in a vast sheet of yellow flame followed by black smoke rising to a great height, according to the raid report. The raid was very satisfactory and finally put the plant permanently out of action. Some bombs also fell to the south west of the target and a bridge was believed to have been hit. Not everything went completely according to plan, however, with seven of the squadron's aircraft were damaged by flak, though the ORB does not contain further details. At least one aircraft, NF968 JI-L, released its bombs early to the west of the target. LM684, JI-C was seen to explode as the aircraft approached the target. It is believed to have been hit by flak. There were no survivors from the crew of F/O Ron Limbert, whose DFC for his earlier exploits was to be announced at the end of the month. The aircraft crashed next to a heavy flak emplacement named 'Grossbatterie Daubenspeckhof' on a farm approximately 1 km NW of Moers city centre, this battery being the most likely culprit for so much carnage amongst 3 Group's squadrons.

Sgt Roger Scott was the flight engineer in LM684. The previous day he had posted a letter to his sister[34]:

20-11-44
2205999 Sgt Scott R
c/o No 2. Sergeants Mess
R.A.F Waterbeach
Nr Cambridge

Dear Ede.
Here's hoping you will forgive me for not having written for some time, or having neglected visiting you, but we are working really hard + it has a strange fatiguing effect on us. I have done as much as two trips to Duisberg in the same day, + I have done ten trips to Germany during the past fifteen days. We have had our photograph in the Sunday Dispatch + the Daily Express some time ago when the Daily Express reporter came with us to Duisberg twice the same day; I have only a few more to do now, + I give you my promise to come + stay with you for a few days when I have finished.
I think it will be safe to tell you (as long as you don't tell ma) that, were it not by the grace of God, I should be pushing German daisies up at the moment; Bomber Command have commended my crew + myself on the fact, that we are the only people in the record of flying, who have had 5 bombs dropped on us in Germany + got home again;
The Pilot + Navigator are each being presented with the D.F.C. for bringing a Lancaster back to this country, after having three of our engines bombed off + one bomb stuck in the fuselage (which we brought back to this country) all our instruments had gone + we flew for three hours (from Dortmund to Cambridge) on one engine; We may all get medals but we can't be sure; Well Ede; I have a lot to tell you when I see you: + I am sure, after the above account of our activities you will forgive my not writing etc. This is all for the time being so cheerio + give my love to Ron + Brian.

[34] Text of letter is from Garry Scott, nephew of Sgt Scott.

love

Roger x x x

PS I shall probably be finished in the next fortnight as I have only 3 more to do.

A wartime wedding. The crew of F/O Geoff France celebrate the marriage of their bomb aimer, F/O Ken Barker RCAF to Doris Brown in Polar, London. The marriage ended in widowhood for Doris Barker within six weeks. L-R: F/O Fred Eisberg (Navigator), F/O Geoff France (Pilot), Sgt Ron Harding (WOP), F/O Ken Barker RCAF (Bomb Aimer), and the three Petes: F/O Pete Slater (MU Gunner), Sgt Pete Coles (Rear Gunner), Sgt Pete Gosnold (Flight Engineer) (France family).

According to Axel Heyermann in Moers, 'November 21st 1944 became notorious as Black Tuesday. The bomb run began at approximately 1500 hrs. Exactly above Kamp-Lintfort Lancaster LM684 of 514 Squadron., flown by F/O Limbert, was hit by flak. The bomb aimer jettisoned the bomb load in emergency and the bomber crashed. The whole crew died. These bombs fell into residential area of Kamp- Lintfort. Some following bombers were misled and dropped their bomb load into the city as well. 74 civilians died within the destroyed buildings. Yet most of the bombers found their target and damaged the plant repeatedly.'

F/O Geoff France was a GH Leader for the operation and the outbound trip had been relatively uneventful following the earlier delay. Immediately after bombing the target, however, PD265 was hit by flak between the starboard inner engine and the cockpit, killing the flight engineer, Sgt Pete Gosnold, and injuring F/O France, in the thigh. F/O France believed the aircraft was also hit in the tail as it became uncontrollable. He remembered bracing his feet on the instrument panel whilst attempting to pull the aircraft out of its dive. He did not remember what happened immediately after that as he then found himself outside the aircraft at what he believed was more than 20,000 feet, so pulled his ripcord. France saw below him another parachute, which he presumed had come from his Lancaster. In fact the navigator F/O Freddie Eisberg, had decided to put on his own parachute when he saw the severity of the flak. He had also been thrown clear. Such decisions, made on the spur of the moment, made the difference between life and death for bomber aircrew.

France noted the tail of the Lancaster becoming detached, and saw the aircraft eventually explode though whether this was on or above the ground he does not know. He landed in a cabbage field, breaking his left leg, so was unable to effect an escape. Having lost consciousness he came too in a school building to find he was under guard by a member of the local Volkssturm (Home Guard) who had taken the opportunity to relieve him of his cigarettes. F/O Eisberg also landed in farmland whilst the aircraft came down in the moat surrounding the Grafschafter Castle in the centre of Moers. France and Eisberg were captured separately but their five crew mates perished.

F/O France was denied treatment to his wounds and subsequently lost his right leg due to untreated wounds turning gangrenous. Both F/O France and F/O Eisberg survived the war, albeit as POWs. F/O Eisberg was in a camp liberated by Soviet forces and found himself chilled by their behaviour and demeanour which he considered to bode ill for the future. Neither man ever forgot his crew mates[35].

[35] Geoff France returned to his studies after the war, becoming an architect. He was subsequently ordained as a vicar. His grandson is Yorkshire and England cricketer Will Rhodes

The third of the squadron's Lancasters to be affected on this raid was NG121, JI-H, flown by F/O John Tolley on his eighth op. The Report on Loss of Aircraft on Operations states:

'The aircraft was flying as a 'follower'; on the run up to the target it was 50 yards to the port quarter of the Leader, and slightly below. There was considerable flak, presumed predicted, during the run up.

'Normally a 'follower' aircraft in this position releases its bombs as soon as it sees the Leader do so. Consequently 'H' opened its bomb doors as soon as the Leader did, and the bomb aimer was waiting with his hand on the bomb release. Just as the formation neared the release point, the pilot and bomb aimer saw that the Leader was jettisoning his bombs all together. They could see no reason why the Leader was not bombing normally, and the bomb aimer prepared to release his bombs. Just as he did so, there was a blinding flash and explosion below the Leader, as if one of his bombs had exploded. The Perspex in the bomb aimer's compartment, the pilot's cockpit and the Mid-Upper turret was shattered, and the fuselage was scarred on the starboard side with small holes. The faces of both the pilot and the bomb aimer were pitted with minute cuts, and both were temporarily blinded by the flash, and by blood streaming over their eyes.

'The pilot lost control of the aircraft, and while he groped for the controls, with the wind lashing his face, the aircraft lost some three thousand feet. His intercom had gone unserviceable, and he could not reach the emergency signal light so he waved the crew forward with his hand, intending to that they should bale out.

'While they were putting on their chutes, however, the pilot regained control and signaled the crew to wait. He could see better by now, and managed to rejoin the stream, though the aircraft, now at 15,000 feet, was well below the others. The engineer had previously tried, without success, to plug the pilot's intercom into a different socket, but the pilot was now able to do so himself, and called up the rest of the crew.

'All the crew replied, except the rear gunner, so the pilot told the wireless operator to go back and investigate. The wireless operator opened the bulkhead doors and saw through the inspection panels that the bomb doors were open and he could see the ground below; air was rushing through the fuselage with the force of a gale. The wireless operator told

the pilot all this, and the pilot told the mid-upper gunner to go instead. The mid-upper gunner, who had already left his turret which when the Perspex was smashed, managed to reach the rear of the fuselage, where he found that the rear hatch was open, and on opening the rear bulkhead doors discovered that the rear gunner had gone. His parachute was missing; he must have baled out within a few miles of the target.

'The Lancaster was now flying normally and on track. Suddenly the starboard inner engine burst into flames, apparently due to an oil leak. This engine was feathered, the Graviner (extinguisher) used and the fire put out. A few minutes later the starboard outer engine revs began to fluctuate, and dense white fumes poured out of it suggesting a coolant leak. This engine was also successfully feathered.

'The wireless operator sent a distress message back to base, though as the aerials were badly damaged he did not think that the message would be received. 'H' had by now formatted on another Lancaster (115/B) and the wireless operator also signaled to this aircraft with the Aldis lamp.

'The Lancaster had by now flown for some 20 minutes since the flash had occurred, when the port outer revs began to fluctuate, and the engine finally burst into flames. Fire drill was again carried out correctly and with success. The Intercom then failed completely.

'The aircraft, now flying on one engine and unable to maintain height, cleared a belt of cumulus cloud at 12,000 feet. Below this cloud the weather was bad, with poor visibility. The pilot brought the aircraft down to 2,000 feet and at this height passed over an airfield near Antwerp. It was impossible to turn the aircraft to land here, so he flew on, and seeing three suitable adjacent fields ahead, he decided to land.

Since the Intercom had failed, all his instructions had to be given either by gesticulation, or written down on paper. Nevertheless, as he touched down, the MU gunner, engineer and navigator were at crash stations. The wireless operator remained in his seat firing off Verey lights to show their position, and the Flight Engineer braced himself in the navigator's seat.

'The pilot had managed to get the flaps down about 10 degrees and he made a perfect belly landing. The aircraft came to rest after travelling about 50 yards over the soft mud. No one in the crew was even bruised, though the pilot was not strapped into his seat and though he was unable,

owing to the Intercom failure, to warn the crew as he touched down. All the top hatches opened easily and the crew quickly scrambled out. The position was Doorn, near Antwerp, behind our own lines.

'The flash and explosion may have been flak, or a falling bomb, as the crew suggest, but it was more probably the explosion of 514/G or 514/C, both of which were lost, since other crews reported seeing an aircraft explode over the target. The incident was too sudden for a clear picture to be formed. The action of the rear gunner in baling out can be well understood, as the suddenness of the incident, the failure of the pilot's intercom, and the fact that the aircraft was then out of control would have been enough to convince him that he ought to bale out; the pilot considered him to be an extremely reliable, level-headed person. The remainder of the crew, particularly the pilot, showed considerable determination and coolness in bringing their aircraft back to friendly territory under extremely difficult conditions, displaying a commendable confidence in their aircraft and in each other.'

F/Lt. Harry Yates DFC of 75(NZ) Squadron from Mepal, who was flying on the operation, described the loss of the three 514 Squadron aircraft[36]:

'The familiar shell-bursts began to hang in the sky, multiplying every few seconds. An aircraft about a mile in front of us was hit, and then a second. Both began to trail smoke and flame. Their noses turned slowly, irrevocably downwards and their fate was sealed. A third aircraft, again about a mile ahead, took a direct hit, obviously in the bomb bay. The prodigious explosion distributed hundreds of burning fragments across the sky. There could be no parachutes but, sickened, I searched for them all the same.'

In conversation with the author six decades afterwards, Harry Yates still remembered the incident with great clarity. He described Homberg as 'a jinx target' which filled him with dread whenever it was tasked. The consolation for F/L Yates, and probably the rest of 3 Group, was that this raid had finally put the important oil plant at Homberg out of action

[36]'Luck and a Lancaster' by Harry Yates DFC (Airlife Publishing 1999).

The Rheinpreussen synthetic oil plant at Homberg, Moers, lies in ruins after a sustained campaign by Bomber Command. The target cost 514 Squadron eight aircraft, more than any other single target.

permanently as the Germans decided it was no longer worth the effort of trying to repair the facility.

On 23rd November, therefore, there was a change of scene as the Nordstern oil plant at Gelsenkirchen received unwanted attention from 168 Lancasters from 3 Group, including nineteen from the squadron. Amidst slight to moderate scattered heavy flak and despite complete cloud cover the force carried out an accurate attack for the loss of a single Lancaster, HK683 4-M of 195 Sqn, which caught fire and crashed off Walcheren Island on the outbound leg. There were no survivors from the crew.

After a short break 514 Squadron was called on to supply twenty two crews on 27th November for a GH raid by 169 Lancasters on marshalling yards at Cologne / Kalk. Although the bombing was largely concentrated there was some scattering to the west and south-west. Large fires were seen with, inevitably, much smoke and five large explosions. Once again the Luftwaffe pilots failed to put in an appearance but their colleagues on the ground made up for their absence with moderate to intense predicted heavy flak which was accurate for height. This accounted for two Lancasters, one of which, 90 Sqn's NN698, WP-U, struggled on despite being hit in the starboard inner engine. The crew of F/O D Jones bombed the target then sustained further hits before crash-landing at high speed near Valenciennes in France, the crew emerging remarkably unscathed. The other aircraft, HK624, IL-J of the ever-unfortunate 115 Sqn, was shot down by flak with the loss of all on board, these numbering nine as the aircraft was carrying additional air gunners.

514 Squadron's crews had an uneventful trip, with a couple of exceptions. P/O Donald Crome's NG203, JI-A was hit by flak sustaining damage to the windscreen and fuselage. F/L Ron Pickler in PB423, A2-G bombed at 1504 hours from 19,800 feet on a red TI. The aircraft's GH set was unserviceable. At 1501 hours PB423 was hit by flak making it very difficult to control. The bombing run was completed and the aircraft kept under control and flown back by the combined efforts of pilot, engineer, air bomber, navigator and rear gunner on the stick plus a length of rope.

F/L Ron Pickler and crew needed courage, strength and ingenuity to bring their damaged Lancaster home from Germany (Ron Pickler).

The mid upper gunner, F/S G Coulson RCAF, was wounded in the head by flak. The ORB noted: *'Captain comments that the crew behaved splendidly.'* F/L Pickler understandably received a DFC for his heroic effort in saving his crew and aircraft.
Before dawn on 29th November eighteen aircraft from Waterbeach went to Neuss as part of another GH raid, this time involving 145 Lancasters. Flak was negligible and, whilst two fighters were seen, no combats were reported and the entire force returned to England unharmed. The crews had seen the glow of fires through the ten tenths cloud cover, though a brief local report noted only 'modest' property damage, mostly residential.
The final operation of the month was on 30th November as sixty Lancasters, including seventeen from the squadron, carried out a GH raid on a benzol plant at Osterfeld. Flak was slight in intensity, heavy calibre, to the chagrin of P/O Alexander Munro RAAF who had to bring NG350, JI-C home from his first operation with slight damage. Bombing was concentrated and a large pall of smoke rose through the cloud layer. Two aircraft were lost to the flak, one each from 33 Base squadrons 75(NZ) and, once again, 115 Sqn.
The Station Commander's Report for November stated:
The intensity of operations has fallen off slightly during the month, largely because of adverse weather, although the Squadron was standing by much of the time and stand-downs were few. The armourers' work was eased to an appreciable extent because changes of bomb load were avoided when targets were changed. This saving of effort, however, was largely offset by the change of working conditions – the wintry weather turning the bomb dump into a flood of mud.
All attacks throughout the month have been made on GH runs and the Squadron has now gained considerable experience in this form of attack. Several of the attacks have been most satisfactory, although equipment and manipulation failures are still too common. The attack on Homberg on the 21st was also a failure, it is thought because markers were dropped early in the attack, four miles short of the target on the run in, and following aircraft bombed these visually thinking their GH set must be unserviceable.

A view from the office window. P/O Brian Haslam leans nonchalantly from the open pilot's window of LM717, JI-T shortly after enjoying an evening out together over Dortmund on 6th October 1944. Lancaster and pilot both survived the war (WMHM).

The morale of aircrews is still good, but daylight GH attacks are not as popular as they were owing to the fact that casualties caused by flak and by falling bombs are seen to happen. GH attacks over the Ruhr in clear skies are also unpopular because of the known accuracy of German flak.

The new month was barely thirty six hours old when on 2nd December the squadron despatched fifteen Lancasters to Dortmund, 93 aircraft being tasked with attacking a benzol plant there. By now the GH raids on oil plants were falling into a pattern; complete cloud cover, accurate bombing, no fighters but moderate heavy flak which caused damage, in this case, to five of the squadron's aircraft.

Fortunately none of the attacking force was lost. Rank had no privileges when it came to anti-aircraft fire; S/L John Timms, Flight Commander of C Flight, was on the final trip of his tour when he brought PD325, A2-L home with flak damage to both starboard engines and the mid upper turret. The unfortunate gunner, W/O John Moran was wounded by flak. PD333, A2-K flown by F/O Bill Coyle was a repeat victim with the tail plane and fuselage damaged. C Flight's tribulations continued with NG141, A2-J sustaining bad damage from a flak shell through the wingtip, though F/O Hugh Richford was able to nurse her back to Waterbeach. F/O Campbell Fiset RCAF, in LM733, JI-F was welcomed to operational flying by flak damage to the cockpit perspex. Finally, F/O Don Gordon was again targeted by the defences, sustaining fuselage damage to NG350, JI-C.

DON'T WASTE BOMBS is the motto of F.O. C. G. Fiset, Montreal. When his oxygen failed on a raid against Hamm, he made a one-bomber raid on Bochal on the German border and got badly shot up, too. With him here, left, are his crew members: W.O. R. J. Hamilton, Toronto, air bomber, and Flt.-Sergt. Larry Mulhall, Woodslee

A Canadian newspaper reported the exploits of F/O Campbell Fiset RCAF and crew as technical problems meant that they had to carry out a single-handed raid on Bocholt, rather than Hamm as planned (WMHM).

F/O Joe Gallicano (centre) and crew, including navigator W/O Peter Lowen. Squadron records do not show PB142 operating with code A2-D though F/O Gallicano's crew usually flew in other aircraft with that code. PB142 also appears to have had its original code painted over. The crew also look particularly pleased with themselves (WMHM).

On 4th December it was Oberhausen's turn to host a visit by 3 Group, with 160 Lancasters carrying out a precision attack on the railway station. Twenty of the visitors were from Waterbeach and the attack was generally considered to have been carried out very well despite the slight heavy flak. This accounted for the sole loss, a Lancaster from XV Sqn at Mildenhall whose crew averaged twenty years of age. Although no results of this GH raid could be observed directly, local reporting mentions heavy damage in the centre of the town. The Station ORB describes the raid as '*the best GH attack yet.*'

Railways were regaining their earlier popularity for the raid planners at 3 Group, with an attack the following morning on the marshalling yards at Hamm. The 91 Lancasters despatched included 21 from Waterbeach, though F/O Campbell Fiset in NN717, JI-E suffered oxygen failure and returned early depositing his 4,000lb cookie and 1,950 four-pound incendiaries on the built-up area of the unfortunate town of Bochalt (possibly a mis-spelling of Bocholt). Over the railway yards at Hamm, there was complete cloud cover but little or no heavy flak. A good concentration of bombing was achieved, to the delight of the GH leaders,

and nearly forty percent of Hamm's built up area was destroyed. Even better, there were no losses incurred by the force.
On 6th December the target was another significant oil plant, at Leuna, Merseburg near Leipzig in eastern Germany. Whilst the trip to Hamm had taken around five hours, this operation lasted between seven and eight, and was carried out at night. The weather over Europe had deteriorated and was poor, with an electrical storm and icing over France. The attacking force was larger than most for oil targets, involving 487 aircraft. The squadron's contribution started at nineteen, but four had to return early. F/O WF Burrows RCAF suffered a loss of ASI and Gee equipment in PB426, JI-D, landing at RAF Oakington. F/O Brian Haslam, in LM728, JI-T had to return to Waterbeach with his mid upper turret unserviceable. P/O Joseph Gallicano RCAF, on his second op, brought his crew home early in NG236, A2-C because his rear gunner, Sgt LG Watson was too sick to guard the aircraft from attack. Sgt J Deighton was also too unwell to fight off any fighters seeking to attack LM733, JI-F so his pilot, F/O Ray Foreman also did the decent thing and took him back to base. F/O Fred Hendy in PD334, A2-D suffered intercom, then wireless, problems but the crew elected to press on. F/S Frank Bell was able to rectify the wireless problem and the crew completed the sortie, remaining on tenterhooks for the 6½ hour trip.
The remaining aircraft arrived over the target to find the clouds lit from below by searchlights and, shortly after the arrival of the force, by the red glow of fires. A 'terrific' explosion was seen at 2052hrs, followed by one that was merely 'large' six minutes later and the post-raid photos showed that considerable damage had been caused. The heavy calibre flak was moderate to intense whilst fighter flares were noted from the front line to the target, with the occasional night fighter being seen. However, no combats were noted in the ORB and all the squadron's Lancasters returned safely. Five Lancasters were lost overall, two to a mid-air collision, one to icing and only two to enemy action, in this case the flak. One crew thought they were fired at by another Lancaster.

Back at Waterbeach, Mr. JJ Bevan of Air Ministry, W8, inspected the bomb stores and discussed plans to increase the explosive storage capacity to 2,000 tons, with the Station Commander and Station Armament officer.

'JC', a small stray dog that lived on the station, flew on a number of operations with the Gallicano crew.

The oft-visited city of Duisburg awaited 3 Group on 8th December, 163 Lancasters carrying out a GH raid on the railway yards. Their number included eighteen of the squadron's crews, all of whom attacked the primary target on this occasion. GH Leader F/O Irvine Bittner in NF966, JI-L released his thirteen 1,000lb bombs and a red and green flare from 21,000 feet. The bomb load now featured American munitions in the form of ANM59 bombs, these semi armour-piercing bombs being used increasingly as the capacity of Bomber Command to deliver explosives to the enemy outstripped the ability of the British munitions industry to keep up with demand. Over ten tenths cloud, the target marking was good and the GH-led aircraft kept together well despite the adverse weather making

formation keeping difficult. F/O Joe Gallicano in NG118, A2-E found his navigational aids were unserviceable through icing but still managed to bomb on a timed run from a Gee fix by the navigator, W/O Peter Lowen. There were no losses from the force on this daylight raid to the Ruhr, though F/O Alexander Munro had to land NG350, JI-C at the emergency airfield at Woodbridge as the aircraft's flaps were unserviceable.
W/O Lowen later recounted to the author how he and his crew adopted a stray terrier which was lurking around Waterbeach, naming the dog 'JC', after a popular, though possibly blasphemous, exclamation uttered whenever anything went wrong. There were no concerns about JC stealing the crew's rations as the dog was apparently adept at hanging around the station kitchens, scrounging scraps and usually eating better than they did. Peter did point out that, although JC accompanied the crew on ops, these were limited to low level flights as they could not find a way of successfully fitting an oxygen mask to the dog. On higher altitude flights,

'Air Force Doggie' was a more conventional lucky mascot for W/O Peter Lowen and the Gallicano crew when their canine crewmate 'JC' was unable to fly due to no one having yet designed an oxygen mask for dogs (Peter Lowen).

Peter explained, JC's stand in was a small knitted dog, his personal mascot. Christened 'Air Force Doggie' by his young daughter, Felicity, it is still in Peter's possession. It appears that a small dog was resident at RAF Waterbeach from 1942 or 1943, having appeared in a photograph with ground crew working on aircraft of 1651 Conversion Unit. It is not known how many ops and other flights JC undertook as, contrary to King's Regulations, JC did not fill in a log book. Peter revealed that JC was not the only illicit passenger carried by the squadron's crews on the less risky ops; WAAFs were also treated to the occasional flight.

After a couple of days off, the squadron was called to arms on 11th December with a combined attack on Osterfeld, near Oberhausen by 98 Lancasters on the railway yards and 52 on a benzol plant. Seventeen aircraft were from Waterbeach but it is not stated which of the two targets was attacked by 514 Squadron's aircraft. Few marker flares were seen, but the aircraft were in good formation while bombing. The ORB notes that two aircraft were seen to blow up; however the official records note only that the only loss was of the squadron's NG350, JI-C flown by F/O Ellis Hill. The aircraft was hit by flak and fell into the built-up area of Sterkrade. There were no survivors from the crew, who were on their eleventh op. The two air gunners, Sgt John Balman (mid upper) and Sgt Alan Bowen (rear), were nineteen years old.

On 12th December the Ruhrstahl steel plant at Witten which, notwithstanding its location between Bochum and Dortmund, had not previously been subject to a major bombing raid. The 140 Lancasters involved included fifteen from Waterbeach, the perennially unfortunate F/O Irvine Bittner having returned early when the port outer and starboard inner engines of NF968, JI-L let the side down. Bombing was reported as slightly scattered at first but improving towards the end of the attack when the flares and bombing became very concentrated. Results unobserved due to cloud; however a local report stated that the steelworks had not been hit and the bombing was scattered all over the town. 126 houses and five industrial premises were hit, and some 400 people were killed or missing on the ground. Things did not go well in the air either; eight Lancasters were posted missing and one crash-landed successfully at Grimbergen airfield in Belgium after flak and fighters were more effective than of late. Four of the Lancasters, including the one that landed in Belgium, were from 195 Sqn at Wratting Common. All the Waterbeach aircraft returned safely.

F/O Bill Coyle (left) and crew, who had a narrow escape when hit by flak on the penultimate operation of their tour (WMHM).

On 15th December it was the turn of Siegen's railways yards to test the accuracy of GH, though the attack was scratched because the escorting fighters were unable to take to the air. It was rescheduled for the 16th when 108 Lancasters were tasked. 514 Squadron despatched twenty one Lancasters, but five of the crews returned early. The weather, on the outbound leg at least, was diabolical with severe icing, which prevented F/O Glen Hanson RCAF in NG142, A2-C and F/O Les Sutton in PB482, JI-P from carrying out their mission. F/O John Crooks was on his first op for the squadron in PB419, JI-N. He had to give up after climbing as high as possible and, even at 21,000 feet, not being able to make any contact with the rest of the bomber stream. F/O Stan Wright in ME355, JI-B suffered technical problems, losing his starboard outer engine and Constant Speed Unit. Finally, F/O Don Parks in ME841, JI-J had to return early to the emergency airfield at Woodbridge with failures to the aircraft's port outer engine and hydraulic system. The remaining aircraft struggled on through the foul weather, and the formation was accordingly ragged until the concentration improved shortly before the target was reached. The crews considered that the attack was good but most of the bombs landed in the town itself and neighbouring Weidenau, rather than the railway yards. A few bombs did actually hit their intended target, however. A number of Me109s were seen, though the squadron noted no combats and, whilst there was slight heavy flak from Bonn and the vicinity of the front line, it was absent over the target. However, F/L Ron Pickler's PA186, A2-G sustained flak damage to the bomb doors, though this did not stop him bombing. His colleague from 'C' Flight, F/O Bill Coyle in NG298, A2-K was also hit, with flak causing damage to the aircraft's mid upper turret and smashing an elevator. The crew were on the penultimate trip of their tour. Only one aircraft failed to return, another Lancaster of the hard-hit 115 Sqn from Witchford falling to an enemy fighter with the loss of four of the crew.

F/O Hugh 'Richie' Richford concentrates on flying NG118, A2-E to Siegen on his penultimate operation, 16th December 1944 (Harry Dison).

A postscript to this raid is given by F/S Frank Bell, wireless operator in LM627, A2-H: 'The weather was atrocious. It seemed this target should be dealt with immediately but they were only sending GH trained crews. It looked odds-on we wouldn't be able to land at our base on our return. We bombed OK but apparently some aircraft had not dropped their bombs and had to unload them into the North Sea on the way back. On the same day band leader Glenn Miller set off to Paris in a light aircraft and disappeared. They shouldn't have set off. Rumour had it that his aircraft was hit accidentally by one of the bombs jettisoned by the Lancasters over the sea. We couldn't understand why some Lancasters hadn't dropped their bombs over the target.'

Hugh 'Richie' Richford had by now been promoted to Flying Officer. He recalled the Siegen op: 'We climbed into a warm front. We were in cloud at the rendezvous height for our formation. Then up to the alternative height and, still in cloud, it was time to set our course out of touch with the others. We carried on climbing becoming well frosted on the outside. Then all four engines began to surge disconcertingly with the less common carburettor icing, quickly identified by the engineer and rectified with 'hot air'.

We were well over the continent by the time we broke horizontally out of the wall of cloud, soon followed by a gaggle of Lancasters. There was no chance of finding our own leader but, by that time in the GH story, such a contingency had been catered for by painting yellow stripes on the tail fins of all leader aircraft. A leader could then be sorted out and followed to the bomb release point. A good idea but, unfortunately, all aircraft with yellow markings were not always flown by GH qualified crews. This applied to us that day flying our own pet Lanc, A2 Easy. Worse still, we were ahead of all the others and almost immediately the gunners were reporting other aircraft seeking to formate on us. For an awful minute or two we were leading some hundred aircraft to a target, obscured by a cloud layer below, with no means of aiming the bombs. In those days of R/T silence there was no easy way of warning others not to follow us. All I could do was to waggle the wings, tell the wireless op to fire a red Very, and turn steeply to port hoping that no one would follow. Looking round I saw a few Lancs turn to follow us but I also saw, thankfully, that some stalwart was pressing on in the lead.

We came out of a 360° turn at the rear end of the stream and I sought some leader to formate on with great urgency, knowing we must be close to the target. The seconds ticked by. Suddenly there was a Lanc a bit above us to starboard with its bomb doors open. There followed moments of confusion. I yelled to the bomb aimer that this was the leader to bomb on, opened the bomb doors and pulled up to formate on him. The bomb aimer and others who could see outside knew better than I but I had given them no time to speak. Another moment and I too knew what was wrong - the other aircraft closed its bomb doors. We had overflown the target without bombing.

There was nothing else for it; once more it was round again. I turned quickly to port on to the reciprocal course. There had been some flak on the way in, two squadron aircraft being damaged, but fortunately there now appeared to be none over the target. There were some groans of disapproval over the intercom; after all it was our 29th op and the poor gunners could see the rest of the stream rapidly disappearing in the distance. After what seemed an age, but no doubt far too soon for accuracy, I turned in and we hurriedly bombed on the green sky markers that the GH leaders always dropped.

The rest of the Lancs were but dots miles ahead and there was no sign of the escort, though they may well have been keeping an eye on us. Boost and revs were quickly pushed up to plus seven, twenty-six fifty, and we went roaring after the others. It was not long before a lone Lanc came into view, a bit below and to starboard. It had one engine feathered. I lost sight of it as it fell behind. We had not reached the tail end of the main stream but I felt we could slow down a bit and reduced power. As I did so, the urgent voice of the rear gunner was warning that the lone Lanc behind had been attacked by fighters and was on fire. Suddenly out to port were two Lightnings and two Mel09s locked in tight turns just above the cloud tops. I looked back into the cockpit to push up the power again and seconds later looked back for the fighters. Just as suddenly they had disappeared.

We soon caught up with the others and were back in the frontal cloud again, heading for home with kind thoughts for our US escort. Records show that the Lanc shot down came from 115 Squadron, up the road at Witchford. Sadly only three of the crew survived.'

Another break in ops was due partly to very poor weather over the battle area as the Germans launched their counter-offensive in the Ardennes, in an ultimately-doomed attempt to break through to Antwerp. During the break, on 19th December the Station ORB welcomed His Excellency the Turkish Ambassador, who visited the station. He was taken round the bomb dump, hangars and Flying Control by the Base Commander and Station Commander, and 'given an unfair picture of activities at a Bomber Station.' No further comment was made as to why or how this was so.

The squadron was spared further ops until 21st December when 113 Lancasters, including fourteen from Waterbeach, attacked the railway yards at Trier, considered vital to the Germans in supplying their attacking force.
It was a wasted trip for F/L Kenneth Condict in LM724, JI-H as he was unable to release his bombs when he reached the target. However his colleagues all pressed home their own attacks whilst he looked on. The cloud was still 10/10ths, albeit to no higher than six to nine thousand feet, and the flak, moderate heavy at first dwindled to nil for an unstated reason, though the gunners had more reason to maintain their interest in proceedings than the frustrated F/L Condict. The cessation of flak did not happen before they struck one of the squadron's aircraft, though the ORB does no more than mention the fact in passing. No aircraft were lost from

Press photograph on the occasion of the final operation for F/O Richie Richford and crew (to Trier on 21st December 1944). The two women were Mlle H Edouard and Mlle H Carion, members of the French Resistance who had assisted shot-down airmen. Crew L to R: Sgt Denis Ratcliffe (MU gunner); Sgt Harry Dison, flight engineer; F/S Geoff Norris, wireless operator; F/O Bill Ledingham, navigator; P/O Ernie Emmett, bomb aimer; Sgt Wally Morrison, rear gunner; F/O Richie Richford, pilot (Harry Dison).

the attacking force. F/L Ron Pickler in PA186, A2-G was joined by the BBC's Richard Dimbleby and recorded a radio broadcast to add to the general cheer as the final Christmas of the war drew close. The crews were unable to see the results of the raid due to the poor visibility, though a large column of smoke suggested that something worthwhile had been hit. A subsequent report indicated that the raid had caused heavy casualties, and under the circumstances it can be speculated that this would include German troops making their way to join the Battle of the Bulge.

On the ground, Mlle H Edouard and Mlle H Carion, members of the FFI and guests of the Air Ministry, were escorted by the Station Commander when they paid a special visit to the station in order to talk to members of aircrew and see a take-off. A party for the children of all ranks was held in the Airwomen's Mess. It proved, as usual, a great success, culminating in the arrival of Father Christmas in the person of No. 1306441, Mackenzie, J. There were many happy faces when the toys, made by personnel of the station workshops, were distributed.

Poor weather then returned to ground the squadron for 48 hours, but they went back to Trier on 23rd December contributing fourteen of the 153 Lancasters deployed. This time, the weather over the target was clear and marking was concentrated. The Master Bomber was able to give precise directions, the target was easily identified with the force leaving the town one mass of brown smoke rising to eight thousand feet. Numerous explosions were seen and, whilst there was moderate heavy flak, no fighters were seen. The ORB went so far as to describe the attack as an unqualified success, and this appears to have been the case, though on this occasion a 90 Sqn Lancaster was lost to flak with her entire crew. The only local report found simply describes the attack as the town's worst raid of the war.

The continuing inclement weather ensured that the squadron was kept on the ground over Christmas. The Station ORB described the festivities: *On Christmas Eve an impromptu concert and smoking party in the station Institute was well attended by an audience already full of the Christmas Spirit in spite of the weather and frequent calls to duty.*

Christmas Day proved a busy one for officers. A football match against NCOs in the morning was followed by waiting on airmen and airwomen in their respective Messes. Catering arrangements and organisation were exceptionally good and everybody sat down to a first class Christmas Dinner. At night the Officers' Mess staff were served with their dinner, the officer waiters washing up afterwards with every appearance of enjoyment. A happy day finished with a crowded but merry All-Ranks Dance in the Airmens' Mess and Station Institute.

On Boxing Day the Officers' Mess held their Christmas Dinner as a 'Guest Night'. In replying to toasts both the Station and Squadron Commanders testified to the good relationship and cooperative spirit which exists on the station.'

No ops were undertaken until 27th December, the marshalling yards at Rheyd being the target for 211 aircraft including six from Waterbeach. Again the weather was clear and the target well-marked. According to the squadron ORB, *'the yards were left a mass of billowing smoke and attack was thought highly successful'*. Two aircraft were lost, a 75(NZ) Sqn Lancaster which was struck by a bomb from another aircraft, with the loss of six crew, and a Mosquito of 106 Sqn which crashed in Holland, its pilot being killed. There being no sign of an official raid report, history will doubtless cite the 514 Squadron ORB as the authoritative account of this raid.

28th December saw 167 Lancasters carrying out another in the continuing series of GH raids on marshalling yards, these being at Köln Gremberg. Fourteen aircraft from the squadron were involved. Crews reported aircraft over the target as being so close together as to present a risk of collision. The attack was accurate and large plumes of smoke were seen to rise through the undercast. With negligible flak and no fighters, all aircraft returned safely to their respective bases, though landing at Waterbeach was made more difficult by fog.

Tragedy struck Waterbeach on 29th December as the squadron prepared its aircraft for an operation, presumably to 3 Group's target at the Lützel marshalling yards in Koblenz. The Station ORB described the catastrophe: *'At 1015hrs a violent explosion occurred on Dispersal No. 27 when Lancaster Aircraft PD325 blew up during bombing-up preparations. The Station Fire Tenders and Ambulance were quickly on the scene of the accident. Little remained of the aircraft and the force of the explosion had rendered seven other aircraft unserviceable. Three bodies were recovered and identified as LAC Derrick Bichard, Radar Mechanic B; AC2 Donald*

Brewer, Armament Assistant and LAC Geoffrey Hayden, Radar Mechanic B. After a Roll Call of all sections on the station had been taken, the following members of the ground staff were classified as Missing Believed Killed:- LAC Laurence Smales, Flight Mechanic A; LAC Samuel Bolton, Flight Mechanic A; LAC Ronald Davies, Flight Mechanic A; Cpl John Westgarth, Armourer; AC1 Harry Leach, Electrician II; LAC Frederick Watson, Flight Mechanic E. Injured:- LAC P Thompson, Flight Mechanic A, Cpl NR Garnham, Flight Mechanic E, LAC R Roberts, Flight Mechanic E, LAC LA Southway, Flight Mechanic E. Members of No. 5133 Bomb Disposal Squadron arrived shortly after the accident, and proceeded to remove unexploded bombs from the affected aircraft. The fires which started after the explosion were quickly extinguished by the Station Fire Section under the direction of the Station Commander and the Station Fire Officer. The National Fire Service turned out but were not required. Blast damaged windows and doors in hangars, workshops, huts and Messes. Severe damage was done to a concrete hut adjoining the dispersal point where the accident occurred. Windows were also broken in the villages of Waterbeach and Landbeach, and the explosion was heard as far away as Mildenhall. The accident is attributed to a 250lb bomb falling and detonating when being loaded onto the aircraft, though there is but little to substantiate this.'

'Mel' Melluish, a Corporal Armourer, suspected that the likely cause was a 250 pound bomb. 'These were old bombs that would have been declared unfit for use in peace time conditions, but someone in authority had the bright idea that they may as well drop them on the enemy. It seems that with age they could exude some of their explosive content which crystallised on the casing.

Regulations stated that these crystals should be removed with hot soapy water and a wooden scraper, but under pressure of work there wasn't time to do the necessary. There were also problems with the Whitlock Carriers holding pairs of the 250 lb bombs, which may have been a causative factor.

On the previous day, Thursday 28th Dec 1944, the Squadron was engaged on daylight raids and the armament staff had been warned to go for early tea as a maximum effort was required for the next day, for a deadline of 9.30am. I was suffering from a severe case of dermatitis and consequently on light duty, which meant no handling of bombs or loading. I was doing a permanent duty crew and doing the job of NCO i/c the servicing crew. The armourers were being pushed to the limit, loading two loads per day plus the occasional load change plus the normal servicing and were working up to 20 hours per day.

My best mate, Cpl John Westgarth, was another ex-regular airman who on this day had asked me if I would swap jobs with him, as he had become engaged to a WAAF and they wished to go out to celebrate. I had some doubts and a funny feeling about it, but after all he was my pal and it seemed only fair to do him a favour. So he was free to seal his engagement that night and I carried on and did his bomb loading.

We finished around 0800 hrs and after a late breakfast tried to get some sleep before being called out to reload the planes again after their short operation. Upon hearing the horrendous explosion we all rushed round on our bikes to the armament office to discover the cause.'

Mel's friend who had swapped shifts with him was among the dead, his engagement not lasting a full day. Lancaster PD325, A2-L was destroyed along with NG141, A2-J.

The final operation of 1944 took place in the early afternoon of 31st December, the target this time being the marshalling yards at Vohwinkel, near Solingen. Winds had been troublesome, making navigation difficult. The force of 155 Lancasters, including ten from Waterbeach, had become split into two streams approximately half a mile apart laterally. As a result there were two areas of bombing, with the northern part of the town receiving some of the bombs intended for the railway yard which was at least hit by the other stream. Flak over the target was negligible, though intense over Duisburg on the route in and no fighters were seen. Two Lancasters from 218 Sqn crashed near Solingen, the cause not being stated.

After the squadron's only full calendar year, the RAF Station Waterbeach Summary of Events notes: *'The WAAF Camp was a scene of animation and vivid colour on the occasion of the New Year's Eve Fancy Dress Dance. Many picturesque and original costumes were seen in the Grand Parade – the gentlemen in some cases vying quite successfully with the ladies – and the Judges' task was no easy one. A happy evening ended with the traditional Greeting of the New Year.'* Amidst the carnage of war, life went on. F/O Rob Simons was navigator in the crew of F/O Fred Hendy. In conversation with the author Rob's widow, Audrey, recalled: 'There were occasional very luxurious mess parties where for a few hours we could forget realities; the evening I remember most was when the Skipper came up to us while we were dancing and said "Sorry, but we've got to break it up and get some sleep. We didn't do a very good job today and we've got to return early tomorrow." I think the target must have been Vohwinkel.'

New Year's Eve at Waterbeach and a good time was had by all, with the exception of the crew of F/O Fred Hendy, who were sent to bed early as they had to bomb Vohwinkel in the morning (WMHM).

The Station Commander's Summary for December noted:
Operations during the month have been severely curtailed by bad weather. Towards the end of the month, in particular, icy conditions and persistent ground fog limited the effort. No. 514 Squadron stood down one flight for GH and H2S Mk.III training from the 19th December. This became necessary in order to train more GH leaders, a sudden reduction in the length of the Operational tour from 35 to 30 sorties, together with the heavy operational demand for GH leaders during the past six weeks

having resulted in some twenty crews having completed their tours during the month. Opportunity is also being taken to train Air Bombers in H2S Mk.III operation in view of the re-equipment of the Squadron with this set so that they may undertake marking duties using it in conjunction with GH.
Admin: The month has been notable for Christmas and for bad weather. Most personnel seem to have been satisfied with the former, while the latter has given many some purposeful exercise in sanding icy runways and perimeter tracks and in de-icing aircraft. Health has been fairly good except for the normal colds. Accommodation for Officers and NCOs has become unduly congested because of the large number of tour-expired aircrew, many of whom do not wish to go on indefinite leave, pending a much delayed posting.

1945 started precisely as 1944 had left off, with the squadron participating in a 3 Group GH return to Vohwinkel. On the evening of New Year's Day nine Lancasters left Waterbeach, part of 146 returning to the railway yards. With clear weather, this time marking was concentrated and the bombing was much more accurate. As it was a night raid, there were searchlights but these, despite being numerous, did not cause much trouble. Two Me109s were seen but no combats reported. F/S Frank Bell, wireless operator in PB482, A2-K noted: 'Night flying is a totally different experience. You fly in complete darkness knowing there are four to seven hundred aircraft in the stream on the same heading, going to the same target. Turning on to the runway there were blue lights on both sides of the perimeter track for taxiing and various red, yellow and green lights along the sides of the runway in use, denoting how much of the runway was left for you to get airborne. All high buildings such as towers and hangers had red lights to warn low flying aircraft. Once the last aircraft is airborne, all lights are switched off except 'Pundit', a continuously-flashing red identification beacon. Waterbeach was WJ (.-- .---). The lights would be switched back on as soon as the first homebound aircraft crossed the Suffolk coast. Tonight, on our way to Vohwinkel I was in a world of my own, listening for broadcasts. I would also concentrate on the 'Fishpond' radar watching for the fast-moving blips that would denote fighter aircraft in the stream. It was up to the gunners to make sure they weren't Mosquitoes which might be mistaken for German night fighters. When I looked out of my window I wondered how the enemy pilots could avoid seeing us, with two huge Merlin engines roaring away on each wing, their exhaust shields glowing red or white hot. On a clear night you could see the flashes of guns and, seconds later, the explosion, a burst of flame and crump, crump, crump, then a splattering of shrapnel against the aircraft. Most times it was hell on earth both down there and up here too. When I allowed myself to think like that I felt sorry for those on the ground, especially the children. But the majority of the civilian population supported the Nazi regime; they knew as well as anyone the indescribable crimes and atrocities committed in their name, especially those perpetrated in the concentration camps. The final argument was what it would be like if the Germans won; we would be faced with slavery and extermination. Approaching Vohwinkel the flak was intense and searchlights were numerous and very active. The ordinary search lights had a yellowish beam but there were two in this bunch that had a bluish light. These were

Lucky escape. F/S 'Doc' Strathdee RCAF and Sgt Pip Joyce, air gunners in the crew of F/O Donald Crome. The crew was twice hit by flak including on the final trip of their tour (Joyce family).

radar-controlled and once they latched on to an aircraft were almost impossible to shake off. As soon as an aircraft was caught the others swung on to it, the unfortunate aircraft in the apex of the lights being a target for the flak. Nine times out of ten it was doomed, exploding in the air or spinning down in flames.
The raid itself was uneventful over the target but returning over southern Holland we were fired on by American anti-aircraft guns. We took a risk of attracting any German night fighters by firing off the colours of the day but they didn't stop. Our language was blue; we cursed them, calling them all the names under the sun. At the debrief we played merry hell.'
Officially, only one aircraft is noted as lost on this raid; however 'Bomber Command Losses 1945' by WR Chorley lists one Lancaster, from 218 Sqn, damaged by flak over the target and then shot down by American AA fire over Namur, Belgium whilst two more, one each from 75(NZ) and 115 Sqns, were lost. The 115 Sqn aircraft was near Namur on its return to Witchford when it was also caught in the American AA barrage. The 75(NZ) Sqn crew came down near Maastricht, cause unstated. The only survivor was F/O G Ingram from the 218 Sqn aircraft. It was noted that a further Lancaster, from XV Sqn, made a forced landing near Juvincourt after also being hit by American 'friendly fire'.
On 2nd January another evening operation was arranged, this being a 519-strong area attack on Nuremberg. 514 Squadron contributed ten aircraft in clear weather, though on this occasion there was no moon. Compared with the terrible night nine months earlier, the night fighter force was a mere shadow of its former self and only a few fighters were seen. This did not prevent them engaging with the bomber force and F/O Christopher Nicholl RCAF in PD389, A2-J, submitted a combat report after his rear gunner was compelled to open fire on an encroaching twin-engined aircraft and he successfully evaded the attacker with a corkscrew manoeuvre. The Luftwaffe was using fighter flares, but there was no further attack. Over the target itself there were no searchlights and the heavy flak was slight and inaccurate. All told, nine aircraft were lost to a variety of causes, including 419 Sqn's famous Canadian-built Lancaster 'Ruhr Express', which caught fire after colliding with an excavator after running off the runway on landing at Middleton St George. The Master Bomber was clear and concise, PFF produced good marking in clear visibility, and the city

centre was destroyed. The Rathaus, castle and some 2,000 preserved medieval buildings succumbed to the attack, along with 4,640 dwellings, mostly flats, and industrial premises including those of MAN and Siemens.

The busy start to the year continued on 3rd January, at least for four crews who drew the short straw in joining 95 other aircraft in a GH attack on benzol plants in Dortmund and Castop-Rauxel. 514's crews were briefed to bomb the Hansa plant in Huckarde, Dortmund. Formation over the target, in the middle of the afternoon, was described as good though slightly elongated and the bombing was concentrated. Results were not observed, due to the usual complete cloud cover, but the record considers the attack to be accurate. The only casualty was a 622 Sqn Lancaster, which exploded over the Hansa plant with the loss of all onboard. As was often the case on GH raids, it is not clear whether this was due to flak or to being hit by bombs from another aircraft in the closely-packed formation.

5th January saw the squadron send fourteen aircraft as part of a 160-strong GH attack on railway yards at Ludwigshaven. Thirteen of the squadron's

F/O Glen Hanson RCAF and crew suffered flak damage on two of their ops but survived the war otherwise unscathed (WMHM).

Lancasters attacked the primary target whilst F/O Murray Muggeridge RNZAF, DFM, flying PD482, A2-K on his second trip with the squadron, was unable to release his bombs after his bomb doors were hit by flak, so unloaded them on a last resort target at Schifferstadt. His was not the only Lancaster that brought battle damage back to the maintenance crews at Waterbeach; eleven of the fourteen were hit by the moderate to intense predicted flak which was unnervingly accurate. The flak, helped by the clear weather over the target, had the effect of splitting up the formation and affecting bombing accuracy, which was scattered at first. Whilst it did later improve, and the marshalling yard was definitely hit, the ORB notes that the attack could not be classified as a first class effort.

The damage sustained by the squadron's aircraft was as varied as ever. F/O Donald Crome's PB426, JI-D suffered damage to the bomb aimer's Perspex and pilot's windshield. The crew was on the last trip of their tour. F/O Frederick Hendy in PA186, A2-G had to contend with damage to the fuselage; hydraulic leads were hit in F/O Alexander Munro's LM717, JI-C; the port fin of LM275, JI-F flown by F/O Leonard Baines RNZAF, was damaged; F/O George Orr in LM728, A2-B had to contend with the pilot's half panel and starboard wing being hit; F/O Alfred Tasker endured NG142, A2-C being bracketed by flak with damage to nose and tail, the middle of the aircraft fortunately being unaffected; F/O Joe Gallicano in PD334, A2-D reported damage to his mid upper turret; it was the rear turret and port wing damage that focused the mind of F/O Glen Hanson in LM285, A2-F; F/O John Tolley, returning to ops following his crash-landing after being hit by flak over Homberg found the welcome equally hostile on this occasion as the bomb aimer's panel on LM685, JI-K was hit. The recording officer was probably losing the will to live by the time he got round to noting that F/O Christopher Nicholl's PB902, JI-A was 'hit by flak'. The only 514 Squadron aircraft not to return to Waterbeach was NF968, JI-B which F/O Stan Wright landed at Woodbridge despite no noted flak damage. Two Lancasters were lost, one each from XV and 90 Squadrons. The latter was shot down by flak and no cause is given for the loss of the former though it appears to have crashed close to the target area and flak is a likely culprit on this occasion.

The busy week continued on 6th January with another visit to Neuss. The squadron managed to put seven Lancasters in the air amongst the 147 detailed to attack the railway yards. The target was well marked though ground identification was impossible through the cloud cover. Once more flak played a part, slight to moderate this time, though accurate for height. Few results were seen apart from an explosion at 1850hrs, but crews reported a good concentration of bombing. There were no fighters seen and the Waterbeach contingent returned undamaged. One aircraft from another squadron reportedly crashed.

There was a change of scene on the late evening of 7th January when the squadron visited Munich for the only time. 645 aircraft took part in the last major raid on the city, including ten from the squadron. F/O Les Sutton in PB426, JI-D returned early with intercom problems and F/S Campbell Fiset had to bring back his bombs when the DR compass in NG298, JI-E packed up. The remaining eight aircraft bombed the primary target, the concentration of markers being rated 'average'. Visual assessment was difficult through the clouds though the reflection of fires could be seen. The crews were met by slight to moderate flak and a few fighters were also trying to interfere with the smooth running of the raid, but to no avail as far as the squadron was concerned. However, fifteen aircraft were lost from the raid, four of these crashing in France. There was no local report available detailing the results of the raid but it is believed that the centre of the city and some industrial areas were severely damaged.

The squadron enjoyed a few days' break before returning to the fray on 11th January. 152 Lancasters carried out a GH attack on marshalling yards at Krefeld, eleven crews from the squadron taking part. Visibility was poor with complete cloud cover, but crews formed the impression that the attack was concentrated, though it was noted that some aircraft were seen to bomb from above 20,000 feet. With flak only slight and no fighters, all the attacking aircraft returned safely. Local reports noted only that this had been '*a large raid*'.

On 13th January it was the turn of Saarbrucken's marshalling yards to receive attention. The 158 Lancasters included thirteen from Waterbeach, though F/O Alfred Tasker in LM627, A2-H was unable to join the party, having returned with his wireless equipment unserviceable. The weather over the target was relatively clear and all crews could see the yards, which were left covered with smoke. Mention was made of the blue puffs, which were reported as an excellent means of marking. Once again there was little flak and no fighters impeding this daylight raid; the only aircraft lost was a 195 Sqn Lancaster. This developed an oil leak which resulted in an engine fire, the aircraft crashing in France. The crew got out though with some injuries. F/S Frank Bell in PA186, A2-G, commented: 'The weather was bad but they said it was possible to take off, though it would deteriorate later. After a smooth take off we were orbiting, waiting for our followers but were on our own. Then suddenly they showed themselves, popping up through the clouds and off we flew. The opposition was not as bad as we expected but there was still plenty of flak. We bombed the target and wheeled out quickly, setting course for home. One hour from home I received a message, using my code book to decipher it. We were to divert to RAF Exeter, adding another hour and a half to the trip. When we got there, many more Lancasters were already in the circuit. The airfield was a small Spitfire station which quickly became crowded with 25 Lancasters. After an overnight stay and breakfast we were taken out to our aircraft but had to wait until refueling was complete. There were crowds of people watching the take-off; they had never seen so many Lancasters. I wondered how the Germans felt seeing four or five hundred passing overhead.' Bell's crew was not alone as all the squadron's aircraft had in fact been diverted to Exeter on their return due to poor weather at Waterbeach. On 15th January, having made their way home from Devon, fourteen crews formed a large part of the 63-strong force tasked with bombing the Robert Muser benzol plant at Lagendreer, a suburb of Bochum. Thirteen of the squadron's aircraft attacked the primary target whilst F/O Glen Hanson in NN717, A2-E was forced to abort his sortie and divert to Manston with an oil leak in both starboard engines and all his navigational equipment unserviceable. The formation was described as good en-route and at bombing. However after leaving the target the stream turned off early and passed over the north Ruhr defences too far to the east.

Flak over the Ruhr, perhaps unsurprisingly, was slight to moderate, heavy and the ORB notes simply that five aircraft were hit, without going into further detail. No aircraft were lost from the bomber force, and there is no assessment available of the results of the raid.

A Halifax flies over the Wanne-Eickel benzol plant on a daylight raid. Photographed by the bomb aimer of a higher-flying aircraft, the Halifax crew were not in a particularly safe position!

The Wanne-Eickel benzol plant, between Bochum and Gelsenkirchen in the Ruhr, was the target on the night of 16th / 17th January, the GH raid comprising 138 Lancasters with the squadron putting up fourteen. Most of the aircraft arrived late over the target with the result that marking was spread out, though the bombing did appear concentrated through the thin low cloud cover. The heavy flak barrage was slight to moderate in intensity and the defences of Düsseldorf also added to the party atmosphere. A single Ju88 night fighter was seen in the target area by the squadron's crews, but no combats were reported.
The only aircraft lost was from 514 Squadron on this occasion, PB906 A2-B and the crew of F/O George Orr being lost without trace. The crew, who included F/O Merlin Matkin RCAF as 'second dickey', are commemorated on the Runnymede Memorial. An RAF report mentioned in 'Nachtjagd War Diaries' notes simply that '*an RAF bomber exploded*'.

F/O Merlin Matkin RCAF was one of several new pilots lost on their experiential 'second dickey' trip.

There is no record of night fighter claims of specific aircraft shot down though there were clearly night fighters active, as mentioned above. It is therefore considered likely that PB906 was lost to an unidentified night fighter at an unknown location. F/O Orr had previously been disciplined for failing to fly at a specified altitude, which had been due, he explained, to icing conditions.

The squadron was not deployed again until 22nd January, when the Thyssen steelworks at Hamborn, Duisburg were targeted by 302 aircraft including twelve of the squadron's crews. All twelve attacked their primary target in clear weather, conditions being described in the ORB as '*almost as bright as day*'. The TIs were reported as very concentrated and correctly placed, bombing was good and the target was left covered in smoke and fires, numerous heavy explosions being heard. The heavy flak was slight to moderate, decreasing as the attack progressed, though F/O John Ness RCAF in PB426, JI-D noted '*bomb sight not used as aircraft had to take evasive action from flak*'. No fighters were reported in the ORB. However, F/S Frank Bell in PA186, A2-G, recalled: 'Ten minutes after leaving the target we were attacked by an Me210 fighter. The first I knew of it was when the skipper threw us into a corkscrew and the guns started chattering. The G force that ensued was so great that I couldn't move. I just sat there and hung on. The skipper continued to twist and turn with the guns exchanging fire between aircraft. I became aware of the smell of cordite and my stomach didn't know where I was. We lost him; he probably went after easier prey but we couldn't relax, knowing he was roaming the skies looking for victims. Fifteen minutes later came another fright when a Lancaster whizzed across in front of us, missing us by a whisker. We were a shaken crew and there was little conversation after this. We were so relieved to see the Waterbeach circuit

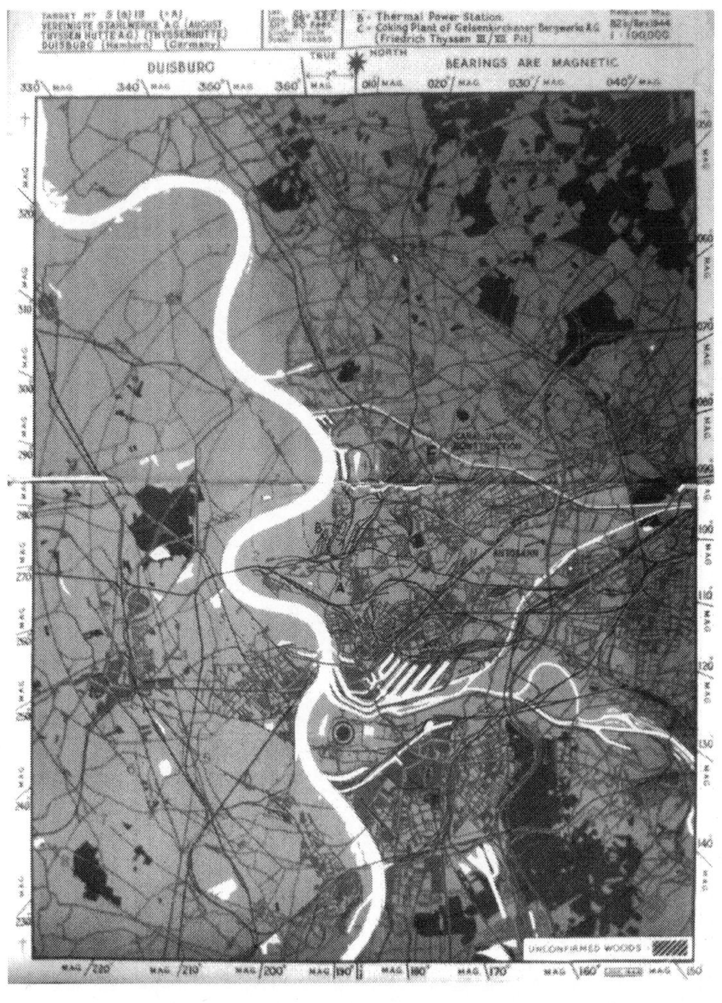

A bombing chart of Duisburg. The original has built up areas and targets highlighted in red and pink, designed to be clear to read under very dim light. The features in white are shown in a similar way to how they would appear on the H2S set. This chart also indicated the location of the Thyssenhutte steelworks at Hamborn (WMHM).

lights and the Pundit flashing the red WJ letters.' Losses amounted to two Lancasters, both from 153 Sqn at Scampton. No cause is recorded. According to 'Bomber Command War Diaries', and other sources, the target was officially intended to be the benzol plant in the Bruckhausen district, with the Thyssen works being hit by accident. However the 514 Squadron ORB clearly states the target to be '*Thyssen works at Hamborn*' so there was clear intent by the squadron to attack the plant. The steelworks were hit by 500 HE bombs, bringing the plant to a permanent standstill. Whether by accident or design, 514 Squadron had scored a significant hit on this important part of Germany's industrial war effort.

Fog and snow kept the squadron on the ground for the following week, until on the afternoon of 28th January another raid was carried out on the Köln-Gremberg marshalling yards. This attack by 153 Lancasters included fourteen from the squadron. The bombing, assisted by the weather clearing over the target, started as scattered but improved with the yards being straddled for their whole length. The force was met by accurate slight to moderate flak. The officer compiling the ORB noted that eight of the squadron's aircraft were damaged without giving more details. Four Lancasters failed to return, two from 218 Sqn being hit by flak whilst an XV Sqn aircraft was shot down outbound. A further, though unidentified, Lancaster crashed in France.

The month ended with twelve crews leaving Waterbeach to join a raid by 148 Lancasters on the Ürdingen marshalling yards at Krefeld. Ten of the squadron's aircraft bombed successfully but two were unable to release their munitions over the target so were unable to contribute to the damage. There was only slight heavy flak over the target and the trip was, apparently, uneventful. No aircraft were lost on this op. Brownish smoke was seen rising above the cloud. The ORB states '*crews reported the bomber stream and bombing to be very concentrated and the attack should prove a success*'. However a short report compiled in Krefeld afterwards stated that the bombs fell over a wide area, without giving further details.

The Station Commander's Report for January 1945 stated:

Operational effort during the month has continued to be curtailed by one flight being 'stood down below the line' for training in H2S Mk.III and GH. Snow and fog also seriously limited operations, only one attack being possible between 16th and 26th January inclusive.

Admin: The month was notable in that the snow plan No. 2 had to be put into operation for the first time in three years. Falls were comparatively light but sufficient to test the snow ploughs on two occasions. It was found that the main runways could be cleared of a fall of three to four inches and sanded in approximately two hours each using four ploughs and the Snogo. Heavier falls would take longer as the small plough would be of little use.

Moenchengladbach marshalling yards were the target on 1st February as 160 Lancasters paid a visit. Fourteen crews joined in from Waterbeach in the late afternoon attack, which appears to have been a less well-organised affair than most. The formation arrived late and the stream was somewhat elongated. The effects are unknown as results were unobserved through the complete cloud cover and there was no local report. Flak was slight and only one aircraft was lost from the attacking force. All the squadron's aircraft landed safely.
They were up and about the following day, thirteen crews taking part in Bomber Command's only large attack on Wiesbaden. The force comprised 507 aircraft, with erratic winds hampering navigation. As a result the bombing effort was spread over a wide area. One aircraft was forced down to 3,000 feet in an explosion and its crew was able to report that the built up area of the town was a mass of flames. A few fighters were seen and the flak was described in the ORB as '*slight*'. However that was no consolation to two crews who sustained damage nor to the crew of NN772, A2-C, flown by F/O William McLean RCAF, on their third operation. Having just bombed NN772 was hit by heavy flak and brought down. F/O McLean remained at the controls despite his boots and clothing being set alight by a piece of white hot shrapnel between his feet. He ordered his crew to bale out, and was last seen by the bomb aimer, Sgt SW Moore, to be enveloped in flames. Only Sgt Moore and the mid upper gunner, Sgt GHS Berridge, survived. Sgt Trevor Blackshaw, the wireless operator, was able to escape the aircraft but on the ground he suffered the extreme misfortune to be captured by an SS Corporal. SS-Rottenführer Heinrich Franke who summarily executed Sgt Blackshaw by shooting him in the head. Franke had also killed an American flier and justice caught up with him in 1948 when he was hanged for the murder of the two airmen.

The ORB also relates that a bomber was seen to explode over the target. This was probably a 428 Sqn Lancaster Mk.X, the crew of which were on their thirtieth op so might have been stood down had they survived the sortie. The sole survivor was the rear gunner. Three other aircraft were lost due to mid-air collisions whilst flak, incendiaries and night fighters accounted for the twelve aircraft lost. Nearly six hundred buildings were destroyed and the railway station was damaged, though several important industrial sites were untouched.

F/O William McLean RCAF sacrificed his own life, staying at the controls of his Lancaster despite his own clothing being on fire. Bomber Command considered his actions worthy of a VC but sadly Churchill did not agree.

When his actions to save his crew became known, F/O McLean was subsequently recommended for the Victoria Cross by the new squadron commander, Wing Commander Philip Morgan:

'*On the night of the 2nd/3rd February 1945, the above named officer was detailed as pilot and captain of a four engined heavy bomber to attack Wiesbaden.*

The target was a heavily defended one, and just after the bombs had been released there was a loud explosion in the aircraft. Flying Officer McLean was then heard to ask the Flight Engineer if the starboard inner engine had been hit. He got no reply but almost immediately he himself confirmed that it was the starboard inner engine and that it was now out of action. At this moment the Mid- Upper Gunner saw that the starboard inner engine was on fire.

The air bomber, who was down in the bomb aimer's position when the explosion occurred, then came up to see if he could give any assistance.

At this moment, a large piece of white-hot metal came into the aircraft and lodged between the pilot's feet just aft of the rudder bar. The Air Bomber attempted to remove this with the aid of a flying jacket, but was unable to do so. Seeing this, Flying Officer McLean ordered the crew to carry out the emergency procedure for abandoning the aircraft. Flying Officer McLean continued to control the aircraft in spite of the white hot metal, which by now was quickly setting fire to everything in its vicinity, including Flying Officer McLean's boots and clothing.

Just prior to leaving his turret, the Mid-Upper Gunner saw that the whole of the front part of the aircraft was on fire but the aircraft was still being kept steady which enabled him to reach the emergency exit and abandon the aircraft.

The Air Bomber, on his way to the emergency exit, noticed the Flight Engineer lying on the floor, apparently wounded or killed, so he called for a parachute pack, which he fastened to the Flight Engineer's harness. The pilot then told them to get out quickly. The Air Bomber then noticed that Flying Officer McLean was enveloped from head to foot in flames and that the whole cockpit was on fire. He then received a blow to the stomach and fell out of the aircraft.

The Air Bomber and the Mid-Upper Gunner were the only two survivors of the crew but they undoubtedly owe their lives to the outstanding bravery of the captain, Flying Officer McLean, who remained at the controls in order to steady the aircraft sufficiently to let his crew abandon it, completely disregarding his own safety and enduring what must have been extreme agony. Had he chosen, Flying Officer McLean was in a position to save himself but, crippled as the aircraft was, it is unlikely that any other members of the crew would have survived.
By his action, Flying Officer McLean set the highest example for outstanding bravery and courage, sacrificing his own life in attempting to save the lives of his crew and comrades.
It is very strongly recommended that this outstanding example of heroism be recognised by the posthumous award of the Victoria Cross to Flying Officer W.E. McLean.'
The recommendation was further endorsed by Bomber Command. The final decision was made by the RAF Awards Committee:
'Bomber Command recommend the award of VC to F.O. W.E. McLean (missing believed killed) for remaining at the controls of a burning aircraft while other members of the crew escaped.
Recommendation has been reviewed by the RAF Awards Comm. In the light of the rule that the VC should be generally awarded for getting into danger (in furtherance of operations), rather than getting out of a desperate situation latent in all Air operations. F.O. McLean comes within the latter category.
The RAF Awards Committee concluded with reluctance that this officer's gallant action does not quite reach the standard required for V.C.
If death is assumed 6months after the date he became missing a Mention in Dispatches is the only alternative award'.
The decision was countersigned by Sir Winston Churchill. 514 Squadron's Victoria Cross was not to be, but that in no way detracts from the valour shown by F/O William McLean.

Sgt Trevor Blackshaw survived the loss of his aircraft, only to be murdered by an SS Corporal on the ground. (Blackshaw family).

The action continued on 3rd February when eleven aircraft were despatched to the Dortmund-Huckarde coking plant. LM627, A2-H flown by F/O John Chadwell returned early when the starboard outer engine overheated. The weather over the target was clear with slight haze and target marking was reported as good, the bombing also being concentrated. A few fires were seen and some explosions. The heavy flak was slight to moderate in intensity from Dortmund and the Ruhr, with 'terrific' searchlight activity around the Ruhr. Although many fighter flares were seen around the target area, only one Ju88 and a few single-engined fighters were seen. S/L Ernest Cozens RCAF, 'C' Flight Commander in PA186, A2-G had his starboard wing flap damaged by the flak whilst F/L John Ness in LM728, JI-F returned from an otherwise successful op with flak damage to the aircraft's fuselage.

The raid is described in Bomber Command records as an attack on the Hansa benzol plant. 514 Squadron records show it as a coking plant. A local report (unverified) suggests that the target was, in fact, the Grosskokerei der Zeche Hansa. The same report notes that widespread damage was caused to the coking plant, coal mine and surrounding area. Of the 149 Lancasters taking part, four failed to return including LM685, A2-B whose crew, piloted by F/O Warren Fisher RCAF, were on their sixth op. According to 'Nachtjagd War Diaries', '*Two Lancasters, HK688*[37] *and LM685, were lost during the run up to the target, probably to the Flak, in combination with the searchlights*' though the same source notes that LM685 was possibly shot down by Maj. Heinz-Wolfgang Schnaufer of Stab NJG4. There were no survivors from the crew, who are buried in Reichswald Forest War Cemetery. The flight engineer, F/S William Warr, is shown in RAF records as a pilot. At this stage of the war, with aircrew training in full swing and losses being, thankfully, reduced, there was now a surplus of pilots, many of whom were for the time being acting as flight engineers.

The squadron now enjoyed a few days' respite from operations. On 7th February, the squadron's popular commander, Wing Commander Mike Wyatt DFC relinquished his post, being posted to the Air Ministry. He survived the war. Command of 514 Squadron passed to Wing Commander Philip Morgan, who remained in post for the rest of the unit's existence. Wing Commander Mike Wyatt later recalled:

'As a Wing Commander I joined 514 Squadron as Commanding Officer at the age of 33 years on 24th May 1944 having entered the RAF in 1934. The Squadron was a good one and easy to command as I had the support of three excellent Flight Commanders. However, shortly after my arrival one of these Flight Commanders completed his tour of operations and he transferred to a second tour of operations with No 7 Pathfinder Squadron. He was replaced by an equally good Squadron Leader who had been a flying instructor just prior to his posting to 514.

During my time with the Squadron I made recommendations for a number of decorations for many brave acts by crews in the air. These were mainly DFCs with a few DSOs. As an example, one aircraft had most of the tail

[37] AP-W of 186 Squadron.

plane shot away, but the pilot managed to fly the aircraft home without further incident. Unfortunately, on a later flight this pilot was killed. He was awarded a DSO.

I left the Squadron on 7th February 1945 to take up a posting to the Air Ministry in the new Directorate of Navigation as the Assistant Director.'

At 0300hrs on 9th February the squadron despatched eleven crews to the Hohenbudberg marshalling yards, Krefeld, in a further attempt to stop the German railways from running on time. Ten of them attacked the target whilst F/O H MacLean RCAF in PB902, JI-A returned early with his starboard engine feathered and the aircraft unable to climb above 12,000 feet. Through broken cloud the TIs were clearly visible and bombing was well concentrated, though subsequent photographic reconnaissance was unable to spot any new damage. There was only slight flak and no fighters were seen by the squadron. 151 Lancasters took part in the dawn raid, for the loss of two aircraft. One of these was a XV Sqn Lancaster carrying a crew of nine, having a second pilot and a mid under gunner.

The next operation for the squadron was destined to be the most controversial of the war for Bomber Command as a whole and set the scene for sustained condemnation of the aircrews by those who enjoyed the comfortable benefit of hindsight. The target was announced to the crews of the thirteen aircraft from Waterbeach directed to take part in the 805-bomber attack on supply and communications lines in Dresden. One unidentified aircraft remained on the ground at Waterbeach with an intercom failure affecting both turrets. Eleven attacked the target, though F/O Ted Henderson RCAF, on his first op, suffered an oil leak, Gee failure and fuel shortage in NN775, A2-F and had to land at Manston on his return having failed to bomb the target. Cloud cover over the target was 5/10ths, target marking was good and the Master Bomber gave clear and precise instructions.

Flak was slight, heavy in the target area whilst two of the squadron's aircraft reported combats. F/O H MacLean RCAF in NN782, JI-F was able to evade a prowling Ju88 with his fellow Canadian in the rear turret, Sgt Vern Flatekval, sending 500 rounds its way as the Lancaster executed a prompt corkscrew. It was even more fraught for F/L Bertram Audis in PB482, A2-K who was attacked by an Me410 which fired on the

Lancaster as it made the first of two passes. Evidently unable or unwilling to follow the Lancaster through its corkscrew, the Me410 broke away after aborting its second pass and was not seen again. On this occasion, two waves of aircraft three hours apart totaled 805 aircraft, dropping between them 1,478 tons of HE and 1,182 tons of incendiaries. 514 Squadron took part in the second wave, itself consisting of 529 Lancasters. Six Lancasters were shot down with another three crashing in the combined attack.

The squadron ORB states '*The whole area on leaving was reported as one mass of flames and smoke, all crews highly delighted.*' This delight must be considered in the context of the crews, from their point of view, carrying out a disciplined and effective attack on a defined target with military value. The routine nature of the operation is shown by the fact that it is recorded in the same perfunctory manner as all others.

F/S Frank Bell, in PA186, A2-G, recorded: 'We knew something was brewing though nothing had been officially announced. In the briefing room all eyes went to the map. We looked at the red tapes goggle-eyed; what a distance! There were three long legs and a short run to the target in the south east corner of Germany, then three long legs back to base. The navigator had all his maps and charts plotting the route and identifying the heavily-defended places we had to avoid but it wasn't possible to miss them all. We were told that the raid would be in two waves; the first was actually going on as we were being briefed and would be returning just as we took off. This would be our longest trip so far, with nine hours' flying.

We were told the raid was to help the Russian advance and each pilot was given a Union Jack to tie around his waist under his clothes. If a crew was shot down they were to press on to the Russian lines, get out the Union Jack to show they were English and hope the Russians didn't shoot them. Dresden, we were told, was filled with German troops coming and going to and from the Eastern Front. There were also armament works and aircraft component factories.

There was an unusual atmosphere that day. We were concerned that with the first wave having been over the target all the defences and fighters would be alert and would have plenty of time to land and refuel and be ready for us before we arrived.

About an hour from the target we could see a glow in the distance. After another twenty minutes we knew it was Dresden. With another half hour to go we were mesmerized by the huge glow which presented itself to us. We couldn't believe it; it was a holocaust. The city was ablaze, no one could be alive down there and we had to add to it. It literally looked like Hell down there; it's a night I will never forget. We dropped our bomb load, a 4,000 lb blockbuster and eight 500 lb bombs. Imagine multiplying that five hundred times. After allowing the automatic camera time to take its battery of photographs we swung out of that glare. If there had been any enemy fighters above us we would have been silhouetted for them and sitting ducks. There was little flak but the ground defences must have been saturated. We could still see the glare half an hour away from Dresden on the return. We landed at 0615hrs. As usual the ground crew were waiting for us. Some Flying Control staff stepped out on to the verandah and gave us the thumbs up. We were de-briefed then went to the Mess for our eggs and bacon. Still etched into our minds was the sight of the city burning; it was devastating.'[38]

On the following night, 514 Squadron was involved in the second part of Operation Thunderclap, its contribution of fourteen aircraft bringing the total force to 617 bombers. Conditions were not so favourable and much of the bombing fell outside the built up area of Chemnitz, which had been singled out for attention as the Third Reich contracted. There were at least two areas of bombing and it was believed that the bulk of the attack was NW of Chemnitz, probably on the existing fires at Rositz. The heavy flak was slight in intensity but many scarecrows were noted. Although the squadron's crews all returned safely and no combats were reported, there were thirteen aircraft lost from the attacking force. F/S Frank Bell, this time in NN776, A2-D, noted: 'Chemnitz was thirty miles west of

[38] Much has been written about the series of raids on Dresden in the closing stage of the war, part of Operation Thunderclap. The cataclysm that befell those present in the city was not known to the crews, several of whom simply noted that this was 'a good effort'. It would only be later that the true human cost of the attack would be made clear. The ensuing firestorm was claimed by the Nazis to have resulted in up to 250,000 deaths on the ground, and this inflated figure was later propagated by the occupying Soviet power in the Cold War to discredit its former Western allies. It has subsequently been estimated that the number was much lower, though still around 25,000. Josef Goebbels allegedly added a zero to the total, thereby turning a tragedy of war into a cynical piece of propaganda. There is a school of thought that, as the Allies had recently discovered the abomination at Auschwitz, this was a ruse by the Nazis to divert attention from their abominable deeds.

Dresden and another long trip. Once again it was to help the Russian army as it was full of German troops resting. Our aim was to annihilate them. The captains again wore Union Jacks under their clothes. When we crossed the Belgian coast the searchlights and flak started. A little to the north we saw a huge flash and explosion as someone took a direct hit. We saw tracers across the sky and knew some poor devil was taking it from an enemy fighter. We were worried about enemy aircraft being around after the previous day's raid on Dresden so were glad when we heard the bomb aimer say "Bombs away." We wheeled round and flew like the clappers till we were well away and settled down to cruising speed. Fifteen minutes from Waterbeach the Captain got in touch by radio and was immediately told "Bandits!" We were given a heading to fly for RAF Tempsford and told to orbit there for a while, until the all clear was given. This happened now and again at night; the German fighters would infiltrate the bomber stream and fly along with it, playing havoc when they reached an airfield. It was pitch black flying at night and we couldn't see what was happening. That was why IFF was so useful.'

The afternoon of 18th February saw the first of a series of raids on the town of Wesel, which was a staging point for German supplies and reinforcements as the Allies prepared to cross the Rhine into Germany. Twelve aircraft took off from Waterbeach as 160 Lancasters conducted a GH attack through ten tenths cloud. Marking was concentrated but the bombing appeared scattered, though admittedly results were unobserved. There was only slight flak, and no fighters were seen. The entire force emerged unscathed.

On the following afternoon the attack was repeated by twenty one of the squadron's crews as 162 Lancasters returned to the town. The cloud cover over Wesel had broken somewhat and a clear patch showed the red puff markers, enabling good concentration of bombs to be achieved. The attack was considered to be a good one overall. Flak was still nil to slight, though one 'scarecrow' was reported above the target. It is possible that is was, in fact, Lancaster PD336, WP-P, of 90 Sqn, the only loss of the raid. The aircraft crashed at Xanten which is near the target area. The aircraft was flown by W/C PF Dunham DFC who lost his life along with his crew.

Dortmund was back on the agenda on 20th February, the 518-strong night

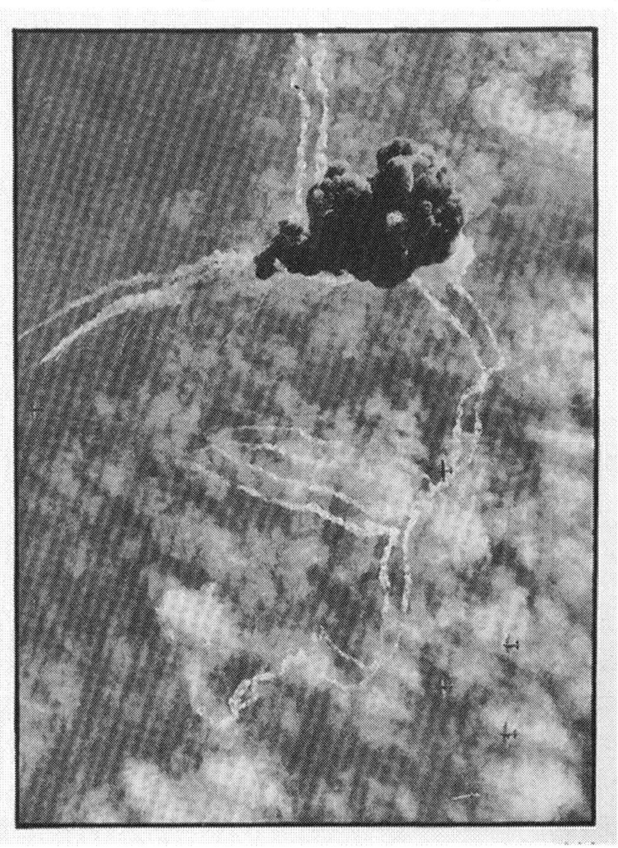

Death of a Lancaster. PD336 of 90 Sqn explodes after being hit by flak over Wesel (Crown).

raid including ten aircraft from the squadron, nine of which attacked the primary. F/O Campbell Fiset in NG298, JI-E had to return early with an unserviceable starboard outer engine, jettisoning its bomb load in the sea. The bombing was considered mostly concentrated and some fires were noted along with a large explosion at 0109hrs. With almost complete cloud cover the searchlights were rendered ineffective though the heavy flak, slight to moderate in intensity, was bursting well below the bombing height of around twenty thousand feet. This did not prevent four aircraft being seen to be shot down over the target, along with a further two over France.

Whilst the Ruhr defences were noticeably quiet several night fighters were seen. PB142, JI-G, flown by F/L JDK Crooks, endured three combats on the homeward leg. An Me109 was the first to have a go, opening fire at 0111hrs during a frontal attack but making only a single pass. Three minutes later an Me110 tried its luck but had been silhouetted against a cloud bank and was seen in time by the rear gunner, W/O George Copland, who shouted for evasive action and opened fire as the fighter closed in. His four Browning machine guns stopped firing, as faulty tracer ammunition gave insufficient recoil, but fortunately Sgt J Deighton in the mid upper turret was able to keep up the fight. The Me110 came back for a second attempt but was engaged again by Sgt Deighton who saw his rounds strike the enemy aircraft and bits break off. The fighter dived into a cloud bank and did not come back. At 0123hrs, a Ju88 approached from the port bow and the bomb aimer, F/O WL Combes RNZAF manning the front turret, fired fifty rounds before his guns failed for the same reason. Fortunately Sgt Deighton's ammunition was unaffected and he was able to join in, the Ju88 also losing interest after the brief encounter.

This attack on Dortmund was the last major raid of the war on the city and Bomber Command assessed that it was successful in destroying the southern half of the city. It came at a cost, however, with fourteen aircraft failing to return.

On 22nd February oil plants at Osterfeld and Gelsenkirchen were selected for a joint attack by 167 Lancasters. The twenty one from Waterbeach were part of the force of 82 tasked with the refinery at Osterfeld in the late afternoon. Although the target was clear of cloud haze and, later, smoke obscured the aiming point. Moderate to intense heavy flak caused much evasive action over the target, increasing the risk of damage by falling bombs as aircraft moved erratically. However, no aircraft were lost from the Osterfeld raid and only one from Gelsenkirchen and, despite the flak, both targets were bombed accurately.

The following day it was 514 Squadron's turn to bomb the Alma Pluto benzol plant in Gelsenkirchen in a mid-afternoon raid featuring fourteen Lancasters among 133 involved in the GH attack. The formation was initially straggly but then the collective act came together with a good formation over the target. Flak was slight with only two burst noted. On their return to England the weather was low stratus cloud over Waterbeach so the squadron dispersed, only four landing at their home base, six at Acklington and the remainder landing individually at Hutton Cranswick, Chipping Ongar, Witchford and Stradishall. No results were obtained from the raid and no aircraft were lost.

On February 25th the squadron sent thirteen aircraft to Kamen on yet another GH raid against an oil target. The formation consisted of 153 Lancasters and the bombing was reported to be concentrated in the factory area. Clouds of black smoke were seen billowing up through the haze and crews were confident that the attack had been successful. The flak had been slight on the outbound route and over the target but the defences of Solingen and Köln were in action and four of the squadron's aircraft were damaged, though no further details are contained in the ORB. All 514 Squadron aircraft landed safely at Waterbeach, the sole casualty being a 75(NZ) Sqn Lancaster which was hit by flak over Wesel. The crew all survived, having to endure what would be a relatively short period as POWs.

Hoesch Benzin at Dortmund was the destination on 26th February, 514 Squadron contributing eighteen Lancasters to the force of 149. GH worked well and the crews felt that bombing was concentrated. With a robust fighter escort visible to the bomber crews, there was no interruption from Luftwaffe pilots, though the flak arm of the service did its best to spoil the occasion, hitting an unspecified squadron aircraft. 'The Lancashire Lass', NG142, JI-J was hit on the tailplane by a bomb from another aircraft, though F/O Gerry Gibson was able to fly the aircraft safely back to base. There were no losses on this operation.

27th February saw a repeat attack on the Alma Pluto benzol plant at Gelsenkirchen. The 149 Lancasters included twenty one from 514 Squadron, twenty of which attacked the primary target whilst S/L Clayton Wilcox, 'B' Flight Commander in ME387, JI-N, was compelled to release his 4,000lb 'cookie' on Solingen as a last resort. The blue puff markers were concentrated and the bombing considered good from the long, narrow stream.

'The Lancashire Lass', NG142, here bearing code JI-J, was another high-scoring Lancaster, surviving 59 operations despite several close calls.

The formation was better on the way home than outbound. Over the target the heavy flak was slight to moderate and accurate, though there were no fighters seen. However, one aircraft was seen to be shot down at 1429hrs with a single parachute noted. This was NG175, AP-J from 186 Sqn at Stradishall. In fact two crew members survived, albeit as POWs. F/S Frank Bell in NG203, A2-C witnessed the loss: 'The flak was terrific on the last leg in. Just before commencing the run in I saw a Lancaster receive a direct hit. It went down in flames and exploded.' February ended with another GH raid on the 28th, this time on the Nordstern synthetic oil plant at Gelsenkirchen. Nineteen aircraft joined a force totalling 156 Lancasters which attacked the plant at midday. With a good formation, the marking and bombing were concentrated and greyish smoke was seen to rise above the almost inevitable ten tenths cloud. No enemy aircraft were in attendance and the heavy flak was only of slight intensity. There were, again, no losses from the bomber force.

The Station Commander's Report for February noted:

GH and H2S Mk.III training continued during the month, but the third flight of 514 Squadron was moved 'above the line' and became operational again on 22nd February. The intensity of flying remained

unchanged throughout the month and the ground staff received rather a set back from the extensive flak damage sustained by aircraft on the 22nd. Landing on return from operations has been fraught with some difficulty owing to poor weather and low visibility on several occasions, and diversions were necessary in two instances.
Admin: The increasing proportion of aircrew officers to NCOs made some reorganisation of accommodation necessary, and the Officers' Mess on the communal site was taken over from the NCOs for officers' sleeping accommodation.

In a still from an official film, a 4,000lb 'Cookie' and 500lb 'GP' bomb are shown a split second after leaving the bomb bay (Crown).

9. Marching on Together: March and April 1945

It fell to Kamen's oil facility to host a GH attack by 151 Lancasters on 1st March, including eighteen from 514 Squadron. There was a glitch as the stream approached the target when the leading formation missed its turning point for the run in. Those aircraft turned later and, guided by their GH equipment, approached the target on various headings whilst following groups stuck to the original plan. The result was a measure of chaos as the risk of being hit by falling bombs meant that some aircraft had to break off the attack and orbit until they could carry out a bombing run without being brought down by their comrades. Fortunately there was no flak, and enemy fighters were again conspicuous by their absence so, although the bombing was scattered, no aircraft were lost.

The late afternoon of 2nd March saw a large raid on Köln by 885 bombers, split into two waves. The eighteen from Waterbeach were part of the second prong, which featured 155 of 3 Group's Lancasters carrying out a GH raid. By now Köln was almost on the front line and could potentially have been the scene of bitter house to house fighting. The first wave was highly destructive but the second attack was beset by problems with the GH transmitters in England, and only fifteen aircraft bombed. Amongst the casualties were 160 German troops, mostly of the notorious and ruthless SS, for whom few tears would be shed. Köln fell to the Allies four days later. Nine bombers were lost in total, though all the squadron's aircraft returned safely.

The operation had been witnessed by several members of the press. Mr RK Powell of Planet Newspapers Ltd and Mr G Bocca of the Daily Express, Mr F Lesser of the Daily Worker, Mr H Procter of the Daily Mail, Mr LJ Smith of the Daily Sketch, Mr GPW Clapton, Miss Mary Munton of the Daily Telegraph and Mr VM Evans of the News Chronicle visited the station in order to photograph the squadron's return from a sortie (Köln), and describe the sortie after interviews with the crews.

The following day all sections of the Camp visited the Station Information Rom to listen to a recorded and illustrated talk on the war in the Far East, which was done by means of a Synchrophone. The talk was concise and

interesting, and admirably illustrated by an illuminated map which was synchronised with the records.
The Consolidated Benzol plant in Gelsenkirchen was the destination for 170 Lancasters of 3 Group on the early afternoon of 5th March, the squadron helping out with nineteen crews. The target was cloud-covered and there was also cirrus cloud at the bombing height of around 21,000 feet. The aircraft held formation well to the target and bombing was reported as concentrated, though the actual results were not observed. There was slight to moderate heavy flak which was accurate for height and two of the squadron's aircraft were damaged. A Lancaster of 149 Sqn at Methwold, NF962, OJ-H, was seen to be shot down by flak over the target at 1404hrs, five parachutes being seen. There were no Luftwaffe fighters present, as was now usually the case on daylight operations.
The only other aircraft lost was 514's NN775, A2-F with no survivors from the crew of 23 year old F/O Holman Kerr, from Lurgan, Northern Ireland. The aircraft crashed at Bunsbeek, province of Brabant, Belgium.

Flight Sergeant Allen Olsen RAAF (front row, right) with other members believed to be from the crew of F/O Holman Kerr (Sally Olsen).

Circumstances of the loss are not stated, the aircraft coming down over Belgium which by now had been fully liberated but it was possibly due to flak or 'friendly bomb' damage as no fighter activity was noted on this daylight raid. The crew members are buried at Heverlee War Cemetery, 30 km from Brussels. Reports indicate that the aircraft was in small pieces suggesting it exploded in midair.

The Wintershall refinery at Salzbergen hosted 3 Group on 6th March, the 119 Lancasters including seventeen from 514 Squadron. The weather was ideal for GH, the ten tenths cloud rising to 10,000 feet. The equipment worked well and the GH navigators were very enthusiastic about the results, at least in theory as none could actually be observed through the cloud. The effort of providing such accuracy proved too much for the Gee receiver installed in F/L Arthur Southward's NN773, JI-K as the set caught fire over the French coast. Fortunately the fire was promptly extinguished.

The squadrons from 33 Base, those from Waterbeach, Witchford and Mepal, held their formation well and the whole stream appeared better than normal. The flak over the target was slight and the only casualty sustained was ME365, JI-T. The Lancaster was seen to explode over the target at 1204hrs when its bombs had dropped twenty to thirty feet. There were no survivors from the crew of F/O Leslie Flack RCAF who are buried at Reichswald Forest War Cemetery. It is not known if the aircraft was hit by flak or by bombs. As it turned out they were to be the last 514 Squadron crew lost in action. The explosion of ME365 caused serious damage to PD334, A2-B, flown by F/O CA Dunn RCAF, and also damaged NG298, JI-E flown by F/O Campbell Fiset. Fragments also caused damage to the mid upper turret and elsewhere on W/O Harry Butcher's NN717, A2-E.

Later the same evening, three aircraft were despatched from Waterbeach to join another 135 attacking German troop concentrations at Wesel. This was to be a 'round the clock' operation, and all aircraft that had just returned from Salzbergen were also to be made ready for a dawn attack on the same target.

The three crews carrying out the evening raid bombed shortly after 2100hrs through the cloud cover which by now extended to 16,000 feet. Crews reported several large explosions early on and we're delighted to

note an extra-large one at 2111hrs. The heavy flak, though slight, was accurate for height and crews reported two jet-propelled fighters.
The dawn operation, for which the squadron put up seven aircraft, took part in two waves as German troops massed in the town. The cloud had thinned in places and the flashes of Bomb bursts and glow of fires could be seen. Already pleased with the GH results, the crews believed the bombing to have been concentrated. A twin-engined fighter was seen, but no combats were reported by the squadron.
On 7th March, the squadron carried out its first and only attack on Dessau, which lies in eastern Germany. Due to the distance over what remained of enemy territory, the raid was carried out at night, with bombing taking place around 2200hrs. Fifteen went from Waterbeach while the overall force was 536 aircraft. Most crews bombed on sky markers, but some crews arrived on the wrong heading, had to orbit and due to the strong following wind were late in getting back and bombed fires. Fires and explosions covered a large area. The Master Bomber was enthusiastic about results. A very large explosion was seen at 2217 hours. Heavy flak was slight to moderate heavy and several fighters seen in target area and Magdeburg. Many fighter flares were seen between the Ruhr and Magdeburg, with activity particularly noticeable over the Ruhr, Magdeburg, Brunswick and Wuppertal. Crews noted that 'a new type of scarecrow was seen in several places' though no further information is noted. F/O CA Dunn, flying ME442, JI-Q was outbound to the target at 2017hrs, between Cologne and Solingen when rear gunner F/S IP Cahill, RCAF sighted an Me109 400 yards astern. Both he and Sgt WH Wylie in the mid upper turret opened fire and the enemy fighter was lost in the corkscrew.
There was considerable damage caused to the town centre, with residential, industrial and transport facilities all being hit. There was considerable night fighter activity against the bomber stream, starting in the vicinity of Cologne and continuing either side of the target. Eighteen aircraft were shot down though all those from Waterbeach returned unscathed.
After a day on the ground, fifteen 514 Squadron aircraft joined 144 others from the group on 9th March in attacking the Emscher Lippe Benzol plant in Datteln. Bombing was concentrated and flak was nil to slight in the

early afternoon raid; no enemy fighters put in an appearance. The only loss was a 90 Sqn Lancaster shot down by flak, with one survivor.
Another of Gelsenkirchen's numerous oil plants was on the agenda for 10th March. 3 Group arranged for 155 Lancasters to take a day trip to the Scholven-Bauer refinery, 514 Squadron contributing thirteen. Once again the formation got its act together on the run up to the target and bombing was accurate and effective. The heavy flak, though slight, hit two of the squadron's aircraft over the plant but there were no losses. 'The Lancashire Lass, NG142, JI-J, was hit once again with some of her Perspex damaged, though F/O William Winkworth was still able to get her home. F/L John Ness in PB142, JI-G also reported the bomb aimer's panel damaged in his aircraft.

Survivors. NG142, JI-J 'The Lancashire Lass' with F/O Jim Eley and crew, after her 59th and final operational flight, the trip to Regensburg on 20th April 1945 (WMHM).

A change of emphasis the following day saw Bomber Command's largest force to a single target to date, 1079 bombers, carry out a daylight raid on German supply lines at Essen, something that would previously have been unthinkable. By now the Luftwaffe appeared to be largely ineffective, if not actually on its knees, with no fighters and no flak observed by the squadron's fifteen crews. The fact that only half 514's aircraft were involved was a further testament to the strength of Bomber Command by this stage of the war. The force dropped 4,661 tons of bombs through complete cloud cover ahead of Allied ground forces. The bombing was accurate, effectively taking Essen out of the war, and the city fell to the Allies shortly afterwards. Three aircraft were lost. Needless to say, this was the last of many attacks on the city of Essen and its war industries.

Bomber Command promptly broke its new record the following day as 1,108 aircraft, including fifteen from Waterbeach, decided that enough was enough as far as Dortmund was concerned. The formation was, again, good and GH continued to work well. The attack was deemed to be successful, with only slight, albeit accurate, heavy flak over the target. F/L Bertram Audis brought home NN781, A2-B having been hit by flak in the trailing edge of her port wing two minutes before bombing. A single FW190 fighter was seen by squadron crews over the city, and even that had three Mustangs on its tail vying for the chance to shoot it down. F/S Frank Bell was in ME529, A2-F: 'We were told there would be 1030 aircraft on this raid, the sky was going to be crowded. The raid had been planned meticulously and everyone had to keep to their heights. The weather would be fine all day and Dortmund wouldn't know what hit it. Looking out of the astrodome I had never seen so many four-engined aircraft on a raid before. We had flak from time to time en-route. I noticed in the distance the white vertical vapour trail of a V2 rocket; in a few minutes that would land on London. Over Dortmund the flak was thick and furious. One Lancaster away on the port side was ablaze and I noticed another with an engine feathered and smoke coming from it. With luck he might get back. For us, everything went according to plan. We dropped our load of bombs, swung away from the target and flak and set off for home. We were first back at Waterbeach. At the de-briefing we reported the plight of the two Lancasters and the V2 rocket and its approximate launch position. Someone would shortly be paying a visit to that site...'

Whilst two Lancasters were lost, the massive raid ensured that, as with Essen the previous day, Dortmund would play no further part in the war. The record tonnage of bombs, 4,851, fell mainly in the centre and south of the city.

The Oil Plan took precedence on 14th March, the 169 Lancasters of 3 Group tasked with putting the Heinrichshutte benzol plant at Hattingen out of action. Two of the squadron's nineteen Lancasters returned early but the rest attacked their target. The plant's defenders put on a formidable show, the heavy flak being moderate to intense. NF968, JI-B was being flown by F/L LR Worthing when the aircraft was hit by flak, causing unstated damage. PB142, JI-G was again hit, being flown on this raid by F/O Campbell Fiset. Her port outer engine was holed by flak, requiring it to be feathered. The mid upper turret was also holed and the hydraulics rendered unserviceable. F/L WF Burrows had to report holes in the tail and port inner engine of ME336, JI-S on the crew's eventual safe return.
F/S William Sparkes, wireless operator for S/L Kenneth Condict in LM724, JI-H, became the last of 514 Squadron's aircrew to fall to enemy action when at 1642hrs he was killed instantly by a flak burst. According to F/S Frank Bell, a friend of F/S Sparkes, he was decapitated when flak shrapnel removed the astrodome in which he was standing. Four of the squadron's aircraft were damaged whilst a 75(NZ) Sqn Lancaster was shot down with the loss of her crew.
The next operation, on 17th March, was a 167 Lancaster effort against the August Viktoria benzol plant at Hüls and another similar facility in Dortmund. The Secretary of State for Air, The Rt. Hon. Sir Archibald Sinclair, Bt., KT, CMG, MP, paid a fleeting visit to Waterbeach in a Grumman Goose aircraft, the ORB records. He spent an hour talking in the briefing room to those aircrew who were available, presumably those of the twenty one attacking August Viktoria who had just landed, before he departed. He was, presumably, told about the high cloud up to 23,000 feet, the contrails to the same height and the sighting by seven crews of a V2 rocket. It might be that he was not told about the problems encountered by the crews flying in and out of cloud, the GH Leaders frequently getting lost and the congestion over the target. The attack was, however, deemed to be successful, with slight to nil heavy flak, no fighters and no losses. Reports of a 'scarecrow' explosion cannot, on this occasion, be accounted for by an exploding bomber. F/O Bill Allan was on his first op but he had to abort when the port outer engine of NG118, A2-H failed 25 minutes before the target and he could not keep up with the formation on three engines

On 18th March 100 Lancasters targeted plants at Hattingen and Lagendreer, 514's sixteen crews being directed to the Bruchstrasse coking plant at the latter location. This appears to have been as run of the mill as would be possible in the context of a bombing raid, with slight accurate heavy flak, no fighters, no losses, GH working correctly and concentrated accurate bombing.

There were still some railway lines left intact in Germany, at least at the Hamm marshalling yards, so at lunchtime on 20th March 3 Group despatched 99 Lancasters, including twenty one from the squadron, to change that. F/L Harold Lunson in NG298, JI-E had to return with an overspeed problem in his starboard outer engine, which would not feather and eventually caught fire. Fear of the fire spreading prompted him to land at the emergency airfield at Manston. The leading squadrons took the stream eight to ten miles to starboard whilst twenty miles out from the target, though fortunately this was corrected in time. The heavy flak was described as slight to moderate, though many crews would believe that to be an understatement with nine aircraft being damaged. F/O Gerry Gibson

F/O Gerry Gibson and crew with ME530, JI-C (WMHM).

in LM627, JI-B sustained three holes in the fuselage and one in a bomb door. F/O William Winkworth's NN782, JI-F sustained unspecified flak damage, as were PB482, A2-K flown by F/O Glen Hanson and ME351, JI-U flown by F/O FE Sider. The perspex on ME355, JI-L was holed, making life more difficult for F/O AH Pickersgill, the same thing happening to NE776, A2-D flown by F/O Joe Gallicano. F/O Thomas Pashley in ME336, JI-S reported damage to the mid upper turret of his aircraft. Not to be out-done, F/L Robert Rice put up with heavy flak holes between the two port engines and damage to the Perspex in the mid upper turret of ME529, A2-F. Despite the damage, and undoubtedly disgruntled chuntering from the ground crews, all the aircraft returned safely. Bombs were seen to hit the target and results expected to be good.
Another significant effort by the squadron saw seventeen aircraft amongst 3 Group's 160, attack Munster Viaduct on 21st March. All but one of the Waterbeach aircraft bombed, whilst F/L Montague Allen in ME336, JI-S was unable to correct being off track so bombed the built up area at Dorstern instead. For the rest, the bombing was concentrated in the viaduct area and to the north on the marshalling yards. F/O Joe Gallicano in NN776, A2-D, reported hitting a bridge with his 4,000lb 'cookie'. Once again the flak caused plenty of patching up work for the ground crews with eight of the squadron's aircraft damaged. F/O G Robertson in ME529, A2-F suffered flak holes in the nacelles of the starboard engines. F/L Robert Rice, having swapped ME529 for NN781, A2-B was grazed on the forehead by a piece of flak which came through the perspex. F/O FE Sider was back in the patched-up ME351, JI-U and suffered further unspecified damage, as did F/O Gerry Gibson in ME535, JI-G. NN782, JI-F, flown by F/O Peter Dean RAAF, was holed between the two port engines whilst S/L Kenneth Condict in NF968, JI-B suffered slight damage to his port engine at Dorstern. Two aircraft were seen to be shot down, these and one other all being from 75(NZ) Sqn at 33 Base's Mepal. Between four and six parachutes were seen. In fact, nine of the 21 crew survived. It was subsequently believed that one or more of these Lancasters might have been hit by bombs from higher aircraft. The raid was assessed as being vital to the hindrance of enemy reinforcements moving towards the Ruhr. Back at Waterbeach F/L PJ Harding of Directorate of Accident Prevention, Air Ministry and Mr E Holmes, Air Ministry PR8 visited the

Station in order to sketch the interior of a Lancaster aircraft. The Station ORB gives no further details as to why the two gentlemen from the Ministry needed to travel to Cambridgeshire when one might have expected the Air Ministry to know what the inside of their most important bomber looked like.

Wesel, which claimed with some credibility to be the most intensively-bombed town of its size in Germany, was the target for the last time on 23rd March. The squadron contributed ten aircraft to the attack by 218 bombers, though F/O Glen Hanson had to bring back his bombs when ME355, JI-L refused to let go of them over the target. The weather was perfect and the GH sets working well, with crews able to see their bombs falling on the eastern bank of the Rhine and the town being completely obliterated by brown smoke. There was no flak and no fighters were seen, no damage and no lost aircraft. The attack immediately preceded Field Marshal Montgomery's crossing of the Rhine and was later reported to have been most accurate and successful. As a result of Bomber Command's continued attention, which was in preparation for and support of the Rhine crossing, 97 percent of the main town area had been destroyed and the population reduced from 25,000 to less than 2,000.

The next raid was not until 27th March when another two benzol plants were noticed, this time at Hamm, and promptly bombed. The 150 Lancasters deployed included 18 from 514 Squadron. Black smoke was seen rising through the cloud over the Hamm-Sachsen plant targeted by 514's crews and indeed from the second plant. There was only slight flak, mainly from Hamm itself and no fighters. There were no aircraft lost and the trip was described as uneventful, which was by now an acceptable result for the crews. Meanwhile back at Waterbeach the 'Cambridgeshire' YMCA hut opposite the Guardroom was formally presented to the Station by Captain RG Briscoe, MP, MC, Lord Lieutenant of the County of Cambridgeshire on behalf of the People of the Town and County of Cambridge.

As March drew to a close there was time for a final outing of the month for seventeen of the squadron's crews, part of the 130 Lancasters attacking the Hermann Goering benzol plant at Salzgitter. On this occasion, the formation was good until fifty miles from the target when high icing clouds caused the raid to go haywire, in the words of the ORB. The green

puff markers were lost in the clouds and followers had difficulty in knowing when to bomb. The results were unobserved, with slight to moderate heavy flak being accurate. Four aircraft were damaged including ME355, JI-L flown by F/L Alexander Munro with damage to the fuselage. Back on the ground, a slight tweak was carried out with ramifications for all pilots and navigators, as all stations were to change aircraft instruments from 'miles' to 'knots' by dusk.
The Station Commander's Summary for March 1945 noted the impending end of hostilities:
The month has been noteworthy for the intensive operational effort, the flying hours for which represent a new record for the Squadron (1707.25). The Squadron has also done a considerable amount of training, both in the initial training of GH crews and in the combined training of GH and H2S Mk.III. The Squadron was called upon to 'mark' using the H2S Mk.III technique for the first time on the 29th March but unfortunately the attack was spoilt by conditions of solid cloud over the target, which dispersed the other Squadrons and made it impossible for individuals to find the coloured smoke puffs.
Admin: Discipline and morale, with particular reference to problems likely to arise on cessation of the German war, have been under constant consideration throughout the month. The matter has been discussed at welfare meetings and at a conference of Section Commanders and Senior NCOs have been addressed on the subject by the Station Commander.

The end of the war was now in sight. A lecture on the 'Release Scheme' was given to personnel by F/L WH Gibson at 1400hrs. The WAAF monthly dance for all ranks was held in the evening which was very successful and well attended.
The Leuna synthetic oil plant was still functioning, although by now the production and delivery of fuel was being strangled by Bomber Command's continuing efforts. On 4th April 341 aircraft made a further attempt to eradicate the facility, twenty aircraft joining in from Waterbeach. It was a mixed effort from the squadron. F/L Robert Rice in PB419, A2-C suffered very low oil pressure so had to feather his starboard outer engine and return to base. 'C' Flight's commander, S/L Ernest Cozens, was interrupted by heavy flak on the bomb run and could not see

any markers when back on track. He elected to bring his bombs back in NN781, A2-B as they were close to the bomb line, a restriction imposed to protect advancing troops from becoming inadvertent victims of 'friendly fire'.
F/L Frederick Morrish had to return early after suffering two engine fires in PB142, JI-K. The event lived on in the memory of his bomb aimer, Sgt Ken Staveley, who recalled the awful loneliness felt by crews having to return alone through enemy skies. PB142 suffered the problems after encountering some flak en route to the target. Faced with a long trip back through hostile skies, the aircraft was at risk of losing altitude so the crew had to save as much weight as possible. This included taking the risk of dumping all their ammunition. Everything that would fit into the flare chute was unceremoniously dropped overboard. The crew jettisoned their bombs, Ken commenting on the impressive sight of their 4,000lb cookie exploding in the sea[39].
PFF were late with their marking and TIs appear to have been scattered over a very wide area, including some over Magdeburg, fifty miles to the north west. Over the plant itself there was complete cloud cover, so some of the crews bombed on sky markers, whereas the markers at Magdeburg were more clearly visible, leading to those being bombed in error. The Master Bomber was faint and gave contradictory instructions, telling crews first to bomb sky markers then to bomb visually. Possibly as a result the raid was very scattered.
Heavy flak was moderate and a number of fighters were seen, including jet propelled aircraft. F/O HA Pickersgill in ME523, A2-G reported being holed by flak in the bomb doors. F/L Ted Henderson in PB389, A2-J, was one of those to bomb Magdeburg on red and green TIs. The crew narrowly avoided colliding with another Lancaster over the target area, the other aircraft fortunately having its navigation lights on. They then had two combats in the target area, with a Ju88 and an Me109, though no combat report remains. Fighter flares were noted following the stream back to the English Channel. Two Lancasters, from 115 and 186 Sqns, collided on the outbound route with a single survivor. Another 186 Sqn machine was hit by flak over the target, struggled home and crashed on landing at

[39] Ken Staveley in conversation with the author, February 2015.

Stradishall, the crew surviving. Less fortunate were the seven men aboard a 424 Sqn RCAF Lancaster which returned to England but crashed into a hillside only three miles from Bomber Command HQ at High Wycombe. Later on 4th April final arrangements were made for a performance by BBC Theatre Orchestra under Conductor Stanford Robinson in the Dining Hall and NAAFI. Special stage lighting and broadcasting facilities required, also messing arrangements for musicians and technicians which numbered over 100. Extra seating for an audience of over 600 arranged. Bookings included HQ 3 Group, RAF Mepal and Witchford. The concert was broadcast on General Forces programme. After this excellent and well conducted performance official guests were entertained in the Officers' Mess where light refreshments were available. The whole of the

ME336, JI-S 'The Impatient Virgin' poses with the crew of F/O Harry Huyton. It is likely that this was taken very shortly after the end of 514 Squadron's bombing war (WMHM).

arrangements reflected great credit on the part of all who contributed their services to make the evening's entertainment such a success. Meanwhile the following evening at 1900hrs an interesting lecture was given by Captain EC Baker on 'Why we should fight Japan'. Given the brutality of the Japanese forces when it is, perhaps, surprising that anyone would need persuading

RAF raid capsizes the Scheer

GERMANY'S 10,000-ton battleship Admiral Scheer capsized at Kiel after an attack by 600 R.A.F. planes on Monday. Below, the Scheer before the attack.—Story in BACK Page.

Scheer delight. The destruction of the cruiser 'Admiral Scheer' by Bomber Command Lancasters was a significant blow to any lingering hopes that the Kriegsmarine might be able to work a last-minute miracle for the Nazis. The papers, in Britain at least, loved it (Paul Sieloff).

On 9th April, Bomber Command arranged a large raid against the docks and U-boat yards at Kiel. The 599 bombers included a near maximum effort from 514 Squadron, with twenty six crews being detailed. A2-L failed to take off due to engine and fuel problems whilst F/L Alexander Munro brought ME336, JI-S home early with wireless and intercom problems, these systems being critical. In clear weather the crews could see that the markers were well placed and they accurately bombed the TIs. The resulting fires could be seen from as far away as Sylt on the return leg and the crews were enthusiastic about their impact.

There was much light flak bursting at 15,000 feet, with the heavy flak, initially moderate, dying off through the raid. Two FW190 fighters were seen, and night fighters are believed to be responsible for the loss of two Lancasters that failed to return, these being from 170 and 622 Sqns. A Lancaster of 300 Sqn, crewed by airmen of the Polish Air Force, was coned by searchlights over the target and shot down by flak.

F/L 'Wes' Hurley and crew who, along with another 514 Squadron crew and some Mosquitoes, carried out their own diversionary raid over Hamburg (WMHM).

The shipyard and U-boat works were badly damaged by this attack. Whilst this raid has not been widely celebrated it achieved the distinction of taking three of Germany's few remaining naval assets out of the war. The pocket battleship Admiral Scheer capsized after being hit, whilst the Admiral Hipper and the Emden were both badly damaged. There had been fears that these three ships might have been crucial in protecting a staged retreat by German forces to Norway in order to continue the war from there. The Kriegsmarine could not effectively do that without ships such as these.

F/O RC Foord in ME535, JI-G bombed a city he tentatively identified as Hamburg, taking an H2S image so that the crew might find out later where he had attacked. Whatever the target might have been his bomb bursts were well concentrated, causing several explosions. After bombing, he then saw the target at Kiel. F/O Foord was not alone in attacking Hamburg, as he was joined by F/L Thomas 'Wes' Hurley in PD389, A2-J who also carried out an accurate attack, the ORB giving details of what appeared to be a significant air raid on the city. So effective was the secondary attack that comments were made by a crew bombing Kiel that they could see explosions over Hamburg.

Sgt Gwyn Morgan, mid upper gunner in ME422, JI-Q, was involved in the squadron's last contact with an enemy night fighter. Sgt Morgan is visible in this photo, waving from the mid upper turret. The photo also shows clearly the stripes on the aircraft's fins denoting it as a GH leader. The serial is suffixed 'G' indicating that it was to be guarded whilst on the ground, because of the still secret GH equipment on board (Morgan family).

The Bomber Command Night Raid Report notes only that a small force of 24 Mosquitoes carried out an accurate attack on Hamburg, whilst omitting to mention that two 514 Squadron Lancasters added their considerable weight to what was obviously an effective raid. 'Nachtjagd War Diaries' mentions a diversionary raid to Hamburg intended to draw night fighters away from the main force attacking Kiel and, indeed, Bomber Command's various tactics did reduce the effectiveness of the Luftwaffe. It is unlikely that P/O Foord or F/L Hurley were knowingly trying to attract the attention of the enemy to themselves, however.

A family portrait of Sgt Gwyn Morgan, who engaged in the squadron's last gunfight with the Luftwaffe (Morgan family).

After another short break, 514 Squadron was back in action on 13th April with another trip to Kiel. Twenty one crews attended on this occasion as part of 475 bombers returning to the U-boat yards. LM724, JI-M flown by F/O Peter Dean had to return early when one engine failed and another started to play up. The ORB noted that markers were concentrated and the Master Bomber gave clear instructions. The intention was to destroy the naval arsenal, Deutsche Werke U-boat construction yards and shipping, with post-raid reports noting fresh damage to buildings and a power station, though on this occasion no further ships were sunk. A couple of crews reported seeing a large explosion at 2330hrs, this possibly being an ammunition store that was also hit. There was slight heavy flak and a few ineffective searchlights, these being joined by more searchlights and light flak from Sylt and the Frisian Islands.

Once again the Luftwaffe took to the skies with what remained of its fighters, pilots and fuel but was thrown off the scent once more by effective diversionary tactics, even without the efforts of any 514 Squadron crews this time. F/L 'Marco' Marks in ME422, JI-Q had the pleasure of reporting the squadron's last direct contact with an enemy night fighter, his mid upper gunner Sgt Gwyn Morgan firing sixty rounds at a Ju88 which was lurking with apparent intent seven hundred yards away. The Luftwaffe pilot decided that discretion was the better part of valour and flew away without pressing home an attack. Two more 186 Sqn Lancasters were lost in particularly tragic circumstances, colliding in the circuit as they prepared to land at their base, Stradishall with the loss of all but two crewmen. A 428 Sqn Lancaster was hit by flak and ditched, six of the crew surviving as POWs. Another Lancaster, from 419 Sqn, was lost without trace.

On 18th April another very large force was assembled for an operation to bomb Heligoland, this comprising 969 aircraft including twenty five from Waterbeach. With no cloud and only a slight haze, visibility was good with many crews bombing visually. Soon, though, the whole target area was obscured by smoke and flame and few markers could be seen, with only the northeastern tip of the island visible. However, the Master Bomber was effective, telling crews to bomb the upwind edge of the smoke. There was evidence of a large oil fire and a very large explosion was seen at 1327hrs. Neither flak nor fighters significantly troubled the squadron, though four Halifax bombers were lost at various stages of the operation, two more were damaged beyond repair in ground accidents and one sustained unknown damage in flight and was struck off charge. F/O Ron Goulding recalled 'On a daylight raid on Heligoland, April 18th 1945, while on the bombing run, a fighter, which I believe was a twin-engined ME262, made an attack. We only saw it as it dived past our Lanc. It was a lucky escape. That incidentally was our last operation before the European war ended.' No Lancasters were harmed in this operation which

was summed up in the 514 Squadron ORB by F/L Ted Henderson who commented *'Wizard effort, no troubles.'*
The same day, the 'Father of the RAF', Marshal of the RAF the Viscount Trenchard GCB, GCVC, DSO, DCL, LLD visited the station and delivered an address to personnel of 514 Squadron and Station ground staff who paraded near the Control Tower. The Marshal had informal chats with numerous officers and men. He was entertained to lunch in the Officers' Mess.

Viscount Trenchard, popularly considered 'The Father of the RAF', addresses ground and aircrew at RAF Waterbeach as the end of the war approaches (WMHM).

20th April 1945 was the last birthday to be celebrated by the German Führer and Bomber Command was never one to let an opportunity pass to rain on his parades. 3 Group marked the occasion by dispatching one hundred Lancasters, including twenty from Waterbeach, to destroy a fuel storage depot at Regensburg. The weather was clear over target and for the whole route. The GH runs were good and bombing concentrated, but it appeared to have overshot and undershot, in effect straddling the target. Fires and smoke were noted whilst a railway bridge was seen to be hit. There was a large fire and column of smoke ten to fifteen miles east of target, and another a similar distance to the south west. Flak was nil increasing to slight and no enemy fighters were seen. One aircraft was seen shot down at 1400hrs, this being Lancaster PA285, GI-O of 622 Sqn which was the only aircraft lost on this raid. One crew member survived. This was Bomber Command's final operation in its ten-month campaign against oil targets. It was assessed that the reduction in oil and fuel supplies had, despite the great cost to Bomber Command, been of immeasurable assistance to the Allies in their efforts against the Germans on all fronts.

The end was nigh for the squadron's combat operations. On 22nd April, Bomber Command despatched a large force of 767 bombers, including twenty one from the squadron, to soften up the areas of the city of Bremen due to be attacked by British ground forces. Eighteen of 514's crews bombed the target collectively dropping eighteen 4,000lb 'cookies' and 288 500lb bombs in the space of seven minutes. However, bombing was affected by cloud and smoke, with the Master Bomber ordering the attack to stop after 195 aircraft had bombed. The first major German port to be captured, Bremen surrendered after 3 days of ground attack, with 6,000 German troops deciding that, for them, the war was now over. Flak, though slight to moderate, was accurate and eleven of the squadron's aircraft were damaged, most of the damage being slight, though F/L Murray Muggeridge had to land ME355 JI-M with his port tyre burst. F/O Steve Abel, with whose crew Sgt Ken Staveley had originally trained, was piloting LM285, JI-A when his aircraft was hit by flak near Wilhelmshaven. Further damage was caused as he continued with his bombing run. As a result the aircraft had a damaged rear turret, fuselage and starboard wing whilst it was losing petrol from the port wing. Furthermore, the port inner engine had to be feathered. Lancasters LM627, JI-D and ME387, JI-N, flown by F/L Fred Morrish and S/L Clayton Wilcox, escorted F/O Abel's stricken aircraft back over friendly territory where he effected a difficult though successful crash landing at Venlo. F/L Morrish's bomb aimer, Sgt Ken Staveley, had a personal interest in the well-being of Steve Abel's crew as he had been one of their number right through their training. Ken remembered: 'We stuck with them all the way until they made a crash landing in a field. We circled round until we could the crew flashing an Aldis lamp to indicate they were OK, then we had to get home.'

The crew survived unscathed, and all returned to Waterbeach on 25th April[40]. One Lancaster from 622 Sqn was also badly damaged by flak, its crew baling out safely, whilst another, from 153 Sqn was lost for an unknown reason with all her crew. A 218 Sqn Lancaster turned back with serious engine trouble but crashed near its base at Chedburgh with the loss of five crew.

Pilot Officer Steve Abel (centre) with air gunners Sgt Freddie Gillett (right) and Sgt CA Cook, (Ken Staveley). Right – Sgt Freddie Gillett (Jo Bulbrook)

ME523, A2-G, was on a training flight on 23rd April when the aircraft carried out a belly landing 1½ miles SW of Topcliffe in Yorkshire[41]. No details are given in the ORB. 514 Squadron's final operation took place on 26th April with thirteen Lancasters participating in a one hundred bomber raid on the railway marshalling yards at Bad Oldesloe. With only very patchy cloud and GH working well, the railway yards, junction and roads were clearly visible and bombing was concentrated on them. The

[40] The full official report of the incident is reproduced in *'Striking Through Clouds'* from the same authors and publisher.

[41] Noted in *'3 Group Bomber Command An Operational Record'*, by Chris Ward & Steve Smith, Pen & Sword Aviation, 2008.

town, between Hamburg and Lübeck, was described as 'unprepared for air attack' and its precautions were 'slack'.

A particularly large explosion was noted, as if an ammunition train had been hit. There were no fighters and no flak over the target, though aircraft were fired on and one was damaged as they flew over isolated German-held areas on the Dutch coast. F/O John Tolley had the previous November crash-landed his Lancaster after being badly damaged over Homberg. At 1054½hrs he commenced his bombing run in RE123, A2-K, the last 514 Squadron pilot to do so. The ORB notes his report:

There was only one bombing raid on Bad Oldesloe but it was the last of many for 514 Squadron. The post-raid reconnaissance photo shows the damage done to the marshalling yards. The air raid apparently came as something of a surprise to the civic authorities (Ken Staveley).

Attacked primary target: Bad-Oldesloe. Bomb load 6 x 1000 ANM 65 and 10 x 500 ANM 64. Bombed on GH 1054½ from 17,300ft. Good GH run. Heavy smoke over centre of target area, and explosions along rail tracks. Good concentration in centre of M/Y some bombs fell along residential area. Smoke and fires on junction. Bang on. Formation good but our followers not with us over target.

These were the last of a total of 14,652½ tons of bombs to fall from 514 Squadron aircraft in the course of the war and indeed in the squadron's history. However it was still some way from the end of matters for the squadron which by now comprised 173 aircrew officers, 276 aircrew NCOs and the Adjutant.

F/O John Tolley and crew flew RE123, A2-K, to Bad Oldesloe and dropped the last bomb load in the course of 514 Squadron's war. In the background is ME354, JI-M with GH Leader markings on her fins (WMHM).

The Station Commander's Report for April 1945 stated:

During the month operations have been limited owing to the reduction in the number of targets available as a result of the sweeping advance of our land forces. The most interesting feature of the month's operations was the changeover on 29th April 1945 to the dropping of food to the people of Holland, a task which has been carried out with a great deal of pleasure. Normal training has continued on days when there were no operations and the weather was suitable.

Admin: On the technical side there has been great activity and long hours have been necessary in order to cope with the task of the manufacture of panniers for food dropping operations. A call for volunteers to assist in this work met with an enthusiastic response. A great deal of thought has been given to the problems which are likely to arise after the cessation of hostilities in Europe. Steps are being taken to endeavour to anticipate

Station requirements in accommodation and training facilities for the Educational and Vocational Training Scheme. So far there is little evidence of much enthusiasm in this direction, but it is hoped that as soon as the official announcement is made of the end of the war in Europe, personnel will realise that it is very much in their own interest that they should take advantage of any facilities which may be provided which will improve their chance of successful re-settlement in civil life.

S/L Clayton Wilcox RCAF (centre) was 'B' Flight Commander for the closing period of the war. The ops markers on the nose of ME387, JI-N indicate that this photo was taken on 22nd or 23rd March 1945. Sgt Donald Poole, 2nd from right, was the crew's flight engineer (Tony Poole).

10. For You the War is Over: May to August 1945

ME364, JI-P 'Princess Patricia', is loaded with hessian sacks containing food for starving Dutch citizens. Her first operation under Operation Manna was piloted by F/O John Chadwell (WMHM).

Although the squadron was warned for a new operation on 25th April, it was destined not to happen. Training continued as ever and then details emerged of a temporary new assignment. Though most of Western Europe was now back in the hands of its rightful owners, parts of Holland were still in German hands. Isolated from the tattered remnants of the Third Reich, the enemy forces were living off the food supplies that were insufficient even for the needs of the Dutch population. People were starving to death. Remarkably, and possibly with an eye on trying to

Manna from Heaven. A Dutch citizen welcomes a food drop from a 3 Group Lancaster.

convince a skeptical world of their residual humanity, German commanders eventually agreed to allow the RAF to drop crucial food supplies to the civilians caught up in the German occupiers' last stand. This was to be Operation Manna.

The briefing called for Lancasters to fly low and slow so that bundles of food could be dropped on to marked targets without it being destroyed in the process. The territory still being occupied by armed enemy troops, still in possession of flak defences, the operation required a huge leap of faith on the part of the aircrews who would be vulnerable to an unprecedented degree, should someone decide to open fire.

On 29th April fourteen Lancasters left Waterbeach laden with food and bound for The Hague. The crews dropped sixty four packs on to red TIs or white crosses, to the delight of cheering crowds, people being seen to sit on top of their houses waving flags. Some difficulty was encountered in releasing the loads, with aircraft sometimes having to orbit two or three

times. The German flak crews could also clearly be seen sitting and awaiting any move that they might deem hostile.
Eric Basford, Fitter for 'A' Flight, explained more about Operation Manna. *The food was packed in hessian sacks, secured within the bomb bay by means of a double canvas door arrangement. Most of the food was in dried form and would have to be reconstituted.*
514's dropping zone was near the Hague. The German`s had specified the flight path, directly over their flak batteries, and also the height. Many of the crews were apprehensive of such an arrangement. They had to fly straight and low with bomb doors open, and at the dropping point, trigger the canvas doors to release the sacks of food.
The crews returned in good spirits, having flown at low level over the top of the flak defences and observed the gunners in position, but there were no incidents. They said the whole population seemed to be there to greet them with much cheering and waving. Horses and carts, wheelbarrows and trolleys of various kinds had been drawn up ready to move the food. Several other drops were made that day in West Holland. Next day there was a repeat operation, but this time 514's dropping zone was near Rotterdam, with the same ecstatic reception from the Dutch.
These operations continued for a little while, but as the German Commanders were surrendering one after the other, food supplies were able to move in by road and the food drops by air were terminated.
Despite unseasonal snow on 30th April, sixteen aircraft departed the following day with food for Rotterdam, sixty two packs being delivered. No TIs were noted this time, crews seeing only a white cross. F/L HC Mottershead in ME225, A2-L reported a house on fire which he thought might well have been caused by a missing red TI. Unfortunately, whilst dropping was largely concentrated, some packs fell into water and some onto marshland. Crews could see people picking up the food almost as it hit the ground and it was evident that there was great enthusiasm from the population.
A further sixteen aircraft dropped food at The Hague on 1st May, to the unbridled joy of more flag-waving crowds. This was repeated on each of the following four days. After a day's break, two more drops were made, these being to The Hague on 6th May and Rotterdam on the following day. 8th May 1945 was VE Day. The Station ORB marked the event:

'A muster parade was held and addressed by the Base Commander, Air Commodore HH Down, AFC and the Station Commander, K Lea-Cox. A short Thanksgiving Service conducted by the Station Chaplain (The Rev RS Hawkins) provided a fitting conclusion to this Parade.
In view of Air Ministry Instructions the Release Procedure was brought into operation at Waterbeach. In the evening a VE All Ranks Dance was held in 'F' hangar.'
The war was now effectively at an end in Europe and there was a massive task awaiting the Allies, that of repatriating tens of thousands of prisoners of war, many of whom had been behind the wire since before Dunkirk. A precious few thousand were the survivors of Bomber Command's horrendous losses over the previous six years or thereabouts. The massed fleet of Bomber Command, now lacking things in Europe to bomb, was to be put to good use flying POWs home to freedom.
For 514 Squadron, unfortunately, there was to be a sting in the tale of events. The squadron's first task under Operation Exodus, on 9th May, was for ten aircraft to collect liberated POWs from Juvincourt, near Reims.
F/L Don Beaton, DSO left Waterbeach at 0726hrs in RF230 JI-B. Having collected its 24 passengers, the aircraft took off from Juvincourt in France at 1215hrs. A message giving the aircraft's estimated time of arrival was received at RAF Waterbeach at 1219 and shortly afterwards the pilot reported he was experiencing trouble with the controls and was putting back to Juvincourt. A further message sent by the aircraft at 1225hrs stated that it was making a forced landing. Flares were fired off from an airfield en route indicating permission to land but no acknowledgment was received.
At 1230hrs RF230 was seen by a number of witnesses on the ground to approach Roye Ami airfield from the west. After circling the airfield twice the aircraft was seen to go into a steep bank to port, before going into a flat spin and crashing into the ground one mile east of Roye Ami. On investigation the aircraft seemed to be fully serviceable and it was not possible to establish the cause of the crash. The position of the passengers to the rear of the fuselage however indicated that the aircraft may have been tail heavy which could have resulted in the pilot believing that there was something seriously wrong with the aircraft, subsequently losing control and crashing. Whether the passengers' positions were taken

up before or after difficulties arose could not be determined. All the passengers and crew lost their lives and were buried at Clichy Northern Cemetery, which is on the northern boundary of Paris.
In conversation with the author, W/O Ken Staveley related that a number of the squadron's pilots had reported control problems when flying with POW passengers. The consensus of opinion amongst crews was that it was the passengers themselves who were the cause of the problem. The Lancaster was not, after all, a passenger aircraft and had neither cabin wall cladding nor fixed seating, not that the liberated POWs had any complaints. The control cables and rods ran along the interior of the fuselage, a fact that was known by the aircrew who left them well alone. However, most of their passengers had never flown before and were unused to the changes in the aircraft's attitude that were a result of climbing, turning and descending. Passengers had an apparent tendency to grab hold of anything they thought might give them some stability, including the control connections. This caused difficulty in operating the elevators and rudders in particular, leading to a loss of control. Once this was known, a member of the crew was given a wooden stick with which they would rap the knuckles of anyone who grabbed the controls. Whether or not the cause was as they feared, this remedy led to an absence of further such incidents.
One happy passenger the following day was returning POW Fred Brown: 'Late on the night of 10th May we landed on a temporary airfield in Northern France. On our arrival we were allocated to areas, and given coffee but no food. I sat with a couple of army types, they had been POWs for some time. We sat and talked through the night. We were to be shipped out the following afternoon.
In the morning, we decided to have a walk around the village, no point in just sitting and waiting. We carried all our gear with us, didn't want to lose any at this stage. There was nothing of interest in the village, we decided to ask one of the locals to brew us a coffee. A lady answered the door we had knocked on. She invited us in and was about to make a brew of ersatz coffee. We said "No" and gave her a large tin of Nescafe. She was beside herself and had to explain to her two young children what it was. The only coffee they had tasted was the ersatz kind. They marvelled at the taste. We

thanked them and left them the coffee and all the other rations we were carrying.
Back to the airfield, we had lots of time to kill. We watched the Yanks moving German POWs, this was something we savoured. Some Germans were being loaded onto a big Yankee truck. The Germans complained that there were too many on the truck. My thoughts went back to the crowded cattle trucks. None of us had any sympathy for the Hun. We had all suffered at their hands. The next scene was a delight to watch, especially for this ex-captive audience. The truck driver pulled away along the tarmac, gathering speed, then applied the pneumatic brakes. All those aboard were swept toward the front of the truck, now there was room for as many again. We cheered encouragement to the driver.

All aboard for Blighty. POWs await their flight home, this group about to embark for their flight home in ME422, JI-Q, flown by F/O CA Dunn RCAF and crew (Dunn family).

Early afternoon we were marshalled along the edge of the runway and numbered off into aircraft loads. In came the Lancasters, squadrons of them, tears came to my eyes. Such a stirring sight. As an aircraft came to rest, a batch of men would board. When it came to our turn, again tears and a lump in my throat, the aircraft letters JI, my squadron. 514 squadron Waterbeach.
I spoke to a member of the crew, told him I was 514. He took me up front, I sat alongside the navigator. The deck of the Lanc was numbered, just

enough space for each man to squat a number. I was given a spare headset, I passed it to one of the army lads, who would never have heard aircrew on intercom before.
Take off, the French coast, the white cliffs of Dover, Vera Lynn. Tears again. A beautiful day, our destination Ford near Brighton. The date May llth 1945. I had been away just a year to the day.'

After several years in exile, Belgian refugees await their flight back to Brussels aboard RA601, JI-J in August 1945 (WMHM).

The final Station Commander's Summary of the war noted:
'Operations during the month have consisted of food dropping in Holland, returning Belgian refugees to their native country and bringing back a return load of released Allied POWs. Flights have also been carried out over Germany viewing bomb damage. These tasks have proved a pleasant change for the crews after a period of intense operational activity. Unfortunately, one aircraft loaded with returning prisoners of war crash landed resulting in the death of 26 persons.
Admin: During the month two important events took place, i.e. VE Day in Europe and an Inspection by the AOC No. 3 Group. Victory in Europe was celebrated by a Parade and Thanksgiving Service and in the evening by an All Ranks Dance which proved very enjoyable.

The AOC's Inspection 'in order to discover how near the accepted 'Peace Time' standard the station was', caused a big stir, but thanks to the strenuous efforts of all officers, airmen and airwomen, passed off very smoothly and the whole station was congratulated on getting so near to our objective in such a short space of time.
All arrangements are in hand to deal with Release procedure, Educational and Vocational Training and voting at the forthcoming General Election.'

W/O Ken Staveley, having survived ten operations remarkably unscathed, found that peacetime flying could still present some serious hazards: 'We were ferrying refugees home and when you came back to England, now the war was over, you had to go through Customs as they expected we would be bringing back all sorts of things. For us on this trip we had to land at Tangmere. We'd left our POWs and set off to fly back to our base at Waterbeach. As we took off, we were affected by a hefty gust of wind, so when we called base to land, they told us Tangmere believed we'd burst a tyre on take-off and that we'd have to land on the grass alongside the runway as 514 were expecting a few kites in after us and didn't want us crashing and fouling it up for them. They were prepared to sacrifice us for the greater good! They were all heart. You can maybe picture our reactions and comments about this but we all took up our crash positions. As bomb aimer mine was braced against the stair side rails underneath the flight engineer's position. The skipper put the Lancaster down on the grass and, what do you know, but the tyre hadn't burst after all. We thought they must have been seeing things at Tangmere. We landed OK, as we'd expected, and then we relaxed and I let go of the rails. Mistake! I had completely forgotten that we had a cross runway to face and there was a bit of a lip where the concrete was higher than the grass. The Lanc's wheel hit that and I got flung forward and hit the bomb sight with my chest, badly bruising it but not, I thought, too seriously. However, pleurisy developed and I had terrible coughing bouts and all the Medical Officers did was give me linctus and tablets. They were keen to get their demob, though that didn't worry me as I had signed on for another eighteen months with the intention of taking an advanced navigation course.
But then a few months later, after the squadron was disbanded, I had been posted to the RAF Photographic Unit at Colerne, near Bath. We had to

'Ot-Az-Ell, ME358, JI-O at the end of the war with a crew believed to be that of F/L William Bainbridge. The 'raid tallies' appear to show a mixture of bombing raids, Operation Manna food drops and POW repatriation flights (WMHM).

walk into Bath quite a lot and I started coughing blood. I went for an aircrew medical in London where an X-ray showed a cavity the size of a fifty pence piece in my left lung. They found out I'd got TB so that x-ray had saved my life.

I wound up getting sent to the RAF Hospital at Kirkham where I stayed for the next two years. You can imagine what it was like with a load of young lads at a loose end as we recuperated. One of the chaps had fluid on his lungs so the doctors gave him a packet of Players cigarettes to help him cough the fluid up, which worked a treat. We were also given a bottle of stout every other day which we used to save up for two or three weeks. Then one night after Matron had gone home we would push a couple of beds together, play poker and have a right old party. You can't imagine being able to get away with that nowadays!'

The war, whilst finished in Europe, still had three months to run in the Far East before its apocalyptic conclusion in Hiroshima and Nagasaki. In common with the rest of Bomber Command, 514 Squadron was in a state of hiatus, its main purpose having been achieved. Crews were kept busy with routine training, jettisoning incendiary bombs, repatriating the dispersed citizens of the formerly occupied countries and bringing home POWs from Germany via France, and Italy. Fortunately this was all achieved without further tragedy, though one Lancaster, RE137, JI-D, was shown as having crashed on a cross-country flight at 2345hrs on 21st August. The crew was unhurt and there is no apparent record other than the single sentence to this effect in the ORB. The aircraft appears not to

RA599, JI-L joined 514 Squadron after the end of hostilities. This crew is believed to be that of F/O R Jones (WMHM).

have been too badly damaged as it was moved to Air Service Training and subsequently the National Gas Turbine Establishment.

The squadron also enthusiastically flew ground crew from Waterbeach and elsewhere in Bomber Command on 'Cook's Tours' over the devastated cities of Germany. This afforded the hard-working and essential support staff of the Command, without whose tireless efforts operations could not have been sustained, an opportunity to see and understand what they had achieved. One such member of the ground crew

was WAAF Joan Harrington (nee Williams) of the Base Registry, RAF Waterbeach, who recalled: 'When crews were due back after a bombing operation, we were asked to be up at the Camp one hour before, to prepare coffee, rum, etc. My friend and I (in the same hut) volunteered, and the WAAF Officer always woke us up in good time. Off we would go on our bikes (transport if bad weather) up to the base. It was rewarding for us to greet the crews who were usually very exhausted and glad of their coffee and rum. We found it very sad when crews were reported missing. After the War finished, we were asked if we would like to have a trip in the Lancaster. The day chosen was 9th July 1945. We were briefed, weather forecast etc., and equipped with a parachute.
We flew out over RAF Woodbridge and then to the Continent and on to our journey over the Ruhr. This will be forever in my memory. After seeing the dreadful devastation I wondered how ever all the places could be restored. I will always be grateful for the opportunity I had to fly in a Lancaster. The journey lasted five hours'.
An overview of the 'Waterbeach Experience' in the final days of the war was given by F/O Peter Dean: 'My crew and I were assigned to A Flight commanded then by S/Ldr K.G. Condict, DFC. The C.O. was Wing Commander P.L.B. Morgan, both of whom I remember as excellent officers. My first operation was a screened trip to Wesel, followed two days later by a trip with my full crew to the same target. Then followed a series of operations to a number of targets in the Ruhr and other places, and night operations, with the final operation to Bad Oldesloe on 24th April '45. I believe that this was the last operation carried out by 514 Squadron on bombing operations. On 30th April we took part in a food dropping mission to Rotterdam, and on May 2nd a similar food drop at The Hague. On 14th May we flew to Juvincourt to uplift ex-prisoners of war, and on 17th, 18th and 23rd May we flew Belgian refugees to Brussels.
In retrospect, our short period spent with 514 Squadron was quite uneventful, bearing in mind the casualties and hazards suffered by some crews who had preceded us. We took some slight flak damage in the course of our short tour, had some fleeting contact with enemy aircraft, enough to experience severe frights, but suffered no casualties.

All in all, our time on the Squadron seems to be very mundane compared with others, who appeared to be dogged with ill fortune. We watched with some interest the launching of V1 flying bombs from sites in France (by daylight) and the launch of V2 rockets towards London. I recall an incident which occurred at dispersal when we had run up our aircraft, and were about to return to the flight office by coach, when we heard a shout of alarm and looked up to see a 'cookie' which had fallen off a bomb trolley, and was rolling in our direction ! That put the wind up us for a while!

My life at Waterbeach was spent with my new wife in digs at Waterbeach awaiting the birth of our daughter. I vividly recall one day walking out with my wife near the village when we came across what I can only now recall as a 'hole in the wall' in a stone wall enclosing an order of nuns. My wife and I purchased a small quantity of honey from one of the nuns, who was permitted to speak to customers after ringing a bell or some such device to attract their attention. We were never able to see any part of the face, only the hands of the nun as she handed us our small purchase and change. On completing our purchase, the nun blessed us both, and this we found to be very touching and something that I shall remember for the rest of my life. Since my wife came from a town in Lancashire we were unable to have time enough to take leave away from Waterbeach, and so we spent a good deal of time visiting Cambridge and lazy afternoons on the Cam in a punt. Memories I shall cherish.'

A final task, Operation Post Mortem, involved flying Lancasters towards captured German radar systems and equipment in order for it to be assessed and evaluated. This might have been beneficial in case the same equipment had been shared with the Nazis' allies in Japan, against whom Bomber Command expected to operate in forthcoming months.

Events, however, overtook the plans and concerns of Bomber Command when the USAAF dropped atomic bombs on Hiroshima and Nagasaki, precipitating the surrender of the Japanese. The 'Tiger Force', intended to conduct long-range strategic bombing against the Japanese mainland, was no longer required. Neither, therefore, were the heavy bomber squadrons, their ranks of aircrew and lines of Lancasters and Halifaxes. On 14th August 1945 514 Squadron received official word that the war would finally end the next day, VJ Day. 514 Squadron was now entirely surplus

to requirements and, on 22nd August 1945, Wing Commander Philip Morgan, Officer Commanding 514 Squadron, posted a final entry in the ORB:
'514 Squadron has now disbanded. Aircrew Personnel have been posted according to instructions, and remainder have been sent on leave to await instructions.'

F/O Hubert Merrett commissioned and owned this painting of a 514 Squadron Lancaster, ME422, JI-Q. F/O Merrett flew several aircraft marked JI-Q (WMHM).

514 Squadron Statistics

Bombing raids:		220
Operational sorties (bombing and mining):		3678
Other operational sorties:		624
Total sorties:		4302
Tons of bombs dropped		14,652½
Strength of Squadron at disbandment		134 Officers
		196 Senior NCOs
Aircraft lost:		**88**
Failed to return from operations	69	
Crashed on operations	7	
Crashed on landing or take-off	3	
Crashed on training flight	3	
Damaged beyond repair on ops	4	
Lost or damaged on ground	2	
Personnel lost:		**437**
Aircrew lost in action:		410
Pilots	57	
Second pilots	7	
Flight Engineers	56	
Navigators	54	
Bomb Aimers	51	
Wireless Operators	63	
Mid Upper Gunners	59	
Rear Gunners	63	
Aircrew lost otherwise than in action:		13
Ground crew lost:		14
Aircrew loss rate per operation (KIA):		1.6%

The Sacrificed: There are twenty 514 Squadron graves in Berlin War Cemetery. Some 437 men were lost by the unit in 18 months of operations. 101 airmen have no known grave and are commemorated on the Runnymede Memorial (John Saddler).

The Survivors. The second 514 Squadron Reunion, 2nd April 1948 in London. (1) Mr. N Brazier, (2) Mr. Hugh Woodcraft, (3) W/Cdr Mike Wyatt, (4) Mr. Frank Bell, (5) Mr. Les Holt (WMHM).

A Veteran's Comments on Bombing– Harry Dison.

I wish to comment on some aspects of bombing in World War Two as RAF bombing has been subjected to controversial criticism from time to time by sections of the media, possibly for sensationalistic gain. We seem to hear much about Dresden, where probably 30,000 people sadly died in a fire storm, but little else of the accomplishments of Bomber Command. In truth RAF bombers significantly reduced Germany's ability to wage war efficiently. Apart from attacks on German cities they operated in many other areas including provision of invaluable support for the invasion in Normandy and following land battles. They destroyed six of Germany's twelve major warships and probably more than 75 U-boats and prevented the construction of as many more again. Air mining resulted in the sinking of over 700 ships plus over 600 damaged. Numerous industrial, communication, oil, missile and other specific targets were attacked, increasingly so as the war progressed. Due to the destruction being inflicted by RAF bombing, Germany needed to employ over a million men in defence and other related services. These men and the weaponry involved would otherwise have been available for the fighting fronts.

United States bombing in Europe was generally confined to industrial and military targets. Although they commenced with this policy against Japan, in order to bring the war to an earlier conclusion they switched to area bombing in March '45. Firstly Tokyo was attacked on the night of March 9th / 10th with fire-bombs, resulting in a fire storm and the death of over 80,000 people. Similar attacks followed on 60 other cities and towns culminating in the ultimate area bombing of Hiroshima and Nagasaki with atomic bombs. Germany in WW2 was a tyranny of immense proportions. Hitler didn't attain power by the use of force but was elected into power by the German people. In the November 1932 elections the Nazis were again voted in as the largest party in the Reichstag leading to Hitler being offered the role of Chancellor, from which position it was relatively easy for him to acquire total dictatorial control. The German people knew, or should have known what he was like before they voted; his hatred of the Jews, his expansionist aims in the east and his desire for revenge against France. This was all stated in his book Mein Kampf. The German electorate had let the evil genie out of the bottle and would live to regret it, along with most of Europe.

Following the fall of Poland and France Hitler was acclaimed by most of the population of Germany. His armies and other armed services, who fought for him with courage and skill, were supported and sustained by the German nation. Germany possessed the world's leading nuclear scientists and might well have been the first to produce the atomic bomb. They invented nerve gas against which there was no defence, but didn't use it in the mistaken belief that we had it also. They were inventive, well ahead of us in missile and rocket development. It was essential to strike at this resourceful and powerful enemy in any and every way and the only feasible way for Britain up to mid-1944 was by bombing at night. During this time all that could normally be targeted at night were areas of cities and towns, in which much of the power of Germany was concentrated.
Briefly the Nazis invaded and enslaved well over half of Europe and large areas of Russia, killing in the process at least 26 million people, including, amongst others, millions of persecuted and helpless Jews (men, women and children) who were put to death or died in their horror camps. Even while our crew was flying over Germany, from August to December 1944, this process continued. Anne Franke, to name but one, was taken in September 1944. I have no regrets that we took the war back to Germany where it belonged.
Following D Day in June '44 when areas of N France were being liberated and allied fighters had gained control of the skies over Germany by day, RAF bombers could have been, and possibly should have been at this stage of the war, used more frequently in daylight against military, industrial and other specific targets. Fortunately 514 Squadron, because of its specialist equipment, operated mainly in this role. The decision to permit Sir Arthur Harris to resume the bombing of German cities after the D Day Invasion period was a strategic decision and as such the responsibility of the War Cabinet and Defence Committee. London at this time was being indiscriminately bombarded by VI and V2 missiles.
With regard to the attack on Dresden in February '45 it should not be forgotten that Churchill himself, for various reasons, was pressing for heavy attacks on certain eastern German cities including Dresden, which lay in the path of the advancing Russians.
Any blame in the choice of targets in the later stages of the war rests solely with those at the highest levels of command. No blame can be placed on the aircrews nor any others in Bomber Command. The crews never questioned the targets they were sent to, trusting they were chosen by knowledgeable and wise counsels way above them. Despite heavy losses,

they did all that was asked of them in the dangerous skies over Europe and should be proud that they took part in the destruction of perhaps the world's greatest tyranny. They also assisted in great measure in bringing freedom back to much of Europe including Germany itself which happily is now one of the world's great democracies.

55,573 AIRCREW DIED IN SERVICE WITH BOMBER COMMAND.

514 Squadron attacked Leipzig on a number of occasions, with considerable damage caused to the city and, later, to the oil plants in and around it. However it was often at considerable cost to the attacking force. The raid of 19th / 20th February 1944 was the second bloodiest of the war for Bomber Command with 78 aircraft failing to return, three of which were from 514 Squadron (Robert Fletcher).

Glossary

A/Bomber	Air Bomber Bomb Aimer
A/C	Aircraft
A/C Instruments	Aircraft Instruments
AC1	Aircraftman - 1st Class
AC2	Aircraftman - Class
ACH/GD	Aircrafthand – General Duties
ACW1	Aircraftwoman – 1st Class
ACW2	Aircraftwoman – 2nd Class
Adj/Adjutant	The Administrative Officer of the Squadron
AFC	Air Force Cross
AFM	Air Force Medal
A - G Firing	Air to Ground Firing
A/G	Air Gunner
Air Tests	Test flight after maintenance or prior to an operational flight
A/G/C	Acting Group Captain
AOC	Air Officer Commanding
ASF	Air to Sea Firing
Assist	Assistant
Astro - Compass	Navigational instrument to obtain a position fix by sighting stars.
A/Ts	Air Tests
ATC Cadets	Air Training Corps Cadets
Baedeker Operation	After hostilities ended, ground crew were flown over bombed German cities so that they could see the results of bombing operations, in which they had also played a vital part. These are referred to in the 514 Squadron ORB as 'Baedeker Tours' after the travel guide. They were more commonly referred to as 'Cooks Tours', whilst 'Baedeker Raids' referred to bombing raids by the Luftwaffe on historic British cities and towns such as York and Canterbury.

BC	Bomber Command
Beam Approach Training	Training in instrument approach to landing.
Beam sorties	Training flights involving beam approaches.
Bombed - up	Aircraft loaded with bombs, awaiting an operation.
Bomb loads	The Avro Lancaster was designed for one purpose; delivering as many bombs as possible to enemy targets. Whilst special variants of the Lanc could carry a bomb load of up to 22,000 lbs, in the form of a single 'Grand Slam' bomb, the standard aircraft generally carried up to 14,000 lbs in a variety of configurations. Bomb loads were described in the individual sortie reports in the format number x weight of each bomb type. Incendiary bombs were small and clustered in packs, so the description was number of packs x bombs in each pack x weight of individual bombs. See 'Bomb Types' at the end of the Glossary.
Bullseye	A navigational sortie where the crew was required to navigate to a spot point, be observed and logged by ground observers.
CB	Companion of the Order of the Bath
CBE	Commander of the Order of the British Empire
CO	Commanding Officer
Cpl	Corporal
Cross Country/ies	Non-operational flights away from the home airfield, usually for navigational practice.
Derby Figures	The maximum effort from operational squadrons excluding crews which have operated on both of the two previous nights and crews screened for training, re-equipping or for any similar purpose.
Derby Signal	Instruction to bomb up 'Derby' number of aircraft.
DFC	Distinguished Flying Cross
DFC and Bar	An award of a further DFC to a person already holding this award.

DFM	Distinguished Flying Medal (Other Ranks equivalent of DFC).
Discip	Discipline
Ditch	Land aircraft in the sea.
DR Navigation	Dead Reckoning Navigation. Calculating the aircraft's position without use of radio aids or other external assistance.
DSC	Distinguished Service Cross
DSO	Distinguished Service Order
ENSA	Entertainments National Service Association. Organisation providing entertainment to military personnel.
Eric Exercise	Non-operational flights to provide practice for Home defences.
ETA	Estimated Time of Arrival
F/Eng	Flight Engineer
Fighter Affiliation	Mock attacks by 'friendly' fighter aircraft to train crews in fighter evasion.
Fighter Flares	Flares dropped by enemy aircraft to mark and illuminate the bomber stream.
Flak	Anti-aircraft fire (also AA, ack-ack). Flak was described by its intensity (slight, moderate or intense) and its calibre (light, medium or heavy).
Flak Suits	Body armour for aircrew to protect them from shrapnel. Heavy and cumbersome, they had to be removed prior to putting on a parachute, so were not adopted by the RAF.
F/L or F/LT	Flight Lieutenant
F/O	Flying Officer
F/Sgt or F/SGT	Flight Sergeant
Formation Flying	Flying in a tight group, either for protection against fighters or to drop their bombs in a concentrated pattern.
FW190	Focke-Wulf 190, a German single-engined fighter aircraft.
Gardening Exercises	Dropping of sea mines

Gee Signals	Radio signals used by RAF to establish the aircraft's position.
GH / Gee-H	A more accurate development of Gee, more resistant to jamming. 3 Group squadrons were specialists in the use of GH as a blind-bombing aid. It allowed the aircraft's position to be pin-pointed with sufficient accuracy to allow bombing through 10/10ths cloud cover with a great degree of confidence that the target would be hit. A proportion of aircraft and their crews were designated 'GH Leader'. These would bomb using GH and other aircraft, formating closely on them, would release their own bombs as soon as they saw the GH Leader's bombs falling. The close proximity of aircraft in a tightly-packed stream, with aircraft at different heights, often led to aircraft being hit by 'friendly' bombs. Several 514 Squadron aircraft, possibly up to ten percent of losses, are believed to have been lost due to being hit by falling bombs and others were damaged.
Goodwood (figures)	The maximum possible effort from Operational Squadrons, including all suitable 'freshmen'. All crews whether screened for training, re-equipping or for any similar purpose, irrespective of the number of previous consecutive nights on which they have operated are to be employed.
Goodwood (Operation)	British Army operation in Normandy, 18th – 20th July 1944.
GRU	Gunnery Research Unit
H and L Tests	Height and load tests. Training in flying heavy aircraft at high altitude.
HF	Heavy flak
High-level Bombing	Tactic of dropping bombs from high altitude, as opposed to ground attack or dive-bombing.
HQ	Headquarters
HRH	His/ Her Royal Highness
H2S	Airborne radar navigation and target location system

Ic	Aircraft on the squadron's operational strength.
IFF	Identification – Friend or Foe. A device on RAF aircraft intended to do exactly that.
Incendiaries	Bombs designed to burst into flames on impact, starting fires.
Inst	Instrument/s
Ir	Aircraft in immediate reserve with the squadron.
Ju88	Junkers 88, a German twin-engined night-fighter aircraft.
KIA	Killed In Action. Death due directly or indirectly to contact with the enemy, as opposed to in an accident.
LAC	Leading Aircraftman
LACW	Leading Aircraftwoman
Local Flying	Non-operational flying in the vicinity of the home airfield.
Lt	Lieutenant
Lt Col	Lieutenant Colonel
Luftwaffe	German Air Force
Make and Mend	Kit and equipment repairs and modification.
M/B	Master Bomber. Experienced pilot and crew directing aircraft on where to release their bombs. This was to improve accuracy and prevent bombing becoming too dispersed.
Me/Bf109	Messerschmitt Bf-109, a single-engined German fighter aircraft. Particularly famous for its role opposite the Spitfire and Hurricane during the Battle of Britain, the Me109 was later used in a night-fighting role. Technically, the designation Bf-109 is correct but contemporary accounts by RAF crews referred to the aircraft as Me109 so this term is used throughout the book.
Me/Bf110	Messerschmitt Bf-110, a German twin-engined fighter aircraft. Designed and deployed as a fighter/bomber in the Battle of Britain, the Me110 was not particularly successful against Spitfires and Hurricanes. However, when used as a night-fighter against heavy bombers, the aircraft proved extremely deadly and Me110

	crews accounted for many 514 Squadron aircraft. As above, the contemporary term Me110 is used rather than the correct Bf-110.
Me210 / Me410	Messerschmitt 210 and 410, twin-engined German fighters, used for night-fighting or intruder role.
Mech	Mechanic
Monica	A warning radar fitted to RAF bombers to warn of approaching night-fighters. However, the Germans developed their own radar device, Flensburg, to home in on Monica signals leading night-fighters to the bomber. It was withdrawn in July 1944.
MUG	Mid Upper Gunner
Nav	Navigator/Navigation
Nav Table	Navigators' Table
NCOs	Non – Commissioned Officer. For aircrew, these were Sergeants, Flight Sergeants and Warrant Officers.
No 3 Group	Bomber Command was organised into a number of 'Groups', each of which consisted of airfield clusters ('Bases') at which the operational squadrons were based. No. 3 Group in 1945 comprised 11 squadrons, which operated from 27 airfields at various times. RAF Waterbeach was the base station for 33 Base, which also included RAF Mepal and RAF Witchford.
OBE	Order of the British Empire
Operation Dodge	Deployment of Lancasters after the end of hostilities to bring home members of the British Eight Army from Italy. Many had been away from home for four or five years.
Operation Manna	Flights over German-occupied Holland to drop food parcels to starving residents. These were undertaken with the agreement of the German forces in the area.
Operation Post Mortem	Flights undertaken to measure and assess the performance of German radar systems.
OPS	Operations
ORB	Operational Record Book

ORs	Other Ranks
Pathfinders / PFF	Path Finder Force was a specific group within Bomber Command tasked with finding and marking targets for 'main force' squadrons to bomb. From mid-1944, 3 Group mostly operated independently of PFF once GH was fully operational. As with all 'elite' forces, any shortcomings in their performance was noted by those not considered elite, hence the numerous comments in crew reports concerning PFF timeliness and accuracy.
PFF Flares	Target-marking flares dropped by PFF to indicate where the main force aircraft should drop their bombs. The flares were used for ground marking, i.e. burning on the ground (Parramatta marking) or sky-marking, i.e. burning as they dropped (Wanganui marking). Wanganui marking was used if the target was obscured by cloud.
P/O	Pilot Officer
POW	Prisoner of War
Prang	Attack or crash.
RAF	Royal Air Force
RAAF	Royal Australian Air Force
RCAF	Royal Canadian Air Force
RDF Methods	Radio Direction Finding (Radar).
RG	Rear Gunner
RN	Royal Navy
RNZAF	Royal New Zealand Air Force
SASO	Senior Air Staff Officer
SBAs	Standard Beam Approaches. Approach to landing using radio aids.
Scarecrow	Believed by crews to be a special shell fired by German anti-aircraft defences to simulate a bomber exploding, thereby demoralising the crews and disrupting the bombing effort. Whilst this explanation was never officially quashed, there is no evidence that such devices existed,

	and almost every report of a scarecrow did, in fact, relate to the explosion of an aircraft.
Serrate	Airborne radar detection equipment designed to home in on Luftwaffe *Liechtenstein* radar fitted to night fighters.
Sgt	Sergeant
Sky Markers	See PFF flares above.
S/LDR or S/L (as rank)	Squadron Leader. Rank usually held by the Flight Commander.
S/L (in raid reports)	Searchlights
SNCOs	Senior Non – commissioned Officers
Special Exercises / Training	Training for a specific operational purpose, e.g. navigation. In the case of 514 Squadron, although no details are given due to secrecy, this was probably GH training.
Sun Ray Treatment	Use of ultraviolet lamps to counteract vitamin deficiency.
Tame Boar	Night fighters acting on the directions of ground controllers. To a certain extent these could be confounded by jamming of their communication channels, or misdirection by German-speaking RAF controllers issuing spurious commands.
TIs	Target Indicators. Long-lasting incendiaries to mark the aiming point.
Up with the lark	A very early start, particularly after an evening in the pub or bar.
U/s	Unserviceable.
USAAF	United States Army Air Force (predecessor of USAF).
Vegetable planting	Laying Sea Mines (see also Gardening).
Very / Verey Light	An emergency signalling light stowed with the inflatable raft
VJ Day	Victory over Japan Day. The end of the Second World War.
WAAF	Women's Auxiliary Air Force
W/Cdr	Wing Commander. Rank held by the squadron's Commanding Officer.

W/O	Warrant Officer. The highest non-commissioned rank.
W/OP	Wireless Operator
W/OP/AG	Wireless Operator/Air Gunner
W/T	Wireless Telegraphy. Radio transmission by Morse code.
Wild Boar	Freelancing (undirected) night fighter. Usually single-engined aircraft such as Me109 or FW190, these aircraft did not rely on control from the ground. See also *Tame Boar.*

Bomb Types:

GP (General purpose)	Heavy-cased bombs for general use. These ranged in weight from 40lb to 4,000 lb and, as the name suggests, were used for general bombing purposes. They had a low charge/weight ratio, typically less than 20%.
MC (Medium Capacity)	Designed for general purpose use, MC bombs had a significantly higher proportion of explosive, typically 50%, meaning that they were more destructive than their GP equivalents. Typical weights ranged from 250 lbs to 4,000 lbs.
HC (High Capacity)	HC bombs were thin-walled with a high charge/ weight ratio, typically 70%. In 514 Squadron use these bombs were 2,000 lbs, 4,000 lb 'Cookies' or 8,000 'Blockbusters'. The larger HC bombs were intended to break down large buildings, especially factories or housing, for incendiary bombs to ignite.
ANM	ANM bombs were American in origin and used for exactly the same purpose as British bombs. L/D bombs had Long Delay fuses, to cause inconvenience to the enemy in their attempts to clear up the damage caused by the raid.

Rank Structures

	Royal Air Force	Luftwaffe
Non-Commissioned Ranks		
AC2	Aircraftman 2nd Class	Flieger / Gefrieter
AC1	Aircraftman 1st Class	Obergefrieter
LAC	Leading Aircraftman	
Cpl	Corporal	Unteroffizier
Sgt	Sergeant	Feldwebel (FW)
F/S	Flight Sergeant	Oberfeldwebel
W/O	Warrant Officer	Oberfeldwebel (Ofw)
Commissioned Ranks		
P/O	Pilot Officer	Leutnant (Lt)
F/O	Flying Officer	Oberleutnant
F/L	Flight Lieutenant	Hauptmann (Hptm)
S/L	Squadron Leader	Major
W/Cdr	Wing Commander	Oberstleutnant
Gp Capt	Group Captain	Oberst
Air Cdre	Air Commodore	Generalmajor
AVM	Air Vice Marshal	Generalleutnant
Air Mshl	Air Marshal	General
Air Chf Mshl	Air Chief Marshal	Generaloberst
MRAF	Marshal of the RAF	Generalfeldmarschall

514 Squadron RAF Roll of Honour

Rank	Forename	Surname	Role	Aircraft	Operation	Date	Age	Buried / Commemorated	Grave
P/O	Thomas	Adams	Bomb Aimer	LM286	Homberg	20/11/1944	28	Reichswald F War Cem	Coll. grave 29. B. 1-16.
Sgt	Lawrence	Adkin	Navigator	DS706	Berlin	30/01/1944	21	Runnymede Memorial	Panel 223.
F/O	Stanley	Anderson	Pilot	HK571	Homberg	21/07/1944	23	Reichswald F War Cem	29. F. 12.
Sgt	Frederick	Ansell	MU Gunner	LL690	Valenciennes	16/06/1944	34	Rieux	Grave 2.
F/S	William	Anthony	Wireless Op	HK570	Homberg	21/07/1944		Runnymede Memorial	Panel 224.
F/O	Leonard	Arkless	Pilot	LM277	Calais	20/09/1944	24	Runnymede Memorial	Panel 204.
Sgt	Cyril	Atter	Wireless Op	NG350	Osterfeld	11/12/1944	21	Reichswald F War Cem	31. B. 13.
F/O	Paul	Bailey	Navigator	DS787	Kamen	11/09/1944	20	Reichswald F War Cem	28. E. 15.
Sgt	Keith	Baker	MU Gunner	DS818	Gelsenkirchen	13/06/1944		Nunspeet	Plot 2. Grave 396.
Sgt	William	Baker	Bomb Aimer	LL627	Magdeburg	22/01/1944	22	Runnymede Memorial	Panel 249.
F/S	William	Ball	Bomb Aimer	DS823	Leipzig	20/02/1944	30	Rheinberg War Cem	7. C. 9.
Sgt	John	Balman	MU Gunner	NG350	Osterfeld	11/12/1944	19	Reichswald F War Cem	31. B. 10.
Sgt	Clive	Banfield	Flt Engineer	LL639	Aachen	11/04/1944		Heverlee War Cem	Coll. grave 5. E. 6-8.
Sgt	John	Barker	MU Gunner	LL680	Magdeburg	21/01/1944	19	Hanover War Cem	Coll. grave 8. A. 8-10.
F/O	Kenneth	Barker	Bomb Aimer	PD265	Homberg	21/11/1944		Reichswald F War Cem	25. G. 6.
F/S	Roger	Basey	Bomb Aimer	LL671	Berlin	24/12/1943	20	Durnbach War Cem	5. D. 4.
Sgt	William	Bates	Bomb Aimer	LL681	Leipzig	20/02/1944	23	Runnymede Memorial	Panel 224.

F/O	Donald	Beaton	Pilot	RF230	Exodus	09/05/1945	22	Clichy Northern	Plot 16. Row 12. Coll. grave 7-18.
F/O	Frederick	Beers	Navigator	PB185	Stuttgart	25/07/1944	26	Runnymede Memorial	Panel 245.
Sgt	Albert	Benham	Wireless Op	LL678	Gelsenkirchen	13/06/1944	21	Bathmen Cem	Coll. grave 173-176.
Sgt	Alfred	Bennett	Flt Engineer	DS823	Leipzig	20/02/1944	20	Rheinberg War Cem	9. A. 8.
Sgt	Philip	Bennett	Flt Engineer	LL625	Berlin	24/03/1944	19	Berlin War Cem	Coll. grave 1. L. 7-12.
F/S	Richard	Bennett	Pilot	LL627	Magdeburg	22/01/1944	20	Runnymede Memorial	Panel 249.
F/O	Richard	Bennett	Bomb Aimer	DS813	Stuttgart	29/07/1944	21	Choloy War Cem	Coll. grave 4. A. 18-20.
P/O	Bertil	Bergquist	MU Gunner	DS785	Schweinfurt	25/02/1944	22	Durnbach War Cem	11. J. 6.
LAC	Derrick	Bichard	Radar Mechanic		Waterbeach	29/12/1944	20	Southgate	Sec. H.B. Grave 661
Sgt	Jack	Birch	Rear Gunner	DS781	Duisburg	22/05/1944	22	Runnymede Memorial	Panel 225.
Sgt	Arthur	Bird	MU Gunner	DS817	Frankfurt	20/12/1943	23	Rheinberg War Cem	Joint grave 10. A. 10-11.
F/S	Henry	Bishop	MU Gunner	PB906	Wanne-Eickel	17/01/1945		Runnymede Memorial	Panel 270.
Sgt	Joseph	Black	Flt Engineer	LL690	Valenciennes	16/06/1944	21	Rieux	Joint grave 1.
Sgt	Leonard	Blackford	Rear Gunner	LL703	Frankfurt	23/03/1944	24	Chadwell Heath	Sec. F. Grave 1314.
Sgt	Arthur	Blackshaw	Wireless Op	NN772	Wiesbaden	02/02/1945	20	Durnbach War Cem	6. B. 5.
Sgt	William	Blake	MU Gunner	LL731	Frankfurt	12/09/1944	29	Rheinberg War Cem	8. F. 2.
F/S	Benjamin	Bloom	Wireless Op	LL690	Valenciennes	16/06/1944		Runnymede Memorial	Panel 225.
Sgt	William	Blore	MU Gunner	ME858	Homberg	21/07/1944		Hunsel	Grave 5.
Sgt	Arthur	Blunden	Flt Engineer	LL641	Le Mans	20/05/1944	37	Cambridge	Grave 13764.

F/S	John	Boanson	MU Gunner	DS822	Massy Palaiseau	08/06/1944	21	La Celle-Les-Bordes	Grave 2.
F/S	Derek	Bolton	Wireless Op	LM684	Homberg	21/11/1944	20	Reichswald F War Cem	Coll. grave 29. B. 1-16.
LAC	Samuel	Bolton	Flight Mechanic		Waterbeach	29/12/1944		Runnymede Memorial	Panel 241.
F/O	William	Bonell	Navigator	LL733	Caen	30/07/1944	25	Runnymede Memorial	Panel 245.
Sgt	Alfred	Booth	MU Gunner	PB185	Stuttgart	25/07/1944	20	Runnymede Memorial	Panel 225.
Sgt	Leslie	Bostock	Flt Engineer	LL671	Berlin	24/12/1943	22	Durnbach War Cem	5. D. 3.
F/O	Philip	Boulter	Flt Engineer	LL685	Brunswick	14/01/1944	23	Hanover War Cem	1. A. 10.
Sgt	Alan	Bowen	Rear Gunner	NG350	Osterfeld	11/12/1944	19	Reichswald F War Cem	31. B. 12.
F/L	George	Boyd	Pilot	DS706	Berlin	30/01/1944	25	Runnymede Memorial	Panel 201.
Sgt	Alfred	Braine	Rear Gunner	LM206	Stuttgart	29/07/1944	19	Neufchateau	Grave 3.
Sgt	James	Brent	Navigator	DS784	Mannheim	18/11/1943	21	Assesse Cem	Grave 2.
Sgt	Arthur	Brettell	MU Gunner	LL627	Magdeburg	22/01/1944	22	Harlingen	Plot E. Row 4. Grave 3.
AC2	Donald	Brewer	Armament Asst		Waterbeach	29/12/1944	19	Cambridge	Grave 15119
F/O	William	Brickwood	Pilot	LL731	Frankfurt	12/09/1944	21	Rheinberg War Cem	8. F. 4.
F/S	John	Brittain	Wireless Op	RF230	J Exodus	09/05/1945	20	Clichy Northern	Plot 16. Row 12. Grave 6.
F/S	Reginald	Bromley	Rear Gunner	LL639	Aachen	11/04/1944	28	Heverlee War Cem	5. E. 4
Sgt	Cyril	Brown	Rear Gunner	PB185	Stuttgart	25/07/1944	37	Runnymede Memorial	Panel 225.
F/O	David	Brown	Navigator	ME858	Homberg	21/07/1944		Hunsel	Grave 2.
Sgt	George	Brown	Wireless Op	DS818	Gelsenkirchen	13/06/1944		Nunspeet	Plot 2. Grave 393A.

W/O	William	Brown	Bomb Aimer	DS781	Duisburg	22/05/1944	21	Runnymede Memorial	Panel 254.
W/O	Kenneth	Bryan	Wireless Op	DS822	Massy Palaiseau	08/06/1944	21	La Celle-Les-Bordes	Grave 1
F/O	Harold	Bryant	MU Gunner	LL732	Chambly	02/05/1944	32	Rouen	Block S. Plot 4. Row U. Coll. Grave 8-14.
F/S	James	Bryson	Navigator	PB906	Wanne-Eickel	17/01/1945		Runnymede Memorial	Panel 270.
Sgt	George	Bumstead	Flt Engineer	LM181	Homberg	21/07/1944	19	Reichswald F War Cem	15. D. 11.
F/O	Arnold	Burgess	Bomb Aimer	PB185	Stuttgart	25/07/1944	20	Runnymede Memorial	Panel 204.
Sgt	Anthony	Buttling	Rear Gunner	DS669	Dusseldorf	23/04/1944		Reichswald F War Cem	7. C. 10.
Sgt	Lawrence	Buxton	Wireless Op	DS633	Duisburg	22/05/1944	22	Great Bircham	Plot 1. Row 4. Grave 11.
Sgt	Robert	Byth	MU Gunner	LL698	Nuremburg	31/03/1944		Rheinberg War Cem	Coll. grave 11. E. 11-13.
F/S	Colin	Campbell	MU Gunner	DS828	Dusseldorf	23/04/1944	19	Reichswald F War Cem	7. C. 9.
F/O	Maurice	Cantin	Pilot	DS814	Berlin	26/11/1943	21	Berlin War Cem	9. D. 16.
Sgt	Harold	Carter	Flt Engineer	DS813	Stuttgart	29/07/1944		Choloy War Cem	Coll. grave 4. A. 18-20.
Sgt	William	Casey	Wireless Op	LL671	Berlin	24/12/1943	22	Durnbach War Cem	5. D. 5.
F/O	Henry	Chapman	MU Gunner	DS813	Stuttgart	29/07/1944		Choloy War Cem	Coll. grave 4. A. 18-20.
F/S	Wilbur	Chapman	Wireless Op	DS824	Magdeburg	26/01/1944	26	Hindeloopen	Plot D, Row 1, Grave 1
P/O	Thomas	Charlton	Pilot	PB143	Stettin	30/08/1944	21	Estruplund	
F/L	George	Chequer	Pilot	DS735	Berlin	30/01/1944	22	Berlin War Cem	8. Z. 36.
Sgt	Victor	Childs	Rear Gunner	LL691	English Channel	01/05/1944	19	Runnymede Memorial	Panel 289.
F/L	Walter	Chitty	Pilot	LL733	Caen	30/07/1944	23	Runnymede Memorial	Panel 256

Sgt	Cecil	Clarke	MU Gunner	LL728	Kiel	26/08/1944	29	Kiel War Cem	3. F. 16.
Sgt	Frank	Clarke	Bomb Aimer	NN775	Gelsenkirchen	05/03/1945		Heverlee War Cem	Coll. grave 10. F. 1-7.
F/O	Ronald	Clements	2nd Pilot	DS725	Leipzig	20/10/1943	27	Berlin War Cem	9. E. 11
F/S	Robert	Cole	Wireless Op	LL732	Chambly	02/05/1944		Rouen	Block "S". Plot 4. Row U. Coll. grave 8-14.
Sgt	Eric	Coles	Flt Engineer	LL620	Villers Bocage	30/06/1944		Coulvain	Coll. grave 3.
Sgt	Leslie	Coles	Rear Gunner	PD265	Homberg	21/11/1944	20	Reichswald F War Cem	29. C. 4.
F/S	Ronald	Collender	Wireless Op	LL731	Frankfurt	12/09/1944	21	Rheinberg War Cem	8. F. 3.
Sgt	Thomas	Combe	MU Gunner	LL733	Dortmund	22/05/1944	19	Inveresk	Sec. C. North Extn. Grave 1281.
F/S	Patrick	Constable	Navigator	DS828	Dusseldorf	23/04/1944	33	Reichswald F War Cem	7. C. 13.
Sgt	Alfred	Cooke	Rear Gunner	LL698	Nuremburg	31/03/1944	19	Rheinberg War Cem	Coll. grave 11. E. 11-13.
Sgt P/O	Bernard	Cooper	MU Gunner	HK570	Homberg	21/07/1944	19	Runnymede Memorial	Panel 249.
Sgt	Gilbert	Cosgrove	Flt Engineer	LL653	Stuttgart	16/03/1944	22	Villars-le-Pautel	Grave 5.
F/O	Reginald	Cowles	Navigator	NG350	Osterfeld	11/12/1944	23	Reichswald F War Cem	31. B. 8.
Sgt	Kenneth	Cragg	Bomb Aimer	DS736	Leipzig	20/02/1944	22	Runnymede Memorial	Panel 227.
F/O	Harold	Crampton	Bomb Aimer	LL697	Lens	11/08/1944	26	Loos	Plot 18. Row G. Grave 32.
P/O	Donald	Crombie	Pilot	DS836	Nuremburg	31/03/1944	29	Runnymede Memorial	Panel 258
Sgt	Robert	Curle	Rear Gunner	DS738	Berlin	02/12/1943	20	Runnymede Memorial	Panel 146.

F/L	Robert	Curtis	Pilot	LL732	Chambly	02/05/1944	26	Rouen	Block "S". Plot 4. Row U. Coll. grave 8-14.
F/O	James	Daly	Navigator	DS813	Stuttgart	29/07/1944		Choloy War Cem	Coll. grave 4. A. 18-20.
LAC	Ronald	Davies	Flight Mechanic		Waterbeach	29/12/1944	24	Runnymede Memorial	Panel 241.
Sgt	Daniel	Davis	Rear Gunner	LL690	Valenciennes	16/06/1944	27	Rieux	Grave 4.
Sgt	Richard	Day	Wireless Op	LL684	Frankfurt	22/03/1944	22	Emmen	Plot 9. Row B. Grave 22.
P/O	Herbert	Delacour	Pilot	LL678	Gelsenkirchen	13/06/1944	20	Bathmen	Coll. grave 173-176.
F/O	Ronald	Dell	Wireless Op	PB143	Stettin	30/08/1944		Frederickshavn	Allied Plot. Grave 68.
Sgt	Norman	Derham	Flt Engineer	ME858	Homberg	21/07/1944	25	Hunsel	Grave 4.
Sgt	Peter	Devlin	MU Gunner	PB143	Stettin	30/08/1944		Estruplund	
Sgt	Ronald	Digby	MU Gunner	LM181	Homberg	21/07/1944	23	Reichswald F War Cem	15. I. 10.
F/S	Arthur	Dimock	Bomb Aimer	LL679	Brunswick	14/01/1944	24	Hanover War Cem	Coll. grave 8. G. 12-18.
W/O	Leslie	Ding	Bomb Aimer	LL733	Caen	30/07/1944	31	Runnymede Memorial	Panel 213.
F/S	Thomas	Dodd	Navigator	LL627	Magdeburg	22/01/1944	22	Runnymede Memorial	Panel 250.
W/O	James	Dodding	2nd Pilot	LL681	Leipzig	20/02/1944		Runnymede Memorial	Panel 253
P/O	Hilary	Doherty	Rear Gunner	LL620	Villers Bocage	30/06/1944	32	Coulvain	Grave 2.
Sgt	Frank	Dolamore	Flt Engineer	DS781	Duisburg	22/05/1944	28	Runnymede Memorial	Panel 217.
Sgt	John	Dowding	Wireless Op	DS706	Berlin	30/01/1944		Runnymede Memorial	Panel 228.
F/O	Alan	Downward	Navigator	LM685	Dortmund-Huckarde	03/02/1945	20	Reichswald F War Cem	Coll. grave 20. C. 13-15.
Sgt	Kenneth	Drummond	2nd Pilot	LL653	Stuttgart	16/03/1944	23	Villars-le-Pautel	Grave 4.

Sgt	James	Dunbar	Bomb Aimer	DS633	Duisburg	22/05/1944	21	Cambridge	Grave 13566.
Sgt	Malcom	Duncan	Rear Gunner	LM181	Homberg	21/07/1944	32	Reichswald F War Cem	15. D. 13.
F/S	Thomas	Durie	Wireless Op	LM181	Homberg	21/07/1944	37	Reichswald F War Cem	15. D. 12.
W/O2	Richard	Eason	Bomb Aimer	LL691	English Channel	01/05/1944		Runnymede Memorial	Panel 250.
F/S	Desmond	Edwards	Navigator	LL671	Berlin	24/12/1943		Durnbach War Cem	5. D. 6.
W/O	James	Edwards	Wireless Op	LL728	Kiel	26/08/1944		Kiel War Cem	3. F. 17.
F/S	Arthur	Elliott	Wireless Op	DS815	Frankfurt	23/03/1944	20	Longueness	Plot 4. Row AA. Grave 58.
F/S	Orval	Evers	Rear Gunner	RF230	Juvincourt - Ford	09/05/1945	19	Clichy Northern	Plot 16. Row 12. Coll. grave 7-18.
Sgt	Leslie	Eyre	MU Gunner	DS814	Berlin	26/11/1943	36	Berlin War Cem	9. D. 18.
Sgt	John	Fenwick	Navigator	DS785	Schweinfurt	25/02/1944	21	Durnbach War Cem	Coll. grave 8. E. 33-35.
Sgt	Thomas	Fenwick	Bomb Aimer	LM735	Emmerich	07/10/1944		Reichswald F War Cem	2. B. 15.
W/O	Harold	Fidge	Rear Gunner	LL681	Leipzig	20/02/1944	29	Runnymede Memorial	Panel 259
F/O	Warren	Fisher	Pilot	LM685	Dortmund-Huckarde	03/02/1945		Reichswald F War Cem	Coll. grave 20. C. 13-15.
F/O	Leslie	Flack	Pilot	ME365	Salzbergen	06/03/1945	25	Reichswald F War Cem	13. E. 5.
Sgt	Ronald	Fontaine	Bomb Aimer	DS784	Mannheim	18/11/1943		Assesse Cem	Grave 3.
F/L	Alba	Fowke	Pilot	DS813	Stuttgart	29/07/1944	26	Choloy War Cem	Coll. grave 4. A. 18-20.
Sgt	Kenneth	Fox	Flt Engineer	PB178	Villers Bocage	30/06/1944	20	Acomb	Row G. Grave 31.
Sgt	Kenneth	Foyle	Flt Engineer	LL680	Magdeburg	21/01/1944	19	Hanover War Cem	Joint grave 8. A. 6-7.

Sgt	James	Fraser	Flt Engineer	DS633	Duisburg	22/05/1944	27	Buckie	Sec. D. Grave 25.
Sgt	Alexander	Freeburn	Navigator	DS633	Duisburg	22/05/1944	28	Cookstown	Sec. A. Grave 967.
Sgt	Sanford	Frith	Flt Engineer	LL698	Nuremburg	31/03/1944	19	Rheinberg War Cem	Coll. grave 11. E. 11-13.
Sgt	J	Gallagher	Rear Gunner	DS633	Duisburg	22/05/1944	19	Glasgow	Sec. 17. Grave 475.
F/S	James	Gallagher	Navigator	LL679	Brunswick	14/01/1944	22	Hanover War Cem	Coll. grave 8. G. 12-18.
Sgt	Leslie	Gardiner	Rear Gunner	LL680	Magdeburg	21/01/1944		Hanover War Cem	Coll. grave 8. A. 8-10.
Sgt	Andrew	George	MU Gunner	PB178	Villers Bocage	30/06/1944	30	Brookwood	54. A. 2.
W/O	Matthew	George	Wireless Op	LM286	Homberg	20/11/1944	23	Reichswald F War Cem	25. G. 12.
F/O	Walter	Gibbs	Rear Gunner	PB143	Stettin	30/08/1944	36	Estruplund	
F/S	Thomas	Gibson	Pilot	DS633	Duisburg	21/05/1944	22	Clogh Holy Trin	
F/O	Robert	Giffin	2nd Pilot	LL692	Stuttgart	29/07/1944		St. Cloud	
P/O	Thomas	Gilchrist	Pilot	LM735	Emmerich	07/10/1944	21	Reichswald F War Cem	2. B. 17.
Sgt	Richard	Gill	Rear Gunner	LL652	Aachen	28/05/1944	35	Geraardsbergen	Grave 11.
Sgt	Harry	Glansford	Bomb Aimer	ME858	Homberg	21/07/1944	23	Hunsel	Joint grave 6.
Sgt	Ernest	Gledhill	Wireless Op	DS682	Dusseldorf	23/04/1944	22	Runnymede Memorial	Panel 230.
Sgt	Geoffrey	Goddard	Bomb Aimer	DS828	Dusseldorf	23/04/1944	23	Reichswald F War Cem	7. C. 4.
W/O	Osmond	Goddard	Wireless Op	LL738	Nuremburg	31/03/1944	20	Rheinberg War Cem	10. C. 10
Sgt	Kenneth	Goodman	Bomb Aimer	PB143	Stettin	30/08/1944	21	Estruplund	
Sgt	Peter	Gosnold	Flt Engineer	PD265	Homberg	21/11/1944	20	Reichswald F War Cem	Coll. grave 29. B. 1-16.
F/S	Wallace	Granbois	Rear Gunner	DS828	Dusseldorf	23/04/1944	26	Reichswald F War Cem	7. D. 13.

F/S	Robert	Gray	Navigator	LM286	Homberg	20/11/1944		Reichswald F War Cem	Coll. grave 29. B. 1-16.
F/S	Alan	Green	Navigator	DS682	Dusseldorf	23/04/1944	23	Runnymede Memorial	Panel 218.
F/S	Bryan	Green	Bomb Aimer	LL732	Chambly	02/05/1944		Rouen	Block "S". Plot 4. Row U. Coll. grave 8-14.
F/S	Frederick	Gregory	Pilot	LL698	Nuremburg	31/03/1944	31	Rheinberg War Cem	Coll. grave 11. E. 11-13.
F/S	Frank	Guest	Bomb Aimer	NG350	Osterfeld	11/12/1944	21	Reichswald F War Cem	31. B. 11.
Sgt	Charles	Guy	Flt Engineer	LL733	Caen	30/07/1944	21	Runnymede Memorial	Panel 230.
F/S	Robert	Guy	Rear Gunner	DS822	Massy Palaiseau	08/06/1944	21	La Celle-Les-Bordes	Grave 3.
F/S	Ernest	Hack	Flt Engineer	HK570	Homberg	21/07/1944	30	Runnymede Memorial	Panel 218.
Sgt	Ernest	Haigh	MU Gunner	DS781	Duisburg	22/05/1944		Kiel War Cem	3. C. 16.
W/O	John	Hall	Wireless Op	DS787	Kamen	11/09/1944	28	Reichswald F War Cem	28. E. 16.
F/S	Norman	Hall	Pilot	DS736	Leipzig	20/02/1944	24	Runnymede Memorial	Panel 218.
W/O	Raymond	Hall	Rear Gunner	LL732	Chambly	02/05/1944	24	Rouen	Block "S". Plot 4. Row U. Coll. grave 8-14.
F/O	Herbert	Hallam	Navigator	LM684	Homberg	21/11/1944	35	Reichswald F War Cem	29. C. 1.
F/S	Jack	Hannesson	Pilot	PB178	Villers Bocage	30/06/1944	21	Brookwood	54. A. 3.
Sgt	Ronald	Harding	Wireless Op	PD265	Homberg	21/11/1944		Reichswald F War Cem	Coll. grave 29. B. 1-16.
F/S	Ronald	Hardy	Wireless Op	LM685	Dortmund-Huckarde	03/02/1945	30	Reichswald F War Cem	Coll. grave 20. C. 13-15.
F/O	John	Harland	Pilot	LM286	Homberg	20/11/1944		Reichswald F War Cem	Coll. grave 29. B. 1-16.
Sgt	J	Harman	MU Gunner	LM277	Calais	20/09/1944		Wissant	Grave 2.

P/O	John	Harrison	Pilot	DS669	Dusseldorf	23/04/1944	24	Reichswald F War Cem	7. C. 14.
Sgt	Robert	Harrison	Rear Gunner	DS785	Schweinfurt	25/02/1944	28	Durnbach War Cem	11. J. 7.
Sgt	William	Harvey	Rear Gunner	NN772	Wiesbaden	14/01/1944	23	Hanover War Cem	1. A. 12.
P/O	William	Harvey	Wireless Op	LL685	Brunswick	02/02/1945	21	Durnbach War Cem	6. B. 4.
LAC	Geoffrey	Hayden	Radar Mechanic		Waterbeach	29/12/1944	20	Cambridge	Grave 15118
Sgt	Herbert	Hayward	Rear Gunner	DS682	Dusseldorf	23/04/1944	27	Runnymede Memorial	Panel 231.
F/O	Frank	Hebditch	Pilot	LL728	Kiel	26/08/1944		Kiel War Cem	3. F. 18.
Sgt	Dennis	Heeley	Rear Gunner	ME365	Salzbergen	06/03/1945	21	Reichswald F War Cem	13. E. 10.
F/S	Clement	Henn	MU Gunner	LL639	Aachen	11/04/1944	22	Heverlee War Cem	5. E. 3
Sgt	John	Hennis	Rear Gunner	LL679	Brunswick	14/01/1944		Hanover War Cem	Coll. grave 8. G. 12-18.
P/O	Walter	Henry	Pilot	DS823	Leipzig	20/02/1944	31	Rheinberg War Cem	7. C. 8.
F/O	Donald	Henshaw	Bomb Aimer	DS824	Magdeburg	22/01/1944	27	Runnymede Memorial	Panel 206.
Sgt	Kenneth	Heron	Wireless Op	LL620	Villers Bocage	30/06/1944	20	Coulvain	Coll. grave 3.
F/O	Ray	Hilchey	Navigator	RF230	Exodus	09/05/1945	22	Clichy Northern	Plot 16. Row 12. Coll. grave 17-18.
P/O	Ellis	Hill	Pilot	NG350	Osterfeld	11/12/1944		Reichswald F War Cem	31. B. 9.
F/O	Frederick	Hill	MU Gunner	LL652	Aachen	28/05/1944	26	Geraardsbergen	Grave 12.
Sgt	Harold	Hill	Rear Gunner	DS836	Nuremburg	31/03/1944	20	Runnymede Memorial	Panel 231.
Sgt	Arthur	Hodson	Flt Engineer	DS736	Leipzig	20/02/1944	20	Runnymede Memorial	Panel 231.
Sgt	Christopher	Hogg	MU Gunner	NN775	Gelsenkirchen	05/03/1945	20	Heverlee War Cem	Coll. grave 10. F. 1-7.

Sgt	Arthur	Holmes	MU Gunner	DS816	Valenciennes	16/06/1944		Croisilles	7. A. 1.
Sgt	George	Holt	Wireless Op	ME858	Homberg	21/07/1944	22	Hunsel	Grave 3.
Sgt	Allan	Hope	Bomb Aimer	HK570	Homberg	21/07/1944	23	Runnymede Memorial	Panel 218.
Sgt	George	Hubbard	Bomb Aimer	DS787	Kamen	11/09/1944		Reichswald F War Cem	28. E. 17.
F/S	John	Hudson	Pilot	DS828	Dusseldorf	23/04/1944	22	Runnymede Memorial	Panel 264.
W/O	Dennis	Hughes	Rear Gunner	LL627	Magdeburg	22/01/1944	22	Runnymede Memorial	Panel 214.
P/O	Garth	Hughes	Pilot	LL738	Nuremburg	31/03/1944	25	Rheinberg War Cem	10. C. 5
Sgt	Patrick	Hughes	Wireless Op	LL639	Aachen	11/04/1944		Heverlee War Cem	5. E. 5.
F/S	Raymond	Hutt	Navigator	LL690	Valenciennes	16/06/1944		Iwuy	Row C. Grave 36.
F/O	George	Jacobson	Bomb Aimer	DS682	Dusseldorf	23/04/1944	27	Runnymede Memorial	Panel 257
Sgt	Kenneth	Jeffery	MU Gunner	HK571	Homberg	21/07/1944	20	Reichswald F War Cem	29. F. 8.
F/S	Edward	Jenner	MU Gunner	LL733	Caen	30/07/1944	21	Runnymede Memorial	Panel 219.
Sgt	Howell	John	Rear Gunner	LL684	Frankfurt	22/03/1944		Emmen	Plot 9. Row B. Joint grave 24.
Sgt	Albert	Johnson	Flt Engineer	LL684	Frankfurt	22/03/1944	20	Emmen	Plot 9. Row B. Joint grave 24.
F/S	Frank	Jones	Wireless Op	LM206	Stuttgart	29/07/1944	22	Neufchateau	Grave 2.
Sgt	Graham	Jones	Flt Engineer	DS828	Dusseldorf	23/04/1944		Reichswald F War Cem	7. C. 2.
F/L	Robert	Jones	Pilot	LM206	Stuttgart	29/07/1944	21	Neufchateau	Grave 1.
F/O	Stanley	Jones	Rear Gunner	LL728	Kiel	26/08/1944	30	Kiel War Cem	3. F. 19
F/S	Thomas	Jones	Wireless Op	PB185	Stuttgart	25/07/1944	22	Runnymede Memorial	Panel 219.

Sgt	Thomas	Jones	Wireless Op	LM277	Calais	20/09/1944		Calais Canadian	6. G. 5.
F/O	William	Jones	Navigator	LL732	Chambly	02/05/1944	35	Rouen	Block "S". Plot 4. Row U. Coll. grave 8-14.
Sgt	Alfred	Kay	Pilot	DS785	Schweinfurt	25/02/1944		Durnbach War Cem	Coll. grave 8. E. 33-35.
Sgt	James	Keenen	Flt Engineer	DS824	Magdeburg	22/01/1944		Runnymede Memorial	Panel 232.
F/S	Lancelot	Kell	Wireless Op	LL679	Brunswick	14/01/1944	29	Hanover War Cem	Coll. grave 8. G. 12-18.
Sgt	George	Kemp	MU Gunner	DS633	Duisburg	22/05/1944	30	Tynemouth	Sec. K. Grave 14499.
Sgt	Douglas	Kenny	MU Gunner	DS823	Leipzig	20/02/1944	25	Rheinberg War Cem	Coll. grave 9. A. 14-16.
F/O	Holman	Kerr	Pilot	NN775	Gelsenkirchen	05/03/1945	23	Heverlee War Cem	Coll. grave 10. F. 1-7.
Sgt	Donald	Kilner	Bomb Aimer	LL653	Stuttgart	16/03/1944	21	Villars-le-Pautel	Grave 2.
Sgt	Kerry	King	Flt Engineer	DS814	Berlin	26/11/1943	19	Berlin War Cem	9. D. 20.
Cpl	William	King			Circs not stated	22/05/1944	51	Widdrington	Grave B.9
P/O	Ernest	Kingham	Pilot	LL690	Valenciennes	16/06/1944		Rieux	Grave 3.
F/L	Leonard	Kingwell	Pilot	LL681	Leipzig	20/02/1944	22	Runnymede Memorial	Panel 202.
F/S	Roy	Kirkpatrick	Bomb Aimer	DS669	Dusseldorf	23/04/1944	21	Reichswald F War Cem	7. C. 11.
Sgt	George	Knight	Navigator	LL681	Leipzig	20/02/1944	21	Runnymede Memorial	Panel 232.
Sgt	Henry	Knight	Flt Engineer	LM735	Emmerich	07/10/1944		Reichswald F War Cem	2. B. 14.
F/S	Jack	Knights	Bomb Aimer	LL625	Berlin	24/03/1944	26	Berlin War Cem	Coll. grave 1. L. 7-12.
F/O	John	Laing	Pilot	LL625	Berlin	24/03/1944	23	Berlin War Cem	Coll. grave 1. L. 7-12.
Sgt	Ronald	Laishley	Flt Engineer	LL679	Brunswick	14/01/1944	19	Hanover War Cem	Coll. grave 8. G. 12-18.

Sgt	William	Lamond	Flt Engineer	LL691	English Channel	01/05/1944	26	Runnymede Memorial	Panel 232.
F/S	Ernest	Lane	Rear Gunner	DS824	Magdeburg	22/01/1944		Wonseradeel	Row O. Grave 39.
Sgt	Robert	Lane	MU Gunner	LM206	Stuttgart	29/07/1944	30	Neufchateau	Grave 5.
F/S	Robert	Langford	Wireless Op	DS781	Duisburg	22/05/1944	23	Runnymede Memorial	Panel 219.
Sgt	William	Lannigan	Rear Gunner	DS823	Leipzig	20/02/1944	24	Rheinberg War Cem	9. A. 18.
W/O	William	Larmouth	Navigator	HK571	Homberg	21/07/1944	26	Reichswald F War Cem	29. F. 9.
W/O	John	Lassam	Pilot	HK570	Homberg	21/07/1944	22	Runnymede Memorial	Panel 214.
F/S	John	Lawrie	Pilot	LM180	Russelsheim	13/08/1944	21	Schoonselhof	IV. D. 15.
Sgt	Bernard	Le Neve-Foster	Flt Engineer	LL645	Frankfurt	22/03/1944	22	Sevenoaks	Sec. A. Cons. Grave 125.
AC1	Harry	Leach	Electrician		Waterbeach	29/12/1944	34	Runnymede Memorial	Panel 243.
F/S	Beverley	Lee	Navigator	PB178	Villers Bocage	30/06/1944	31	Brookwood	4. L. 14
Sgt	Frank	Lewis	Wireless Op	DS736	Leipzig	20/02/1944	24	Runnymede Memorial	Panel 233.
F/S	Gordon	Lewis	Navigator	DS818	Gelsenkirchen	13/06/1944	23	Nunspeet	Plot 2. Grave 394.
F/O	Ronald	Limbert	Pilot	LM684	Homberg	21/11/1944	22	Reichswald F War Cem	Coll. grave 29. B. 1-16.
F/O	Kenneth	Loder	Bomb Aimer	LM206	Stuttgart	29/07/1944	21	Neufchateau	Grave 4.
Sgt	Harold	Long	Rear Gunner	ME858	Homberg	21/07/1944	20	Hunsel	Grave 1.
F/O	Francis	Longston	Navigator	LL620	Villers Bocage	30/06/1944	22	Coulvain	Coll. grave 3.
Sgt	Edward	Lowe	Navigator	LL680	Magdeburg	21/01/1944		Hanover War Cem	Coll. grave 8. A. 8-10.
Sgt	Kenneth	Lowery	Flt Engineer	LL627	Magdeburg	22/01/1944	20	Runnymede Memorial	Panel 233.

Sgt	Stanley	Lucas	MU Gunner	LM286	Homberg	20/11/1944		Reichswald F War Cem	25. G. 13.
F/O	Alan	Lundie	Bomb Aimer	LM684	Homberg	21/11/1944		Reichswald F War Cem	29. C. 6.
P/O	James	Lupton	Rear Gunner	LL731	Frankfurt	12/09/1944	20	Rheinberg War Cem	8. F. 5
Sgt	Clarence	MacKenzie	MU Gunner	LL696	Nuremburg	31/03/1944	19	Durnbach War Cem	5. J. 8.
P/O	Donald	Manchul	Rear Gunner	HK570	Homberg	21/07/1944		Runnymede Memorial	Panel 251.
W/O	Gerald	Manlow	Navigator	LM735	Emmerich	07/10/1944	24	Reichswald F War Cem	2. B. 16.
Sgt	Edward	Marchant	Flt Engineer	DS785	Schweinfurt	25/02/1944	20	Durnbach War Cem	Coll. grave 8. E. 33-35.
Sgt	William	Marsden	Flt Engineer	NN775	Gelsenkirchen	05/03/1945	20	Heverlee War Cem	Coll. grave 10. F. 1-7.
Sgt	Reginald	Marshall	Wireless Op	LL641	Le Mans	20/05/1944	22	Woodkirk	Sec. C. Row 25. Grave 24.
F/O	John	Martin	Navigator	LL685	Brunswick	14/01/1944		Hanover War Cem	Coll. grave 1. A. 8-9.
Sgt	Stanley	Martin	Flt Engineer	LL732	Chambly	02/05/1944	32	Rouen	Block "S". Plot 4. Row U. Coll. grave 8-14.
F/S	Peter	Martindale	Bomb Aimer	DS706	Berlin	30/01/1944	23	Runnymede Memorial	Panel 220.
F/S	Paul	Mason	Pilot	LL679	Brunswick	14/01/1944	23	Hanover War Cem	Coll. grave 8. G. 12-18.
Sgt	Joseph	Masson	MU Gunner	LL641	Le Mans	20/05/1944		Brookwood	49. C. 4.
F/O	Merlin	Matkin	2nd pilot	PB906	Wanne-Eickel	17/01/1945	21	Runnymede Memorial	Panel 279.
Sgt	Frederick	Maunder	Flt Engineer	NN772	Wiesbaden	02/02/1945	19	Durnbach War Cem	6. B. 3.
Sgt	John	McCormick	Wireless Op	DS785	Schweinfurt	25/02/1944	20	Durnbach War Cem	Coll. grave 8. E. 33-35.
F/S	James	McCreary	Bomb Aimer	LL698	Nuremburg	31/03/1944	20	Rheinberg War Cem	Coll. grave 11. E. 11-13.
Sgt	James	McGahey	Flt Engineer	DS836	Nuremburg	31/03/1944		Runnymede Memorial	Panel 233.

F/S	Anthony	McGlone	Wireless Op	PB906	Wanne-Eickel	17/01/1945	23	Runnymede Memorial	Panel 271.
F/S	William	McIlRaith	Bomb Aimer	LM181	Homberg	21/07/1944	27	Reichswald F War Cem	15. D. 6.
F/S	William	McIntosh	Navigator	LM265	Russelsheim	13/08/1944	25	Reichswald F War Cem	22. D. 9.
Sgt	John	McKeown	Bomb Aimer	DS785	Schweinfurt	25/02/1944	20	Durnbach War Cem	Coll. grave 8. E. 33-35.
F/O	Lamont	McLean	Pilot	LM181	Homberg	21/07/1944	23	Reichswald F War Cem	15. D. 7
F/S	Stanley	McLean	Wireless Op	LM735	Emmerich	07/10/1944	20	Reichswald F War Cem	2. B. 13
F/O	William	McLean	Pilot	NN772	Wiesbaden	02/02/1945	25	Durnbach War Cem	6. B. 2.
Sgt	Charles	McLoughlin	Bomb Aimer	LL680	Magdeburg	21/01/1944		Hanover War Cem	Joint grave 8. A. 6-7.
F/S	Alfred	McMurrugh	Flt Engineer	RF230	Exodus	09/05/1945	23	Clichy Northern	Plot 16. Row 11. Grave 18.
Sgt	John	McNeil	MU Gunner	DS813	Stuttgart	15/03/1944	27	Cambridge	Grave 13756.
Sgt	Peter	McQueeney	Flt Engineer	LL672	Magdeburg	21/01/1944	19	Berlin War Cem	8. K. 2.
Sgt	Albert	McWhinney	MU Gunner	LM685	Dortmund-Huckarde	03/02/1945	23	Reichswald F War Cem	Coll. grave 20. C. 13-15.
Sgt	William	Michell	Wireless Op	DS814	Berlin	26/11/1943	22	Berlin War Cem	Joint grave 9. D. 21-22.
F/O	Thomas	Middleton	Pilot	PB185	Stuttgart	25/07/1944		Runnymede Memorial	Panel 208.
F/O	Douglas	Millar	Pilot	ME858	Homberg	21/07/1944	28	Hunsel	Joint grave 6.
F/S	Leslie	Millis	Navigator	DS824	Magdeburg	22/01/1944	22	Wonseradeel	Row O. Grave 32.
Sgt	Reginald	Mirams	MU Gunner	DS706	Berlin	30/01/1944	19	Runnymede Memorial	Panel 234.
Sgt	Robert	Montgomery	Wireless Op	DS735	Berlin	30/01/1944		Berlin War Cem	5. C. 1.
Sgt	Harry	Morgan	Rear Gunner	PB178	Villers Bocage	30/06/1944	24	West Alvington	Near North boundary.

F/O	Maurice	Morgan-Owen	Pilot	DS682	Dusseldorf	23/04/1944	20	Runnymede Memorial	Panel 208.
Sgt	Hugh	Morris	Wireless Op	DS817	Frankfurt	20/12/1943	20	Rheinberg War Cem	Joint grave 10. A. 10-11.
P/O	Alfred	Morrison	Rear Gunner	LM685	Dortmund-Huckarde	03/02/1945	32	Reichswald F War Cem	20. C. 18.
W/O	Kenneth	Mortimer	Navigator	LL735	Berlin	19/04/1945	22	Berlin War Cem	6. B. 18.
F/S	John	Moulsdale	Bomb Aimer	LL639	Aachen	11/04/1944	32	Heverlee War Cem	Coll. Grave 5. E. 6-8
F/O	Gordon	Murphy	Rear Gunner	DS813	Stuttgart	29/07/1944	24	Choloy War Cem	Coll. grave 4. A. 18-20.
Sgt	Frederick	Nash	Wireless Op	DS669	Dusseldorf	23/04/1944	22	Runnymede Memorial	Panel 235.
Sgt	Per	Nelson	Rear Gunner	LL671	Berlin	24/12/1943	22	Durnbach War Cem	5. D. 1.
Sgt	Dennis	Newbury	Flt Engineer	LL681	Leipzig	20/02/1944		Runnymede Memorial	Panel 235.
F/S	Stanley	Newman	Wireless Op	LL652	Aachen	28/05/1944	20	Geraardsbergen	Coll. Grave 13-14
Sgt	Alexander	Nicholson	Rear Gunner	DS706	Berlin	30/01/1944	25	Runnymede Memorial	Panel 235.
F/S	Norman	Nightingale	Navigator	NN772	Wiesbaden	02/02/1945	22	Durnbach War Cem	6. B. 1.
Sgt	Ronald	Norris	Flt Engineer	DS669	Dusseldorf	23/04/1944		Reichswald F War Cem	7. C. 3.
Sgt	Ernest	Oakley	MU Gunner	LL679	Brunswick	14/01/1944		Hanover War Cem	Coll. grave 8. G. 12-18.
F/S	John	O'Brien	MU Gunner	DS735	Berlin	30/01/1944	23	Berlin War Cem	8. Z. 37
Sgt	Walter	O'Dea	Rear Gunner	DS817	Frankfurt	20/12/1943	20	Rheinberg War Cem	10. A. 9
F/S	Patrick	O'Donohue	Wireless Op	ME365	Salzbergen	06/03/1945	21	Reichswald F War Cem	13. E. 6
F/S	Allan	Olsen	Wireless Op	NN775	Gelsenkirchen	05/03/1945	21	Heverlee War Cem	Coll. grave 10. F. 1-7.
F/O	George	Orr	Pilot	PB906	Wanne-Eickel	17/01/1945	34	Runnymede Memorial	Panel 267.
Sgt	Henry	Osborn	Flt Engineer	DS816	Valenciennes	16/06/1944	20	Croisilles	7. A. 3.

Sgt	Thomas	Owen	Wireless Op	LL653	Stuttgart	16/03/1944	21	Villars-le-Pautel	Joint grave 6.
F/O	Ian	Partington	Navigator	LM277	Calais	20/09/1944	23	Calais Canadian	7. G. 8.
Sgt	Robert	Paterson	Flt Engineer	LM286	Homberg	20/11/1944	19	Reichswald F War Cem	25. G. 11.
Sgt	Allen	Pattison	Bomb Aimer	LL645	Nuremburg	31/03/1944	23	Brookwood	48. D. 2.
Sgt	Claude	Payne	MU Gunner	DS836	Nuremburg	31/03/1944	34	Runnymede Memorial	Panel 221.
Sgt	Kenneth	Peake	MU Gunner	LL653	Stuttgart	16/03/1944		Villars-le-Pautel	Grave 7.
F/O	Kaiho	Penkuri	Pilot	LL653	Stuttgart	16/03/1944	21	Villars-le-Pautel	Grave 3.
F/O	Samuel	Phillips	2nd Pilot	LL678	Gelsenkirchen	13/06/1944		Bathmen Cem	Grave 172.
F/O	Roy	Picton	Navigator	LL678	Gelsenkirchen	13/06/1944		Bathmen Cem	Coll. grave 173-176.
Sgt	Sydney	Picton	Wireless Op	DS813	Stuttgart	29/07/1944	21	Choloy War Cem	Coll. grave 4. A. 18-20.
Sgt	Edward	Pitman	Wireless Op	LL680	Magdeburg	21/01/1944	21	Hanover War Cem	Coll. grave 8. A. 8-10.
Sgt	Joseph	Plant	Flt Engineer	LL728	Kiel	26/08/1944	35	Kiel War Cem	3. F. 15.
Sgt	Reginald	Pomroy	Flt Engineer	PB143	Stettin	30/08/1944	23	Estruplund	
Sgt	Eric	Pond	Wireless Op	LL698	Nuremburg	31/03/1944		Rheinberg War Cem	Coll. grave 11. E. 11-13.
Sgt	John	Porrelli	Rear Gunner	DS816	Valenciennes	16/06/1944	35	Croisilles	7. A. 2.
Sgt	Arthur	Pratt	MU Gunner	DS824	Magdeburg	22/01/1944		Runnymede Memorial	Panel 236.
Sgt	Albert	Prescott	MU Gunner	LM684	Homberg	21/11/1944	22	Reichswald F War Cem	29. C. 3.
F/S	Charles	Prowles	Pilot	DS816	Valenciennes	16/06/1944	21	Croisilles	7. A. 5.
Sgt	Norman	Readman	Flt Engineer	NG350	Osterfeld	11/12/1944		Reichswald F War Cem	31. B. 14.

Sgt	Andrew	Reilly	MU Gunner	ME365	Salzbergen	06/03/1945	21	Reichswald F War Cem	13. E. 9.
Sgt	Kenneth	Rhodes	Bomb Aimer	HK571	Homberg	21/07/1944		Reichswald F War Cem	29. F. 6.
F/O	Ivor	Rich	Navigator	LL684	Frankfurt	22/03/1944	35	Emmen	Plot 9. Row B. Grave 23.
F/S	Edgar	Richardson	Pilot	LM265	Russelsheim	13/08/1944	20	Reichswald F War Cem	Coll. grave 22. D. 12-15.
F/S	John	Richardson	Wireless Op	LL733	Caen	30/07/1944	21	Runnymede Memorial	Panel 221.
Sgt	Stanley	Ricketts	Navigator	DS823	Leipzig	20/02/1944	20	Rheinberg War Cem	9. A. 17.
AC2	Charles	Riman			Circs not stated	09/09/1944	19	Putney Vale	Block W, Grave 743
Sgt	Bleddyn	Roberts	MU Gunner	LM735	Emmerich	07/10/1944		Reichswald F War Cem	2. B. 18.
Sgt	Eric	Roberts	Navigator	DS817	Frankfurt	20/12/1943	21	Rheinberg War Cem	10. A. 8.
F/S	Cecil	Robertshaw	Wireless Op	LM265	Russelsheim	13/08/1944		Reichswald F War Cem	22. D. 11.
AC1	George	Robinson	Passenger	LL691	English Channel	01/05/1944		Runnymede Memorial	Panel 243.
Sgt	Alan	Roderick	Flt Engineer	LL652	Aachen	28/05/1944	24	Geraardsbergen	Coll. grave 13-14.
W/O	Henry	Rolph	Wireless Op	DS828	Dusseldorf	23/04/1944	24	Runnymede Memorial	Panel 214.
P/O	Henry	Roome	2nd Pilot	LM265	Russelsheim	13/08/1944	20	Reichswald F War Cem	Coll. Grave 22. D. 12-15
Sgt	Charles	Rose	MU Gunner	LL695	Duisburg	22/05/1944	20	Groesbeek	XVI. B. 7.
P/O	Frank	Rosher	Rear Gunner	LL685	Brunswick	14/01/1944		Hanover War Cem	1. A. 11.
Sgt	William	Saddler	Navigator	DS814	Berlin	26/11/1943	20	Berlin War Cem	Joint grave 9. D. 21-22.
Sgt	Henry	Sadler	Flt Engineer	DS682	Dusseldorf	23/04/1944		Sage	3. D. 16.
Sgt	Charles	Salt	Rear Gunner	LL625	Berlin	24/03/1944		Berlin War Cem	Coll. grave 1. L. 7-12.
Sgt	Charles	Samson	Rear Gunner	HK571	Homberg	21/07/1944		Reichswald F War Cem	29. F. 7.

F/S	George	Savage	Rear Gunner	LL678	Gelsenkirchen	13/06/1944	20	Bathmen Cem	Coll. grave 173-176.
F/S	Gerald	Scott	Wireless Op	LL625	Berlin	24/03/1944	20	Berlin War Cem	Coll. grave 1. L. 7-12.
Sgt	Roger	Scott	Flt Engineer	LM684	Homberg	21/11/1944		Reichswald F War Cem	29. C. 5.
Sgt	Anthony	Sealtiel	Flt Engineer	LL695	Duisburg	22/05/1944	19	Eindhoven	Plot KK. Grave 50.
Sgt	Reginald	Seddon	Bomb Aimer	DS817	Frankfurt	20/12/1943		Rheinberg War Cem	10. A. 7.
F/S	Ernest	Shanks	Bomb Aimer	LL620	Villers Bocage	30/06/1944		Coulvain	Coll. grave 3.
F/S	Edward	Shearing	Pilot	LL641	Le Mans	20/05/1944	21	Bournemouth	Plot N. Row 5. Grave 160.
Sgt	Patrick	Sheehy	Rear Gunner	LM735	Emmerich	07/10/1944		Runnymede Memorial	Panel 237.
Sgt	Joseph	Shepherd	MU Gunner	LL645	Nuremburg	31/03/1944	19	Heywood	Sec. J. C. of E. Grave 883.
Sgt	Robert	Shields	Rear Gunner	LM277	Calais	20/09/1944		Runnymede Memorial	Panel 237.
AC2	James	Simpson			Circs not stated	01/10/1944	20	Belfast	Sec. B.5 Grave 316
F/O	Peter	Slater	MU Gunner	PD265	Homberg	21/11/1944		Reichswald F War Cem	Coll. grave 29. B. 1-16.
Sgt	Leonard	Slocombe	Rear Gunner	LM286	Homberg	20/11/1944	33	Reichswald F War Cem	Coll. grave 29. B. 1-16.
S/L	Ernest	Sly	Pilot	LL685	Brunswick	14/01/1944		Hanover War Cem	Coll. grave 1. A. 8-9.
LAC	Laurence	Smales	Flight Mechanic		Waterbeach	29/12/1944	23	Runnymede Memorial	Panel 242
Sgt	James	Smethurst	Flt Engineer	DS817	Frankfurt	20/12/1943		Rheinberg War Cem	10. A. 6.
F/S	Llewellyn	Smith	Navigator	LL738	Nuremburg	31/03/1944	26	Rheinberg War Cem	14. B. 3.
Sgt	Philip	Smith	Rear Gunner	LM265	Russelsheim	13/08/1944	21	Reichswald F War Cem	Coll. grave 22. D. 12-15.
F/S	Sidney	Smith	Navigator	NN775	Gelsenkirchen	05/03/1945	21	Heverlee War Cem	Coll. grave 10. F. 1-7.

Sgt	Stuart	Smith	Bomb Aimer	DS814	Berlin	26/11/1943		Berlin War Cem	9. D. 17.
F/O	James	Sneddon	MU Gunner	LL685	Brunswick	14/01/1944		Hanover War Cem	1. A. 13.
F/S	William	Sparkes	Wireless Op	LM724	Hattingen	14/03/1945	23	Lodge Hill	Plot 7AC. Grave 601.
F/S	Frank	Spencer	Bomb Aimer	LL690	Valenciennes	16/06/1944	19	Rieux	Joint grave 1.
F/S	George	Spencer	Rear Gunner	PB906	Wanne-Eickel	17/01/1945	32	Runnymede Memorial	Panel 273.
F/S	Ronald	Spencer	Bomb Aimer	DS816	Valenciennes	16/06/1944	29	Croisilles	7. A. 6.
F/S	Keith	Stafford	Navigator	LL731	Frankfurt	12/09/1944	26	Rheinberg War Cem	8. F. 1.
Sgt	Richard	Stafford	Flt Engineer	PB185	Stuttgart	25/07/1944		Runnymede Memorial	Panel 238.
Sgt	Harry	Stagg	Flt Engineer	DS784	Mannheim	18/11/1943	29	Assesse Cem	Grave 5.
Sgt	William	Steger	Rear Gunner	DS818	Gelsenkirchen	13/06/1944	20	Nunspeet	Plot 2. Grave 395.
F/O	Donald	Stephens	Bomb Aimer	LM685	Dortmund-Huckarde	03/02/1945	20	Reichswald F War Cem	20. C. 16.
Sgt	Charlie	Stepney	Rear Gunner	LM684	Homberg	21/11/1944	30	Reichswald F War Cem	29. C. 7.
Sgt	Norman	Stevens	Navigator	PB143	Stettin	30/08/1944	20	Estruplund	
F/S	Arthur	Stone	Navigator	LM181	Homberg	21/07/1944	22	Reichswald F War Cem	15. D. 9.
F/S	Gordon	Stromberg	Wireless Op	LL727	Massy Palaiseau	09/06/1944	19	St. Pierre	Plot 7. Row E. Grave 13.
Sgt	Raymond	Surtees	Wireless Op	DS816	Valenciennes	16/06/1944		Croisilles	7. A. 4.
Sgt	William	Sutherland	Rear Gunner	LL653	Stuttgart	16/03/1944	32	Villars-le-Pautel	Grave 1.
Sgt	Harry	Taylor	MU Gunner	LL681	Leipzig	20/02/1944	21	Runnymede Memorial	Panel 238.
F/L	Lloyd	Taylor	Pilot	LL652	Aachen	21/07/1944	27	Bergen-Op-Zoom	14. A. 8.
Sgt	Walter	Taylor	Navigator	HK570	Homberg	20/05/1944	35	Coventry	Square 283. Grave 130.

F/S	Victor	Tayton	Navigator	LL641	Le Mans	20/05/1944	35	Coventry	Square 283. Grave 130.
F/O	Alec	Teece	Bomb Aimer	LM277	Calais	20/09/1944	20	Runnymede Memorial	Panel 209.
Sgt	Alfred	Tetley	MU Gunner	DS682	Dusseldorf	23/04/1944	23	Sage	5. D. 6.
P/O	Noel	Thackray	Pilot	LL639	Aachen	11/04/1944	27	Heverlee War Cem	Coll. Grave 5. E. 6-8
F/S	Cecil	Thomas	Bomb Aimer	LL652	Aachen	28/05/1944	23	Geraardsbergen	Coll. Grave 13-14
P/O	Edwin	Thomas	Bomb Aimer	LL685	Brunswick	14/01/1944	28	Hanover War Cem	Coll. grave 1. A. 8-9.
Sgt	Frank	Thomas	Wireless Op	DS784	Mannheim	18/11/1943		Assesse Cem	Grave 1.
Sgt	Herbert	Thomas	Rear Gunner	NN775	Gelsenkirchen	05/03/1945	23	Heverlee War Cem	Coll. grave 10. F. 1-7.
P/O	Stanley	Thomas	Pilot	DS784	Mannheim	18/11/1943		Assesse Cem	Grave 4.
Sgt	George	Thornton	Rear Gunner	LL738	Nuremburg	31/03/1944	22	Runnymede Memorial	Panel 239.
W/O	Robert	Thornton	Pilot	DS787	Kamen	11/09/1944	22	Reichswald F War Cem	28 E. 14.
F/S	Robert	Toms	MU Gunner	RF230	Exodus	09/05/1945	20	Clichy Northern	Plot 16. Row 11. Grave 19.
Sgt	George	Trigwell	Bomb Aimer	LM265	Russelsheim	13/08/1944	21	Reichswald F War Cem	22. D. 10.
F/S	Norman	Turner	Pilot	LL691	English Channel	01/05/1944		Runnymede Memorial	Panel 223.
Sgt	Morris	Tyler	Wireless Op	DS836	Nuremburg	31/03/1944	20	Runnymede Memorial	Panel 239.
Sgt	William	Udell	MU Gunner	LL620	Villers Bocage	30/06/1944		Coulvain	Grave 1.
F/S	John	Underwood	Pilot	LL684	Frankfurt	22/03/1944	21	Emmen	Plot 9. Row B. Grave 25.
F/S	Peter	Upton	Wireless Op	LL627	Magdeburg	22/01/1944	21	Harlingen	Plot E. Row 4. Grave 2.
Sgt	Francis	Vallance	Wireless Op	DS823	Leipzig	20/02/1944		Rheinberg War Cem	Coll. grave 9. A. 14-16.

Sgt	Albert	Vickers	Navigator	LL625	Berlin	24/03/1944	22	Berlin War Cem	Coll. grave 1. L. 7-12.
Sgt	Bernard	Vince	MU Gunner	LM265	Russelsheim	13/08/1944	21	Reichswald F War Cem	Coll. grave 22. D. 12-15.
Sgt	James	Vincent	Navigator	LL652	Aachen	28/05/1944	24	Geraardsbergen	Coll. grave 13-14.
F/S	Frederick	Wall	Bomb Aimer	ME365	Salzbergen	06/03/1945	29	Reichswald F War Cem	13. E. 7.
Sgt	Robert	Walne	Rear Gunner	DS814	Berlin	26/11/1943	20	Berlin War Cem	9. D. 19.
AC1	James	Ware			Circs not stated	12/01/1944	35	Scarborough	Sec. C. Row 10. Grave 18.
F/S	William	Warr	Flt Engineer	LM685	Dortmund-Huckarde	03/02/1945	22	Reichswald F War Cem	20. C. 17.
Sgt	Lewis	Warren	Rear Gunner	LL703	Frankfurt	23/03/1944	19	Beck Row	Row F. Grave 2.
Sgt	Clifford	Washington	Navigator	LL728	Kiel	26/08/1944	20	Kiel War Cem	3. F. 14.
Sgt	William	Watkins	MU Gunner	DS736	Leipzig	20/02/1944	21	Runnymede Memorial	Panel 240.
LAC	Frederick	Watson	Flight Mechanic		Waterbeach	29/12/1944	29	Runnymede Memorial	Panel 242
Sgt	William	Watson	Flt Engineer	ME365	Salzbergen	06/03/1945	20	Reichswald F War Cem	13. E. 8.
Sgt	Peter	Webb	Flt Engineer	DS706	Berlin	30/01/1944	28	Runnymede Memorial	Panel 240.
F/S	George	Wells	Rear Gunner	LL733	Caen	30/07/1944	21	Runnymede Memorial	Panel 223.
Sgt	Roy	Werrill	Flt Engineer	PB906	Wanne-Eickel	17/01/1945	21	Runnymede Memorial	Panel 277.
Sgt	Harry	West	Flt Engineer	LL738	Nuremburg	31/03/1944	20	Runnymede Memorial	Panel 240.
Cpl	John	Westgarth			Waterbeach	29/12/1944	23	Runnymede Memorial	Panel 241.
Sgt	Percival	Whale	MU Gunner	LL691	English Channel	01/05/1944	39	Runnymede Memorial	Panel 240.
Sgt	Harold	Whichelow	Wireless Op	LL681	Leipzig	20/02/1944	33	Runnymede Memorial	Panel 223.
F/S	Leslie	Whitbread	MU Gunner	LL738	Nuremburg	31/03/1944	20	Runnymede Memorial	Panel 223.

Sgt	Alan	White	Flt Engineer	LM277	Calais	20/09/1944	20	Runnymede Memorial	Panel 240.
Sgt	Raymond	Whitehall	Wireless Op	HK571	Homberg	21/07/1944		Reichswald F War Cem	Joint grave 29. F. 10-11.
Sgt	Augustine	Whitehead	Navigator	LL691	English Channel	01/05/1944		Runnymede Memorial	Panel 240.
P/O	Kenneth	Whitting	Pilot	LL671	Berlin	24/12/1943	25	Durnbach War Cem	5. D. 2
F/S	Thomas	Wilcox	Bomb Aimer	PB906	Wanne-Eickel	17/01/1945	25	Runnymede Memorial	Panel 273.
F/S	Edward	Wilde	Navigator	DS669	Dusseldorf	23/04/1944	23	Reichswald F War Cem	7. D. 10.
Sgt	Benjamin	Williams	Rear Gunner	LL695	Duisburg	22/05/1944	20	Eindhoven	Plot KK. Grave 48.
P/O	John	Williams	Pilot	DS824	Magdeburg	22/01/1944		Staveren	Row K. Grave 31.
Sgt	John	Williams	Navigator	DS736	Leipzig	20/02/1944		Runnymede Memorial	Panel 240.
Sgt	Albert	Williston	Rear Gunner	LL672	Magdeburg	21/01/1944	27	Berlin War Cem	8. K. 1.
Sgt	John	Wilson	Flt Engineer	HK571	Homberg	21/07/1944		Reichswald F War Cem	Joint grave 29. F. 10-11.
Sgt	William	Wilson	MU Gunner	DS669	Dusseldorf	23/04/1944	20	Reichswald F War Cem	7. C. 12.
Sgt	Leo	Wilton	Rear Gunner	DS783	Berlin	02/12/1943	26	Cambridge	Grave 13736.
P/O	Bernard	Windsor	Pilot	DS781	Duisburg	22/05/1944	29	Runnymede Memorial	Panel 263.
Sgt	William	Winkley	Wireless Op	LL691	English Channel	01/05/1944		Runnymede Memorial	Panel 240.
Sgt	Thomas	Woodford	Rear Gunner	DS736	Leipzig	20/02/1944		Runnymede Memorial	Panel 241.
P/O	Douglas	Woods	Pilot	LL620	Villers Bocage	30/06/1944	22	Coulvain	Coll. grave 3.
Sgt	Gordon	Woodward	Navigator	DS781	Duisburg	22/05/1944		Runnymede Memorial	Panel 241.
W/O	Lawrence	Wry	Navigator	LL653	Stuttgart	16/03/1944		Villars-le-Pautel	Joint grave 6.
F/O	Roy	Young	Navigator	ME365	Salzbergen	06/03/1945	34	Reichswald F War Cem	13. E. 4.

Key: Full Names of Cemeteries

Acomb	ACOMB (ST. STEPHEN) CHURCHYARD
Assesse Cem	ASSESSE COMMUNAL CEMETERY
Bathmen Cem	BATHMEN GENERAL CEMETERY
Beck Row	BECK ROW (ST. JOHN) CHURCHYARD
Belfast	BELFAST (DUNDONALD) CEMETERY
Bergen-Op-Zoom	BERGEN-OP-ZOOM WAR CEMETERY
Berlin War Cem	BERLIN 1939-1945 WAR CEMETERY
Bournemouth	BOURNEMOUTH EAST CEMETERY
Brookwood	BROOKWOOD MILITARY CEMETERY
Buckie	BUCKIE NEW CEMETERY
Calais Canadian	CALAIS CANADIAN WAR CEMETERY, LEUBRINGHEN
Cambridge	CAMBRIDGE CITY CEMETERY
Chadwell Heath	CHADWELL HEATH CEMETERY
Choloy War Cem	CHOLOY WAR CEMETERY
Clichy Northern	CLICHY NORTHERN CEMETERY
Clogh Holy Trin	CLOGH (HOLY TRINITY) CHURCHYARD
Cookstown	COOKSTOWN NEW CEMETERY
Coulvain	COULVAIN CHURCHYARD
Coventry	COVENTRY (LONDON ROAD) CEMETERY
Croisilles	CROISILLES BRITISH CEMETERY
Durnbach War Cem	DURNBACH WAR CEMETERY
Eindhoven	EINDHOVEN (WOENSEL) GENERAL CEMETERY
Emmen	EMMEN (NIEUW DORDRECHT) GENERAL CEMETERY
Estruplund	ESTRUPLUND CHURCHYARD
Frederikshavn	FREDERIKSHAVN CEMETERY
Geraardsbergen	GERAARDSBERGEN COMMUNAL CEMETERY
Glasgow	GLASGOW (ST. PETER'S) ROMAN CATHOLIC CEMETERY
Great Bircham	GREAT BIRCHAM (ST. MARY) CHURCHYARD
Groesbeek	GROESBEEK CANADIAN WAR CEMETERY
Hanover War Cem	HANOVER WAR CEMETERY
Harlingen	HARLINGEN GENERAL CEMETERY
Heverlee War Cem	HEVERLEE WAR CEMETERY
Heywood	HEYWOOD CEMETERY, LANCASHIRE

Hunsel	HUNSEL ROMAN CATHOLIC CHURCHYARD
Inveresk	INVERESK PARISH CHURCHYARD
Iwuy	IWUY COMMUNAL CEMETERY
Kiel War Cem	KIEL WAR CEMETERY
La Celle-Les-Bordes	LA CELLE-LES-BORDES COMMUNAL CEMETERY
Lodge Hill	BIRMINGHAM (LODGE HILL) CEMETERY
Longuenesse	LONGUENESSE (ST. OMER) SOUVENIR CEMETERY
Loos	LOOS BRITISH CEMETERY
Neufchateau	NEUFCHATEAU COMMUNAL CEMETERY, VOSGES
NKG	No Known Grave
Nunspeet	ERMELO (NUNSPEET) NEW GENERAL CEMETERY
Putney Vale	PUTNEY VALE CEMETERY AND CREMATORIUM
Reichswald F War Cem	REICHSWALD FOREST WAR CEMETERY
Rheinberg War Cem	RHEINBERG WAR CEMETERY
Rieux	RIEUX COMMUNAL CEMETERY
Rouen	ST. SEVER CEMETERY EXTENSION, ROUEN
Runnymede Memorial	RUNNYMEDE MEMORIAL
Sage War Cem	SAGE WAR CEMETERY
Scarborough	SCARBOROUGH (WOODLANDS) CEMETERY
Schoonselhof	SCHOONSELHOF CEMETERY
Sevenoaks	SEVENOAKS (GREATNESS PARK) CEMETERY
Southgate	SOUTHGATE CEMETERY
St. Cloud	ST. CLOUD-EN-DUNOIS COMMUNAL CEMETERY
St. Pierre	ST. PIERRE CEMETERY, AMIENS
Staveren	STAVEREN GENERAL CEMETERY
Tynemouth	TYNEMOUTH (PRESTON) CEMETERY
Villars-le-Pautel	VILLARS-LE-PAUTEL COMMUNAL CEMETERY
West Alvington	WEST ALVINGTON (ALL SAINTS) CHURCHYARD
Widdrington	WIDDRINGTON (HOLY TRINITY) CHURCHYARD
Wissant	WISSANT COMMUNAL CEMETERY
Wonseradeel	WONSERADEEL (MAKKUM) PROT. CHURCHYARD
Woodkirk	WOODKIRK (ST. MARY) CHURCHYARD

514 Squadron Aircraft Losses

The hazardous business of night bombing is clearly shown in this photo of an unidentified Lancaster running the gauntlet of flak over a target. For every tracer shell there were others that remained unseen until they exploded (TNA).

Ops Date	A/C Type	Serial	Code	Duty	Target	Pilot	Name	Fate	Details	Location
18/11/1943	Lancaster II	DS784	JI-C	Ops	Mannheim	P/O	Thomas	FTR	Shot down - night fighter.	Assesse (Namur) 16 km SE of Namur, Belgium.
26/11/1943	Lancaster II	DS814	JI-M	Ops	Berlin	F/O	Cantin	FTR	Shot down - flak.	Germendorf, 4 km w of Oranienburg.
02/12/1943	Lancaster II	DS738	JI-J	Ops	Berlin	F/L	Hinde	FTR	Shot down - night fighter.	Potsdam
20/12/1943	Lancaster II	DS817	JI-P	Ops	Frankfurt	F/S	Davis	FTR	Shot down - night fighter.	Rettert, WNW of the target
24/12/1943	Lancaster II	LL671	A2-B	Ops	Berlin	P/O	Whitting	FTR	Shot down - night fighter.	Ostheim, approx 10 miles North of Frankfurt.
29/12/1943	Lancaster II	DS821	JI-S	Ops	Berlin	F/O	Greenburgh	Forced landing	Ditched in the sea following attacks by night fighters. Crew rescued.	North Sea
14/01/1944	Lancaster II	LL679	A2-J	Ops	Brunswick	F/S	Mason	FTR	Shot down - night fighter.	Lauenberg, SE of Dassel.
14/01/1944	Lancaster II	LL685	A2-G	Ops	Brunswick	S/L	Sly	FTR	Shot down - night fighter.	800 metres W of Bennebostel, 5 km S of Celle
21/01/1944	Lancaster II	DS824	JI-K	Ops	Magdeburg	P/O	Williams	FTR	Shot down - night fighter.	Ijsselmeer
21/01/1944	Lancaster II	LL627	JI-U	Ops	Magdeburg	F/S	Bennett	FTR	Shot down - night fighter.	Ijsselmeer
21/01/1944	Lancaster II	LL672	A2-C	Ops	Magdeburg	F/L	Bourke	FTR	Shot down - night fighter.	Perlesberg
21/01/1944	Lancaster II	LL680	A2-H	Ops	Magdeburg	P/O	Vizer	FTR	Shot down - night fighter.	Not recorded

27/01/1944	Lancaster II	LL674	A2-D	Ops	Berlin	F/S	Symmons	Crashed	Overran the runway on landing and crashed into a ditch. No injuries reported.	RAF Waterbeach
30/01/1944	Lancaster II	DS706	JI-G	Ops	Berlin	F/L	Boyd	FTR	Shot down - probably night fighter.	Lost without trace.
30/01/1944	Lancaster II	DS735	JI-A	Ops	Berlin	F/L	Chequer	FTR	Shot down - probably night fighter.	Approximately 10 miles North of Brandenburg.
19/02/1944	Lancaster II	DS736	A2-D	Ops	Leipzig	F/S	Hall	FTR	Probably shot down - night fighter.	Lost without trace.
19/02/1944	Lancaster II	DS823	JI-M	Ops	Leipzig	F/S	Henry	FTR	Shot down - night fighter.	Essern-Osterloh on the SW edge of Hrosses Moor, 11 km NE of Rahden.
19/02/1944	Lancaster II	LL681	JI-J	Ops	Leipzig	F/L	Kingwell	FTR	Probably shot down - night fighter.	Lost without trace.
24/02/1944	Lancaster II	DS785	JI-D	Ops	Schweinfurt	Sgt	Kay	FTR	Shot down - night fighter.	Heidingsfeld, near Würzburg.
15/03/1944	Lancaster II	LL653	JI-E	Ops	Stuttgart	F/O	Penkuri	FTR	Shot down - night fighter.	Between Blondefontaine and Villars-le-Pautel.
17/03/1944	Lancaster II	DS820	JI-R	Training		F/S	Shearing	Crashed	Crashed during training flight. No details recorded. No casualties.	Martlesham Heath
17/03/1944	Lancaster II	LL669	JI-K	Training		F/S	Medland	Crashed	Crashed while practising flapless landings. No casualties.	RAF Woodbridge

22/03/1944	Lancaster II	DS815	JI-N	Ops	Frankfurt	F/L	Nichol	FTR	Aircraft crash-landed in occupied territory after being damaged by night fighter.	Nordausques, about twenty miles south east of Calais.
22/03/1944	Lancaster II	LL684	A2-B	Ops	Frankfurt	F/S	Underwood	FTR	Shot down - night fighter.	Nieuw Dordrecht (Drenthe), 8 km SE of Emmen, Holland.
24/03/1944	Lancaster II	LL625	JI-C	Ops	Berlin	F/O	Laing	FTR	Shot down - night fighter.	Worlitz, 12 km ENE of Dessau.
30/03/1944	Lancaster II	DS836	JI-L	Ops	Nuremburg	P/O	Crombie	FTR	Shot down - night fighter.	Wulferhausen.
30/03/1944	Lancaster II	LL645	JI-R	Ops	Nuremburg	P/O	Chitty	Crashed	While approaching to land, another aircraft forced pilot tried to go round again. Aircraft crash landed, ripping the undercarriage off. Bomb aimer and mid upper gunner killed.	RAF Waterbeach
30/03/1944	Lancaster II	LL683	JI-P	Ops	Nuremburg	W/O	McGown	Forced landing	Forced landing in field due to fuel shortage and fog on return from Nuremburg.	Sawbridgeworth, Herts.
30/03/1944	Lancaster II	LL696	JI-A	Ops	Nuremburg	F/O	Hood	FTR	Shot down - night fighter.	Memmelsdorf, 6.5 km NE of Bamberg.
30/03/1944	Lancaster II	LL698	A2-J	Ops	Nuremburg	F/S	Gregory	FTR	Shot down - night fighter.	Oberpleis, 12 km ESE of Bonn.
30/03/1944	Lancaster II	LL738	JI-D	Ops	Nuremburg	P/O	Hughes	FTR	Shot down - night fighter.	Southern outskirts of Sinzig at Westum

11/04/1944	Lancaster II	LL639	JI-R	Ops	Aachen	P/O	Thackray	FTR	Shot down - night fighter or flak.	Near Molenbeersel, Belgium.
22/04/1944	Lancaster II	DS669	JI-C	Ops	Dusseldorf	F/S	Harrison	FTR	Believed hit by Flak, or may have collided with another 514 Squadron Lancaster DS828.	Ecke Rethel and Schubertstrasse, Dusseldorf.
22/04/1944	Lancaster II	DS682	JI-N	Ops	Dusseldorf	F/O	Morgan-Owen	FTR	Crashed in the sea. It is believed that the aircraft sustained damage earlier in the raid and failed to make it home.	North Sea.
22/04/1944	Lancaster II	DS828	JI-D	Ops	Dusseldorf	F/S	Hudson	FTR	Either hit by flak or collided with DS669, crashed in the target area.	Dusseldorf.
30/04/1944	Lancaster II	LL691	A2-D	Training		F/S	Turner	Crashed	Whilst on a training flight, crashed in the English Channel off Dover. Possibly shot down in error by local AA defences.	English Channel
01/05/1944	Lancaster II	LL732	A2-H	Ops	Chambly	F/L	Curtis	FTR	Shot down - night fighter.	Approximately 3 km SW of Chaumont-en-Vexin (Oise), 25 km SW of Beauvais.
11/05/1944	Lancaster II	LL739	JI-M	Ops	Louvain	P/O	Cunningham	FTR	Shot down - night fighter.	Brussels.
19/05/1944	Lancaster II	LL641	JI-K	Ops	Le Mans	F/S	Shearing	Crashed	Aircraft crashed on return near Newmarket, when it entered a spin for unknown reason.	Chippenham, near Newmarket, Cambs.

19/05/1944	Lancaster II	LL703	JI-L	Ops	Le Mans	F/O	Gray	DBR	Severely damaged by flak.	
21/05/1944	Lancaster II	DS633	A2-B	Ops	Duisburg	F/S	Gibson	FTR	Probably shot down - night fighter.	The Wash.
21/05/1944	Lancaster II	DS781	JI-R	Ops	Duisburg	P/O	Windsor	FTR	Probably shot down - night fighter.	North Sea.
21/05/1944	Lancaster II	LL695	JI-A	Ops	Duisburg	F/S	Medland	FTR	Shot down - night fighter.	Geldrop (Noord-Brabant), 6 km ESE from the centre of Eindhoven.
27/05/1944	Lancaster II	LL652	JI-C	Ops	Aachen	F/L	Taylor	FTR	Shot down - night fighter.	Ophasselt (Oost-Vlaanderen) approximately 5 km N of Geraardsbergen.
07/06/1944	Lancaster II	DS822	JI-T	Ops	Massy Palaiseau	P/O	McGown	FTR	Shot down - night fighter.	La Celle les Bordes, France.
07/06/1944	Lancaster II	LL727	A2-C	Ops	Massy Palaiseau	F/O	Greenburgh	FTR	Shot down - night fighter.	St-Eusoye, 20 km NE of Beauvais.
12/06/1944	Lancaster II	DS818	JI-Q	Ops	Gelsenkirchen	P/O	Duncliffe	FTR	Shot down - night fighter.	Nunspeet, Gelderland, Netherlands.

12/06/1944	Lancaster II	LL678	A2-L	Ops	Gelsenkirchen	P/O	Delacour	FTR	Shot down - night fighter.	Zuid Loo (Overjssel), a small hamlet 3 km SE of Bathmen, Netherlands.
15/06/1944	Lancaster II	DS816	JI-O	Ops	Valenciennes	F/S	Prowles	FTR	Shot down - night fighter.	Croisilles, Pas de Calais.
15/06/1944	Lancaster II	LL690	JI-J	Ops	Valenciennes	P/O	Kingham	FTR	Shot down - night fighter.	Between Iwuy (Nord) and Rieux-en-Cambresis, 9 km from Cambrai.
30/06/1944	Lancaster II	LL620	JI-T	Ops	Villers Bocage	P/O	Woods	FTR	Shot down - flak.	Coulvain (Calvados), 5 km SW of Villers-Bocage.
30/06/1944	Lancaster III	PB178	JI-P	Ops	Villers Bocage	F/S	Hannesson	FTR	Mid-air collision.	Midhurst, Sussex
20/07/1944	Lancaster I	HK570	JI-P	Ops	Homberg	W/O	Lassam	FTR	Shot down - night fighter.	North Sea, off Dutch coast.
20/07/1944	Lancaster I	HK571	JI-L	Ops	Homberg	P/O	Anderson	FTR	Shot down - night fighter.	Daubenspeckhof, 1 km W of Moers
20/07/1944	Lancaster I	LM181	JI-E	Ops	Homberg	F/O	McLean	FTR	Shot down - night fighter.	Homberg.
20/07/1944	Lancaster I	ME858	JI-J	Ops	Homberg	F/O	Millar	FTR	Shot down - night fighter.	Limburg.
24/07/1944	Lancaster III	PB185	A2-F	Ops	Stuttgart	F/O	Middleton	FTR	Shot down - night fighter.	Trier.

28/07/1944	Lancaster II	DS813	JI-N	Ops	Stuttgart	F/L	Fowke	FTR	Probably shot down - night fighter.	Deinvillers, near St. Die.
28/07/1944	Lancaster II	LL692	A2-C	Ops	Stuttgart	F/L	Campbell	FTR	Shot down - night fighter.	4 km. East of Chateaudun.
28/07/1944	Lancaster I	LM206	JI-C	Ops	Stuttgart	F/L	Jones	FTR	Shot down - night fighter.	Neufchateau, France.
30/07/1944	Lancaster II	LL733	JI-S	Ops	Caen	F/L	Chitty	FTR	Probably mid-air collision.	English Channel, off coast of Normandy.
03/08/1944	Lancaster II	LL716	A2-G	Ops	Bois de Casson	F/O	Topham	FTR	Hit by bombs from another aircraft.	10 km S of Beaumont (Oise), France.
11/08/1944	Lancaster II	LL697	A2-B	Ops	Lens	W/O	Brickwood	DBR	Hit by bombs from another aircraft.	
12/08/1944	Lancaster I	LM180	JI-G	Ops	Russelsheim	F/S	Lawrie	FTR	Shot down - night fighter.	Havelange.
12/08/1944	Lancaster I	LM265	JI-E	Ops	Russelsheim	F/S	Richardson	FTR	Shot down - night fighter.	Engegstadt, about 10 miles south west of Mainz, Germany.
25/08/1944	Lancaster II	LL624	JI-R	Ops	Vincly	P/O	Saltmarsh	Crashed	Burst tyre on take-off.	RAF Waterbeach.
25/08/1944	Lancaster II	LL635	JI-M	Ops	Vincly	F/O	Cossens	DBR	Severely damaged by flak over target.	
26/08/1944	Lancaster II	LL728	A2-L	Ops	Kiel	F/O	Hebditch	FTR	Shot down - night fighter.	Near Kleve, 10 km SSE of Friedrichstadt.
29/08/1944	Lancaster III	PB143	JI-B	Ops	Stettin	F/S	Charlton	FTR	Shot down - night fighter.	North Sea near Estruplund, Denmark.

08/09/1944	Lancaster II	LL677	A2-E	Ops	Le Havre	F/O	Beaton	DBR	Severely damaged by flak over target.	
11/09/1944	Lancaster II	DS787	A2-G	Ops	Kamen	W/O	Thornton	FTR	Probably hit by bombs from another aircraft.	Kamen, Germany.
12/09/1944	Lancaster II	LL731	JI-U	Ops	Frankfurt	F/O	Brickwood	FTR	Shot down - night fighter.	Kordel, Ehranger Wald, 8 km NW of Trier.
20/09/1944	Lancaster I	LM277	JI-F	Ops	Calais	F/O	Arkless	FTR	Crashed in the sea near the target after being hit by flak or bombs from another aircraft.	English Channel, off Calais, France.
07/10/1944	Lancaster III	LM735	A2-G	Ops	Emmerich	F/S	Gilchrist	FTR	Probably shot down - flak.	Believed Emmerich, Germany.
20/11/1944	Lancaster I	LM286	A2-F	Ops	Homberg	F/O	Harland	FTR	Crashed near the target after being hit by flak or bombs from another aircraft.	Homberg.
21/11/1944	Lancaster III	LM684	JI-C	Ops	Homberg	F/O	Limbert	FTR	Shot down - flak.	1 km NW of Moers.
21/11/1944	Lancaster I	NG121	JI-H	Ops	Homberg	F/O	Tolley	Forced landing	Severely damaged by flak over target.	Antwerp, Belgium
21/11/1944	Lancaster I	PD265	JI-G	Ops	Homberg	F/O	France	FTR	Shot down - flak.	Grafschafter Castle, Moers.
11/12/1944	Lancaster I	NG350	JI-C	Ops	Osterfeld	P/O	Hill	FTR	Shot down - flak.	Sterkrade, Germany.
29/12/1944	Lancaster I	NG141	A2-J	Ground				Ground accident	Destroyed when PD325 exploded on the ground.	RAF Waterbeach.
29/12/1944	Lancaster I	PD325	A2-L	Ground				Ground accident	Exploded on ground during bombing-up.	RAF Waterbeach.

16/01/1945	Lancaster III	PB906	A2-B	Ops	Wanne-Eickel	F/O	Orr	FTR	Probably shot down - flak.	Lost without trace.
02/02/1945	Lancaster I	NN772	A2-C	Ops	Wiesbaden	F/O	McLean	FTR	Shot down - flak.	Springen, 6km W of Bad Schwalbach.
03/02/1945	Lancaster III	LM685	A2-B	Ops	Dortmund-Huckarde	F/O	Fisher	FTR	Shot down - flak or night fighter.	Between Krefeld and Dortmund, Germany.
05/03/1945	Lancaster I	NN775	A2-F	Ops	Gelsenkirchen	F/O	Kerr	FTR	Exploded over allied territory.	Bunsbeek, Brabant, Belgium.
06/03/1945	Lancaster III	ME365	JI-T	Ops	Salzbergen	F/O	Flack	FTR	Believed hit by flak or bombs from other aircraft.	Salzbergen.
22/04/1945	Lancaster I	LM285	JI-A	Ops	Bremen	F/O	Abel	Forced landing	Severely damaged by flak over target.	Venlo.
23/04/1945	Lancaster III	ME523	A2-G	Training				Forced landing	Belly-landed during training flight.	1.5 miles SW of Topcliffe.
09/05/1945	Lancaster III	RF230	JI-B	POW flight		F/O	Beaton	Crashed	Whilst carrying POWs from Juvincourt to Ford, aircraft crashed after control problems. 6 crew and 24 passengers killed.	Roye Amy, France.

DBR Damaged beyond repair.
FTR Failed to return from ops.